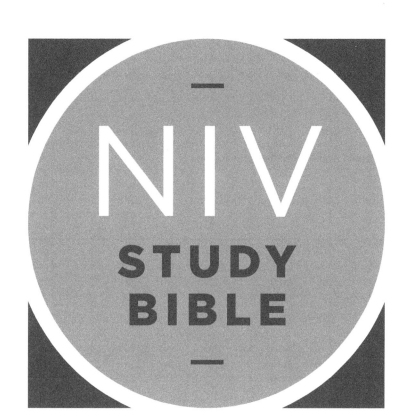

NIV

STUDY
BIBLE

ESSENTIAL GUIDE TO
PSALMS

ZONDERVAN®

The NIV Study Bible Essential Guide to Psalms

Published by Zondervan, 2022

Adapted from the *The NIV Study Bible* Copyright © 1985, 1995, 2002, 2008, 2011, 2020 by Zondervan
Grand Rapids, Michigan, 49546, USA

www.Zondervan.com

Library of Congress Catalog Card Number 2022930440

Welcome to the *NIV Study Bible Essential Guide to Psalms*. You have in your hands a book designed for personal or group study that has been created specifically to enhance your understanding of and appreciation for God's Word.

About the *NIV Study Bible Essential Guides*

The *NIV Study Bible Essential Guide to Psalms* contains the full text of the book of Psalms, a book introduction, selected study notes and space for notetaking, questions for reflection and study, and other study helps adapted from the bestselling *NIV Study Bible, Fully Revised Edition.* The team of evangelical scholars who wrote and edited notes for the *NIV Study Bible* has also served over the years on the translation committee for the New International Version itself. Since the release of the *NIV Study Bible* in 1985, its editors have diligently worked to revise the notes to provide readers with the most up-to-date, relevant study notes available today. Find out more about the New International Version itself by reading the Preface, beginning on page vii.

What Are the *NIV Study Bible Essential Guides*?

The *NIV Study Bible Essential Guides* are books of the Bible with study aids adapted from the *NIV Study Bible.* The books contain the full text of the Bible book from the NIV translation and a library of study features alongside interactive prompts to help individual readers or groups to grasp, understand, and apply what the text is saying.

What Help Do the Study Features Offer Me?

- Book introductions answer the Who? What? Where? Why? and When? questions readers have about the book.
- Study notes have been placed close to the text that they amplify and explain. These notes have been designed to provide background and context to the Scripture text and will also answer questions that may arise as one reads through the Bible.
- Certain kinds of material have been made more accessible through the use of the following symbols:
  - The trowel points out references containing study notes that provide light from archaeology.
  - The seedling calls attention to Scripture references containing study notes that have practical principles for personal application.
  - The character symbol occurs in front of Scripture references containing study notes that provide descriptions and/or characterizations of a person or a people group. It also sometimes appears in book introductions and essays.
- Full-color in-text maps, charts and models, along with well-crafted articles, summarize and explain important information and ideas from Scripture.
- Questions for reflection, Insight callouts, and space for journaling allow readers to fully engage and interact with the text.

May God bless you as you study and come to understand the timeless truths of the Bible as priceless treasures for today.

TABLE OF CONTENTS

The goal of the New International Version (NIV) is to enable English-speaking people from around the world to read and hear God's eternal Word in their own language. Our work as translators is motivated by our conviction that the Bible is God's Word in written form. We believe that the Bible contains the divine answer to the deepest needs of humanity, sheds unique light on our path in a dark world and sets forth the way to our eternal well-being. Out of these deep convictions, we have sought to recreate as far as possible the experience of the original audience — blending transparency to the original text with accessibility for the millions of English speakers around the world. We have prioritized accuracy, clarity and literary quality with the goal of creating a translation suitable for public and private reading, evangelism, teaching, preaching, memorizing and liturgical use. We have also sought to preserve a measure of continuity with the long tradition of translating the Scriptures into English.

The complete NIV Bible was first published in 1978. It was a completely new translation made by over a hundred scholars working directly from the best available Hebrew, Aramaic and Greek texts. The translators came from the United States, Great Britain, Canada, Australia and New Zealand, giving the translation an international scope. They were from many denominations and churches — including Anglican, Assemblies of God, Baptist, Brethren, Christian Reformed, Church of Christ, Evangelical Covenant, Evangelical Free, Lutheran, Mennonite, Methodist, Nazarene, Presbyterian, Wesleyan and others. This breadth of denominational and theological perspective helped to safeguard the translation from sectarian bias. For these reasons, and by the grace of God, the NIV has gained a wide readership in all parts of the English-speaking world.

The work of translating the Bible is never finished. As good as they are, English translations must be regularly updated so that they will continue to communicate accurately the meaning of God's Word. Updates are needed in order to reflect the latest developments in our understanding of the biblical world and its languages and to keep pace with changes in English usage. Recognizing, then, that the NIV would retain its ability to communicate God's Word accurately only if it were regularly updated, the original translators established the Committee on Bible Translation (CBT). The Committee is a self-perpetuating group of biblical scholars charged with keeping abreast of advances in biblical scholarship and changes in English and issuing periodic updates to the NIV. The CBT is an independent, self-governing body and has sole responsibility for the NIV text. The Committee mirrors the original group of translators in its diverse international and denominational makeup and in its unifying commitment to the Bible as God's inspired Word.

In obedience to its mandate, the Committee has issued periodic updates to the NIV. An initial revision was released in 1984. A more thorough revision process was completed in 2005, resulting in the separately published TNIV. The updated NIV you now have in your hands builds on both the original NIV and the TNIV and represents the latest effort of the Committee to articulate God's unchanging Word in the way the original authors might have said it had they been speaking in English to the global English-speaking audience today.

Translation Philosophy

The Committee's translating work has been governed by three widely accepted principles about the way people use words and about the way we understand them.

First, the meaning of words is determined by the way that users of the language actually use them at any given time. For the biblical languages, therefore, the Committee utilizes the best and most recent scholarship on the way Hebrew, Aramaic and Greek words were being used in biblical times. At the same time, the Committee carefully studies the state of modern English. Good translation is like good communication: one must know the target audience so that the appropriate choices can be made about which English words to use to represent the original words of Scripture. From its inception, the NIV has had as its target the general English-speaking population all over the world, the "International" in its title reflecting this concern. The aim of the Committee is to put the Scriptures into natural English that will communicate effectively with the broadest possible audience of English speakers.

Modern technology has enhanced the Committee's ability to choose the right English words to convey the meaning of the original text. The field of computational linguistics harnesses the power of computers to provide broadly applicable and current data about the state of the language. Translators can now access huge databases of modern English to better understand the current meaning and usage of key words. The Committee utilized this resource in preparing the 2011 edition of the

NIV. An area of especially rapid and significant change in English is the way certain nouns and pronouns are used to refer to human beings. The Committee therefore requested experts in computational linguistics at Collins Dictionaries to pose some key questions about this usage to its database of English — the largest in the world, with over 4.4 billion words, gathered from several English-speaking countries and including both spoken and written English. (The Collins Study, called "The Development and Use of Gender Language in Contemporary English," can be accessed at *http://www.thenivbible. com/about-the-niv/about-the-2011-edition/*.) The study revealed that the most popular words to describe the human race in modern U.S. English were "humanity," "man" and "mankind." The Committee then used this data in the updated NIV, choosing from among these three words (and occasionally others also) depending on the context.

A related issue creates a larger problem for modern translations: the move away from using the third-person masculine singular pronouns — "he/him/his" — to refer to men and women equally. This usage does persist in some forms of English, and this revision therefore occasionally uses these pronouns in a generic sense. But the tendency, recognized in day-to-day usage and confirmed by the Collins study, is away from the generic use of "he," "him" and "his." In recognition of this shift in language and in an effort to translate into the natural English that people are actually using, this revision of the NIV generally uses other constructions when the biblical text is plainly addressed to men and women equally. The reader will encounter especially frequently a "they," "their" or "them" to express a generic singular idea. Thus, for instance, Mark 8:36 reads: "What good is it for someone to gain the whole world, yet forfeit their soul?" This generic use of the "distributive" or "singular" "they/them/their" has been used for many centuries by respected writers of English and has now become established as standard English, spoken and written, all over the world.

A second linguistic principle that feeds into the Committee's translation work is that meaning is found not in individual words, as vital as they are, but in larger clusters: phrases, clauses, sentences, discourses. Translation is not, as many people think, a matter of word substitution: English word *x* in place of Hebrew word *y*. Translators must first determine the meaning of the words of the biblical languages in the context of the passage and then select English words that accurately communicate that meaning to modern listeners and readers. This means that accurate translation will not always reflect the exact structure of the original language. To be sure, there is debate over the degree to which translators should try to preserve the "form" of the original text in English. From the beginning, the NIV has taken a mediating position on this issue. The manual produced when the translation that became the NIV was first being planned states: "If the Greek or Hebrew syntax has a good parallel in modern English, it should be used. But if there is no good parallel, the English syntax appropriate to the meaning of the original is to be chosen." It is fine, in other words, to carry over the form of the biblical languages into English — but not at the expense of natural expression. The principle that meaning resides in larger clusters of words means that the Committee has not insisted on a "word-for-word" approach to translation. We certainly believe that every word of Scripture is inspired by God and therefore to be carefully studied to determine what God is saying to us. It is for this reason that the Committee labors over every single word of the original texts, working hard to determine how each of those words contributes to what the text is saying. Ultimately, however, it is how these individual words function in combination with other words that determines meaning.

A third linguistic principle guiding the Committee in its translation work is the recognition that words have a spectrum of meaning. It is popular to define a word by using another word, or "gloss," to substitute for it. This substitute word is then sometimes called the "literal" meaning of a word. In fact, however, words have a range of possible meanings. Those meanings will vary depending on the context, and words in one language will usually not occupy the same semantic range as words in another language. The Committee therefore studies each original word of Scripture in its context to identify its meaning in a particular verse and then chooses an appropriate English word (or phrase) to represent it. It is impossible, then, to translate any given Hebrew, Aramaic or Greek word with the same English word all the time. The Committee does try to translate related occurrences of a word in the original languages with the same English word in order to preserve the connection for the English reader. But the Committee generally privileges clear natural meaning over a concern with consistency in rendering particular words.

Textual Basis

For the Old Testament the standard Hebrew text, the Masoretic Text as published in the latest edition of *Biblia Hebraica*, has been used throughout. The Masoretic Text tradition contains marginal notations that offer variant readings. These have sometimes been followed instead of the text itself. Because such instances involve variants within the Masoretic tradition, they have not been indicated in the textual notes. In a few cases, words in the basic consonantal text have been divided differently than in the Masoretic Text. Such cases are usually indicated in the textual footnotes. The Dead Sea Scrolls contain biblical texts that represent an earlier stage of the transmission of the Hebrew text. They have been consulted, as have been the Samaritan Pentateuch and the ancient scribal traditions concerning deliberate textual changes. The translators also consulted the more important early versions. Readings from these versions, the Dead Sea Scrolls and the scribal traditions were occasionally followed where the Masoretic Text seemed doubtful and where accepted principles of textual criticism showed that one or more of these textual witnesses appeared to provide the correct reading. In rare cases, the translators have emended the Hebrew text where it appears to have become corrupted at an even earlier stage of its transmission. These departures from the Masoretic Text are also indicated in the textual footnotes. Sometimes the vowel indicators (which are later additions to the basic consonantal text) found in the Masoretic Text did not, in the judgment of the translators, represent the correct vowels for the original text. Accordingly, some words have been read with a different set of vowels. These instances are usually not indicated in the footnotes.

The Greek text used in translating the New Testament has been an eclectic one, based on the latest editions of the Nestle-Aland/United Bible Societies' Greek New Testament. The translators have made their choices among the variant readings in accordance with widely accepted principles of New Testament textual criticism. Footnotes call attention to places where uncertainty remains.

The New Testament authors, writing in Greek, often quote the Old Testament from its ancient Greek version, the Septuagint. This is one reason why some of the Old Testament quotations in the NIV New Testament are not identical to the corresponding passages in the NIV Old Testament. Such quotations in the New Testament are indicated with the footnote "(see Septuagint)."

Footnotes and Formatting

Footnotes in this version are of several kinds, most of which need no explanation. Those giving alternative translations begin with "Or" and generally introduce the alternative with the last word preceding it in the text, except when it is a single-word alternative. When poetry is quoted in a footnote a slash mark indicates a line division.

It should be noted that references to diseases, minerals, flora and fauna, architectural details, clothing, jewelry, musical instruments and other articles cannot always be identified with precision. Also, linear measurements and measures of capacity can only be approximated (see the Table of Weights and Measures).

Although *Selah*, used mainly in the Psalms, is probably a musical term, its meaning is uncertain. Since it may interrupt reading and distract the reader, this word has not been kept in the English text, but every occurrence has been signaled by a footnote.

As an aid to the reader, sectional headings have been inserted. They are not to be regarded as part of the biblical text and are not intended for oral reading. It is the Committee's hope that these headings may prove more helpful to the reader than the traditional chapter divisions, which were introduced long after the Bible was written.

Sometimes the chapter and/or verse numbering in English translations of the Old Testament differs from that found in published Hebrew texts. This is particularly the case in the Psalms, where the traditional titles are included in the Hebrew verse numbering. Such differences are indicated in the footnotes at the bottom of the page. In the New Testament, verse numbers that marked off portions of the traditional English text not supported by the best Greek manuscripts now appear in brackets, with a footnote indicating the text that has been omitted (see, for example, Matthew 17:[21]).

Mark 16:9 – 20 and John 7:53 — 8:11, although long accorded virtually equal status with the rest of the Gospels in which they stand, have a questionable standing in the textual history of the New Testament, as noted in the bracketed annotations with which they are set off. A different typeface has been chosen for these passages to indicate their uncertain status.

Basic formatting of the text, such as lining the poetry, paragraphing (both prose and poetry), setting up of (administrative-like) lists, indenting letters and lengthy prayers within narratives and the insertion of sectional headings, has been the work of the Committee. However, the choice between single-column and double-column formats has been left to the publishers. Also the issuing of "red-letter" editions is a publisher's choice — one that the Committee does not endorse.

The Committee has again been reminded that every human effort is flawed — including this revision of the NIV. We trust, however, that many will find in it an improved representation of the Word of God, through which they hear his call to faith in our Lord Jesus Christ and to service in his kingdom. We offer this version of the Bible to him in whose name and for whose glory it has been made.

THE COMMITTEE ON BIBLE TRANSLATION

PSALMS

INTRODUCTION

Title

The titles "Psalms" and "Psalter" come from the Septuagint (the pre-Christian Greek translation of the OT), where they originally referred to stringed instruments (such as harp, lyre and lute), then to songs sung with their accompaniment. The traditional Hebrew title is *tehillim* (meaning "praises"; see note on Ps 145 title), even though many of the psalms are *tephilloth* (meaning "prayers," including laments). In fact, one of the first collections included in the book is titled "the prayers of David son of Jesse" (72:20).

Collection, Arrangement and Date

The Psalter is a collection of collections and represents the final stage in a process that began in the early days of the first (Solomon's) temple (or even earlier in the time of David), when the temple liturgy began to take shape. Both the scope of its subject matter and the arrangement of the whole collection strongly suggest that this collection was viewed by its final editors as a guide for the life of faith in accordance with the Law, the Prophets and the Writings. By the first century AD it was referred to as the "Book of Psalms" (Lk 20:42; Ac 1:20). At that time Psalms appears also to have been used as a shorthand designation for the entire section of the Hebrew OT canon more commonly known as the Writings (see Lk 24:44). Many collections preceded this final compilation of the Psalms (e.g., "the prayers of David," noted above).

Additional collections expressly referred to in the present Psalter titles are: (1) the songs and/or psalms "of the Sons of Korah" (Ps 42–49; 84–85; 87–88), (2) the psalms and/or songs "of Asaph" (Ps 50; 73–83) and (3) the songs "of ascents" (Ps 120–134).

Other evidence points to further compilations. Ps 1–41 (Book I) make frequent use of the divine name Yahweh ("the LORD"), while Ps 42–72 (Book II) make frequent use of Elohim ("God"). Moreover, Ps 93–100 appear to be a traditional collection (see "The LORD reigns" in 93:1; 96:10; 97:1; 99:1). Other apparent groupings include Ps 111–118 (a series of Hallelujah psalms; see introduction to Ps 113–118), Ps 138–145 (each of which include "of David" in their titles) and Ps 146–150 (each of which begins and ends with "Praise the LORD"; see NIV text note on 111:1).

In its final edition, the Psalter contained 150 psalms. On this the Septuagint (the pre-Christian Greek translation of the OT) and Hebrew texts agree, though they arrive at this number differently.

Psalms written (c. 1400–430 BC)

Israelites enter Canaan (c. 1406 BC)

Judges begin to rule (c. 1375 BC)

Saul's reign (1050–1010 BC)

David's reign (1010–970 BC)

Solomon's reign (970–930 BC)

Division of the kingdom (930 BC)

Fall of Jerusalem (586 BC)

First return of exiles to Jerusalem (538 BC)

The Septuagint has an extra psalm at the end (but not numbered separately as Ps 151); it also unites Ps 9–10 (see NIV text note on Ps 9) and Ps 114–115 and divides Ps 116 and Ps 147 each into two psalms. Both the Septuagint and Hebrew texts number Ps 42–43 as two psalms, though they were evidently originally one (see NIV text note on Ps 42).

In its final form the Psalter was divided into five Books (Book I: Ps 1–41; Book II: 42–72; Book III: 73–89; Book IV: 90–106; Book V: 107–150), each of which was provided with a concluding doxology (see 41:13; 72:18–19; 89:52; 106:48; 150). The first two of these Books were probably preexilic. The division of the remaining psalms into three Books, thus attaining the number five, was possibly in imitation of the five books of Moses. In spite of this five-book division, the Psalter was clearly thought of as a whole, with an introduction (Ps 1–2) and a conclusion (Ps 146–150). Notes throughout the Psalms give additional indications of conscious arrangement.

Authorship and Titles (or Superscriptions)

Of the 150 psalms, only 34 lack superscriptions of any kind (only 17 in the Septuagint, the pre-Christian Greek translation of the OT). These psalms are found mainly in Books III—V, where they tend to occur in clusters: Ps 91; 93–97; 99; 104–107; 111–119; 135–137; 146–150. (In Books I—II, only Ps 1–2; 10; 33; 43; 71 lack titles, and Ps 10 and 43 are actually continuations of the preceding psalms.)

The contents of the superscriptions vary but fall into a few broad categories: (1) author, (2) name of collection, (3) type of psalm, (4) musical notations, (5) liturgical notations and (6) brief indications of occasion for composition. For details, see notes on the titles of the various psalms.

A figurine made of terracotta holding a harp in her left hand, dated 600–480 BC. Metropolitan Museum of Art. Public Domain

Musicians in the palace of the Hittite King Barekup (8th century BC). The Psalms were originally intended to be sung, and several of them (e.g., Ps 150:3–5) mention instruments such as the harp, lyre, trumpet, timbrel, horn and cymbals.

Z. Radovan/www.BibleLandPictures.com

There is no consensus on the antiquity and reliability of these superscriptions. That many of them are at least preexilic appears evident from the fact that the Septuagint translators were sometimes unclear as to their meaning. Furthermore, the practice of attaching titles, including the name of the author, is ancient. On the other hand, comparison between the Septuagint and the Hebrew texts shows that the content of some titles was still subject to change well into the postexilic period.

As for the superscriptions regarding historical occasion of composition, many of these brief notations of events read as if they had been taken from 1,2 Samuel. Moreover, they are sometimes not easily correlated with the content of the psalms they head. This suggests they may be later attempts to fit the psalms into the real-life events of history, though the limited number of such notations and apparent mismatches raises some doubt in this regard.

Regarding authorship, opinions are even more divided. The notations themselves are ambiguous since the Hebrew phraseology used, meaning in general "belonging to," can also be taken in the sense of "concerning" or "for the use of" or "dedicated to." The name may refer to the title of a collection of psalms that had been gathered under a certain name (as "Of Asaph" or "Of the Sons of Korah"). To complicate matters, there is evidence within the Psalter that at least some of the psalms were subjected to editorial revision in the course of their transmission. As for Davidic authorship, there can be little doubt that the Psalter contains psalms composed by that noted singer and musician and that there was at one time a "Davidic" psalter. This, however, may have also included psalms written concerning David, or concerning one of the later Davidic kings, or even psalms written in the manner of those he authored. It is also true that the tradition as to which psalms are "Davidic" remains somewhat indefinite, and some "Davidic" psalms seem clearly to reflect later situations (see, e.g., Ps 30 title—but see also note there; and see introduction to Ps 69 and note on Ps 122 title). Moreover, "David" is sometimes used elsewhere in the OT as a collective for the kings of his dynasty, and this could also be true in some of the psalm titles.

Psalm Types

Hebrew superscriptions to the Psalms acquaint us with an ancient system of classification: (1) *mizmor* ("psalm"); (2) *shiggaion* (possibly a musical term; see note on Ps 7 title); (3) *miktam* (unknown meaning; see note on Ps 16 title); (4) *shir* ("song"); (5) *maśkil* (see note on Ps 32 title); (6) *tephillah* ("prayer"); (7) *tehillah* ("praise"); (8) *lehazkir* ("for being remembered"—i.e., before God, a petition); (9) *letodah* ("for praising" or "for giving thanks"); (10) *lelammed* ("for teaching"); and (11) *shir yedidoth* ("song of loves"—i.e., a wedding song). The meaning of many of these terms, however, is uncertain. In addition, some titles contain two of these (especially *mizmor* and *shir*), indicating that the types are diversely based and overlapping.

Analysis of form of content has given rise to three main types (or genres) of psalms: (1) hymns (e.g., Ps 8, 33, 100, 103, 113, 117, 150); (2) laments (e.g., Ps 5–7, 22, 26, 42, 64, 79, 130); and (3) thanksgiving psalms (e.g., Ps 9, 107, 118, 136). While many other types of psalms have been identified (e.g., wisdom, confidence, redemptive-historical, Zion, royal, etc.) they may be considered subsets of these three main types. For example, redemptive-historical psalms like Psalm 107 fit within the larger category of thanksgiving psalms.

A shepherd leads his sheep (see Ps 23; Jn 10:4).
© Noel Powell/www.BigStockPhoto.com

Hymns are characterized by exuberant praise to God motivated by specific reasons outlined by the psalmist. Thus, hymns usually contain (1) a call to praise God; (2) reasons for that praise; and (3) often an additional call to praise God.

Laments (perhaps surprisingly the most common type of psalm in the Psalter) are at the opposite end of the emotional spectrum from hymns. Laments are identified by several distinct characteristics, though not all of these are present in every lament: (1) an introductory call to God for help; (2) a description of the problem; (3) a confession of sin or an assertion of trust or innocence; (4) a call to God to deal with the problem; and (5) a declaration of confidence in God's response and / or commitment to praise him.

Thanksgiving psalms describe the psalmist's deliverance from some threat and the subsequent commitment to praise God for it. They characteristically contain: (1) a call to praise God that sometimes includes reasons; (2) a description of the threat and what God has done to resolve it; and (3) further praise and / or calls to praise.

As can be seen from the above descriptions, these psalm types are not rigid, and overlap exists. In addition, it is frequently helpful to note whether the psalm originates from or is intended for use by an individual or the larger community. Even here, though, distinctions are difficult inasmuch as an individual (the priest or the king) could be speaking on behalf of the community. Also, the psalm may have had a liturgical use which involved both an individual and the larger community.

Literary Features

The Psalter is poetry from first to last. The psalms are impassioned, vivid and concrete; they are rich in images, in simile and metaphor. Other literary features include assonance, alliteration, wordplays, repetition and the piling up of synonyms. Key words frequently highlight major themes in prayer or song. Inclusio or framing (repetition of a significant word or phrase from the beginning that recurs at the end) frequently wraps up a composition or a unit within it. The notes on the structure of the individual psalms often call attention to literary frames within which the psalm has been set.

Hebrew poetry lacks rhyme and regular meter. Its most distinctive and pervasive feature is parallelism. Most poetic lines are composed of two (sometimes three) balanced segments (the balance is often loose, with the second segment commonly somewhat shorter than the first). The traditional categories of parallelism are synonymous, antithetic, and synthetic. In synonymous parallelism, the same thought is expressed in both segments by means of synonyms. Antithetic parallelism presents a parallel by contrast through the use of antonyms. In synthetic parallelism, the second segment completes the thought of the first segment. Although a traditional classification, synthetic parallelism is not actually parallelism at all and seems to be nothing more than a default category for poetic lines that don't fit the other two categories. When the second or third segment of a poetic line repeats, echoes or overlaps the content of the preceding segment, it intensifies or more sharply focuses the thought or its expression. In the NIV the second and third segments of a line are slightly indented relative to the first. See chart, p. 13.

Determining where the Hebrew poetic lines or line segments begin or end (scanning) is sometimes an uncertain matter. Even the Septuagint (the pre-Christian Greek translation of the OT) at times scans the lines differently from the way the Hebrew texts now available to us do. It is therefore not surprising that modern translations occasionally differ.

A related problem is the extremely concise, often elliptical, writing style of the Hebrew poets. The syntactical connection of words must at times be inferred simply from context. Where more than one possibility presents itself, translators are confronted with ambiguity. They are not always sure with which line segment a border word or phrase is to be read.

The stanza structure of Hebrew poetry is also a matter of dispute. Occasionally, recurring refrains mark off stanzas, as in Ps 42–43; 57. In Ps 110 two balanced stanzas are divided by their introductory prophecies, while Ps 119 devotes eight lines to each letter of the Hebrew alphabet. For the most part, however, no such obvious indicators are present. The NIV has used spaces to mark off poetic paragraphs (called "stanzas" in the notes). Usually this could be done with some confidence, and the reader is advised to be guided by them.

The word *Selah* is found in 39 psalms, all but two of which (Ps 140; 143, both "Davidic") are in Books I—III. It is also found in Hab 3, a psalm-like poem. Suggestions as to its meaning abound, but honesty must confess ignorance. Most likely it is a liturgical notation. The common suggestion that it calls for a brief musical interlude or for a brief liturgical response by the congregation is plausible but unproven (the former may be supported by the Septuagint rendering). In some instances its present placement in the Hebrew text is highly questionable.

Close study of the Psalms discloses that the authors often composed with an overall design in mind. This is true of the alphabetic acrostics, in which the poet devoted to each letter of the Hebrew alphabet one line segment (as in Ps 111–112), a single line (as in Ps 25; 34; 145), two lines (as in Ps 37) or eight lines (as in Ps 119). In addition, Ps 33; 38; 103 have 22 lines each, no doubt because of the number of letters in the Hebrew alphabet. Although the intended purpose of acrostics remains unknown, constructing a psalm around the alphabet may have facilitated memorization or may simply have been aesthetically pleasing.

Other literary devices were also used. For example, there are psalms that devote the same number of lines to each stanza (e.g., Ps 12; 41), or do so with variation only in the introductory or concluding stanza (e.g., Ps 38; 83; 94). Others match the opening and closing stanzas and balance the ones between (e.g., Ps 33; 86). A particularly interesting device is to place a key thematic line at the very center, sometimes constructing the whole or part of the poem around that center (see note on 6:6). Still other design features are pointed out in the notes. The authors of the psalms crafted their compositions very carefully. They were heirs of an ancient art, and they developed it to a state of high sophistication. Their works are best appreciated when carefully studied and pondered.

Theology

The Psalter is for the most part a book of the laments and praises of God's people. But there are also psalms that are explicitly instructional in form and purpose, teaching the way of godliness. As noted before (Collection, Arrangement and Date), the manner in which the whole collection has been arranged suggests that one of its main purposes was instruction in the life of faith, a faith formed and nurtured by the Law, the Prophets and the Writings. Accordingly, the Psalter is theologically rich. Its theology is, however, not abstract or systematic but doxological, confessional and practical. Included here are a number of the major themes of the Psalter.

(1) God rules over all. At the core of the theology of the Psalter is the conviction that the gravitational center of life (of right human understanding, trust, hope, service, morality, adoration), but also of history and of the whole creation (heaven and earth), is God (Yahweh, "the LORD"; see Dt 6:4). He is the Great King over all, the One to whom all things are subject. He created all things and preserves them. Because he ordered them, they have a well-defined and true identity. Because he maintains them, they are sustained and kept secure from disruption, confusion or annihilation. Because he alone is the sovereign God, they serve one divine purpose. Under God creation is an orderly and systematic whole. Through creation the Great King's majestic glory is displayed. He is good (wise, righteous, faithful, amazingly benevolent and merciful—evoking trust), and he is great (his knowledge, thoughts and works are beyond human comprehension—evoking reverent awe). By his good and lordly rule he is shown to be the Holy One.

> Unquestionably the supreme kingship of Yahweh is the most pervasive theological concept in the Psalter. It provides the fundamental perspective in which people are to view themselves, the whole creation, events in nature and history, and the future.

(2) God tolerates no rivals. As the Great King by right of creation and his enduring, absolute sovereignty, God ultimately will not tolerate any worldly power that opposes, denies or ignores him. He will come to rule the nations so that all will be compelled to acknowledge him. This expectation is no doubt the root and broadest scope of the psalmists' long view of the future. Because the Lord is the Great King beyond all challenge, his righteous and peaceful kingdom will come, overwhelming all opposition and purging the creation of all rebellion against his rule.

(3) God opposes the proud and exalts the humble. As the Great King on whom all creatures depend, God opposes the proud, those who rely on their own resources to work out their own destiny. These are the ones who ruthlessly wield whatever power they possess to attain worldly wealth, status and security—who are a law to themselves and exploit others as they will. In the Psalter, this kind of pride is the root of all evil. Those who embrace it, though they may seem to prosper, will be brought down to death, their final end. The humble, the poor and needy, those who acknowledge their dependence on the Lord in all things—these are the ones in whom God delights. Hence the "fear of the LORD"—i.e., humble trust in and obedience to the Lord—is the beginning of all wisdom (111:10). Ultimately, those who embrace it will inherit the earth. Not even death can separate them from God.

(4) God is the righteous Judge. Because God is the Great King, he is the ultimate Executor of justice among humans. God is the mighty and faithful Defender of the defenseless and the wronged. He knows every deed and the secrets of every heart. There is no escaping his scrutiny. No false testimony will mislead him in judgment. And he hears the pleas brought to him. As the good and faithful Judge, he delivers those who are oppressed or wrongfully attacked and redresses the wrongs committed against them (see note on 5:10). This is the unwavering conviction that accounts for the psalmists' impatient complaints when they, as poor and needy, boldly cry to him, "Why, LORD (have you not yet delivered me)?" "How long, LORD (before you act)?"

(5) God chose Israel as his special people. As the Great King over all the earth, the Lord has chosen the Israelites to be his inheritance among the nations. He has delivered them by mighty acts out of the hands of the world powers, has given them a land of their own and has united them with himself in covenant as the initial embodiment of his redeemed kingdom. Thus, both their destiny and his honor came to be bound up with this relationship. To them he also gave his word of revelation, which testified of him, made specific his promises and proclaimed his will. By God's covenant, Israel was to live among the nations, loyal only to their heavenly King. They were to trust solely in his protection, hope in his promises, live in accordance with his will and worship him exclusively. Israel was to sing his praises to the whole world—which in a special sense revealed their anticipatory role in the evangelization of the nations.

(6) God chose David as king. As the Great King, Israel's covenant Lord, God chose David to be his royal representative on earth. In this capacity, David was the Lord's servant. The Lord himself anointed him and adopted him as his royal "son" to rule in his name. Through him God made his people secure in the promised land and subdued all the powers that threatened them. What is more, he covenanted to preserve the Davidic dynasty. Henceforth the kingdom of God on earth, while not dependent on the house of David, was linked to it by God's decision and commitment. In its continuity and strength lay Israel's security and hope as they faced a hostile world. And since

the Davidic kings were God's royal representatives in the earth, in concept seated at God's right hand (110:1), the scope of their rule was potentially worldwide (see Ps 2).

The Lord's anointed, however, was more than a warrior king. He was to be endowed by God to govern his people with righteousness: to deliver the oppressed, defend the defenseless, suppress the wicked and thus bless the nation with internal peace and prosperity. He was also an intercessor with God on behalf of the nation, the builder and maintainer of the temple and the foremost voice calling the nation to worship the Lord.

(7) God chose Jerusalem as his royal residence. As the Great King, God (who had chosen David and his dynasty to be his royal representatives) also chose Jerusalem (the City of David) as his own

Do the Psalms Speak of Christ?

Given the amount of space NT authors give to quoting or alluding to the Psalter to comment on the life, death, and resurrection of Jesus, it might seem obvious to affirm that the Psalms (at least many of them) speak of Christ. Yet how the Psalms speak of Christ is a key question for consideration. Do the Psalms speak of Christ prophetically? Or do they more often than not speak of Christ typologically, with the Psalmist's situation or status paving the way for understanding the coming Messiah?

It is important to remember that the Psalms are not written in the literary form of prophetic literature but in the form of song. Both these genres are primarily poetic (with the Psalms exclusively so), but they differ in their purposes. The Psalms were composed to express the full range of emotions of a life lived in faith before God, from lament to trust to praise. They reveal truth about God and about humanity.

A primary way the Psalms point ahead to the coming Messiah is through their idealized portrait of Israel's king, often with a focus on the Davidic dynasty (18:50; 132:10–11). This portrait emerges primarily in a set of Psalms identified as "royal Psalms." The picture of this prototypical king extends from his enthronement (e.g., 2:6; 110:1) to his just and merciful rule (e.g., 45:4; 72:1–4, 12–14) to his victories in battle because of God's blessing (18:50; 21:1; 110:5). This idealized figure trusts in the Lord and is utterly faithful to him (21:7; 101:2–4). This idealization of a Davidic king provides the Messianic raw material for NT writers, who often draw upon these royal psalms to show how Jesus, as Messiah, is the ultimate and unique Davidic king (Mt 22:44; Ac 13:33; Heb 1:13).

Another way the Psalms point to Jesus as Messiah is through their laments about unjust suffering. Quite a number of psalms highlight the suffering of an innocent individual, with the psalmist calling on God to come to his aid, especially given his blamelessness (e.g., Ps 22; 26). New Testament authors draw upon this category of psalms for their own portraits of Jesus as the consummate person who endures unjust suffering and throughout remains faithful to God (e.g., Ps 22 in Mt 27:38–46; Heb 2:12; and Ps 31:5 in Lk 23:46).

▶ List some ways the psalms point to Jesus.

_____

_____

_____

royal city, the earthly seat of his throne. Thus Jerusalem became the earthly capital and symbol of the kingdom of God. There in his temple he ruled his people. There his people could meet with him to bring their prayers and praise and to see his power and glory. From there he brought salvation, dispensed blessings and judged the nations. And with him as the city's great Defender, Jerusalem was the secure citadel of the kingdom of God, the hope and joy of God's people.

God's goodwill and faithfulness toward his people were most strikingly symbolized by his pledged presence among them at his temple in Jerusalem, the "city of the Great King" (48:2). But no manifestation of his benevolence was greater than his readiness to forgive the sins of those who humbly confessed them and whose hearts showed him that their repentance and professions of loyalty to him were genuine.

Unquestionably the supreme kingship of Yahweh is the most basic metaphor and most pervasive theological concept in the Psalter—as in the OT generally. It provides the fundamental perspective in which people are to view themselves, the whole creation, events in nature and history, and the future. All creation is Yahweh's one kingdom. To be a creature in the world is to be a part of his kingdom and under his rule. To be a human being in the world is to be dependent on and responsible to him. To proudly deny that fact is the root of all wickedness.

God's election of Israel, together with the giving of his word, represents the renewed inbreaking of God's righteous kingdom into this world of rebellion and evil. It initiates the great divide between the righteous nation and the wicked nations, and on a deeper level between the righteous and the wicked generally, a more significant distinction that cuts even through Israel. In the end this divine enterprise will triumph. Human pride will be humbled, and wrongs will be redressed. The humble will be given the whole earth to possess, and the righteous and peaceful kingdom of God will come to full realization. When the Psalter was being given its final form, what the psalms said about the Lord and his ways with his people, with the nations, with the righteous and the wicked, and what the psalmists said about the Lord's anointed, his temple and his holy city—all this was understood in light of the prophetic literature (both Former and Latter Prophets). Relative to these matters, the Psalter and the Prophets were mutually reinforcing and interpretive.

When the Psalms speak of the king on David's throne, they speak of the king who is being crowned (as in Ps 2; 72; 110—though some think 110 is an exception) or is reigning (as in Ps 45) at the time. They proclaim his status as the Lord's anointed and declare what the Lord will accomplish through him and his dynasty. Thus they also speak of the sons of David to come—and in the exile and the postexilic era, when there was no reigning king, they spoke to Israel only of the great Son of David whom the prophets had announced as the one in whom God's covenant with David would yet be fulfilled. So it is not surprising that the NT quotes these psalms as testimonies to Christ, which in a unique way they are. In him they are truly fulfilled.

When in the Psalms righteous sufferers cry out to God in their distress (as in Ps 22; 69), they give voice to the sufferings of God's servants in a hostile and evil world. These cries became the prayers of God's oppressed people, and as such they were taken up into Israel's book of prayers. When Christ came in the flesh, he identified himself with God's humble people in the world. He became for them God's righteous servant *par excellence*, and he shared their sufferings at the hands of the wicked. Thus, these prayers became his prayers also. In him the suffering and deliverance of which these prayers speak are fulfilled. At the same time, they continue to be the prayers of those who take up their cross and follow him.

Similarly, in speaking of God's covenant people, of the city of God and of the temple in which God dwells, the Psalms ultimately speak of Christ's people, the church. The Psalter is not only the prayer book of the second temple; it is also the enduring prayer book of the people of God across generations. Now, however, Christians pray these prayers in the light of the new era of redemption that dawned with the first coming of the Messiah and that will be consummated at his second coming.

QUESTIONS FOR REFLECTION

▶ How were some ways the psalms were originally used?

• LITURICALLY

▶ What are some purposes of the psalms?

• PRAISE AND PRAYER

• CEREMONIAL RITUALS

▶ What themes in the psalms resonate with you the most?

▶ How do you see Jesus in the psalms?

BOOK I

Psalms 1 – 41

Psalm 1

1 Blessed is the one
　who does not walk in step with the
　　wicked
　or stand in the way that sinners take
　or sit in the company of mockers,
2 but whose delight is in the law of the LORD,
　and who meditates on his law day and
　　night.
3 That person is like a tree planted by streams of
　　water,
　which yields its fruit in season
　and whose leaf does not wither —
　whatever they do prospers.

4 Not so the wicked!
　They are like chaff
　that the wind blows away.
5 Therefore the wicked will not stand in the
　　judgment,
　nor sinners in the assembly of the
　　righteous.

6 For the LORD watches over the way of the
　　righteous,
　but the way of the wicked leads to
　　destruction.

Psalm 2

1 Why do the nations conspire[a]
　and the peoples plot in vain?
2 The kings of the earth rise up
　and the rulers band together
　against the LORD and against his anointed,
　　saying,
3 "Let us break their chains
　and throw off their shackles."

4 The One enthroned in heaven laughs;
　the Lord scoffs at them.
5 He rebukes them in his anger
　and terrifies them in his wrath, saying,

---

[a] 1 Hebrew; Septuagint *rage*

Ps 1–2 These two "orphan" psalms (having no title) are bound together by framing clauses ("Blessed is the one . . . whose delight is in the law of the LORD"; "Blessed are all who take refuge in him") that highlight their function as the introduction to the whole Psalter. Together they point on the one hand to God's law and to the instruction of the wisdom teachers (Ps 1) and on the other hand to a central theme in the Prophets, namely, what Yahweh has committed himself to accomplish for and through his anointed king from the house of David (Ps 2).

Ps 1 Godly wisdom here declares the final outcome of the two "ways": "the way that sinners take" (v. 1) and "the way of the righteous" (v. 6). See 34:19–22; Ps 37. The psalmist develops three contrasts that set the righteous apart from the wicked: (1) their "way" of life (vv. 1–2); (2) the life condition they experience ("like a tree," "like chaff," vv. 3–4); and, climactically, (3) God's judgment on their different ways (vv. 5–6).

1:1 *Blessed.* The happy condition of those who revere the Lord and do his will (see 94:12; 112:1; 119:1–2; 128:1; Pr 29:18; cf. Ps 41:1; 106:3; Pr 14:21; Isa 56:2) and who put their trust in him (see 40:4; 84:5,12; 144:15; 146:5; Pr 16:20; Isa 30:18; Jer 17:7; cf. Ps 2:12; 34:8). Reference is not first of all to health and wealth but to the assurance and experience that they live under the guardianship and faithful care of the gracious Lord of life. The Psalter begins by proclaiming the blessedness of the godly and ends by calling all living things to praise God in his earthly and heavenly sanctuaries (Ps 150).

1:2 *meditates on his law.* Seeking guidance for life in God's law rather than in the deliberations of the wicked.

1:5 *will not stand in the judgment.* Will not be able to withstand God's wrath when he judges (see 76:7; 130:3; Ezr 9:15; Na 1:6 and note; Mal 3:2; Mt 25:31–46; Rev 6:17). *righteous.* One of several terms in the OT for God's people; it presents them as those who honor God and order their lives according to his will.

Ps 2 Peter and John ascribed this psalm to David in Ac 4:25—possibly in accordance with the Jewish practice of honoring David as the primary author of the Psalter. A royal psalm, it was likely composed for the coronation of a Davidic king in light of the Lord's covenant with David (see 2Sa 7). As the second half of a two-part introduction to the Psalms, it proclaims the blessedness of all who acknowledge the lordship of God and his anointed and "take refuge in him" (v. 12; see introductions to Ps 1–2 and Ps 1; see also note on 1:1). This psalm is frequently quoted in the NT, where it is applied to Christ as the great Son of David and God's Anointed.

2:1–3 The nations rebel. In the ancient Near East the coronation of a new king was often the occasion for the revolt of peoples and kings who had been subject to the crown.

⁶"I have installed my king
    on Zion, my holy mountain."

⁷I will proclaim the LORD's decree:

He said to me, "You are my son;
    today I have become your father.
⁸Ask me,
    and I will make the nations your
        inheritance,
    the ends of the earth your possession.
⁹You will break them with a rod of iron[a];
    you will dash them to pieces like
        pottery."

¹⁰Therefore, you kings, be wise;
    be warned, you rulers of the earth.
¹¹Serve the LORD with fear
    and celebrate his rule with trembling.
¹²Kiss his son, or he will be angry
    and your way will lead to your
        destruction,
for his wrath can flare up in a moment.
    Blessed are all who take refuge in him.

Psalm 3[b]

*A psalm of David. When he fled
from his son Absalom.*

¹LORD, how many are my foes!
    How many rise up against me!
²Many are saying of me,
    "God will not deliver him."[c]

³But you, LORD, are a shield around me,
    my glory, the One who lifts my
        head high.
⁴I call out to the LORD,
    and he answers me from his holy
        mountain.

⁵I lie down and sleep;
    I wake again, because the LORD
        sustains me.
⁶I will not fear though tens of
        thousands
    assail me on every side.

⁷Arise, LORD!
    Deliver me, my God!
Strike all my enemies on the jaw;
    break the teeth of the wicked.

⁸From the LORD comes deliverance.
    May your blessing be on your people. •

---

a 9 Or *will rule them with an iron scepter* (see Septuagint and
Syriac)   *b* In Hebrew texts 3:1-8 is numbered 3:2-9.
c 2 The Hebrew has *Selah* (a word of uncertain meaning) here
and at the end of verses 4 and 8.

The newly anointed king is here pictured as ruler over an empire.

2:2 *LORD . . . his anointed.* To rebel against the Lord's anointed is also to rebel against the One who anointed him. *anointed.* Refers to the Davidic king and is ultimately fulfilled in Christ. The English word "Messiah" comes from the Hebrew word for "anointed one," and the English word "Christ" from the Greek word for "anointed one."

2:6 *holy mountain.* The site of the Jerusalem temple (see 2Ch 33:15; see also 3:4; 15:1; 43:3; 99:9).

2:7–9 The Lord's anointed proclaims the Lord's decree on the occasion of the king's coronation. For NT application to Jesus' resurrection, see Ac 13:33; to his superiority over angels, see Heb 1:5; to his appointment as high priest, see Heb 5:5.

2:7 *son . . . father.* In the ancient Near East the relationship between a great king and one of his subject kings, who ruled by his authority and owed him allegiance, was expressed not only by the words "lord" and "servant" but also by "father" and "son." The Davidic king was the Lord's "servant" and his "son" (2Sa 7:5,14).

2:9 According to Rev 12:5; 19:15–16 this word will be fulfilled in the triumphant reign of Christ; in Rev 2:26–27 Christ declares that he will appoint those who remain faithful to him to share in his subjugating rule over the nations. *dash them to pieces like pottery.* See Jer 19:11.

2:10–12 The rebellious rulers are warned against dishonoring the Lord and his anointed.

Ps 3–14 A group of 12 psalms composed primarily of laments divided into two groups of five (Ps 3–7; 9–13), each of which has appended to it a sixth that characterizes the human condition (Ps 8; 14).

Ps 3 The first lament in the Psalter, introducing five laments (Ps 3–7). For the typical structure of a lament psalm, see Introduction: Psalm Types. Though threatened by many foes, the psalmist prays confidently to the Lord.

3 title *When he fled.* See 2Sa 15:13—17:22. References to events in David's life stand in the superscriptions of 13 psalms (3; 7; 18; 34; 51; 52; 54; 56; 57; 59; 60; 63; 142), all but one (Ps 142) in Books I and II. See Introduction: Authorship and Titles (or Superscriptions).

3:2 See 22:7–8; 71:10–11. The psalmists frequently quote their wicked oppressors in order to portray how they mock God and his servants. For *Selah,* see NIV text note; see also Introduction: Literary Features.

3:3–4 David's confidence in God, who does not fail to answer his prayers.

3:3 *shield.* That the king is a shield (protector) of his people was a common concept in ancient Israel. That the Lord is the shield of his people is frequently asserted (84:11; 91:4; 115:9–11; Dt 33:29; Pr 30:5). *my glory.* David rejoices in the Lord as his provider and protector, who has raised him to a position of honor. *lifts my head high.* In victory over his enemies (110:7).

3:5 Even while David's own watchfulness is surrendered to sleep, the watchful Lord preserves him (4:8).

3:7 *LORD . . . my God.* That is, "LORD my God"; the two elements of a compound divine name are also frequently distributed between the two halves of a poetic line.

TYPES OF HEBREW **PARALLELISM**

TYPE	CHARACTERISTIC	EXAMPLE
I. Synonymous (Some variations on this category are provided below.)	Each element of the poetic line after the first element uses similar terms as the first while advancing the thought of the entire poetic line in some way.	**Ps 6:1** LORD, do not rebuke me in your anger or discipline me in your wrath. The similar terms between the two elements of the poetic line are "rebuke" / "discipline" and "anger" / "wrath." But in each case, the second term advances the thought of the first in some way. The purpose of the "rebuke" is clarified as "discipline" and "anger" is elevated to "wrath."
I.a. Climactic	Each element of the poetic line after the first element builds on a term presented in the first element until the climactic final element, which breaks the pattern.	**Ps 29:1–2** Ascribe to the LORD, you heavenly beings, ascribe to the LORD glory and strength. Ascribe to the LORD the glory due his name; worship the LORD in the splendor of his holiness. The first element introduces the term "ascribe to the LORD." The second element provides the content of what is ascribed. The third element asserts the Lord's worthiness to receive it. The fourth and final element arrests our attention by climactically breaking the pattern.
I.b. Emblematic	The elements of the poetic line are linked by means of the use of simile or metaphor.	**Ps 42:1** As the deer pants for streams of water, so my soul pants for you, my God. The use of "As" at the beginning of the poetic line signals the simile that will require the second element of the poetic line to complete.
I.c. Pivot Pattern	A word or clause in one element of the poetic line is intended to be read with the words before and after it. In this way the elements of the poetic line are tied more closely together.	**Ps 23:4** Even though I walk through the darkest valley, I will fear no evil, for you are with me. The pivot words in this poetic line are "I will fear no evil." They can be read equally well as the end of the preceding sentence or as the beginning of a new sentence. This ties the poetic line tightly together and also highlights its key idea.
II. Antithetic	The two elements of the poetic line use antonyms to make the same point, but from different perspectives.	**Ps 1:6** For the LORD watches over the way of the righteous, but the way of the wicked leads to destruction. The antonyms between the two elements of the poetic line are "the LORD watches over" / "destruction" and "righteous" / "wicked." Each element of the poetic line encourages people to choose the right path in life. The first element does so by highlighting the security and blessing that accompanies the right choice; the second does so by highlighting the disastrous results of the wrong choice.
III. Synthetic	This traditional category of parallelism is actually not parallelism at all. In poetic lines categorized as synthetic, the subsequent elements after the first element complete or supplement the idea expressed in the first.	**Ps 2:6** I have installed my king on Zion, my holy mountain. The second element of this poetic line simply specifies the place of the installing referred to in the first element.

Adapted from *Expositor's Bible Commentary - Abridged Edition:* The Old Testament by Kenneth L. Barker; John R. Kohlenberger III. Copyright © 1994 by the Zondervan Corporation. Used by permission of Zondervan.

Psalm 4[a]

For the director of music. With stringed instruments. A psalm of David.

[1] Answer me when I call to you,
    my righteous God.
  Give me relief from my distress;
    have mercy on me and hear my prayer.

[2] How long will you people turn my glory into
      shame?
    How long will you love delusions and seek
      false gods[b]?[c]
[3] Know that the LORD has set apart his faithful
      servant for himself;
    the LORD hears when I call to him.

[4] Tremble and[d] do not sin;
    when you are on your beds,
    search your hearts and be silent.
[5] Offer the sacrifices of the righteous
    and trust in the LORD.

[6] Many, LORD, are asking, "Who will bring us
      prosperity?"
    Let the light of your face shine on us.
[7] Fill my heart with joy
    when their grain and new wine abound.

[8] In peace I will lie down and sleep,
    for you alone, LORD,
    make me dwell in safety.

Psalm 5[e]

For the director of music. For pipes. A psalm of David.

[1] Listen to my words, LORD,
    consider my lament.
[2] Hear my cry for help,
    my King and my God,
    for to you I pray.

[3] In the morning, LORD, you hear my voice;
    in the morning I lay my requests before you
    and wait expectantly.
[4] For you are not a God who is pleased with
      wickedness;
    with you, evil people are not welcome.
[5] The arrogant cannot stand
    in your presence.
  You hate all who do wrong;
[6] you destroy those who tell lies.
  The bloodthirsty and deceitful
    you, LORD, detest.

---

[a] In Hebrew texts 4:1-8 is numbered 4:2-9.   [b] 2 Or *seek lies*
[c] 2 The Hebrew has *Selah* (a word of uncertain meaning) here
and at the end of verse 4.   [d] 4 Or *In your anger* (see
Septuagint)   [e] In Hebrew texts 5:1-12 is numbered 5:2-13.

---

break the teeth. Probably comparing the enemies to wild animals (see note on 7:2).

3:8 *From the LORD comes deliverance.* A common feature in the laments of the Psalter is a concluding expression of confidence that the prayer will be or has been heard (as in 4:8; 6:8-10; 7:10-17; 13:5-6; 17:15 and often elsewhere; see note on 12:5-6). Here David's confidence becomes a testimony to God's people.

Ps 4 A lament calling on God for relief from the threat of slanderers who falsely blame the king for some calamity (possibly a drought; see v. 7) that has stricken the nation, thereby undermining his public standing (his "glory," v. 2) and endangering the very security of his throne.

4 title *For the director of music.* Probably a liturgical notation, indicating either that the psalm was to be added to the collection of works to be used by the director of music in Israel's worship services or that when the psalm was used in the temple worship it was to be spoken by the leader of the Levitical choir—or by the choir itself (1Ch 23:5,30; 25; Ne 11:17). *With stringed instruments.* See Ps 6; 54; 55; 61; 67; 76 titles (cf. Hab 3:19). This is a liturgical notation, indicating that the Levites were to accompany the psalm with harp and lyre (see 1Ch 23:5; 25:1,3,6; cf. Ps 33:2; 43:4; 71:22; see also notes on Ps 39; 42 titles).

4:1 *righteous.* Very often the "righteousness" of God in the Psalms (and frequently elsewhere in the OT) refers to the faithfulness with which he acts. This faithfulness is in full accordance with his commitments to his people and with his status as the divine King—to whom the powerless may look for protection, the oppressed for redress and the needy for help. *my distress.* The threat of being publicly discredited by the slander of those who blame him for the nation's troubles.

4:2-3 David challenges those who have turned on him and warns them that the Lord will hear his prayer for deliverance from their attacks (see note on 5:9).

4:2 *How long . . . ?* See Introduction: Theology; see also note on 6:3. *turn my glory into shame.* That is, through slander rob David of the public honor he had enjoyed under the Lord's blessing and care (see 3:3 and note) and bring him into public disrepute. *false gods.* Or "lies," as indicated in the NIV text note (see 5:6 and note on 5:9). For *Selah,* see NIV text note and note on 3:2.

4:3 *his faithful servant.* Hebrew *ḥasid,* which occurs 26 times in the Psalms (once of God: 145:17, "faithful"; cf. 18:25) and is usually rendered (in the plural) in the NIV as "faithful (servants/people)." It is one of several Hebrew words for God's people, referring to them as people who are devoted to God and faithful to him.

4:6 In the face of widespread uncertainty, David prays for the Lord to bless. *Who . . . ?* Because of the slanders being spread, many are looking for another leader to replace the king. *will bring us prosperity.* See 34:10; 84:11; 85:12; 103:5; 107:9; cf. 16:2; Jas 1:17. *Let . . . your face shine on.* David appeals to the Lord to restore the well-being of the nation—employing a common expression for favor (see note on 13:1).

4:7 *heart.* In biblical language the center of the human spirit, from which spring emotions, thoughts, motivations, courage and action—"Everything you do flows from it" (Pr 4:23).

⁷But I, by your great love,
    can come into your house;
  in reverence I bow down
    toward your holy temple.

⁸Lead me, LORD, in your righteousness
    because of my enemies —
    make your way straight before me.
⁹Not a word from their mouth can be
        trusted;
    their heart is filled with malice.
  Their throat is an open grave;
    with their tongues they tell lies.
¹⁰Declare them guilty, O God!
    Let their intrigues be their downfall.
  Banish them for their many sins,
    for they have rebelled against you.
¹¹But let all who take refuge in you be glad;
    let them ever sing for joy.
  Spread your protection over them,
    that those who love your name may rejoice
        in you.

¹²Surely, LORD, you bless the righteous;
    you surround them with your favor as with a
        shield.

Ps 5 This lament, perhaps offered at the time of the morning sacrifice, is the psalmist's cry for help when his enemies spread malicious lies to destroy him.
5:3–7 Seven lines (in the Hebrew text) in which the psalmist declares that he prays to God "in the morning" "toward your holy temple" because he can be confident of God's dealings toward the wicked.
5:6 *tell lies.* Destroy others by slander or false testimony (see v. 9 and note).
5:7 *great love.* See article, p. 16.
5:8 *Lead me.* As a shepherd (23:3). *righteousness.* See note on 4:1. *make your way straight.* May the way down which you lead me be straight, level and smooth, free from obstacles and temptations. The psalmist prays that God will so direct him that his enemies will have no grounds for their malicious accusations (25:4; 27:11; 139:24; 143:8–10).
5:9–10 Accusation and call for judicial action (both are common elements in the laments of the Psalter when the psalmist is under threat or attack from human adversaries).
5:9 *word from their mouth.* The most frequent weapon used against the psalmists is the tongue (for a striking example, see Ps 12; see also note on 10:7). For the psalmists, the tongue is as deadly as swords and arrows (see 55:21; 57:4; 59:7; 64:3–4; cf. Pr 12:18; 25:18; Jas 3:6). *heart.* See note on 4:7. *throat . . . grave.* See note on 49:14.

Imprecatory Psalms
Ps 5:10

The presence of imprecations (curses) in the Psalms has occasioned much discussion and has caused many Christians to wince, in view of Jesus' instructions to turn the other cheek and to pray for one's enemies (Mt 5:39,44), as well as his own example on the cross (Lk 23:34). These imprecations contain appeals to God to take action to right the wrongs perpetrated against the psalmists by imposing penalties commensurate with the violence done (28:4)—in accordance also with God's norm for judicial action in human courts (Dt 25:1–3). The psalmists knew that those who have been wronged are not to avenge that wrong themselves but are to leave justice to the Lord, who says, "It is mine to avenge; I will repay" (Dt 32:35; see also Pr 20:22; Ro 12:19). Therefore, they appeal their cases to the divine Judge (Jer 15:15).

Ultimately that divine Judge would avenge all human wrongs by exercising his divine judgment upon Christ on the cross (1Pe 2:24). In the words of the NT, "Christ redeemed us from the curse of the law by becoming a curse for us" (Gal 3:13). We must therefore read these psalms today in light of the suffering Christ experienced on our behalf. And we can continue to pray that God's judgment against evildoers is realized—we can pray that it be realized by Christ on their behalf when they put their faith in him.

▶ How do imprecatory psalms give a glimpse of the people behind the writing?

Psalm 6[a]

For the director of music. With stringed instruments.
According to sheminith.[b] *A psalm of David.*

[1] LORD, do not rebuke me in your anger
 or discipline me in your wrath.
[2] Have mercy on me, LORD, for I am faint;
 heal me, LORD, for my bones are in agony.
[3] My soul is in deep anguish.
 How long, LORD, how long?

[4] Turn, LORD, and deliver me;
 save me because of your unfailing love.
[5] Among the dead no one proclaims your name.
 Who praises you from the grave?

[6] I am worn out from my groaning.

 All night long I flood my bed with weeping
 and drench my couch with tears.
[7] My eyes grow weak with sorrow;
 they fail because of all my foes.

[8] Away from me, all you who do evil,
 for the LORD has heard my weeping.

[a] In Hebrew texts 6:1-10 is numbered 6:2-11. [b] Title: Probably
a musical term

they tell lies. For the plots and intrigues of enemies, usually involving lies to discredit the king and bring him down, see Ps 17; 25; 27–28; 31; 35; 41; 52; 54–57; 59; 63–64; 71; 86; 109; 140–141—all psalms ascribed to David. Frequently such attacks came when the king was feeling low and abandoned by God (as in Ps 25; 35; 41; 71; 86; 109). See Paul's use of this verse in Ro 3:13.

5:10 *Banish them.* From God's presence, thus from the source of blessing and life (Ge 3:23). See article, p. 15.

5:12 A concluding profession of confidence that God will surely protect the innocent. See note on 3:8. *righteous.* See note on 1:5.

Ps 6 A lament in a time of severe illness, an occasion seized upon by David's enemies to vent their animosity.

6:1–3 Although the clearest threat is the psalmist's enemies (vv. 7–10), this initial stanza might suggest that sickness is another way the psalmist is experiencing God's anger (vv. 2,5). Though the Lord has sent him illness to discipline him for his sin (32:3–5; 38:1–8,17–18), David asks that God would not in anger impose the full measure of the penalty for sin, for then death must come (see v. 5; see also 130:3).

6:2 *bones.* As the inner skeleton, they here represent the whole body.

6:3 *soul.* Not a spiritual aspect in distinction from the physical, nor the psalmist's "inner" being in distinction from his "outer" being, but his very self as a liv-

Ḥesed: God's Unfailing Love
Ps 6:4

The difficulty of translating this Hebrew word (*ḥesed*) is evidenced by the variety of English expressions used to do so. These include "kindness" (Ge 19:19), "love" (Ge 20:13), "loyalty" (Jdg 8:35), "unfailing kindness" (2Sa 22:51), "unfailing love" (Ps 6:5), "devotion" (Jer 2:2), and "mercy" (Hos 6:6). Hebrew lexicons add "joint obligation," "faithfulness," "goodness," and "graciousness" as possibilities. It is important to note that all of these terms are relational. They describe characteristics that are desired and expected by each participant in a healthy relationship.

The term *ḥesed*, therefore, can be defined as behavior that is appropriate for an agreed-upon relationship. This relationship can be between one human being and another or between God and his people. Within God's covenant relationship with his people, God always upholds his side of the relationship; that is, he unfailingly exercises loving care for his relationship partners. God desires, of course, that his relationship partners reciprocate this relational faithfulness. However, it would take the coming of the God-man, Jesus Christ, whose faithfulness represents that of all who put their faith in him, for the human side of God's covenant relationship to finally be upheld as perfectly as God upholds his.

▶ How does Jesus embody the Hebrew word *ḥesed*?

The Israelite View of Death

Ps 6:5

The Israelites at this stage of their history usually viewed death as they saw it—the very opposite of life. And resurrection was not yet a part of their communal experience with God. The grave brought no escape from God (Ps 139:8), but just how they viewed the condition of the godly dead is not clear. (Non-Biblical documents from the ancient Near East indicate a general conception that immortality was reserved for the gods but that the dead continued to have some kind of shadowy existence in the dismal netherworld. Egyptian provisions for their entombed pharaohs, however, testified to a more bodily form of resurrection.)

The OT writers knew that human beings were created for life, that God's will for his people was life and that he had power over death. They also knew that death was everyone's lot, and at its proper time the godly rested in God and accepted it with equanimity (see Ge 15:15; 25:8; 47:30; 49:33; 1Ki 2:2).

Nevertheless, death could be a blessing for the righteous, affording escape from the greater evil that would overtake the living (2Ki 22:20; Isa 57:1–2). Furthermore, the death of the righteous was reputedly better than that of the wicked (Nu 23:10). It seems clear that there was even an awareness that death (as observed) was not the end of hope for the righteous—that God had more in store for them (see especially 16:9–11; 17:15; 49:14–15; 73:24). Later in the OT, of course, there would be a clearer revelation of the final resurrection of all people (Da 12:1–4).

▶ What changed the Israelite view of death over time?

---

9 The LORD has heard my cry for mercy;
  the LORD accepts my prayer.
10 All my enemies will be overwhelmed with
      shame and anguish;
  they will turn back and suddenly be put
      to shame.

Psalm 7[a]

*A shiggaion[b] of David, which he sang to the LORD
concerning Cush, a Benjamite.*

1 LORD my God, I take refuge in you;
  save and deliver me from all who pursue me,
2 or they will tear me apart like a lion
  and rip me to pieces with no one to rescue me.

3 LORD my God, if I have done this
  and there is guilt on my hands —
4 if I have repaid my ally with evil
  or without cause have robbed my foe —

---

[a] In Hebrew texts 7:1-17 is numbered 7:2-18.   [b] Title: Probably a literary or musical term

ing, conscious, personal being. Its use in conjunction with "bones" shows that the person's whole being is in agony. *How long . . . how long?* See Introduction: Theology. Such language of impatience and complaint is found frequently in the laments of the Psalter (usually "how long?" or "when?" or "why?"). It expresses the anguish of relief not (yet) granted and exhibits the boldness with which the psalmists wrestled with God on the basis of their relationship with him and their conviction concerning his righteousness (see note on 4:1).

  6:4 *unfailing love.* See article, p. 16. The Hebrew for this phrase (*ḥesed*) denotes a strong sense of goodwill and loyalty, especially such as can be relied upon in times of need. Appeal to God's "(unfailing) love" (sometimes rendered "kindness" or "mercy" [see Jos 2:12; Hos 6:6]) is frequent in the OT since it summarizes all that the Lord covenanted to show to Israel (Dt 7:9,12), as well as to David and his dynasty (89:24,28,33,49; 2Sa 7:15; Isa 55:3).

  6:5 David insists that God's praise is at stake. It is the living, not the dead, who remember God's mercies and celebrate his deliverances (see article, above). 6:6 *I am worn out from my groaning.* The very center of the poem—thus underscoring the pathos of this lament. This literary device—of placing a key thematic line at the very center of the psalm—was frequently used (see notes

5 then let my enemy pursue and overtake me;
　　let him trample my life to the ground
　　and make me sleep in the dust.[a]

6 Arise, LORD, in your anger;
　　rise up against the rage of my enemies.
　　Awake, my God; decree justice.
7 Let the assembled peoples gather around you,
　　while you sit enthroned over them on high.
8 　Let the LORD judge the peoples.
　Vindicate me, LORD, according to my
　　　righteousness,
　　according to my integrity, O Most High.
9 Bring to an end the violence of the wicked
　　and make the righteous secure —
　　you, the righteous God
　　who probes minds and hearts.

10 My shield[b] is God Most High,
　　who saves the upright in heart.
11 God is a righteous judge,
　　a God who displays his wrath every day.
12 If he does not relent,
　　he[c] will sharpen his sword;
　　he will bend and string his bow.
13 He has prepared his deadly weapons;
　　he makes ready his flaming arrows.

14 Whoever is pregnant with evil
　　conceives trouble and gives birth to
　　　disillusionment.
15 Whoever digs a hole and scoops it out
　　falls into the pit they have made.
16 The trouble they cause recoils on them;
　　their violence comes down on their own heads.

17 I will give thanks to the LORD because of his
　　　righteousness;
　　I will sing the praises of the name of the
　　　LORD Most High.

Psalm 8[d]

*For the director of music. According
to gittith.[e] A psalm of David.*

1 LORD, our Lord,
　　how majestic is your name in all the earth!

　You have set your glory
　　in the heavens.
2 Through the praise of children and infants
　　you have established a stronghold against
　　　your enemies,
　　to silence the foe and the avenger.

---

[a] 5 The Hebrew has *Selah* (a word of uncertain meaning)
here.　　[b] 10 Or *sovereign*　　[c] 12 Or *If anyone does not
repent, / God*　　[d] In Hebrew texts 8:1-9 is numbered 8:2-10.
[e] Title: Probably a musical term

on 8:4; 14:4; 34:8–14; 42:8; 47:5–6; 48:8; 54:4; 55:15; 63:6;
introduction to Ps 69; 71:14; 74:12; 82:5; 86:9; 97:7; introductions to Ps 101 and 106; 113:5; introduction to Ps 138;
141:5; see also Introduction: Literary Features).

Ps 7 A lament with an appeal to the Lord's court of justice
when enemies attack.

7 title *shiggaion.* See NIV text note. The word occurs only
here (but see its plural in Hab 3:1). *Cush.* Not otherwise
known, but as a Benjamite he was probably a supporter of
Saul. Hence the title evokes Saul's determined attempts
on David's life. See Introduction: Authorship and Titles (or
Superscriptions).

7:2 *like a lion.* As a young shepherd, David had been attacked by lions (1Sa 17:34–35). But it is also a convention
in the Psalms to liken the attack of enemies to that of
ferocious animals, especially the lion (10:9; 17:12; 22:12–
13,16,20–21; 35:17; 57:4; 58:6; 124:6).

7:6 *anger.* See v. 11 and note on 2:5. *Awake.* The Lord does
not sleep (121:4) while evil triumphs and the oppressed
cry to him in vain (as they do to Baal; see 1Ki 18:27). But
the psalmists' language of urgent prayer vividly expresses their anguished impatience with God's inaction in the
face of their great need (see 80:2; see also 78:65; Isa 51:9).

7:12–13 *sword . . . bow . . . flaming arrows.* The weapons
of the Divine Warrior used in defense of his people (see Ex
15:3) but also in judgment.

🌿 **7:17** A vow to praise God. Many laments in the Psalter
include such vows in anticipation of the expected
answer to prayer. They reflect Israel's religious consciousness that praise must follow deliverance as surely as
prayer springs from need—if God is to be truly honored.
Such praise was usually offered with thank offerings and
involved celebrating God's saving act in the presence of
those assembled at the temple (see 50:14–15,23; see also
note on 9:1).

🌿👥 **Ps 8** In praise of the Creator (not of human
beings—as is evident from the doxology that
encloses it, vv. 1,9; see also note on 9:1) out of wonder over
his sovereign ordering of the creation. Ge 1 (particularly
vv. 26–28) clearly provides the lens, but David speaks out of
his present experience of reality. Two matters especially
impressed him: (1) the glory of God reflected in the starry
heavens, and (2) the astonishing condescension of God to
be mindful of mere mortals, to crown them with glory almost godlike and to grant them authority and power over
his other creatures. At this juncture in the Psalter this
psalm surprises. After five psalms (and 64 Hebrew poetic
lines—following Ps 1–2, which introduce the Psalter; see
introduction to Ps 1–2) in which the psalmists have called

Additional Insights

The titles "Psalms" and "Psalter"
come from the Septuagint (the pre-
Christian Greek translation of the
OT), where they originally referred
to stringed instruments.

³When I consider your heavens,
  the work of your fingers,
 the moon and the stars,
  which you have set in place,
⁴what is mankind that you are mindful of them,
  human beings that you care for them?ᵃ

⁵You have made themᵇ a little lower than the
    angelsᶜ
  and crowned themᵇ with glory and honor.
⁶You made them rulers over the works of your
    hands;
  you put everything under theirᵈ feet:
⁷all flocks and herds,
  and the animals of the wild,
⁸the birds in the sky,
  and the fish in the sea,
  all that swim the paths of the seas.

⁹LORD, our Lord,
  how majestic is your name in all the earth!

Psalm 9ᵉ,ᶠ

*For the director of music. To the tune of "The Death
of the Son." A psalm of David.*

¹I will give thanks to you, LORD, with all my heart;
  I will tell of all your wonderful deeds.

ᵃ 4 Or *what is a human being that you are mindful of him, / a
son of man that you care for him?*   ᵇ 5 Or *him*   ᶜ 5 Or *than
God*   ᵈ 6 Or *made him ruler . . . ; / . . . his*   ᵉ Psalms 9 and
10 may originally have been a single acrostic poem in which
alternating lines began with the successive letters of the Hebrew
alphabet. In the Septuagint they constitute one psalm.   ᶠ In
Hebrew texts 9:1-20 is numbered 9:2-21.

on Yahweh to deal with human perversity, this psalm's
praise of Yahweh for his astounding endowment of the human race with royal "glory and honor" (v. 5) serves as a
striking and unexpected counterpoint. Its placement here
highlights the glory (God's gift) that characterizes human
beings.

8:1b–2 The mighty God, whose glory is displayed
across the face of the heavens, surprisingly evokes
the praise of little children to silence the dark powers arrayed against him (for a NT application, see Mt 21:16).
8:3–5 The vastness and majesty of the heavens as the
handiwork of God (19:1–6; 104:19–23) evoke wonder for
what their Maker has done for human beings, who are
here today and gone tomorrow (144:3–4). (See Job 7:17–21
for Job's complaint that God takes humans too seriously.)
8:3 *fingers.* See photo, below.
8:5 *angels.* The exalted creatures that surround God in his
heavenly realm (as, e.g., in Isa 6:2); but see NIV text note.
8:6–8 See Ge 1:26–27. The power to exercise benevolent rule over some of God's creatures is even now a
part of humanity's "glory and honor" (v. 5). The full realization of that potential—and vocation—belongs to humanity's appointed destiny (the eschatological import
drawn on by Paul and the author of Hebrews). But this
power—and vocation—to rule is not absolute or independent. It is participation, but not as an equal, in God's
rule; and it is a gift, not a right.
8:9 Repeated verbatim from v. 1a.
Ps 9 That Ps 9 and 10 were sometimes viewed (or used)
as one psalm is known from the Septuagint (the pre-
Christian Greek translation of the OT; see NIV text note).
Whether they were originally composed as one psalm is
not known, though a number of indicators point in that
direction. Ps 9 is predominantly praise (by the king) for
God's deliverance from hostile nations. It concludes with
a short prayer for God's continuing righteous judgments
(v. 4) on the haughty nations. Ps 10 is predominantly
prayer against the unscrupulous people within the realm.
The attacks of "the wicked" (9:5; 10:4), whether from
within or from without, are equally threatening to the
faithful within Israel. Praise of God's past deliverances is
often an integral part of prayer in the Psalter (see 3:3–4,8
and notes; 25:6; 40:1–5), as also in other ancient Near
Eastern prayers.

9:1 *heart.* See note on 4:7. *tell of.* The praise of God in
the Psalter is rarely a private matter between the
psalmist and the Lord. It is usually a public (at the temple)
celebration of God's holy virtues or of his saving acts or
gracious bestowal of blessings. In his praise the psalmist
proclaims to the assembled throng God's glorious attributes or his righteous (see note on 4:1) deeds (see, e.g.,
22:22–31; 56:12–13; 61:8; 65:1; 69:30–33). To this is usually

Babylonian boundary stone. A seated person, perhaps a priest, is
worshiping the four main Babylonian deities: Ishtar, the goddess of
love and fertility, symbolized by the star; the moon-god Sin; the sun-
god Shamash; and the goddess Ishara, symbolized by the scorpion. The
author of Ps 8 recognizes the Lord as the creator of "the moon and the
stars" (Ps 8:3).

Z. Radovan/www.BibleLandPictures.com

²I will be glad and rejoice in you;
    I will sing the praises of your name, O Most
        High.

³My enemies turn back;
    they stumble and perish before you.
⁴For you have upheld my right and my cause,
    sitting enthroned as the righteous judge.
⁵You have rebuked the nations and destroyed
        the wicked;
    you have blotted out their name for ever
        and ever.
⁶Endless ruin has overtaken my enemies,
    you have uprooted their cities;
    even the memory of them has perished.

⁷The LORD reigns forever;
    he has established his throne for judgment.
⁸He rules the world in righteousness
    and judges the peoples with equity.
⁹The LORD is a refuge for the oppressed,
    a stronghold in times of trouble.
¹⁰Those who know your name trust in you,
    for you, LORD, have never forsaken those
        who seek you.

¹¹Sing the praises of the LORD, enthroned
        in Zion;
    proclaim among the nations what he has
        done.
¹²For he who avenges blood remembers;
    he does not ignore the cries of the afflicted.

¹³LORD, see how my enemies persecute me!
    Have mercy and lift me up from the gates of
        death,
¹⁴that I may declare your praises
    in the gates of Daughter Zion,
    and there rejoice in your salvation.

¹⁵The nations have fallen into the pit they
        have dug;
    their feet are caught in the net they have
        hidden.
¹⁶The LORD is known by his acts of justice;
    the wicked are ensnared by the work of their
        hands.ᵃ
¹⁷The wicked go down to the realm of the dead,
    all the nations that forget God.
¹⁸But God will never forget the needy;
    the hope of the afflicted will never perish.

¹⁹Arise, LORD, do not let mortals triumph;
    let the nations be judged in your presence.
²⁰Strike them with terror, LORD;
    let the nations know they are only mortal.

ᵃ 16 The Hebrew has *Higgaion* and *Selah* (words of uncertain meaning) here; *Selah* occurs also at the end of verse 20.

added a call to praise God, summoning all who hear to take up the praise—to acknowledge and joyfully celebrate God's glory, his goodness and all his righteous acts. This aspect of praise in the Psalms has rightly been called the OT anticipation of NT evangelism.

9:4 *enthroned.* See note on v. 7.

🌿 **9:7–10** Celebration of the righteous rule of God (see note on 4:1; see also Ps 93; 96–99), which evokes trust on the part of those who look to the Lord.

9:7 *his throne.* In heaven (11:4). See also v. 4.

🌿 **9:10** *Those who know your name.* Those who acknowledge in their hearts who the Lord is and also faithfully live out that acknowledgment (see 91:14).

9:11 *enthroned in Zion.* God's heavenly throne (v. 7) has its counterpart on earth in his tabernacle or temple at Jerusalem, from which center he rules the world (see 2:6 and note; 20:2). For God's election of Zion as the seat of his rule, see 132:13; see also Introduction: Theology: Major Themes, 7.

🌿 **9:12** *he who avenges blood.* See Dt 32:41,43. *cries of the afflicted.* The psalter highlights God's identification with the oppressed and afflicted, the poor and the needy (see v. 18; 9:12,18; 10:17–18, 22:24; 35:10; 72:12; 76:9; 103:6).

9:14 *declare.* See notes on v. 1; 7:17. *gates.* Having been thrust down by the attacks of his enemies to "the gates of death" (v. 13), David prayed to be lifted up so he could celebrate his deliverance (see note on v. 1) in "the gates of . . . Zion."

9:15 *pit . . . dug . . . net . . . hidden.* In the Psalter, imagery drawn from the hunt is frequently (in 14 psalms) employed to depict the cunning attacks of enemies who sought to destroy by hidden means or surprise attacks, the tongue being the most common weapon (see 5:9 and note). In ancient times hunters used snares, traps, nets and pits, often in combination, and always involving concealment.

9:16 For *Selah,* see NIV text note and note on 3:2.

🌿 **9:18** *God will never forget.* Those who forget God will come to nothing, but the needy and afflicted will not be forgotten by God (v. 12). *needy . . . afflicted.* In this psalm David and Israel are counted among them because of the threat from the enemies.

9:19–20 A prayer at the conclusion of praise, asking that the Lord may ever rule over the nations as he has done in the event here celebrated—that those who "forget God" (v. 17) may know that they are only weak mortals, not gods, and cannot withstand the God of Israel (10:18).

Additional Insights

The traditional Hebrew title [for Psalms] is *tehillim* (meaning "praises"), even though many of the psalms are *tephilloth* (meaning "prayers," including laments).

1 Why, LORD, do you stand far off?
　Why do you hide yourself in times of trouble?

2 In his arrogance the wicked man hunts down
　　the weak,
　who are caught in the schemes he devises.
3 He boasts about the cravings of his heart;
　he blesses the greedy and reviles the LORD.
4 In his pride the wicked man does not seek him;
　in all his thoughts there is no room for God.
5 His ways are always prosperous;
　your laws are rejected by[b] him;
　he sneers at all his enemies.
6 He says to himself, "Nothing will ever shake me."
　He swears, "No one will ever do me harm."

7 His mouth is full of lies and threats;
　trouble and evil are under his tongue.
8 He lies in wait near the villages;
　from ambush he murders the innocent.
　His eyes watch in secret for his victims;
9 　like a lion in cover he lies in wait.
　He lies in wait to catch the helpless;
　　he catches the helpless and drags them off in
　　　his net.
10 His victims are crushed, they collapse;
　they fall under his strength.
11 He says to himself, "God will never notice;
　he covers his face and never sees."

12 Arise, LORD! Lift up your hand, O God.
　Do not forget the helpless.
13 Why does the wicked man revile God?
　Why does he say to himself,
　　"He won't call me to account"?
14 But you, God, see the trouble of the afflicted;
　you consider their grief and take it in hand.
　The victims commit themselves to you;
　　you are the helper of the fatherless.
15 Break the arm of the wicked man;
　　call the evildoer to account for his wickedness
　　that would not otherwise be found out.

16 The LORD is King for ever and ever;
　the nations will perish from his land.
17 You, LORD, hear the desire of the afflicted;
　you encourage them, and you listen to
　　their cry,
18 defending the fatherless and the oppressed,
　so that mere earthly mortals
　will never again strike terror.

---

a Psalms 9 and 10 may originally have been a single acrostic poem in which alternating lines began with the successive letters of the Hebrew alphabet. In the Septuagint they constitute one psalm.　b 5 See Septuagint; Hebrew / they are haughty, and your laws are far from

Ps 10 A prayer for rescue from the attacks of unscrupulous people—containing a classic OT portrayal of "the wicked" (v. 4). See introduction to Ps 9.
10:1 See note on 6:3.
10:2–11 Accusation lodged against the oppressors (see note on 5:9–10). Here the psalmist launches into a characterization of oppressors in general. Their deeds betray the arrogance (see vv. 2–5—so long as they prosper, v. 5) with which they defy God (see vv. 3–4,13; see especially their words in vv. 6,11,13). They greedily seek to glut their unrestrained appetites (v. 3) by victimizing others, taking account of neither God (v. 4) nor his law (v. 5).
10:2 *hunts . . . caught.* The psalmists often use imagery from the hunt (see notes on 7:2; 9:15).
10:6 *shake me.* Take away my well-being, destroy my security.
10:7 *lies and threats.* Two common weapons of the tongue (see note on 5:9). *lies.* Slander and false testimony for malicious purposes (see, e.g., 1Ki 21:8–15).
10:9 See note on 7:2. *lies in wait.* The imagery shifts from the lion to the hunter (see note on 9:15).
10:11 See note on 3:2. The arrogance with which the wicked speak (17:10), especially their easy dismissal of God's knowledge of their evil acts and his unfailing prosecution of their malicious deeds, is frequently noted by the psalmists (see v. 13; 12:4; 42:3,10; 59:7; 64:5; 71:11; 73:11; 94:7; 115:2; see also Isa 29:15; Eze 8:12).
10:12–15 Prayer that God will call the wicked to account.
10:14 Appeal to God's righteous rule (5:4–6).
10:15 *Break the arm.* Destroy the power to oppress.
10:16–18 The psalmist's confidence in the righteous reign of the Lord (see note on 3:8). Reference to the nations (v. 16) and to the humbling of proud humans (see v. 18; see also 9:19–20) suggests links with Ps 9. As the conclusion to Ps 10, this stanza expands the vision of God's just rule to its universal scope and sets the purging of the Lord's land of all nations that do not acknowledge him (v. 16) alongside God's judicial dealing with the wicked who would oppress the most vulnerable.
10:18 *mere earthly mortals.* Who are not God and so constitute no ultimate threat (49:12,20; 56:4,11; 62:9; 78:39; 103:14–16; 118:6,8–9; 144:4; Isa 31:3; Jer 17:5).

> **What emotions do you see expressed in the words of the psalmists?**

_____

_____

_____

_____

_____

▶ How can you delight in God's law (1:2)?

_____

_____

_____

_____

_____

▶ When have you felt overwhelmed and in need of rescue (3:8)?

_____

_____

_____

_____

_____

▶ What does Psalm 5 tell you about David?

_____

_____

_____

_____

_____

▶ What inspires you to praise God (Ps 8)?

_____

_____

_____

_____

_____

Psalm 11

For the director of music. Of David.

¹ In the LORD I take refuge.
    How then can you say to me:
    "Flee like a bird to your mountain.
² For look, the wicked bend their bows;
    they set their arrows against the
        strings
  to shoot from the shadows
    at the upright in heart.
³ When the foundations are being
        destroyed,
    what can the righteous do?"

⁴ The LORD is in his holy temple;
    the LORD is on his heavenly throne.
  He observes everyone on earth;
    his eyes examine them.
⁵ The LORD examines the righteous,
    but the wicked, those who love violence,
    he hates with a passion.
⁶ On the wicked he will rain
    fiery coals and burning sulfur;
    a scorching wind will be their lot.

⁷ For the LORD is righteous,
    he loves justice;
    the upright will see his face.

Psalm 12 [a]

*For the director of music. According
to* sheminith.[b] *A psalm of David.*

¹ Help, LORD, for no one is faithful anymore;
    those who are loyal have vanished from
        the human race.
² Everyone lies to their neighbor;
    they flatter with their lips
    but harbor deception in their hearts.

³ May the LORD silence all flattering lips
    and every boastful tongue —
⁴ those who say,
    "By our tongues we will prevail;
    our own lips will defend us — who is lord
        over us?"

---

[a] In Hebrew texts 12:1-8 is numbered 12:2-9.   [b] Title: Probably
a musical term

Ps 11 A lament psalm of confident trust in the Lord's righteous rule, at a time when wicked adversaries seem to have the upper hand. Two four-line stanzas (in the Hebrew text: vv. 1–3,4–6) are followed by a climactic profession of confident faith (v. 7).

11 title *For the director of music.* See note on Ps 4 title.

11:1–3 David testifies of his unshakable trust in the Lord (his refuge) to apprehensive people around him. These people, possibly his closest counselors, see the power and underhandedness of the enemy (they "shoot from the shadows," v. 2), and fear that the foundations (v. 3) are crumbling and that flight to a mountain refuge is the only recourse. David dismisses their fearful advice with disdain.

11:2 It is not clear whether those who wield the bows and arrows are archers or false accusers (see 57:4; 64:3–4; see also note on 5:9). *heart.* See note on 4:7.

11:3 *foundations.* Of the world order (82:5). To those who counsel flight, the powerful upsurge of evil appears to indicate that the righteous can no longer count on a world order in which good triumphs over evil. *righteous.* See note on 1:5.

11:4–7 Reply to the fearful: The Lord is still securely on his heavenly throne. And the righteous Lord (v. 7) discerns the righteous (v. 5) to give them a place in his presence (v. 7), while his judgment will "rain" (v. 6) on the wicked.

11:4 *The LORD is in his holy temple.* Repeated verbatim in Hab 2:20. Here reference is to his heavenly temple.

11:6 Perhaps recalling God's judgment on Sodom and Gomorrah (see Ge 19:24,28; see also Rev 14:10; 20:10; 21:8).

11:7 *righteous.* See note on 4:1. *the upright.* In spite of the danger to them (v. 2), God will vindicate them (v. 7). *see his face.* The Hebrew for "see the king's face" was an expression denoting access to the king (see Ge 43:3,5; 44:23,26; 2Sa 3:13, "come into my presence"; 14:24,28,32). Sometimes it referred to those who served before the king (see 2Ki 25:19, "royal advisers"; Est 1:14, those "who had special access to the king"). Here David speaks of special favor with and freedom of access before the heavenly King and the blessings that would bring.

Ps 12 A lament when it seems that everyone is faithless and every tongue false (Mic 7:1–7). The psalm is composed of four couplets (vv. 1–2,3–4,5–6,7–8), framed by references to the prevailing evil in the "human race" (vv. 1,8).

12 title *For the director of music.* See note on Ps 4 title.

12:1–2 Initial appeal, with description of the cause of distress.

12:1 *faithful.* See note on 4:3. *those who are loyal.* Those who maintain moral integrity.

12:3 *boastful.* See note on 10:2–11.

⁵"Because the poor are plundered and the
        needy groan,
    I will now arise," says the LORD.
    "I will protect them from those who malign
        them."
⁶And the words of the LORD are flawless,
    like silver purified in a crucible,
    like gold*ᵃ* refined seven times.

⁷You, LORD, will keep the needy safe
    and will protect us forever from the wicked,
⁸who freely strut about
    when what is vile is honored by the human
        race.

Psalm 13*ᵇ*

For the director of music. A psalm of David.

¹How long, LORD? Will you forget me forever?
    How long will you hide your face from me?
²How long must I wrestle with my thoughts
    and day after day have sorrow in my heart?
    How long will my enemy triumph over me?

³Look on me and answer, LORD my God.
    Give light to my eyes, or I will sleep in death,
⁴and my enemy will say, "I have overcome him,"
    and my foes will rejoice when I fall.

⁵But I trust in your unfailing love;
    my heart rejoices in your salvation.
⁶I will sing the LORD's praise,
    for he has been good to me.

Psalm 14

For the director of music. Of David.

¹The fool*ᶜ* says in his heart,
    "There is no God."
    They are corrupt, their deeds are vile;
        there is no one who does good.

²The LORD looks down from heaven
    on all mankind
    to see if there are any who understand,
        any who seek God.
³All have turned away, all have become corrupt;
    there is no one who does good,
        not even one.

⁴Do all these evildoers know nothing?

    They devour my people as though eating bread;
        they never call on the LORD.

ᵃ 6 Probable reading of the original Hebrew text; Masoretic
Text *earth*   *ᵇ* In Hebrew texts 13:1-6 is numbered 13:2-6.
ᶜ 1 The Hebrew words rendered *fool* in Psalms denote one
who is morally deficient.

12:5–6 A reassuring word from the Lord. Such words of
assurance following lament in the Psalms were perhaps
spoken by a priest (1Sa 1:17) or a prophet (see 51:8; 2Sa
12:13).
12:5 *I will now arise.* See Isa 33:10.
12:6 *words of the LORD.* Set in sharp contrast to the boastful words of the adversaries; they are as flawless as thoroughly refined silver. *crucible.* In the metallurgy of the
ancient Near East, heating in special furnaces was used
to extract silver and gold from crushed ore and to remove the dross (base metals such as copper, tin, iron,
bronze and lead). This process provided vivid metaphors
for many of Israel's poets (66:10; Pr 17:3; 27:21; Isa 1:22a,25;
48:10; Jer 6:27–30; 9:7; Eze 22:17–22; Zec 13:9; Mal 3:3).
seven. Signifies fullness or completeness—here thor-
oughness of refining.
12:7 *the needy.* Receiving special care from God (see note
on 9:12). *the wicked.* The enemies of v. 5.
Ps 13 A lament to the Lord seeking deliverance from a se-
rious illness that threatens to be fatal (v. 3), which would
give David's enemies just what they wanted. See introduction to Ps 6.
13:1 *How long . . . ?* See note on 6:3. *forget.* Ignore. *hide
your face.* For use in combination with "forget," see 44:24.
In moments of need the psalmists frequently ask God
why he hides his face (30:7; 44:24; 88:14), or they plead
with him not to do so (27:9; 69:17; 102:2; 143:7). When he
does hide his face, those who depend on him can only
despair (30:7; 104:29). When his face shines on a person,
blessing and deliverance come (see 4:6 and note; 31:16;
44:3; 67:1; 80:3,7,19; 119:135; see also Nu 6:25).
13:2 *heart.* See note on 4:7.
13:5 *unfailing love.* God's covenant faithfulness. See article, p. 16. *heart.* See note on 4:7.

Ps 14 A testimony concerning the moral folly of
those who live as if there were no God and therefore
feel free to cruelly prey on others who are at their mercy
(Ps 53 is a somewhat revised duplicate). In its depiction of
their godless arrogance, it has links with Ps 10; 12 (see also
28:3–5). And it shares with Ps 11 the conviction that the
righteous Lord is on his heavenly throne. This psalm
brings to closure the collection of prayers that began
with Ps 3. Five psalms (and 64 Hebrew poetic lines) after
Ps 8's surprising evocation of humanity's "glory and hon-
or" (8:5), this psalm highlights people's propensity for
evil. In this it serves as a counterpoint to that earlier recollection of the height of humanity's dignity and thereby
exposes more sharply the depth of their disgrace—from
which the petitioners in this and the preceding psalms
have suffered.

14:1 *The fool.* Hebrew *nabal*; see NIV text note (see
also 1Sa 25:25; Isa 32:5–7). *heart.* See note on 4:7. *no
God.* A practical atheism (see 10:4,6,11,13; 36:1). *no one who
does good.* Context limits the scope of this assertion (also
in v. 3) to the "fool" who takes no account of God and
does not hesitate to show his malice toward "the company of the righteous" (v. 5)—as in 9:19–20; 10:2–11,13,18;
12:1–4,7–8 (this is also the situation that Ps 11 describes).
In other psalms the psalmists do include themselves
among those who are not righteous in God's eyes (see
130:3; 143:2; see also 1Ki 8:46; Job 9:2; Ecc 7:20).

⁵But there they are, overwhelmed with dread,
 for God is present in the company of the
 righteous.
⁶You evildoers frustrate the plans of the poor,
 but the LORD is their refuge.

⁷Oh, that salvation for Israel would come out
 of Zion!
 When the LORD restores his people,
 let Jacob rejoice and Israel be glad!

Psalm 15

A psalm of David.

¹LORD, who may dwell in your sacred tent?
 Who may live on your holy mountain?

²The one whose walk is blameless,
 who does what is righteous,
 who speaks the truth from their heart;
³whose tongue utters no slander,
 who does no wrong to a neighbor,
 and casts no slur on others;
⁴who despises a vile person
 but honors those who fear the LORD;
 who keeps an oath even when it hurts,
 and does not change their mind;
⁵who lends money to the poor without interest;
 who does not accept a bribe against the
 innocent.

Whoever does these things
 will never be shaken.

Psalm 16

A miktamᵃ of David.

¹Keep me safe, my God,
 for in you I take refuge.

²I say to the LORD, "You are my Lord;
 apart from you I have no good thing."
³I say of the holy people who are in the land,
 "They are the noble ones in whom is all my
 delight."
⁴Those who run after other gods will suffer
 more and more.
 I will not pour out libations of blood to
 such gods
 or take up their names on my lips.

⁵LORD, you alone are my portion and my cup;
 you make my lot secure.
⁶The boundary lines have fallen for me in
 pleasant places;
 surely I have a delightful inheritance.

ᵃ Title: Probably a literary or musical term

14:3 *turned away.* From God and goodness.
14:4–6 The folly of the wicked exposed.
 14:4 *Do all these evildoers know nothing?* In Hebrew the centered line of the psalm (see note on 6:6), containing the hinge on which the psalm's thematic development turns. *devour . . . as though eating bread.* They attempt to destroy God's people as routinely and casually as picking up a bit of food.
Ps 15–24 Ps 15 and its distinctive counterpart, Ps 24, frame a cluster of psalms that have been arranged in a concentric pattern with Ps 19 serving as the hinge (for the thematic links between Ps 16 and 23, Ps 17 and 22, and Ps 18 and 20–21, see introductions to those psalms). The framing psalms (15; 24) are thematically linked by their evocation of the high majesty of God and their insistence on moral purity "without [which] no one will see the Lord" (Heb 12:14). At the center, Ps 19 uniquely combines a celebration of the divine majesty as displayed in the creation and an exposition of how moral purity is attained through God's law, forgiveness and shepherding care. Together, these three psalms (15; 19; 24) provide instructive words concerning the petitioners heard in the enclosed psalms, offer a counterpoint to Ps 14, and reinforce the instruction of Ps 1.
15:1 *dwell . . . live on.* Not as a priest but as God's welcome guest in his holy, royal house, the tabernacle or temple (see 23:6; 27:4–6; 61:4; 84:10; 2Sa 12:20). *holy mountain.* See note on 2:6.
15:2 *The one . . . righteous.* A summary introduction to the list that follows. *blameless.* That is, uniting loyalty to God and faithfulness to his covenant directives. See Ge 17:1; see also how the Hebrew word is used in 18:23; 37:18; 84:1; 101:2,6; 119:1,80; Jos 24:14 ("all faithfulness"); Jdg 9:16,19 ("honorably") and how a closely related word is used in Ps 7:8 ("integrity"). *righteous.* See note on 1:5.
15:3 *tongue.* See note on 5:9.
 15:4 *despises a vile person.* Or "despises those repudiated" by God—because they have become an offense to him. *those who fear the LORD.* Those who honor God and order their lives in accordance with his will because of their reverence for him.
Ps 16 A prayer for safekeeping (v. 1—the petition element in lament psalms is often relatively short; see 3:7; 22:19–21; 44:23–26), pleading for the Lord's protection against the threat of death. In accordance with its dominant theme, it could also be called a psalm of trust. In this regard it has close thematic links with Ps 23 (compare 16:2 with 23:1; 16:5 with 23:5; 16:7–8 with 23:4; 16:11 with 23:6). Together these two psalms underscore faith/trust as an essential characteristic (alongside conformity to God's law; see introduction to Ps 15–24) of those who bring their prayers to God (see introduction to Ps 1–2; see also note on 34:8–14).
16 title *miktam.* The term remains unexplained, though it always stands in the superscription of Davidic prayers occasioned by great danger (Ps 56–60).
 16:2–4 The Lord is David's one and only good thing (73:25,28); David will have nothing to do with the counterfeit gods to whom others pour out their libations (4:2).
16:3 See Ps 101.

7 I will praise the LORD, who counsels me;
   even at night my heart instructs me.
8 I keep my eyes always on the LORD.
   With him at my right hand, I will not be shaken.

9 Therefore my heart is glad and my tongue
     rejoices;
   my body also will rest secure,
10 because you will not abandon me to the realm
     of the dead,
   nor will you let your faithful*a* one see decay.
11 You make known to me the path of life;
   you will fill me with joy in your presence,
   with eternal pleasures at your right hand.

Psalm 17

A prayer of David.

1 Hear me, LORD, my plea is just;
   listen to my cry.
 Hear my prayer —
   it does not rise from deceitful lips.
2 Let my vindication come from you;
   may your eyes see what is right.

3 Though you probe my heart,
   though you examine me at night and test me,
 you will find that I have planned no evil;
   my mouth has not transgressed.
4 Though people tried to bribe me,
   I have kept myself from the ways of the
     violent
 through what your lips have commanded.
5 My steps have held to your paths;
   my feet have not stumbled.

6 I call on you, my God, for you will answer me;
   turn your ear to me and hear my prayer.
7 Show me the wonders of your great love,
   you who save by your right hand
   those who take refuge in you from their foes.
8 Keep me as the apple of your eye;
   hide me in the shadow of your wings
9 from the wicked who are out to destroy me,
   from my mortal enemies who surround me.

10 They close up their callous hearts,
   and their mouths speak with arrogance.
11 They have tracked me down, they now
     surround me,
 with eyes alert, to throw me to the ground.
12 They are like a lion hungry for prey,
   like a fierce lion crouching in cover.

13 Rise up, LORD, confront them, bring them down;
   with your sword rescue me from the wicked.

a 10 Or holy

16:4 *suffer more and more.* In contrast with David's good "portion" (v. 5), which affords him much joy (73:18–26). *libations of blood.* Blood of sacrifices poured on altars. *take up their names.* Appeal to or worship them (Jos 23:7).
16:5–6 Joy over the inheritance received from the Lord. David refers to what the Lord bestowed on his people in the promised land, either to the gift of fields there (Nu 16:14) or to the Lord himself (as in 73:26; 119:57; 142:5; La 3:24), who was the inheritance of the priests (Nu 18:20) and the Levites (Dt 10:9).
🌿 **16:5** *cup.* A metaphor referring to what the host offers his guests to drink. To the godly the Lord offers a cup of blessing (23:5) or salvation (116:13); he makes the wicked drink from a cup of wrath (Jer 25:15; Rev 14:10; 16:19). *secure.* Just as each Israelite's family inheritance in the promised land was to be secure (Lev 25; Nu 36:7).
16:7 *counsels.* Shows the way that leads to life (v. 11). *heart.* Reference here is probably to conscience.
🌿 **16:9–11** Describes the joy of the total security that God's faithful care provides. David speaks of himself and of the life he enjoys by the gracious provision and care of God. The Lord, in whom the psalmist takes refuge, wills life for him (hence he makes known to him the path of life, v. 11) and will not abandon him to the grave, even though "flesh and . . . heart . . . fail" (73:26). But implicit in these words of assurance (if not actually explicit) is the confidence that, with the Lord as his refuge, even the grave cannot rob him of life (see 17:15; 73:24; see also note on 11:7). If this could be said of David—and of all those godly Israelites who made David's prayer their own—how much more of David's promised Son! So Peter quotes vv. 8–11 and declares that with these words David prophesied of Christ and his resurrection (Ac 2:25–28). See also note on 6:5.
16:10 *faithful one.* Hebrew *ḥasid* (see note on 4:3). Reference is first of all to David, but the psalm is ultimately fulfilled in Christ (see note on vv. 9–11).
Ps 17 A lament to the Lord as Judge when David is under attack by ungodly foes. The circumstances evoked and the petition to which they gave rise show considerable affinity with Ps 22 (see introduction to Ps 15–24). The psalm reflects many of the Hebrew conventions of lodging a judicial appeal before the king.
17 title *A prayer.* See titles of Ps 86; 90; 102; 142; see also 72:20.
17:1 *plea.* For justice. His case is truly "just," not a clever misrepresentation by deceitful lips (for a similar situation, see 1Sa 24:15).
👤 **17:3–5** David's claim of innocence in support of the rightness of his case. He is not guilty of the ungodly ways of his attackers—let God examine him (cf. 139:23–24).
17:6–9 The petition: what David wants the Lord to do for him—motivated by David's trust in him ("for you will answer me," v. 6) and the Lord's unfailing righteousness (v. 7).
17:7 *wonders.* See note on 9:1. *great love.* See article, p. 16.
🌿 **17:8** *apple of your eye.* The object of God's special care. *shadow of your wings.* Image of the safety provided by the wings of a bird as it protects its young (34:15; Dt 32:11). Shade is a conventional Hebrew metaphor for protection against oppression—as shade protects from the oppressive heat of the hot desert sun. Kings were spoken of as the "shade" of those dependent on them for

¹⁴By your hand save me from such people, LORD,
  from those of this world whose reward is in
    this life.
  May what you have stored up for the wicked fill
    their bellies;
  may their children gorge themselves on it,
  and may there be leftovers for their little ones.

¹⁵As for me, I will be vindicated and will see your
    face;
  when I awake, I will be satisfied with seeing
    your likeness.

Psalm 18ᵃ

*For the director of music. Of David the servant of the
LORD. He sang to the LORD the words of this song
when the LORD delivered him from the hand of all
his enemies and from the hand of Saul. He said:*

¹I love you, LORD, my strength.

²The LORD is my rock, my fortress and my
    deliverer;
  my God is my rock, in whom I take refuge,
  my shieldᵇ and the hornᶜ of my salvation,
    my stronghold.

³I called to the LORD, who is worthy of praise,
  and I have been saved from my enemies.
⁴The cords of death entangled me;
  the torrents of destruction overwhelmed me.
⁵The cords of the grave coiled around me;
  the snares of death confronted me.

⁶In my distress I called to the LORD;
  I cried to my God for help.
  From his temple he heard my voice;
  my cry came before him, into his ears.
⁷The earth trembled and quaked,
  and the foundations of the mountains
    shook;
  they trembled because he was angry.
⁸Smoke rose from his nostrils;
  consuming fire came from his mouth,
  burning coals blazed out of it.
⁹He parted the heavens and came down;
  dark clouds were under his feet.
¹⁰He mounted the cherubim and flew;
  he soared on the wings of the wind.
¹¹He made darkness his covering, his canopy
    around him —
  the dark rain clouds of the sky.
¹²Out of the brightness of his presence clouds
    advanced,
  with hailstones and bolts of lightning.

ᵃ In Hebrew texts 18:1-50 is numbered 18:2-51.   ᵇ *2 Or
sovereign*   ᶜ *2 Horn* here symbolizes strength.

protection (as in Nu 14:9, where the same Hebrew word is
translated "protection"; La 4:20, "shadow"; Eze 31:6,12,17).
Similarly, the Lord is the protective "shade" of his people
(see 91:1; 121:5; Isa 25:4; 49:2; 51:16). *wings.* See 36:7; 57:1;
61:4; 63:7; 91:4; Ru 2:12; see also Mt 23:37.
17:10–12 The accusation lodged against the vicious adversaries (see note on 5:9–10).
17:13–14 Petition: how David wants the Lord to deal with
the two parties in the conflict.
17:13 *bring them down.* See note on 5:10. *your sword.* See
7:12–13 and note.
17:14 *such people.* See 9:19–20; 10:18; 12:1–4,8; 14:1–3.
17:15 Concluding confession of confidence (see note on
3:8). *will be vindicated.* The righteous Judge (see note
on 4:1) will acknowledge and vindicate the innocence
(righteousness) of the petitioner. *see your face.* See note
on 11:7.
Ps 18 This thanksgiving psalm of David occurs also (with
minor variations) in 2Sa 22. In its structure, apart from the
introduction (vv. 1–3) and the conclusion (vv. 46–50), the
song is composed of three major divisions: (1) the Lord's
deliverance of David from his mortal enemies in answer
to his cry for help (vv. 4–19); (2) the moral grounds for the
Lord's saving help (vv. 20–29); (3) the Lord's help recount-
ed (vv. 30–45). David's celebration of God's saving help in
answer to prayer when under threat from powerful enemies receives its counterpart in the two closely related
psalms (Ps 20–21; see introductions to those psalms and
introduction to Ps 15–24).
18 title *For the director of music.* See note on Ps 4 title. *servant of the LORD.* See 78:70; 89:3,20,39; 132:10; 144:10. The
title designates David in his royal office as, in effect, an
official in the Lord's own kingly rule over his people (2Sa
7:5)—as were Moses (see Ex 14:31), Joshua (Jos 24:29) and
the prophets (Elijah, 2Ki 9:36; Jonah, 2Ki 14:25; Isaiah, Isa
20:3; Daniel, Da 6:20). *song.* See note on Ps 30 title. *when
the LORD delivered him.* It is possible that David composed his song shortly after his victories over his foreign
enemies (2Sa 8:1–14), but it may have been later in his life.
delivered him . . . from the hand of Saul. See 1Sa 18–27.
18:1–3 A prelude of praise.
18:1 Does not occur in 2Sa 22. *I love you.* From an unusual
Hebrew expression that emphasizes the fervor of David's
love; cf. 116:1. *my strength.* My source of strength.
18:2 *rock . . . rock.* "Rock" is a common poetic figure for
God (or the gods: Dt 32:31,37; Isa 44:8), symbolizing his
unfailing (Isa 26:4) strength as a fortress refuge (vv. 31,46;
31:2–3; 42:9; 62:7; 71:3; 94:22; Isa 17:10) or as deliverer (19:14;
62:2; 78:35; 89:26; 95:1; Dt 32:15). It is a figure particularly
appropriate for David's experiences (1Sa 23:14,25; 24:2,22),
for the Lord was his true security. *shield.* See note on 3:3.
horn. See NIV text note; Dt 33:17; Jer 48:25.
18:4 *torrents of destruction.* See note on 30:1.
18:5 *cords of the grave . . . snares of death.* See 116:3. He
had, as it were, been snared by death (personified) and
bound as a prisoner of the grave (Job 36:8). In 1Sa 20:3
David declared, "There is only a step between me and
death."
18:7–15 The Lord came to the aid of his servant—depicted
as a fearful theophany (divine manifestation) of the heavenly Warrior descending in wrathful attack upon David's

¹³The LORD thundered from heaven;
the voice of the Most High resounded.ᵃ
¹⁴He shot his arrows and scattered the enemy,
with great bolts of lightning he routed
them.
¹⁵The valleys of the sea were exposed
and the foundations of the earth laid bare
at your rebuke, LORD,
at the blast of breath from your nostrils.

¹⁶He reached down from on high and took hold
of me;
he drew me out of deep waters.
¹⁷He rescued me from my powerful enemy,
from my foes, who were too strong for me.
¹⁸They confronted me in the day of my disaster,
but the LORD was my support.
¹⁹He brought me out into a spacious place;
he rescued me because he delighted in me.

²⁰The LORD has dealt with me according to my
righteousness;
according to the cleanness of my hands he
has rewarded me.
²¹For I have kept the ways of the LORD;
I am not guilty of turning from my God.
²²All his laws are before me;
I have not turned away from his decrees.
²³I have been blameless before him
and have kept myself from sin.
²⁴The LORD has rewarded me according to my
righteousness,
according to the cleanness of my hands in
his sight.

²⁵To the faithful you show yourself faithful,
to the blameless you show yourself
blameless,
²⁶to the pure you show yourself pure,
but to the devious you show yourself
shrewd.
²⁷You save the humble
but bring low those whose eyes are
haughty.

ᵃ 13 Some Hebrew manuscripts and Septuagint (see also
2 Samuel 22:14); most Hebrew manuscripts *resounded, / amid
hailstones and bolts of lightning*

enemies (5:4–5; 68:1–8; 77:16–19; Mic 1:3–4; Na 1:2–6; Hab 3:3–15). He sweeps down upon them like a fierce thunderstorm (Jos 10:11; Jdg 5:20–22; 1Sa 2:10; 7:10; 2Sa 5:24; Isa 29:6).

18:8 God's fierce majesty is portrayed in terms similar to those applied to the awesome Leviathan (Job 41:19–21).

18:10 *cherubim.* Heavenly beings who are symbols of royalty (see 80:1; 99:1). In Eze 1 and 10, they appear as the bearers of the throne-chariot of God.

18:14 *arrows.* For shafts of lightning as the arrows of God, see 77:17; 144:6; Hab 3:11; see also photo, below.

18:15 Perhaps recalls the great deed of the heavenly Warrior when he defeated Israel's enemy at the Red Sea (Ex 15:1–12).

18:16–19 Deliverance from the enemy.

18:16 *deep waters.* See note on 32:6.

18:19 *spacious place.* He is free to roam unconfined by the threats and dangers that had hemmed him in (vv. 4–6,16–18). To be afflicted or oppressed is like being bound by fetters (Job 36:8,13). To be delivered is to be set free (Job 36:16). *delighted in me.* God was pleased with David as "a man after his own heart" (1Sa 13:14; see also 1Sa 15:28; 1Ki 14:8; 15:5; Ac 13:22), a man with whom he had made a covenant assuring him of an enduring dynasty (2Sa 7) and who was faithful to that covenant (vv. 20–29).

18:20–24 David's righteousness rewarded. David's assertion of his righteousness (like that of Samuel, 1Sa 12:3; Hezekiah, 2Ki 20:3; Job, Job 13:23; 27:6; 31; see also Ps 17:3–5; 26; 44:17–18; 101) is not a pretentious boast of sinless perfection (51:5). Rather, it is a claim that, in contrast to his enemies, he has devoted himself entirely to the service of the Lord, that his has been a godli-

Plaque of a storm god shows him on top of a horned animal, holding a weapon in his right hand and bolts of lightning in his left. It was common for people in the ancient world to connect natural phenomena with their gods. Psalm 18:14 also describes Israel's God as being God of the storms: The Lord "shot his arrows and scattered the enemy, with great bolts of lightning he routed them."

Oriental Institute Museum, Public Domain

²⁸ You, LORD, keep my lamp burning;
　　my God turns my darkness into light.
²⁹ With your help I can advance against a
　　　troop^a;
　　with my God I can scale a wall.

³⁰ As for God, his way is perfect:
　　The LORD's word is flawless;
　　he shields all who take refuge in him.
³¹ For who is God besides the LORD?
　　And who is the Rock except our God?
³² It is God who arms me with strength
　　and keeps my way secure.
³³ He makes my feet like the feet of a deer;
　　he causes me to stand on the heights.
³⁴ He trains my hands for battle;
　　my arms can bend a bow of bronze.
³⁵ You make your saving help my shield,
　　and your right hand sustains me;
　　your help has made me great.
³⁶ You provide a broad path for my feet,
　　so that my ankles do not give way.

³⁷ I pursued my enemies and overtook
　　　them;
　　I did not turn back till they were
　　　destroyed.
³⁸ I crushed them so that they could not rise;
　　they fell beneath my feet.
³⁹ You armed me with strength for battle;
　　you humbled my adversaries before me.
⁴⁰ You made my enemies turn their backs in
　　　flight,
　　and I destroyed my foes.
⁴¹ They cried for help, but there was no one to
　　　save them—
　　to the LORD, but he did not answer.
⁴² I beat them as fine as windblown dust;
　　I trampled them^b like mud in the streets.
⁴³ You have delivered me from the attacks of the
　　　people;
　　you have made me the head of nations.
　People I did not know now serve me,
⁴⁴　　foreigners cower before me;
　　as soon as they hear of me, they obey me.
⁴⁵ They all lose heart;
　　they come trembling from their
　　　strongholds.

⁴⁶ The LORD lives! Praise be to my Rock!
　　Exalted be God my Savior!
⁴⁷ He is the God who avenges me,
　　who subdues nations under me,

---

^a 29 Or *can run through a barricade*　　^b 42 Many Hebrew manuscripts, Septuagint, Syriac and Targum (see also 2 Samuel 22:43); Masoretic Text *I poured them out*

ness with integrity—itself the fruit of God's gracious working in his heart (51:10–12).

18:23 *blameless.* See note on 15:2.

18:25–29 Because God responds to people in accordance with their ways (Job 34:11; Pr 3:34), David has experienced the Lord's favor.

18:26 *shrewd.* The pattern of God responding in identical fashion (v. 25) is broken because God is pure. But he can respond with that which is cunning or crafty (see 1Ki 22:23).

18:27 The thought of this verse fits well with David's and Saul's reversals of status (see 1Sa 16:13–14). It also echoes the central theme of Hannah's song (1Sa 2:1–10), which the author of Samuel uses to highlight a major thesis of his account of the ways of God as he brings about his kingdom.

18:28 *keep my lamp burning.* God causes his life, his undertakings and his dynasty to flourish (see especially Job 18:5–6; 21:17). *light.* See note on 27:1.

18:30–36 By God's blessing David the king has thrived.

18:30 *is perfect.* Does not fail—and so, because of his blessing, David's way has not failed (v. 32). *The LORD's word.* While the reference is general, it applies especially to God's promise to David (2Sa 7:8–16). *flawless.* See note on 12:6. *shields.* See note on 3:3.

18:37–42 With God's help David has crushed all his foes.

18:43–45 God has made David the head of nations (2Sa 5; 8; 10)—he who had been, it seemed, on the brink of death (see vv. 4–5 and note on v. 5), sinking into the depths (v. 16).

18:43 *attacks of the people.* All the threats he had endured from his own people in the days of Saul, and perhaps also in the time of Absalom's rebellion. *People I did not know.* Those with whom he had had no previous relationship.

18:46–50 Concluding doxology.

18:46 *The LORD lives!* God's interventions and blessings in David's behalf have shown him to be the living God (Dt 5:26).

18:47 *avenges me.* Redresses the wrongs committed against me (see Dt 32:41).

What can you do with God's help?

_____

_____

_____

_____

_____

_____

_____

48 who saves me from my enemies.
You exalted me above my foes;
    from a violent man you rescued me.
49 Therefore I will praise you, LORD, among the
    nations;
    I will sing the praises of your name.

50 He gives his king great victories;
    he shows unfailing love to his anointed,
    to David and to his descendants
        forever.

Psalm 19[a]

For the director of music. A psalm of David.

1 The heavens declare the glory of God;
    the skies proclaim the work of his hands.
2 Day after day they pour forth speech;
    night after night they reveal knowledge.
3 They have no speech, they use no words;
    no sound is heard from them.
4 Yet their voice[b] goes out into all the earth,
    their words to the ends of the world.
In the heavens God has pitched a tent for
    the sun.
5   It is like a bridegroom coming out of his
        chamber,
    like a champion rejoicing to run his
        course.
6 It rises at one end of the heavens
    and makes its circuit to the other;
    nothing is deprived of its warmth.

7 The law of the LORD is perfect,
    refreshing the soul.
The statutes of the LORD are trustworthy,
    making wise the simple.
8 The precepts of the LORD are right,
    giving joy to the heart.
The commands of the LORD are radiant,
    giving light to the eyes.
9 The fear of the LORD is pure,
    enduring forever.
The decrees of the LORD are firm,
    and all of them are righteous.

[a] In Hebrew texts 19:1-14 is numbered 19:2-15.
[b] 4 Septuagint, Jerome and Syriac; Hebrew *measuring line*

Additional Insights

In its final form the Psalter was divided into five Books, each of which was provided with a concluding doxology.

18:49 David vows to praise the Lord among the nations (see note on 9:1). Paul quotes this verse in Ro 15:9.

🌿 **18:50** *his king ... his anointed.* David views himself as the Lord's chosen and anointed king (see 1Sa 16:13). *unfailing love.* Hebrew *ḥesed* (see article, p. 16). David's final words recall the Lord's covenant with him (see 2Sa 7:8–16). The whole song is to be understood in the context of David's official capacity and the Lord's covenant with him. What David claims in this grand conclusion—as, indeed, in the whole psalm—has been and is being fulfilled in Jesus Christ, David's greatest descendant.

Ps 19 A hymn extolling the majestic "glory of God" (v. 1) as displayed in the heavens and in "the law of the LORD" (v. 7), which blesses the lives of those who heed it (vv. 7–13). An embedded prayer (vv. 12–13) asks God to provide what his law cannot: forgiveness for "hidden faults" and a shepherd's care that preserves from "willful sins." Placed next to Ps 18, this psalm completes the cycle of praise—for the Lord's saving acts, for his glory reflected in creation and for his life-nurturing law. Placed at the center of Ps 15–24, it powerfully reinforces the themes of the two framing psalms (see introduction to Ps 15–24) and reminds all who would enter Yahweh's presence that they must come as those who have seen with their eyes his glory on display in the creation and who have in their hearts a deep devotion to his law.

19 title *For the director of music.* See note on Ps 4 title.

19:1–4a The silent heavens speak, declaring the glory of their Maker to all who are on the earth (148:3). The heavenly lights are not divine (see Ge 1:16; Dt 4:19; 17:3), nor do they control or disclose anyone's destiny (Isa 47:13; Jer 10:2; Da 4:7). Their glory testifies to the righteousness and faithfulness of the Lord who created them (see 50:6; 89:5–8; 97:6; see also Ro 1:19–20).

🌿 **19:4** Interpreting this heavenly proclamation eschatologically in the light of Christ, Paul applies this verse to the proclamation of the gospel in his own day (Ro 10:18).

19:4b–6 The heavens are the divinely pitched "tent" for the majestic sun—widely worshiped in the ancient Near East (cf. Dt 4:19; 17:3; 2Ki 23:5,11; Jer 8:2; Eze 8:16), but here, as in 136:7–8; Ge 1:16, a mere creation of God. Of the created realm, the sun is the supreme metaphor of the glory of God (84:11; Isa 60:19–20), as it makes its daily triumphant sweep across the whole extent of the heavens and pours out its warmth on every creature.

19:5 *like a bridegroom.* The sun's radiance at sunrise is like the joy of a bridegroom on his wedding day.

19:7–9 Stately, rhythmic celebration of the life-nurturing effects of the Lord's revealed law (Ps 119).

19:7 *trustworthy.* God's laws are "trustworthy" (111:7; 119:86) or "firm" (19:9) or "true" (119:142,151,160) in the sense that they faithfully represent God's righteous will (119:138,160), they endure generation after generation (they "stand firm," 93:5; see also 119:91,152,160), and they truly fulfill their purpose in the lives of those who honor them (see 119:43,93,98–100,165)—they can be trusted. *the simple.* The naive, those whose understanding and judgment have not yet matured (see 119:98–100; Pr 1:4; cf. also 2Ti 3:15; Heb 5:13–14).

19:8 *heart.* See note on 4:7.

¹⁰ They are more precious than gold,
　　than much pure gold;
　they are sweeter than honey,
　　than honey from the honeycomb.
¹¹ By them your servant is warned;
　　in keeping them there is great reward.
¹² But who can discern their own errors?
　　Forgive my hidden faults.
¹³ Keep your servant also from willful sins;
　　may they not rule over me.
　Then I will be blameless,
　　innocent of great transgression.

¹⁴ May these words of my mouth and this
　　meditation of my heart
　be pleasing in your sight,
　　LORD, my Rock and my Redeemer.

Psalm 20 ᵃ

For the director of music. A psalm of David.

¹ May the LORD answer you when you are in
　　distress;
　may the name of the God of Jacob protect you.
² May he send you help from the sanctuary
　　and grant you support from Zion.
³ May he remember all your sacrifices
　　and accept your burnt offerings.ᵇ
⁴ May he give you the desire of your heart
　　and make all your plans succeed.
⁵ May we shout for joy over your victory
　　and lift up our banners in the name of our God.

　May the LORD grant all your requests.

⁶ Now this I know:
　　The LORD gives victory to his anointed.
　He answers him from his heavenly sanctuary
　　with the victorious power of his right hand.
⁷ Some trust in chariots and some in horses,
　　but we trust in the name of the LORD our God.
⁸ They are brought to their knees and fall,
　　but we rise up and stand firm.
⁹ LORD, give victory to the king!
　　Answer us when we call!

ᵃ In Hebrew texts 20:1-9 is numbered 20:2-10.　ᵇ 3 The Hebrew has *Selah* (a word of uncertain meaning) here.

Additional Insights

In its final edition, the Psalter contained 150 psalms.

19:9 *fear of the LORD.* Honoring God by obeying what the law requires (see note on 15:4).
19:10–11 The matchless worth of God's law and its rich value for life (Dt 5:33).
19:12–13 Humanity's moral consciousness remains flawed; hence people err without realizing it and have reason to seek pardon for "hidden faults" (v. 12; see Lev 5:2–4). "Willful sins" (v. 13), however, are open rebellion; they are the "great transgression" (v. 13) that leads to being cut off from God's people (Nu 15:30–31) apart from God's gracious forgiveness (Ps 51).
19:14 The psalmist presents this hymn as a praise offering to the Lord. *Rock.* See note on 18:2.
Ps 20 A liturgy of prayer for the king just before he goes out to battle against a threatening force (2Ch 20:1–30). Ps 20–21 serve as the counterpart of Ps 18 in the arrangement of Ps 15–24 (see introduction to Ps 15–24); in Ps 18 we hear the voice of the king, while in Ps 20–21 we hear the voices of the people.
20 title *For the director of music.* See note on Ps 4 title.
20:1–5 The people (perhaps his assembled army) address the king, adding their prayers to his prayer for victory.
20:1 *name.* See vv. 5,7.
20:2 *Zion.* See note on 9:11.
20:3 For *Selah*, see NIV text note and note on 3:2.
20:5 *banners.* Probably the troop standards around which the units rallied.
20:6 A participant in the liturgy (perhaps a Levite; see 2Ch 20:14) announces assurance that the king's prayer will be heard. *his anointed.* The king appointed by the Lord to rule in his name (see 2:2 and note).
20:7–8 The army's confession of trust in the Lord rather than in a chariot corps (cf. 33:16–17; Dt 17:16)—the enemy perhaps came reinforced by such a prized corps. See David's similar confession of confidence when he faced Goliath (1Sa 17:45–47).
20:9 The army's concluding petition.

> **List some of your favorite songs and hymns.**

＿＿＿＿＿＿＿＿＿＿＿＿＿＿＿＿＿＿

＿＿＿＿＿＿＿＿＿＿＿＿＿＿＿＿＿＿

＿＿＿＿＿＿＿＿＿＿＿＿＿＿＿＿＿＿

＿＿＿＿＿＿＿＿＿＿＿＿＿＿＿＿＿＿

＿＿＿＿＿＿＿＿＿＿＿＿＿＿＿＿＿＿

＿＿＿＿＿＿＿＿＿＿＿＿＿＿＿＿＿＿

＿＿＿＿＿＿＿＿＿＿＿＿＿＿＿＿＿＿

▶ What do the psalms reveal about human nature (Ps 12)?

_____

_____

_____

_____

_____

▶ Could you ask God to judge your heart (17:3)?

_____

_____

_____

_____

_____

▶ How does nature communicate God's glory (Ps 19)?

_____

_____

_____

_____

_____

▶ When might the Israelites have sung Psalm 20?

_____

_____

_____

_____

_____

Psalm 21[a]

For the director of music. A psalm of David.

¹ The king rejoices in your strength, LORD.
How great is his joy in the victories you
give!

² You have granted him his heart's desire
and have not withheld the request of
his lips.[b]

³ You came to greet him with rich blessings
and placed a crown of pure gold on his
head.

⁴ He asked you for life, and you gave it to
him —
length of days, for ever and ever.

⁵ Through the victories you gave, his glory is
great;
you have bestowed on him splendor and
majesty.

⁶ Surely you have granted him unending
blessings
and made him glad with the joy of your
presence.

⁷ For the king trusts in the LORD;
through the unfailing love of the Most
High
he will not be shaken.

⁸ Your hand will lay hold on all your enemies;
your right hand will seize your foes.

⁹ When you appear for battle,
you will burn them up as in a blazing
furnace.
The LORD will swallow them up in his wrath,
and his fire will consume them.

¹⁰ You will destroy their descendants from the
earth,
their posterity from mankind.

¹¹ Though they plot evil against you
and devise wicked schemes, they cannot
succeed.

¹² You will make them turn their backs
when you aim at them with drawn bow.

¹³ Be exalted in your strength, LORD;
we will sing and praise your might.

---

a In Hebrew texts 21:1-13 is numbered 21:2-14.   *b 2* The Hebrew has *Selah* (a word of uncertain meaning) here.

Ps 21 A psalm of praise for victories granted to the king. It is thus linked with Ps 20. Here the people's praise follows that of the king (v. 1); there (Ps 20) the people's prayer was added to the king's. In its structure, the psalm is framed by vv. 1,13 ("in your strength, LORD" is in both verses).

21:2–7 The people celebrate the Lord's many favors to the king: all "his heart's desire" (v. 2). Verse 2 announces the theme; vv. 3–5 develop the theme; v. 6 climactically summarizes the theme.

21:2 *heart's.* See note on 4:7. For *Selah,* see NIV text note and note on 3:2.

21:3 *came to greet him.* Back from the battles. *placed a crown . . . on his head.* Exchanged the warrior's helmet for the ceremonial emblem of royalty—possibly the captured crown of the defeated king (2Sa 12:30).

21:4 The king's life has been spared—to live "for ever and ever" (see 1Ki 1:31; Da 2:4; 3:9; see also 1Sa 10:24; 1Ki 1:25,34,39).

21:6 *your presence.* Your favor, which is the supreme cause of joy because it is the greatest blessing and the wellspring of all other blessings.

21:7 A participant in the liturgy (perhaps a priest or Levite) proclaims the king's trust in the Lord and the reason for his security. *LORD . . . Most High.* That is, "LORD Most High" (see 7:17; see also note on 3:7). *unfailing love.* God's covenant faithfulness (see article, p. 16). *shaken.* See note on 10:6.

21:8–12 The people hail the future victories of their triumphant king. Verse 8 announces the theme; vv. 9–11 develop the theme; v. 12 summarizes the theme.

21:9 *The LORD . . . in his wrath.* Credits the king's victories to the Lord's wrath.

21:10 The king's royal enemies will be left with no descendants to rise up against him again.

21:13 Conclusion—and return to the beginning: Lord, assert your strength, in which "the king rejoices" (v. 1; see also v. 7, "trusts"), and we will ever "praise your might."

Additional Insights

Both the scope of its subject matter and the arrangement of the [Psalms] strongly suggest that this collection was viewed by its final editors as a guide for the life of faith in accordance with the Law, the Prophets and the Writings.

Psalm 22[a]

For the director of music. To the tune of "The Doe
of the Morning." A psalm of David.

[1] My God, my God, why have you forsaken me?
Why are you so far from saving me,
so far from my cries of anguish?
[2] My God, I cry out by day, but you do not answer,
by night, but I find no rest.[b]

[3] Yet you are enthroned as the Holy One;
you are the one Israel praises.[c]
[4] In you our ancestors put their trust;
they trusted and you delivered them.
[5] To you they cried out and were saved;
in you they trusted and were not put to shame.

[6] But I am a worm and not a man,
scorned by everyone, despised by the people.
[7] All who see me mock me;
they hurl insults, shaking their heads.
[8] "He trusts in the LORD," they say,
"let the LORD rescue him.
Let him deliver him,
since he delights in him."

[9] Yet you brought me out of the womb;
you made me trust in you, even at my
mother's breast.
[10] From birth I was cast on you;
from my mother's womb you have been my God.

[11] Do not be far from me,
for trouble is near
and there is no one to help.

[12] Many bulls surround me;
strong bulls of Bashan encircle me.
[13] Roaring lions that tear their prey
open their mouths wide against me.
[14] I am poured out like water,
and all my bones are out of joint.
My heart has turned to wax;
it has melted within me.
[15] My mouth[d] is dried up like a potsherd,
and my tongue sticks to the roof of my mouth;
you lay me in the dust of death.

[16] Dogs surround me,
a pack of villains encircles me;
they pierce[e] my hands and my feet.
[17] All my bones are on display;
people stare and gloat over me.

[a] In Hebrew texts 22:1-31 is numbered 22:2-32.   [b] 2 Or *night,*
and am not silent   [c] 3 Or *Yet you are holy, / enthroned on the*
praises of Israel   [d] 15 Probable reading of the original
Hebrew text; Masoretic Text *strength*   [e] 16 Dead Sea Scrolls
and some manuscripts of the Masoretic Text, Septuagint and
Syriac; most manuscripts of the Masoretic Text *me, / like a lion*

Ps 22 An anguished lament of David as a godly sufferer victimized by the vicious and prolonged attacks of enemies whom he has not provoked and from
whom the Lord has not (yet) delivered him. No other
psalm fitted quite so aptly the circumstances of Jesus at
his crucifixion. Hence on the cross he recited its opening
line (see Mt 27:46 and parallels), and the Gospel writers,
especially Matthew and John, frequently alluded to it (as
they did to Ps 69) in their accounts of Christ's passion (Mt
27:35,39,43; Jn 19:23–24,28). They saw in the passion of
Jesus the fulfillment of this cry of the righteous sufferer.
The author of Hebrews placed the words of v. 22 on Jesus'
lips (see Heb 2:12).
22 title See note on Ps 4 title.
22:1 *why . . . ? Why . . . ?* See note on 6:3.
22:1a Quoted by Jesus (see Mt 27:46; Mk 15:34).
22:3–5 Recollection of what the Lord has done for Israel
(see note on vv. 9–10).
22:3 *enthroned.* See note on 9:11. *Holy One.* See Lev 11:44.
the one Israel praises. For his saving acts on their behalf
(148:14; Dt 10:21; Jer 17:14).
22:6 *a worm and not a man.* See Job 25:6; Isa 41:14; 52:14.
22:7 *hurl insults, shaking their heads.* See Mt 27:39; Mk
15:29; see also note on 5:9.
22:8 Quoted in part in Mt 27:43; see note on 3:2.
22:9–10 Recollection of what the Lord has done for him
(see note on vv. 3–5).
22:12–18 The psalmist's deep distress. In vv. 12–13,16–18 he
uses four figures to portray the attacks of his enemies; in
vv. 14–15 he describes his inner sense of powerlessness
under their fierce attacks.
22:12–13,16 *bulls . . . lions . . . Dogs.* Metaphors for the enemies (see note on 7:2).
22:12 *Bashan.* Noted for its good pasture, and hence for
the size and vigor of its animals (see Dt 32:14; Eze 39:18;
Am 4:1).
22:14 *bones . . . heart.* See note on 102:4. *heart.* See note
on 4:7.
22:16 *pierce my hands and my feet.* The "dogs" wound his
limbs as he seeks to ward off their attacks. But see also
v. 20 and note on vv. 20–21; Isa 53:5; Zec 12:10; Jn 19:34,37.
22:17 *All my bones are on display.* The figure is probably
that of one attacked by highway robbers or enemy soldiers, who strip him of his garments (see v. 18; see also
note on vv. 20–21).

Additional Insights

[Psalm 22 is an] anguished lament of
David as a godly sufferer victimized by
the vicious and prolonged attacks of
enemies whom he has not provoked
and from whom the Lord has not (yet)
delivered him.

18 They divide my clothes among them
    and cast lots for my garment.

19 But you, LORD, do not be far from me.
    You are my strength; come quickly to
        help me.
20 Deliver me from the sword,
    my precious life from the power of
        the dogs.
21 Rescue me from the mouth of the lions;
    save me from the horns of the wild oxen.

22 I will declare your name to my people;
    in the assembly I will praise you.
23 You who fear the LORD, praise him!
    All you descendants of Jacob, honor him!
    Revere him, all you descendants of Israel!
24 For he has not despised or scorned
    the suffering of the afflicted one;
he has not hidden his face from him
    but has listened to his cry for help.

25 From you comes the theme of my praise in
    the great assembly;
    before those who fear you*a* I will fulfill
        my vows.
26 The poor will eat and be satisfied;
    those who seek the LORD will praise him —
    may your hearts live forever!

27 All the ends of the earth
    will remember and turn to the LORD,
and all the families of the nations
    will bow down before him,
28 for dominion belongs to the LORD
    and he rules over the nations.

29 All the rich of the earth will feast and
    worship;
    all who go down to the dust will kneel
        before him —
    those who cannot keep themselves alive.
30 Posterity will serve him;
    future generations will be told about
        the Lord.
31 They will proclaim his righteousness,
    declaring to a people yet unborn:
    He has done it!

Psalm 23

A psalm of David.

1 The LORD is my shepherd, I lack nothing.
2   He makes me lie down in green pastures,
  he leads me beside quiet waters,
3   he refreshes my soul.

a 25 Hebrew *him*

22:18 See introduction to this psalm; see also Jn 19:23–24.
22:20–21 The psalmist's prayer recalls in reverse order the four figures by which he portrayed his attackers in vv. 12–13,16–18: "sword," "dogs," "lions," "wild oxen." Here "sword" refers back to the scene described in vv. 16–18, and thus many interpret it as an attack by robbers or enemy soldiers, though "sword" is often used figuratively of any violent death.
22:21 *wild oxen.* The aurochs, the wild ancestor of domestic cattle.
22:22–31 Vows to praise the Lord when the Lord's sure deliverance comes (see note on 7:17). The vows proper appear in vv. 22,25. Verses 23–24 call for praise to God that will accompany the psalmist's praise (see note on 9:1). Verses 26–31 describe the expanding company of those who will take up the praise—a worldwide company of persons from every station in life and continuing through the generations. No psalm or prophecy contains a grander vision of the scope of the throng of worshipers who will join in the praise of God's saving acts.
22:23 *fear the LORD.* See v. 25; see also note on 15:4.
22:25 *assembly.* The worshipers gathered at the tabernacle or temple (see note on 1:5).
22:26 *will eat and be satisfied.* As they share in the ceremonial festival of praise (Lev 7:11–27).
22:27 *All the ends of the earth.* All people will be told of God's saving acts (see 18:49 and note on 9:1). The good news that the God of Israel hears the prayers of his people and saves them will move them to turn from their idols to the true God (cf. 1Th 1:9).
22:28 The rule of the God of Israel is universal, and the nations will come to recognize that fact through what he does in behalf of his people (see Ps 47; Ge 12:2–3; see also Dt 32:21; Ro 10:19; 11:13–14).
22:29 *All the rich . . . all who go down to the dust.* The most prosperous and those on the brink of death, and all those whose life situation falls in between these two extremes. *dust.* See v. 15; see also Job 7:21.
22:31 *righteousness.* See note on 4:1.
Ps 23 A profession of joyful trust in the Lord as the good Shepherd-King. In the arrangement of Ps 15–24 it serves as the counterpart of Ps 16, with which it is thematically linked (see introduction to Ps 16; see also introduction to Ps 15–24). The psalm may have accompanied a festival of praise at "the house of the LORD" (v. 6) following a deliverance, such as is contemplated in 22:25–31 (see note on 7:17). The basic theme of the psalm is announced in v. 1a. Verses 1b–3 develop the theme by affirming the psalmist's total security under the Shepherd-King's care. Verse 4 elaborates on this theme by focusing on the Shepherd's protection in times of great danger and distress. Verse 5 describes the psalmist's privileged position as an honored guest at the Shepherd-King's table. In v. 6 the psalmist professes his full confidence for the future—a confidence grounded in the Shepherd-King's faithful covenant love. The psalm is framed by its first and last lines, each of which refers to "the LORD."
23:1 *shepherd.* A widely used metaphor for kings in the ancient Near East, and also in Israel (see 78:70–72; 2Sa 5:2; Isa 44:28; Jer 3:15; 23:1–4; Mic 5:4). For the Lord as the shepherd of Israel, see 28:9; 79:13; 80:1; 95:7; 100:3;

He guides me along the right paths
    for his name's sake.
4 Even though I walk
    through the darkest valley,*a*
I will fear no evil,
    for you are with me;
your rod and your staff,
    they comfort me.

5 You prepare a table before me
    in the presence of my enemies.
You anoint my head with oil;
    my cup overflows.

a 4 Or *the valley of the shadow of death*

Ge 48:15; Isa 40:11; Jer 17:16; 31:10; 50:19; Eze 34:11–16. Here David the king acknowledges that the Lord is his Shepherd-King. For Jesus as the shepherd of his people, see Jn 10:11,14; Heb 13:20; 1Pe 5:4; Rev 7:17.

23:2 *lie down.* For flocks lying down in contented and secure rest, see Isa 14:30; 17:2; Jer 33:12; Eze 34:14–15; Zep 2:7; 3:13. *green pastures.* Metaphor for all that makes life flourish (Eze 34:14; Jn 10:9). *leads me.* Like a shepherd (see Isa 40:11; see also photo, p. 4). *quiet waters.* Calm waters that provide refreshment and well-being (Isa 49:10). See article and photo, below.

23:3 *refreshes my soul.* See 19:7; Ru 4:15; Pr 25:13; La 1:16. *guides me along the right paths.* As a shepherd leads his sheep (77:20; 78:72) in paths that offer safety and well-being, so David's Shepherd-King guides him in ways that cause him to be secure and prosperous. *for his name's sake.*

God as Shepherd
Ps 23:1

When describing the authority and care exercised by a deity or a king who represents the gods, the metaphor of a shepherd was natural in the ancient Near East. Marduk was the chief god in Babylonia for much of its history, and a standard hymn of praise concludes by extolling his care for the weak like a benevolent shepherd. A hymn to Shamash, the Mesopotamian sun-god, states: "You shepherd all living creatures together, you are their herdsman, above and below."

Hammurapi (c. 1750 BC), who wrote that he received kingship from the gods, claims that he fulfilled his royal duty as a shepherd by providing the people with "pastures and watering places," having "settled them in peaceful abodes." Another text affirming the role of Ashurbanipal (c. 650 BC) reports that he was appointed as shepherd to overthrow enemies. The image not only suggested protection; it was an affirmation of the authority to rule (2Sa 5:2; 1Ch 11:2).

Thus the metaphor of shepherd was a royal one, with connotations of strong leadership but tender care. One ancient Sumerian wisdom text offers a particularly good parallel to Psalm 23: "A man's personal god is a shepherd who finds pasturage for him. Let him lead him like sheep to the grass they can eat." For the psalmist, there is but one shepherd, Yahweh, the one true God (Ge 48:15).

▶ How is a king like a shepherd?

_____

_____

_____

Pharaoh Amenhotep I with ruler's shepherd crook
© Lenka Peacock

⁶Surely your goodness and love will
   follow me
   all the days of my life,
and I will dwell in the house of the LORD
   forever.

Psalm 24

Of David. A psalm.

¹The earth is the LORD's, and everything
   in it,
   the world, and all who live in it;
²for he founded it on the seas
   and established it on the waters.

³Who may ascend the mountain of the
   LORD?
   Who may stand in his holy place?
⁴The one who has clean hands and a
   pure heart,
who does not trust in an idol
   or swear by a false god.^a

⁵They will receive blessing from the LORD
   and vindication from God their Savior.
⁶Such is the generation of those who
   seek him,
who seek your face, God of Jacob.^{b,c}

⁷Lift up your heads, you gates;
   be lifted up, you ancient doors,
   that the King of glory may come in.
⁸Who is this King of glory?
   The LORD strong and mighty,
   the LORD mighty in battle.
⁹Lift up your heads, you gates;
   lift them up, you ancient doors,
   that the King of glory may come in.
¹⁰Who is he, this King of glory?
   The LORD Almighty —
   he is the King of glory.

Psalm 25^d

Of David.

¹In you, LORD my God,
   I put my trust.

²I trust in you;
   do not let me be put to shame,
   nor let my enemies triumph over me.

---

^a 4 Or *swear falsely*   ^b 6 Two Hebrew manuscripts and
Syriac (see also Septuagint); most Hebrew manuscripts *face,
Jacob*   ^c 6 The Hebrew has *Selah* (a word of uncertain
meaning) here and at the end of verse 10.   ^d This psalm is
an acrostic poem, the verses of which begin with the
successive letters of the Hebrew alphabet.

The prosperity of the Lord's servant brings honor to the
Lord's name (1Ki 8:41–42; Isa 48:9; Jer 14:21; Eze 20:9,14,22).
23:4 *the darkest valley.* A metaphor for circumstances
of greatest peril (see 107:10 and note). See also NIV text
note.

23:5 The heavenly Shepherd-King receives David at
his table as his vassal king and takes him under his
protection. In the ancient Near East, covenants were often concluded with a meal expressive of the bond of
friendship and loyalty (41:9; Ge 31:54; Ob 7); in the case of
vassal treaties or covenants, the vassal was present as the
guest of the overlord (Ex 24:8–12). *anoint my head with
oil.* Customary treatment of an honored guest at a banquet (see Lk 7:46; see also 2Sa 12:20; Ecc 9:8; Da 10:3). *cup.*
Of the Lord's banquet (see note on 16:5).
23:6 *goodness and love.* Both frequently refer to covenant
benefits (see article, p. 16); here they are personified (see
25:21; 43:3; 79:8; 89:14). *dwell in the house of the LORD.*
See note on 15:1. *forever.* The Hebrew for this word suggests "throughout the years," as in Pr 28:16 ("enjoy a long
reign"). But see also note on 16:9–11.
Ps 24 A processional liturgy (Ps 47; 68; 118; 132) celebrating
the Lord's entrance into Zion—composed either for the
occasion when David brought the ark to Jerusalem (2Sa
6) or for a festival commemorating the event. Together
with Ps 15 it frames the intervening collection of psalms
and with that psalm sharply delineates those who may
approach God in prayer and "dwell in the house of the
LORD" (23:6; see introduction to Ps 15–24). The church has
long used this psalm in celebration of Christ's ascension
into the heavenly Jerusalem—and into the sanctuary on
high (see introduction to Ps 47).
24:1–2 The prelude (perhaps spoken by a Levite), proclaiming the Lord as the Creator, Sustainer and Possessor
of the whole world (19:1–4) and therefore worthy of worship and reverent loyalty as "the King of glory" (vv. 7–10;
see Ps 29; 33:6–11; 89:5–18; 93; 95:3–5; 96; 104).
24:2 An echo of Ge 1:1–10. *founded . . . established.* A
metaphor taken from the founding of a city (Jos 6:26; 1Ki
16:24; Isa 14:32) or of a temple (1Ki 5:17; 6:37; Ezr 3:6–12;
Isa 44:28; Hag 2:18; Zec 4:9; 8:9). Like a temple, the earth
was depicted as having foundations (18:15; 82:5; 1Sa 2:8;
Pr 8:29; Isa 24:18) and pillars (75:3; Job 9:6). In the ancient
Near East, temples were thought of as microcosms of the
created world, so language applicable to a temple could
readily be applied to the earth. *on.* Or "above" (104:5–9;
Ge 1:9; 7:11; 49:25; Ex 20:4; Dt 33:13).
24:4 *clean hands.* Blameless actions. *pure heart.* Right attitudes and motives (51:10; 73:1). Jesus said that the "pure
in heart . . . will see God" (Mt 5:8).
24:7–10 Heralding the approach of the King of glory (perhaps spoken by the king at the head of the assembled
Israelites, with responses by the keepers of the gates).
The Lord's arrival at his sanctuary in Zion completes his
procession. "The LORD Almighty" (v. 10), "the LORD mighty
in battle" (v. 8; see Ex 15:1–18), has triumphed over all his
enemies and comes now in victory to his own city (Ps 46;
48; 76; 87), his "resting place" (132:8,14; see 68:7–8; Jdg
5:4–5; Hab 3:3–7). Henceforth Jerusalem is the royal city
of the kingdom of God (see note on 9:11).
Ps 25–33 A group of nine psalms containing an unusual

³No one who hopes in you
  will ever be put to shame,
 but shame will come on those
  who are treacherous without cause.

⁴Show me your ways, LORD,
  teach me your paths.
⁵Guide me in your truth and teach me,
  for you are God my Savior,
  and my hope is in you all day long.
⁶Remember, LORD, your great mercy and love,
  for they are from of old.
⁷Do not remember the sins of my youth
  and my rebellious ways;
 according to your love remember me,
  for you, LORD, are good.

⁸Good and upright is the LORD;
  therefore he instructs sinners in his ways.
⁹He guides the humble in what is right
  and teaches them his way.
¹⁰All the ways of the LORD are loving and
    faithful
  toward those who keep the demands of his
    covenant.
¹¹For the sake of your name, LORD,
  forgive my iniquity, though it is great.

¹²Who, then, are those who fear the LORD?
  He will instruct them in the ways they
    should choose.ᵃ
¹³They will spend their days in prosperity,
  and their descendants will inherit the land.
¹⁴The LORD confides in those who fear him;
  he makes his covenant known to them.
¹⁵My eyes are ever on the LORD,
  for only he will release my feet from the
    snare.

¹⁶Turn to me and be gracious to me,
  for I am lonely and afflicted.
¹⁷Relieve the troubles of my heart
  and free me from my anguish.
¹⁸Look on my affliction and my distress
  and take away all my sins.
¹⁹See how numerous are my enemies
  and how fiercely they hate me!

²⁰Guard my life and rescue me;
  do not let me be put to shame,
  for I take refuge in you.
²¹May integrity and uprightness protect me,
  because my hope, LORD,ᵇ is in you.

²²Deliver Israel, O God,
  from all their troubles!

ᵃ 12 Or *ways he chooses*   ᵇ 21 Septuagint; Hebrew does not
have LORD.

concentration (even for the Psalter) of pleas for mercy or grace (25:16; 26:11; 27:7; 28:2; 30:8,10; 31:9) accompanied by professions of trust (25:2; 26:1; 27:3; 28:7; 31:6,14; 32:10; 33:21) and appeals to or celebrations of Yahweh's unfailing love (25:6–7,10; 26:3; 31:7,16,21; 32:10; 33:5,18,22).

The series begins with an alphabetic acrostic (see Introduction: Literary Features) prayer for God's saving help (Ps 25; see NIV text note) and culminates in a 22-verse hymn of praise (the number of letters in the Hebrew alphabet) for Yahweh's sovereign rule and saving help (Ps 33). (For thematic links between these two psalms, see note on 25:3.) This prayer and hymn frame a concentrically arranged cluster that hinges on Ps 29. For the significance of Ps 29 as a hinge, see introduction to that psalm.

Ps 25 David prays for God's covenant mercies when suffering affliction for sins (v. 7) and when enemies seize the occasion to attack, perhaps by trying to discredit the king through false accusations (see note on 5:9). Appealing to God's covenant benevolence (his mercy, love, goodness, uprightness, faithfulness and grace, vv. 6–8, 10,16) and his own reliance on the Lord (vv. 1,5,15,20–21), he prays for deliverance from his enemies (vv. 2,19), for guidance in God's will (vv. 4–5,21; see also vv. 8–10,12), for the forgiveness of his sins (vv. 7,11,18) and for relief from his affliction (vv. 2,16–18,20). These are related: God's forgiveness will express itself in removing his affliction, and then his enemies will no longer have occasion to slander him. And with God guiding him in "his way" (v. 9)—i.e., in "the demands of his covenant" (v. 10)—he will no longer wander into "rebellious ways" (v. 7). This psalm is linked with Ps 24 by its reference to putting one's trust in the true "God" (v. 1) instead of a "false god" (24:4).

25:1–3 Prayer for relief from distress or illness and the slander of David's enemies that it occasions.

25:3 *hopes.* The three references to hoping in God occurring here (vv. 3,5,21) are echoed by three references to "hope" in 33:18,20,22.

25:4–7 Prayer for guidance and pardon.

25:5 *your truth.* Here synonymous for "your ways" and "your paths" (see note on 19:7).

25:7 *love.* See v. 10 and article, p. 16.

25:8–15 Confidence in the Lord's covenant favors. In this context of prayer for pardon, David implicitly identifies himself with "sinners" (v. 8), as well as with the "humble" (v. 9)—those who keep God's covenant (vv. 10, 14) and those who fear the Lord (vv. 12,14). As sinner he is in need of forgiveness; as humble servant of the Lord he hopefully awaits God's pardon and guidance in covenant faithfulness.

25:10 *ways of the LORD.* The Lord's benevolent dealings (103:7; 138:5) with those who are true to his ways (see note on v. 4).

25:12 *fear the LORD.* See notes on 15:4; 34:8–14.

25:14 *confides.* Gives them access to God's purposes (Ge 18:17–19; Job 29:4). *fear.* See note on 15:4.

25:16–21 Prayer for relief from distress (probably illness) and related attacks of his enemies.

25:21 *integrity and uprightness.* Personified virtues (see 23:6 and note). Pardon is not enough; David prays that God will enable him to live a life of moral virtue—even as God is "good and upright" (v. 8; see 51:10–12). *integrity.* See note on 15:2.

Psalm 26

Of David.

[1] Vindicate me, LORD,
　for I have led a blameless life;
　I have trusted in the LORD
　and have not faltered.
[2] Test me, LORD, and try me,
　examine my heart and my mind;
[3] for I have always been mindful of your
　unfailing love
　and have lived in reliance on your faithfulness.

[4] I do not sit with the deceitful,
　nor do I associate with hypocrites.
[5] I abhor the assembly of evildoers
　and refuse to sit with the wicked.
[6] I wash my hands in innocence,
　and go about your altar, LORD,
[7] proclaiming aloud your praise
　and telling of all your wonderful deeds.

[8] LORD, I love the house where you live,
　the place where your glory dwells.
[9] Do not take away my soul along with sinners,
　my life with those who are bloodthirsty,
[10] in whose hands are wicked schemes,
　whose right hands are full of bribes.
[11] I lead a blameless life;
　deliver me and be merciful to me.

[12] My feet stand on level ground;
　in the great congregation I will praise the LORD.

Psalm 27

Of David.

[1] The LORD is my light and my salvation—
　whom shall I fear?
　The LORD is the stronghold of my life—
　of whom shall I be afraid?

[2] When the wicked advance against me
　to devour[a] me,
　it is my enemies and my foes
　who will stumble and fall.
[3] Though an army besiege me,
　my heart will not fear;
　though war break out against me,
　even then I will be confident.

[4] One thing I ask from the LORD,
　this only do I seek:
　that I may dwell in the house of the LORD
　all the days of my life,
　to gaze on the beauty of the LORD
　and to seek him in his temple.

a 2 Or *slander*

Ps 26 A prayer for God's discerning mercies—to spare his faithful and godly servant from the death that overtakes the wicked and ungodly. This prayer for vindication (v. 1) because the psalmist has led "a blameless life" (v. 11) and has refused "to sit with the wicked" (v. 5) has its counterpoint in Ps 32 (in the concentric arrangement of Ps 25–33; see introduction to Ps 25–33), which celebrates the blessedness of those who have confessed their sins and been forgiven. The king's prayer for vindication suggests that he is threatened by the "deceitful" (v. 4) and "bloodthirsty" (v. 9) to whom he refers (as in Ps 23; 25; 27–28).

26:1 *blameless life.* A claim of moral integrity (see vv. 2–5; see also note on 15:2). *trusted.* Obedience and trust are the two sides of godliness, as the Abraham story exemplifies (see Ge 12:4; 22:12; see also Ps 34:8–14).
26:3 *your unfailing love . . . your faithfulness.* A single idea of God's unfailing covenant faithfulness (40:10). David keeps his eye steadfastly on the Lord's great love (see article, p. 16) and faithfulness, which are pledged to those "who keep the demands of his covenant" (25:10).
26:4–5 *sit with.* David refuses to settle in or associate himself with that company he describes as "deceitful," "hypocrites," "evildoers," "wicked" (see 1:1 and note; see also Ps 101).

26:6 *wash my hands in innocence.* Reference appears to be to a ritual claiming innocence. "Clean hands and a pure heart" are requisite for those who come to God (see 24:4 and note). *go about your altar.* To vocally celebrate God's saving acts while circling his altar may have been a public act of devotion in which one also invited all the assembled worshipers to praise the Lord (43:3–4).
26:7 *your praise.* See note on 9:1.

26:8 *where your glory dwells.* The presence of God's glory signaled the presence of God himself (Ex 24:16; 33:22). His glory dwelling in the tabernacle (see Ex 40:34) and later the temple (1Ki 8:11) assured Israel of the Lord's holy, yet gracious, presence among them. Jn 1:14 announces that same presence in the Word who became flesh and who "made his dwelling among us" and showed us his "glory."
26:11 *lead a blameless life.* A return to the appeal with which David began (v. 1).

Ps 27 David's triumphantly confident prayer to God to deliver him from all those who conspire to bring him down. The prayer presupposes the Lord's covenant with David (2Sa 7). The psalm consists of an expression of trust (vv. 1–6) along with a lament about being forsaken (vv. 7–10) in the face of slander (vv. 11–12). The conclusion (vv. 13–14) echoes the confidence of vv. 1–6 and adds the psalmist's exhortation to himself—to wait patiently for that which is sure, though not yet seen (Ps 42–43; Heb 11:1).

27:1 *light.* Often symbolizes well-being (97:11; Job 18:5–6; 22:28; 29:3; Pr 13:9; La 3:2) or life and salvation (18:28; Isa 9:2; 49:6; 58:8; 59:9; Jer 13:16; Am 5:18–20). To say "The LORD is my light" is to confess confidence in him as the source of these benefits (see Isa 10:17; 60:1–2,19–20; Mic 7:8–9). *my salvation.* "My Savior" (v. 9).
27:4–6 The Lord's temple (or tabernacle) is the king's stronghold—because the Lord himself is his "stronghold" (v. 1; see notes on 9:11; 18:2).
27:4 *dwell in.* As God's guest in his tabernacle or temple

5 For in the day of trouble
  he will keep me safe in his dwelling;
he will hide me in the shelter of his sacred tent
  and set me high upon a rock.

6 Then my head will be exalted
  above the enemies who surround me;
at his sacred tent I will sacrifice with shouts
    of joy;
  I will sing and make music to the LORD.

7 Hear my voice when I call, LORD;
  be merciful to me and answer me.
8 My heart says of you, "Seek his face!"
  Your face, LORD, I will seek.
9 Do not hide your face from me,
  do not turn your servant away in anger;
  you have been my helper.
Do not reject me or forsake me,
  God my Savior.
10 Though my father and mother forsake me,
  the LORD will receive me.
11 Teach me your way, LORD;
  lead me in a straight path
  because of my oppressors.
12 Do not turn me over to the desire of my foes,
  for false witnesses rise up against me,
  spouting malicious accusations.

13 I remain confident of this:
  I will see the goodness of the LORD
  in the land of the living.
14 Wait for the LORD;
  be strong and take heart
  and wait for the LORD.

Psalm 28

Of David.

1 To you, LORD, I call;
  you are my Rock,
  do not turn a deaf ear to me.
For if you remain silent,
  I will be like those who go down to the pit.
2 Hear my cry for mercy
  as I call to you for help,
as I lift up my hands
  toward your Most Holy Place.

3 Do not drag me away with the wicked,
  with those who do evil,
who speak cordially with their neighbors
  but harbor malice in their hearts.
4 Repay them for their deeds
  and for their evil work;
repay them for what their hands have done
  and bring back on them what they deserve.

(see note on 15:1). *beauty of the LORD.* His unfailing benevolence (see 90:17: "favor of the Lord").
27:7–12 Prayer for deliverance from treacherous enemies. Their chief weapon is false charges intent on discrediting the king (see note on 5:9).
27:10 *the LORD will receive me.* Or "may the LORD receive me."

27:11 *Teach me your way.* Only those who know and do the Lord's will can expect to receive favorable response to their prayers (see Ps 24–26; see also 2Sa 7:14). *lead me in a straight path.* See 5:8 and note.
27:13–14 Concluding note of confidence (see note on 3:8).

27:14 *Wait for the LORD.* The psalmist's exhortation to himself to persevere (42:5,11; 43:5; 62:5).
Ps 28 A lament psalm pleading for deliverance in the face of deadly peril at the hands of malicious and God-defying enemies. As with Ps 25, the lament ends with intercession for all the people of the Lord (see 3:8 and note). Reference in the last verse to the Lord as the shepherd of his people connects this psalm with Ps 23. However, in the concentric arrangement of Ps 25–33 (see introduction to Ps 25–33) it is linked more closely with Ps 30. In Ps 28 the psalmist cries to Yahweh "for mercy" (vv. 2,6) when about to go "down to the pit" (v. 1); in Ps 30 the psalmist praises Yahweh for having heard his cry "for mercy" (vv. 8,11) and sparing him from going "down to the pit" (v. 3).
28:1–2 Initial appeal to be heard.
28:2 *lift up my hands.* In worship and prayer (63:4; 134:2; 141:2). *Most Holy Place.* The inner sanctuary of the temple (1Ki 6:5), where the ark of the covenant stood (1Ki 8:6–8); it was God's throne room on earth.

Write a song or poem describing the goodness of the Lord.

_____

_____

_____

_____

_____

_____

_____

_____

_____

⁵Because they have no regard for the deeds of
the L<small>ORD</small>
and what his hands have done,
he will tear them down
and never build them up again.

⁶Praise be to the L<small>ORD</small>,
for he has heard my cry for mercy.
⁷The L<small>ORD</small> is my strength and my shield;
my heart trusts in him, and he helps me.
My heart leaps for joy,
and with my song I praise him.

⁸The L<small>ORD</small> is the strength of his people,
a fortress of salvation for his anointed one.
⁹Save your people and bless your
inheritance;
be their shepherd and carry them
forever.

Psalm 29

A psalm of David.

¹Ascribe to the L<small>ORD</small>, you heavenly beings,
ascribe to the L<small>ORD</small> glory and strength.
²Ascribe to the L<small>ORD</small> the glory due his
name;
worship the L<small>ORD</small> in the splendor of his^a
holiness.

³The voice of the L<small>ORD</small> is over the waters;
the God of glory thunders,
the L<small>ORD</small> thunders over the mighty
waters.
⁴The voice of the L<small>ORD</small> is powerful;
the voice of the L<small>ORD</small> is majestic.
⁵The voice of the L<small>ORD</small> breaks the cedars;
the L<small>ORD</small> breaks in pieces the cedars of
Lebanon.
⁶He makes Lebanon leap like a calf,
Sirion^b like a young wild ox.
⁷The voice of the L<small>ORD</small> strikes
with flashes of lightning.
⁸The voice of the L<small>ORD</small> shakes the desert;
the L<small>ORD</small> shakes the Desert of Kadesh.
⁹The voice of the L<small>ORD</small> twists the oaks^c
and strips the forests bare.
And in his temple all cry, "Glory!"

¹⁰The L<small>ORD</small> sits enthroned over the flood;
the L<small>ORD</small> is enthroned as King forever.
¹¹The L<small>ORD</small> gives strength to his people;
the L<small>ORD</small> blesses his people with
peace.

---

^a 2 Or L<small>ORD</small> *with the splendor of*   ^b 6 That is, Mount
Hermon   ^c 9 Or L<small>ORD</small> *makes the deer give birth*

28:5 This expression of confidence in God's anticipated deliverance climaxes the prayer and prepares for the shift to praise in vv. 6–7. *deeds of the L<small>ORD</small>.* His redemption of Israel, the establishment of Israel as his kingdom (by covenant, Ex 19–24), and the appointment of the house of David (also by covenant, 2Sa 7) as his earthly regent over his people.
28:8 *anointed one.* The legitimate king from David's line (see note on 2:2).
28:9 *Save . . . bless.* God's two primary acts by which he effects his people's well-being: He saves from time to time as circumstances require; he blesses day by day to make their lives and labors fruitful. *your inheritance.* See Dt 9:29. *shepherd.* See introduction; see also 80:1; Isa 40:11; Jer 31:10; Eze 34; Mic 5:4 and note on Ps 23:1. The answer to this prayer—the last, full answer—has come in the ministry of the "good shepherd" (Jn 10:11,14).
Ps 29 A hymn in praise of the King of creation, whose glory is trumpeted by the thunderclaps that rumble through the cloudy mass of winter's rainstorms as they rise above the Mediterranean ("the mighty waters," v. 3) and move from west to east across the face of the sky, sweeping over the Lebanon range (vv. 5–6) and reaching the wilds of (northern) Kadesh on the upper reaches of the Orontes River (v. 8). The glory of the Lord is not only visible in the creation (19:1–6; see introduction to that psalm; see also Ps 104); it is also audible in creation's most awesome voice. (The most powerful forces in the ancient Near East were earthquakes, the raging sea, and heavy thunderstorms.) This hymn to Yahweh ("the L<small>ORD</small>") served also as a testimony and protest against the worship of the Canaanite god Baal, who was thought to be the divine power present in the thunderstorm (cf. 31:6). Its placement marks it as the hinge psalm in the concentric arrangement of Ps 25–33 (see introduction to Ps 25–33). In the midst of prayer and praise, it reminds those who meditate on the psalms and use them as their own that the One with whom they have to do is the mighty Lord over all that is. All creation displays his power and glory, evoking awe and praise (vv. 1–2), but his gracious ways with his people (v. 11) also invite confident prayer in every need.
29:1 *heavenly beings.* Perhaps reference is to the angelic host (see 103:20; 148:2; Job 1:6 and NIV text note; 2:1 and NIV text note; Isa 6:2) or possibly to all those foolishly thought to be gods—as in Ps 97 (97:7), which has several thematic links with this psalm. The Lord alone must be acknowledged as the divine King.
29:2 *in the splendor of his holiness.* A word-for-word translation of a difficult Hebrew phrase (see NIV text note; see also 96:9; 110:3; 1Ch 16:29; 2Ch 20:21). It is uncertain whether it describes God himself or the sanctuary or the (priestly) garb the worshipers are to wear when they approach God. The use of an almost identical Hebrew phrase in 110:3 (translated "in holy splendor") seems to support the last alternative, but the Hebrew text and the context of 2Ch 20:21 favor "in the splendor of his holiness."
29:5 *cedars of Lebanon.* The most majestic and highly prized trees of the Middle East (see SS 5:15; see also photo, p. 42).
29:6 *leap.* Tremble or shake (see 114:4 and note).

Cedar trees are still common in modern Lebanon today. Psalm 29:5 boasts of the Lord's glory and strength: "The voice of the LORD breaks the cedars; the LORD breaks in pieces the cedars of Lebanon."
© Robert Eisenbach/www.BigStockPhoto.com

Psalm 30ᵃ

A psalm. A song. For the dedication of the temple.ᵇ Of David.

¹ I will exalt you, LORD,
     for you lifted me out of the depths
     and did not let my enemies gloat
       over me.
² LORD my God, I called to you for help,
     and you healed me.
³ You, LORD, brought me up from the realm of
     the dead;
     you spared me from going down to
     the pit.

⁴ Sing the praises of the LORD, you his faithful
     people;
     praise his holy name.
⁵ For his anger lasts only a moment,
     but his favor lasts a lifetime;

ᵃ In Hebrew texts 30:1-12 is numbered 30:2-13.   ᵇ Title: Or *palace*

29:9 *temple.* A primary thematic link with Ps 23–28. Reference may be to the temple in Jerusalem or to God's heavenly temple, where he sits enthroned (2:4; 11:4; 113:5; Isa 6:1; 40:22) as the Lord of all creation. But perhaps it is the creation itself that here is named God's temple (see note on 24:2). Then the "all" (those who cry "Glory!") is absolutely all—all creation shouts his praise (cf. 150:6). *Glory!* See note on 26:8.

29:10–11 The Lord's absolute and everlasting rule is committed to his people's complete salvation and unmixed blessedness—the crowning comfort in a world where threatening tides seem to make everything uncertain.

29:10 *enthroned over the flood.* As the One who by his word brought the ordered creation out of the formless "deep" (Ge 1:2,6–10).

30 title *A song.* See titles of Ps 18; 45–46; 48; 65–68; 75–76; 83; 87–88; 92; 108—all psalms of praise except 83; 88. In addition there are the songs "of ascents" (Ps 120–134). *For the dedication of the temple. Of David.* If "Of David" indicates authorship, the most probable occasion for the psalm is recorded in 1Ch 21:1—22:6. In 1Ch 22:1–6 David dedicated both property and building materials for the temple, and he may well have intended that Ps 30 be used at

weeping may stay for the night,
    but rejoicing comes in the morning.

6 When I felt secure, I said,
    "I will never be shaken."
7 LORD, when you favored me,
    you made my royal mountain*a* stand firm;
but when you hid your face,
    I was dismayed.

8 To you, LORD, I called;
    to the Lord I cried for mercy:
9 "What is gained if I am silenced,
    if I go down to the pit?
Will the dust praise you?
    Will it proclaim your faithfulness?
10 Hear, LORD, and be merciful to me;
    LORD, be my help."

11 You turned my wailing into dancing;
    you removed my sackcloth and clothed me
      with joy,
12 that my heart may sing your praises and not
      be silent.
    LORD my God, I will praise you forever.

a 7 That is, Mount Zion

List some of the things God has done for you.

_____

_____

_____

_____

_____

_____

_____

_____

_____

_____

_____

_____

---

the dedication of the temple itself. Later, the psalm came to be applied to the exile experience of Israel. In Jewish liturgical practice dating from Talmudic times it is chanted at Hanukkah, the festival that celebrates the rededication of the temple by Judas Maccabeus (165 BC) after its desecration by Antiochus Epiphanes (168). In such communal use, the "I" of the psalm becomes the collective "person" of Israel—a common mode of speaking in the OT.

30:1 *lifted me out of the depths.* The vivid imagery that associates distress with "the depths"—so expressive of universal human experience—is common in OT poetry (69:2,15; 71:20; 88:6; 130:1; La 3:55; Jnh 2:2). The depths are often linked, as here, with Sheol ("the realm of the dead," v. 3) and "the pit" (v. 3), together with a cluster of related associations: silence (31:17; 94:17; 115:17; 1Sa 2:9), darkness (88:6,12; 143:3; Job 10:21–22; 17:13; Ecc 6:4; La 3:6), destruction (v. 9; 18:4; 55:23, "decay"; 88:11; Isa 38:17; Hos 13:14), dust (v. 9; 7:5; 22:15,29; Job 17:16; 40:13; Isa 26:19; 29:4), mire (40:2; 69:2,14), slime (40:2) and mud (40:2; Job 30:19). See also note on 49:14.

30:4 *faithful people.* See note on 4:3. *name.* Or "memorial," or "name of renown" (97:12; 135:13; Isa 26:8; Hos 12:5). The Hebrew evokes Ex 3:15 and refers to the name around which clustered memories of all that God had done, especially in Israel's history.

30:6–10 Expanded recollection of the Lord's gracious deliverance.

30:6–7 In his security he had grown arrogant, forgetful of who had made his "mountain stand firm," but the Lord reminded him.

30:6 *never be shaken.* He spoke as do the wicked (10:6), hence lost the blessing of the righteous (15:5). *shaken.* See note on 10:6.

30:7 *made my royal mountain stand firm.* Reference may be to David's security in his mountain fortress, Zion; or that mountain fortress may here serve as a metaphor for David's state as a vigorous and victorious king. *hid your face.* See note on 13:1.

30:8–10 Shattered strength swept away all self-reliance; at the brink of death his cries for divine mercy arose to God.

30:9 See note on 6:5. *your faithfulness.* To your covenant.

30:11–12 God answered—and David vows to prolong his praise forever (see note on 7:17).

30:11 *sackcloth.* A coarse, black fabric (see Isa 50:3; Rev 11:3) woven of goat hair and commonly used for making sacks. It was worn as a symbol of mourning (see 35:13; 69:11).

Additional Insights

The vivid imagery that associates distress with "the depths"—so expressive of universal human experience—is common in OT poetry.

▶ Parts of Psalm 22 are quoted in the New Testament in relation to Jesus. How does this psalm express the lament of David and apply to Jesus?

_____

_____

_____

_____

_____

▶ In what ways do the well-known words of Psalm 23 bring comfort to you?

_____

_____

_____

_____

_____

▶ The psalmist claims to be blameless (Ps 26:1,11), but we know that no one is truly blameless. How can you read psalms like this and understand it in the writer's context?

_____

_____

_____

_____

▶ When has God seemed silent in the face of your prayers (28:1)?

_____

_____

_____

_____

Psalm 31[a]

For the director of music. A psalm of David.

[1] In you, LORD, I have taken refuge;
    let me never be put to shame;
    deliver me in your righteousness.
[2] Turn your ear to me,
    come quickly to my rescue;
  be my rock of refuge,
    a strong fortress to save me.
[3] Since you are my rock and my fortress,
    for the sake of your name lead and guide me.
[4] Keep me free from the trap that is set for me,
    for you are my refuge.
[5] Into your hands I commit my spirit;
    deliver me, LORD, my faithful God.

[6] I hate those who cling to worthless idols;
    as for me, I trust in the LORD.
[7] I will be glad and rejoice in your love,
    for you saw my affliction
    and knew the anguish of my soul.
[8] You have not given me into the hands of the
        enemy
    but have set my feet in a spacious place.

[9] Be merciful to me, LORD, for I am in distress;
    my eyes grow weak with sorrow,
    my soul and body with grief.
[10] My life is consumed by anguish
    and my years by groaning;
  my strength fails because of my affliction,[b]
    and my bones grow weak.
[11] Because of all my enemies,
    I am the utter contempt of my neighbors
  and an object of dread to my closest friends —
    those who see me on the street flee from me.
[12] I am forgotten as though I were dead;
    I have become like broken pottery.
[13] For I hear many whispering,
    "Terror on every side!"
  They conspire against me
    and plot to take my life.

[14] But I trust in you, LORD;
    I say, "You are my God."
[15] My times are in your hands;
    deliver me from the hands of my enemies,
    from those who pursue me.

---

[a] In Hebrew texts 31:1-24 is numbered 31:2-25.   [b] 10 Or *guilt*

Ps 31 A lament over a conspiracy so powerful and pervasive that all David's friends abandoned him. According to Lk 23:46, Jesus on the cross applied Ps 31:5 to his own circumstances; thus those who share in his sufferings at the hands of evil forces are encouraged to hear and use this psalm in a new light (Ac 7:59; 1Pe 4:19). No psalm expresses a sturdier trust in the Lord when powerful human forces threaten. The heart of the prayer itself is found in vv. 9–18, which are both preceded and followed by nine Hebrew poetic lines—stanzas that resound with the theme of trust (v. 14). Verse 13, at the center of the psalm, expresses most clearly the prayer's occasion.

31 title *For the director of music.* See note on Ps 4 title.
31:1–5 Initial appeal to the Lord, the faithful refuge.
31:1 *righteousness.* See note on 4:1.
31:2 *rock.* See note on 18:2.
31:3 *for the sake of your name.* God's honor is at stake in the safety of his servant now under attack (see note on 23:3). *lead and guide.* As a shepherd (see 23:2–3 and notes).
31:4 *trap that is set for me.* By his enemies (see v. 11; see also note on 9:15).
31:5 *Into your hands I commit my spirit.* The climactic expression of trust in the Lord—echoed by Jesus in Lk 23:46. *commit.* Entrust to God's care (Lev 6:4; 1Ki 14:27). *my spirit.* His very life.
31:6–8 Confession of loyal trust in the Lord, whose past mercies to David when enemies threatened are joyfully recalled.
31:6 *hate.* Refuse to be associated with. *who cling to worthless idols.* See Jnh 2:8. *cling to.* Or "watch" (expectantly for the help of; see 59:9 and note).
31:7 *love.* See vv. 16,21; see also article, p. 16. *soul.* See note on 6:3.
31:9–13 The distress described: He is utterly drained physically and emotionally (see vv. 9–10; see also 22:14–15); all his friends have abandoned him like a piece of broken pottery (vv. 11–12); and all this because the conspiracy against him is so strong (v. 13).
31:11–12 Abandonment by friends was a common experience at a time when God seemed to have withdrawn his favor (38:11; 41:9; 69:8; 88:8,18; Job 19:13–19; Jer 12:6; 15:17).
31:13 *many whispering.* See note on 5:9.
31:14–18 His trust in the Lord is unwavering; his defense against his powerful enemies is his reliance on God's faithfulness and discerning judgment.
31:14 Cf. v. 22.
31:15 *My times are in your hands.* All the events and circumstances of life are in the hands of the Lord, "my God" (v. 14).
31:16 *face shine.* See note on 13:1.

16 Let your face shine on your servant;
    save me in your unfailing love.
17 Let me not be put to shame, LORD,
    for I have cried out to you;
  but let the wicked be put to shame
    and be silent in the realm of the dead.
18 Let their lying lips be silenced,
    for with pride and contempt
    they speak arrogantly against the
      righteous.

19 How abundant are the good things
    that you have stored up for those who
      fear you,
  that you bestow in the sight of all,
    on those who take refuge in you.
20 In the shelter of your presence you hide them
    from all human intrigues;
  you keep them safe in your dwelling
    from accusing tongues.

21 Praise be to the LORD,
    for he showed me the wonders of his love
    when I was in a city under siege.
22 In my alarm I said,
    "I am cut off from your sight!"
  Yet you heard my cry for mercy
    when I called to you for help.

23 Love the LORD, all his faithful people!
    The LORD preserves those who are true
      to him,
  but the proud he pays back in full.
24 Be strong and take heart,
    all you who hope in the LORD.

Psalm 32

Of David. A maskil.^a

1 Blessed is the one
    whose transgressions are forgiven,
    whose sins are covered.
2 Blessed is the one
    whose sin the LORD does not count against
      them
    and in whose spirit is no deceit.

3 When I kept silent,
    my bones wasted away
    through my groaning all day long.
4 For day and night
    your hand was heavy on me;
  my strength was sapped
    as in the heat of summer.^b

^a Title: Probably a literary or musical term   ^b 4 The Hebrew has *Selah* (a word of uncertain meaning) here and at the end of verses 5 and 7.

31:17–18 *but let the wicked . . . be silenced.* See note on 5:10.
31:18 *lying lips.* See note on 5:9. *righteous.* See note on 1:5.
31:19–20 Confident anticipation of God's saving help (see note on 3:8).
   31:19 *stored up.* David commits his life into the hands of God to share in the covenant benefits that God has stored up for his faithful servants ("good things," Ex 18:9; Nu 10:29,32; Dt 26:11; Jos 23:15; Ne 9:25; Isa 63:7; Jer 33:9; see Jos 21:45; 23:14, "good promises"; 2Ch 6:41; Ne 9:25,35; Ps 27:13, "goodness"; Jer 31:12,14, "bounty").
31:20 *accusing tongues.* See "whispering" (v. 13) and "lying lips" (v. 18).
31:21–22 Praise anticipating deliverance (see note on 12:5–6).
31:21 *city under siege.* Probably a metaphor for the threat he had experienced.
31:22 *cut off from your sight.* See note on 13:1.
31:23–24 Praise culminates by encouraging the people of God (see 62:8).
   31:23 *faithful people.* See note on 4:3. *those . . . true to him.* Those who maintain moral integrity and faithfulness to the Lord. *the proud.* Those who refuse to live in humble reliance on the Lord. They arrogantly try to make their way in the world either as a law to themselves (see, e.g., v. 18; 10:2–11; 73:6; 94:2–7; Dt 8:14; Isa 2:17; Eze 28:2,5; Hos 13:6) or by relying on false gods (Jer 13:9–10). Hence "the proud" is often equivalent to "the wicked."
   Ps 32 Thanksgiving for God's gift of forgiveness toward those who with integrity confess their sins and are receptive to God's rule in their lives. The psalm appears to be a liturgical dialogue between David and God in the presence of the worshipers at the sanctuary. In vv. 1–2 and again in v. 11 David speaks to the assembly; in vv. 3–7 he speaks to God (in their hearing); in vv. 8–10 he is addressed by one of the Lord's priests (but see note on vv. 8–10). In traditional Christian usage, the psalm has been numbered among the penitential psalms (see introduction to Ps 6). Its placement in the concentric arrangement of Ps 25–33 (see introduction to Ps 25–33) suggests that the editors of the Psalter intended it to stand in counterpoint to Ps 26 (see introduction to that psalm).
32 title *maskil.* Occurs also in the titles of Ps 42; 44–45; 52–55; 74; 78; 88–89; 142. The Hebrew word may indicate that these psalms contain instruction in godliness (see 14:2; 53:2, "any who understand"; 41:1, "those who have regard"; but see also 47:7, where it is rendered "psalm").
   32:1–2 Exuberant proclamation of the happy state of those who experience God's forgiveness. *Blessed . . . Blessed.* See note on 1:1. Repetition is for emphasis. *are forgiven . . . are covered . . . does not count against them.* Repeating the same idea with varied language communicates the depth of God's forgiveness. For Paul's use of these verses, see Ro 4:6–8.
   32:3–5 Testimony to a personal experience of God's pardon. God's heavy hand, pressing down "day and night" on the stubborn silence of unacknowledged sin, filled life with groaning, but full confession brought blessed relief.
32:4 *strength was sapped.* Under God's heavy hand of discipline David wilted like a plant in the heat of summer. For *Selah,* see NIV text note and note on 3:2.

⁵Then I acknowledged my sin to you
  and did not cover up my iniquity.
I said, "I will confess
  my transgressions to the LORD."
And you forgave
  the guilt of my sin.

⁶Therefore let all the faithful pray to you
  while you may be found;
surely the rising of the mighty waters
  will not reach them.
⁷You are my hiding place;
  you will protect me from trouble
  and surround me with songs of deliverance.

⁸I will instruct you and teach you in the way you
    should go;
  I will counsel you with my loving eye
    on you.
⁹Do not be like the horse or the mule,
  which have no understanding
but must be controlled by bit and bridle
  or they will not come to you.
¹⁰Many are the woes of the wicked,
  but the LORD's unfailing love
  surrounds the one who trusts in him.

¹¹Rejoice in the LORD and be glad, you righteous;
  sing, all you who are upright in heart!

Psalm 33

¹Sing joyfully to the LORD, you righteous;
  it is fitting for the upright to praise him.
²Praise the LORD with the harp;
  make music to him on the ten-stringed lyre.
³Sing to him a new song;
  play skillfully, and shout for joy.

⁴For the word of the LORD is right and true;
  he is faithful in all he does.
⁵The LORD loves righteousness and justice;
  the earth is full of his unfailing love.

⁶By the word of the LORD the heavens were
    made,
  their starry host by the breath of his
    mouth.
⁷He gathers the waters of the sea into jars*ᵃ*;
  he puts the deep into storehouses.
⁸Let all the earth fear the LORD;
  let all the people of the world revere him.
⁹For he spoke, and it came to be;
  he commanded, and it stood firm.

¹⁰The LORD foils the plans of the nations;
  he thwarts the purposes of the peoples.

ᵃ 7 Or sea as into a heap

32:5 Again repetition is used (see note on vv. 1–2). *sin . . . iniquity . . . transgressions.* See 51:1–2; the three most common OT words for evil thoughts and actions (Isa 59:12). *confess.* See Ps 51; 2Sa 12:13.
32:6–7 A chastened confession that life is secure only with God.
32:6 Though addressed to God as confession, it is also intended for the ears of the fellow worshipers. He admonishes them to "seek the LORD while he may be found . . . while he is near" (Isa 55:6) and not to foolishly provoke his withdrawal—and the coming near of his heavy hand—as David had done. A God who forgives is a God to whom one can entrust and devote one's life (130:4). *faithful.* See note on 4:3. *mighty waters.* Powerful imagery for threatening forces or circumstances.
32:8–10 A priestly word of godly instruction, either to David (do not be foolish toward God again) or to those who have just been exhorted to trust in the Lord (add obedience to trust). Some believe that the psalmist himself here turns to others to warn them against the ways into which he has fallen (see 51:13 and note).
32:9 Be more open to God's will than horses and mules are to the will of their masters (Isa 1:3).
32:10 *unfailing love.* See article, p. 16.
Ps 33 A liturgy in praise of the Lord, the sovereign God of Israel—a counterpoint to the acrostic prayer of Ps 25. These two psalms frame the intervening psalms (see introduction to Ps 25–33). Most likely the voices of the Levitical choir (1Ch 16:7–36; 25:1) are heard in this psalm. Perhaps the choir leader spoke in vv. 1–3, the choir in vv. 4–19, and the people responded with the words of vv. 20–22. The original occasion is unknown, but reference to a "new song" (see note on v. 3) suggests a national deliverance, such as Judah experienced in the time of Jehoshaphat (2Ch 20) or Hezekiah (2Ki 19); see vv. 10–11,16–17.
Although structurally not an alphabetic acrostic (see Introduction: Literary Features) like the psalm that follows it, the length of the psalm (22 verses) may have been determined by the length of the Hebrew alphabet (22 letters); see Ps 38; 103; La 5.
33:1 *righteous.* The assembly of worshipers (see note on 1:5).
33:3 *new song.* Celebrating God's new saving act, as in 40:3; 96:1; 98:1; 144:9; 149:1; see Isa 42:10; Rev 5:9; 14:3; see also note on 7:17.
33:4–11 Under the Lord's rule by his sovereign "word" (v. 4) his "plans" for his people "stand firm" (v. 11), even as the creation order "stood firm" (v. 9) because it was ordered by his sovereign "word" (v. 6). Hence his chosen people are the blessed nation (vv. 12–19).
33:4 *word.* God's word is effective and accomplishes what he wills (107:20; 147:15,18). *right and true.* Under the Lord's rule, order and goodness are present in the creation.
33:5 *loves.* Delights in doing. *righteousness and justice.* See note on 4:1. *his unfailing love.* Here, his goodness to all his creatures (see 36:5–9; 104:27–28; see also article, p. 16).
33:6 *word.* God's creating word (see v. 9; 104:7; 119:89; Ge 1; Job 38:8–11; Heb 11:3).
33:7 *into jars . . . storehouses.* Like a householder storing up olive oil and grain (104:9; Ge 1:9–10; Job 38:8–11; Pr 8:29; Jer 5:22).
33:8 *all the earth . . . all the people.* Not only Israel, but all humankind, for all experience the goodness of his sovereign

¹¹But the plans of the LORD stand firm forever,
the purposes of his heart through all
generations.

¹²Blessed is the nation whose God is the LORD,
the people he chose for his inheritance.
¹³From heaven the LORD looks down
and sees all mankind;
¹⁴from his dwelling place he watches
all who live on earth—
¹⁵he who forms the hearts of all,
who considers everything they do.

¹⁶No king is saved by the size of his army;
no warrior escapes by his great strength.
¹⁷A horse is a vain hope for deliverance;
despite all its great strength it cannot save.
¹⁸But the eyes of the LORD are on those who
fear him,
on those whose hope is in his unfailing love,
¹⁹to deliver them from death
and keep them alive in famine.

²⁰We wait in hope for the LORD;
he is our help and our shield.
²¹In him our hearts rejoice,
for we trust in his holy name.
²²May your unfailing love be with us, LORD,
even as we put our hope in you.

Psalm 34^{a,b}

*Of David. When he pretended to be insane before
Abimelek, who drove him away, and he left.*

¹I will extol the LORD at all times;
his praise will always be on my lips.
²I will glory in the LORD;
let the afflicted hear and rejoice.
³Glorify the LORD with me;
let us exalt his name together.

⁴I sought the LORD, and he answered me;
he delivered me from all my fears.
⁵Those who look to him are radiant;
their faces are never covered with shame.
⁶This poor man called, and the LORD heard him;
he saved him out of all his troubles.
⁷The angel of the LORD encamps around those
who fear him,
and he delivers them.

⁸Taste and see that the LORD is good;
blessed is the one who takes refuge in him.
⁹Fear the LORD, you his holy people,
for those who fear him lack nothing.

^a This psalm is an acrostic poem, the verses of which begin
with the successive letters of the Hebrew alphabet.   ^b In
Hebrew texts 34:1-22 is numbered 34:2-23.

rule (see note on 9:1)—but he foils all their contrary designs
(vv. 10–11). *fear the LORD.* See v. 18; see also note on 15:4.

33:11 *heart.* See note on 4:7.

33:12–19 Israel is safe and secure under God's protective rule.

33:12 *Blessed.* See note on 1:1.

33:16 *king.* Nation (v. 12) and king constitute an organic
social unit.

33:18,22 *unfailing love.* Here, his covenant favor toward
Israel (see article, p. 16).

33:20–22 The people's response: faith's commitment expressed in confession (vv. 20–21) and petition (v. 22).

Ps 34–37 This small grouping of four psalms is framed by
two alphabetic acrostics (see Introduction: Literary Features) that contain wisdom-like instruction in godliness
and related warnings concerning the fate of the wicked—
instruction and warnings that reinforce key themes in the
two enclosed prayers (Ps 35–36).

Ps 34 An alphabetic acrostic (see Introduction: Literary
Features) that begins with praise of the Lord for deliverance in answer to prayer (vv. 1–7), then shifts to wisdom-like instruction.

34 title The superscription assigns this psalm to the occasion in David's life (see note on Ps 3 title) narrated in 1Sa
21:10–15—but note "Abimelek" rather than "Achish" (perhaps Abimelek was a traditional dynastic name or title
for Philistine kings; see Ge 20; 21:22–34; 26). Not all agree
with this tradition, however; some feel that it is more
likely that early Hebrew editors of the Psalms linked 1Sa
21 with Ps 34 on the basis of word association (the Hebrew
for "pretended to be insane," 1Sa 21:13, comes from the
same root as the Hebrew used here for "Taste," v. 8).

34:2 *glory in the LORD.* That is, give the Lord all the praise.

34:4–7 The occasion: God's saving answer to prayer. The
theme is developed in alternating lines—an *a-b/a-b* pattern (note the shift from first-person singular references
to third-person plural references—what Yahweh has
done for the psalmist he will do for all those who "fear
him," v. 7). For thematic links with vv. 15–18, see note on
those verses.

34:5 *radiant.* With joy (Isa 60:5).

34:6 *poor.* Here, as occasionally in the Psalms, "poor"
characterizes not only those who have no possessions but also those who are (and recognize that they are)
without resources to effect their own deliverance (or secure their own lives, safety or well-being)—and so are
dependent on God.

34:7 *angel of the LORD.* God's heavenly representative, his
"messenger," sent to effect his will on earth (see 35:5–6).
encamps around. The line speaks of the security with
which the Lord surrounds his people, individually and
collectively; it does not necessarily teach a doctrine of
individual "guardian angels."

34:8–14 Instruction in "the fear of the LORD."
These verses are thematically linked, with a title line (v. 11) at the center—Hebrew authors often centered key lines (see note on 6:6). A symmetrical development of the theme "good" dominates the stanza: Because
the Lord is "good" (v. 8), those who trust in him will lack
nothing "good" (v. 10); but in order to experience "good

Does the Psalmist Promise Prosperity? Ps 34:17

It is sometimes easy for believers to focus on single verses in the Psalms and conclude that God will reward righteous behavior with material prosperity in this life. Ps 84:11, e.g., declares, "no good thing does he withhold from those whose walk is blameless." Ps 34:8–13 seems likewise to promise such prosperity. Part of a proper interpretation of such promises is to recall that God made a covenant with Israel, unlike that with any other nation, that material prosperity would be contingent on a general level of national obedience to his Law,

especially on the part of Israel's leaders. But it is also always important to read the promises of a given psalm in the context of the entire psalm.

Here vv. 17–19 temper the notion that the psalmist is promising a trouble-free life. Verse 22 suggests that the ultimate good is rescue from condemnation at the final judgment. Thus, although the psalmist never spells it out (as, e.g., in Ps 73), he may well recognize that some of the righteous receive the good things promised to them only or primarily in the life to come.

▶ Why is understanding a verse's context important when reading any portion of the Bible?

_____

_____

10 The lions may grow weak and hungry,
   but those who seek the LORD lack no good thing.
11 Come, my children, listen to me;
   I will teach you the fear of the LORD.
12 Whoever of you loves life
   and desires to see many good days,
13 keep your tongue from evil
   and your lips from telling lies.
14 Turn from evil and do good;
   seek peace and pursue it.

15 The eyes of the LORD are on the righteous,
   and his ears are attentive to their cry;
16 but the face of the LORD is against those who do evil,
   to blot out their name from the earth.

17 The righteous cry out, and the LORD hears them;
   he delivers them from all their troubles.
• 18 The LORD is close to the brokenhearted
   and saves those who are crushed in spirit.

19 The righteous person may have many troubles,
   but the LORD delivers him from them all;
20 he protects all his bones,
   not one of them will be broken.

21 Evil will slay the wicked;
   the foes of the righteous will be condemned.

days" (v. 12) they must shun evil and "do good" (v. 14). To trust and obey—that is "the fear of the LORD." On the instruction of this stanza, see Ps 37. For Peter's use of vv. 12–16, see 1Pe 3:8–12.
34:8 *blessed.* See note on 1:1.
34:11 *Come, my children.* Conventional language of the wisdom teachers.
34:13 See 15:2–3; Jas 3:5–10. For the tongue as a weapon, see note on 5:9.
34:14 *Turn from evil and do good.* A key link with Ps 37 (see 37:27). *seek peace.* See 37:37; 120:7; Pr 12:20; Zec 8:19 (also Zec 8:16–17); Mt 5:9; Ro 12:18; 1Co 7:15; 2Co 13:11; 1Th 5:13; Heb 12:14; Jas 3:17–18; 1Pe 3:8–12.
34:15 *righteous.* See vv. 8–14; see also note on 1:5.
34:16 *face of the LORD.* See note on 13:1.
34:17–18 See especially 51:17.
34:15–18 Assurance that the Lord hears the prayers of the righteous. He so thoroughly thwarts those who do evil that they are forgotten (v. 16). As in vv. 4–7, which these verses structurally balance, the theme is developed in alternating lines (in an *a-b/a-b* pattern).
34:17 *delivers them from all their troubles.* See 2Co 1:10; see also article, above.
34:19–22 Assurance that the Lord is the unfailing deliverer of the righteous—and that he holds the wicked accountable for their hostility toward the righteous (v. 21). Here, too, an *a-b/a-b* thematic pattern appears to be employed (note the contrast expressed in vv. 19,21 and the reinforcement of v. 20 found in v. 22).
34:20 *all his bones.* His whole being (see note on 6:2). *not one of them will be broken.* Perhaps John's

²² The LORD will rescue his servants;
  no one who takes refuge in him will be
    condemned.

Psalm 35

Of David.

¹ Contend, LORD, with those who contend with me;
  fight against those who fight against me.
² Take up shield and armor;
  arise and come to my aid.
³ Brandish spear and javelin^a
  against those who pursue me.
  Say to me,
  "I am your salvation."

⁴ May those who seek my life
  be disgraced and put to shame;
  may those who plot my ruin
  be turned back in dismay.
⁵ May they be like chaff before the wind,
  with the angel of the LORD driving them
    away;
⁶ may their path be dark and slippery,
  with the angel of the LORD pursuing them.

⁷ Since they hid their net for me without cause
  and without cause dug a pit for me,
⁸ may ruin overtake them by surprise —
  may the net they hid entangle them,
  may they fall into the pit, to their ruin.
⁹ Then my soul will rejoice in the LORD
  and delight in his salvation.
¹⁰ My whole being will exclaim,
  "Who is like you, LORD?
  You rescue the poor from those too strong for
    them,
  the poor and needy from those who rob them."

¹¹ Ruthless witnesses come forward;
  they question me on things I know nothing
    about.
¹² They repay me evil for good
  and leave me like one bereaved.
¹³ Yet when they were ill, I put on sackcloth
  and humbled myself with fasting.
  When my prayers returned to me unanswered,
¹⁴   I went about mourning
  as though for my friend or brother.
  I bowed my head in grief
  as though weeping for my mother.
¹⁵ But when I stumbled, they gathered in glee;
  assailants gathered against me without my
    knowledge.
  They slandered me without ceasing.

^a 3 Or *and block the way*

Gospel applies this word to Jesus (see NIV text note on Jn 19:36)—as the one above all others who could be called "righteous" (v. 19).

Ps 35 An appeal to the heavenly King, as divine Warrior and Judge, to come to the defense of "his servant" (v. 27) who is being maliciously slandered by those toward whom he had shown only the most tender friendship. The attack seems to have been occasioned by some "distress" (v. 26) that had overtaken the king (vv. 15,19,21,25). Ps 35 exemplifies such a "cry" (34:15) to the Lord in expectation of vindication as that spoken of in 34:15–22—except that here the author does not expressly identify himself as one of the "righteous" (34:21); he appeals to the Lord rather as an innocent victim of an unmotivated attack. This psalm has been paired with Ps 36 and placed between the two acrostic wisdom psalms (34 and 37; see introduction to Ps 34–37). Together they evoke terror among people who have "no fear of God" (36:1) but also testify to the security of those who fear the Lord (cf. 34:7) and trust him (cf. 37:3,5), relying on his love (36:5,7,11) and righteousness (35:24,28; 36:6,10).

35:1–3 Appeal for help to the Lord as Warrior-King (Ex 15:1–18). For links with vv. 22–25, see note on those verses.
35:2 *shield and armor.* For defense. For the Lord himself as the psalmists' "shield," see 3:3; 7:10; 18:2,30; 28:7; 33:20; 59:11; 84:9,11; 89:18; 115:9–11; 119:114; 144:2.
35:3 *spear and javelin.* For attack (but see NIV text note on "javelin"). For the Lord wielding a spear, see Hab 3:11.
35:4–6 Appeal to the Lord to deal with the attackers by frustrating all their efforts and totally disabling them. For links with vv. 26–27, see note on those verses.
35:4 *plot my ruin.* See note on 5:9.
35:5–6 *angel of the LORD.* See 34:7 and note.
35:7–10 Appeal to the Lord to match the attackers' violent intent with his saving act (see note on 5:10)—which the psalmist will celebrate with praise (see note on 7:17).
35:7–8 *hid their net . . . dug a pit . . . net they hid . . . fall into the pit.* See 9:15 and note.
35:9 *soul.* See note on 6:3.
35:10 *poor and needy.* A common pairing in the Psalter to describe those who lack resources and need God's justice (see 37:14; 40:17; 74:21; 109:22; see also 34:6, Ex 22:21–27).
35:11–16 The accusation: They repaid my friendship with malicious slander. This accusation stands at the center of the psalm (see note on 6:6).
35:13–14 The psalmist provides a living example of Jesus' later command to "pray for those who persecute you" (Mt 5:44)—as do Job (Job 42:7–10) and Jesus himself (Lk 23:34).

Additional Insights

The Psalter is a collection of collections and represents the final stage in a process that began in the early days of the first (Solomon's) temple (or even earlier in the time of David), when the temple liturgy began to take shape.

16 Like the ungodly they maliciously mocked;[a]
  they gnashed their teeth at me.

17 How long, Lord, will you look on?
  Rescue me from their ravages,
  my precious life from these lions.
18 I will give you thanks in the great assembly;
  among the throngs I will praise you.
19 Do not let those gloat over me
  who are my enemies without cause;
 do not let those who hate me without reason
  maliciously wink the eye.
20 They do not speak peaceably,
  but devise false accusations
  against those who live quietly in the land.
21 They sneer at me and say, "Aha! Aha!
  With our own eyes we have seen it."

22 Lord, you have seen this; do not be silent.
  Do not be far from me, Lord.
23 Awake, and rise to my defense!
  Contend for me, my God and Lord.
24 Vindicate me in your righteousness, Lord
    my God;
  do not let them gloat over me.
25 Do not let them think, "Aha, just what we wanted!"
  or say, "We have swallowed him up."

26 May all who gloat over my distress
  be put to shame and confusion;
 may all who exalt themselves over me
  be clothed with shame and disgrace.
27 May those who delight in my vindication
  shout for joy and gladness;
 may they always say, "The Lord be exalted,
  who delights in the well-being of his servant."

28 My tongue will proclaim your righteousness,
  your praises all day long.

Psalm 36[b]

*For the director of music. Of David
the servant of the Lord.*

1 I have a message from God in my heart
  concerning the sinfulness of the wicked:[c]
There is no fear of God
  before their eyes.

2 In their own eyes they flatter themselves
  too much to detect or hate their sin.
3 The words of their mouths are wicked and
    deceitful;
  they fail to act wisely or do good.

---

a 16 Septuagint; Hebrew may mean *Like an ungodly circle of
mockers,*   *b* In Hebrew texts 36:1-12 is numbered 36:2-13.
c 1 Or *A message from God: The transgression of the wicked /
resides in their hearts.*

35:13 *sackcloth.* See note on 30:11. *fasting.* An act of mourning (69:10).
35:15 *stumbled.* Brought low by circumstances (9:3; 27:2; 37:24; 56:13; 119:165).
35:16 *gnashed their teeth.* In malice (37:12; La 2:16).
35:17–21 Renewed appeal for God's saving help, accompanied by a vow to praise God (v. 18; see note on 7:17). This five-line stanza and the five-line stanza in vv. 7–10 frame the central accusation.
35:17 *How long . . . ?* See note on 6:3. *lions.* See note on 7:2.
35:18 *assembly.* See note on 1:5.
 35:19 *enemies without cause.* See vv. 11–17; an experience frequently reflected also elsewhere in the Psalter (38:19; 69:4; 109:3; 119:78,86,161). See also La 3:52. *hate me without reason.* See 69:4. It is not known which of these passages is referred to in Jn 15:25. Both psalms reflect circumstances applicable also to Jesus' experience (but see introduction to Ps 69).
35:21 *Aha! Aha!* See v. 25; see also note on 3:2.
35:22–25 A return to the opening appeal (vv. 1–3) for God to arouse himself, take up the psalmist's cause and "contend" (v. 23) with those attacking him.
35:22 *do not be silent.* Do not remain inactive (see 28:1; 83:1; 109:1).
35:23 *Awake.* See note on 7:6.
35:24 *righteousness.* See note on 4:1.
35:25 *swallowed.* See 124:3.
35:26–27 Again (see vv. 4–6) an appeal for God to bring "shame" and "disgrace" on the adversaries. For both form and substance, cf. 40:14–16.
35:26 *who gloat over my distress.* In Hebrew, a verbal echo of "who plot my ruin" (v. 4).
35:27 May all who are faithful supporters of the Lord's "servant" (here no doubt equivalent to his "anointed"; see note on 2:2) have reason to rejoice and praise the Lord.
35:28 A concluding vow to praise God (see note on 7:17). *righteousness.* See note on 4:1.
Ps 36 A prayer for God's unfailing protection, as the psalmist reflects on the godlessness of the wicked and the goodness of God. For this psalm's relationship with Ps 35, see introduction to Ps 34–37. Structurally, a short couplet (v. 1) introduces a series of four stanzas of three Hebrew poetic lines each (vv. 2–4, 5–7a,7b–9,10–12). In later Jewish practice, vv. 7–10 became part of the morning prayer.
36 title *For the director of music.* See note on Ps 4 title. *servant of the Lord.* His royal servant (see notes on Ps 18 title; 35:27; see also 2Sa 7:20).
 36:1 *message from God.* Usually reserved for words of revelation from God, such as those spoken by the prophets. Here reference is to an insight into the true character of the wicked. *heart.* See note on 4:7. *no fear of God.* Such as the psalmist calls for in Ps 34 and (implicitly) in Ps 37. See 55:19; Ge 20:11. They take no account of his all-seeing eye, his righteous judgment and his power to deal with them (see note on 10:11). For Paul's use of this verse, see Ro 3:18.
 36:2–4 The wicked characterized (see 10:2–11 and notes; see also introduction to Ps 37).
36:2 *flatter themselves.* Out of the smug, conceited notion that they are accountable to no one.

4Even on their beds they plot evil;
    they commit themselves to a sinful
      course
    and do not reject what is wrong.

5Your love, LORD, reaches to the heavens,
    your faithfulness to the skies.
6Your righteousness is like the highest
      mountains,
    your justice like the great deep.
    You, LORD, preserve both people and
      animals.
7How priceless is your unfailing love,
    O God!
    People take refuge in the shadow of your
      wings.
8They feast on the abundance of your
      house;
    you give them drink from your river of
      delights.
9For with you is the fountain of life;
    in your light we see light.

10Continue your love to those who know you,
    your righteousness to the upright in
      heart.
11May the foot of the proud not come
      against me,
    nor the hand of the wicked drive me
      away.
12See how the evildoers lie fallen —
    thrown down, not able to rise!

Psalm 37[a]

Of David.

1Do not fret because of those who are evil
    or be envious of those who do wrong;
2for like the grass they will soon wither,
    like green plants they will soon die away.

3Trust in the LORD and do good;
    dwell in the land and enjoy safe pasture.
4Take delight in the LORD,
    and he will give you the desires of your
      heart.

5Commit your way to the LORD;
    trust in him and he will do this:
6He will make your righteous reward shine
      like the dawn,
    your vindication like the noonday sun.

7Be still before the LORD
    and wait patiently for him;

---

[a] This psalm is an acrostic poem, the stanzas of which begin with the successive letters of the Hebrew alphabet.

36:3 *words of their mouths.* See note on 5:9. *are . . . deceitful.* See 35:20. *fail to act wisely.* See 94:8–11; Pr 2:9–11. *fail to . . . do good.* In contrast to the wise and godly person (see 34:14; 37:3,27; see also note on 34:8–14).

36:4 *on their beds.* Where one's thoughts are free to range and to set the course for the activities of the day. The wicked do not meditate on God's law "day and night" (1:2; see 119:55). On the other hand, the hearts of the godly instruct them at night (16:7); they commune at night with God (42:8), think of him (63:6) and reflect on his promises (119:148). *plot evil.* See 34:14; 37:27; cf. Mic 2:1.

36:5–7a The trustworthiness of the Lord.

36:5 *love . . . faithfulness.* See note on 26:3. *reaches to the heavens . . . to the skies.* Encompasses all the realms of creaturely existence (57:10; 108:4).

36:6 *righteousness.* See note on 4:1.

36:7a *unfailing love.* See v. 5; see also article, p. 16.

36:7b–9 The Lord's benevolence toward all his creatures (33:4–5).

36:7b *shadow of your wings.* See 17:8 and note.

36:8 *feast . . . drink.* Life-giving food and water. *house.* Here, God's whole estate or realm—i.e., the earth, from which springs the abundance of food for all living things (see note on 24:2). *river.* The "channel" (Job 38:25) by which God brings forth the rain out of his "storehouses" (33:7; see Job 38:8–11,22,37; Jer 10:13) in his "upper chambers" (104:13; see 65:9; Isa 30:25 and the references to "blessings" from heaven in Ge 49:25; Dt 33:23). This vivid imagery—depicting God's control over the waters from heaven, which feed the rivers and streams of earth to give life and health wherever they flow—is the source of the symbol of "the river of the water of life" that flows from the temple of God (Rev 22:1–2; see also Eze 47:1–12). *of delights.* Furnishing many sources of joy.

36:9 The climax and summation of vv. 5–9. *fountain of life.* See Jer 2:13; 17:13. Ultimately, for sinners, God provides the water of life through Jesus Christ (Jn 4:10,14). *your light.* See 27:1 and note. *see.* Experience, have, enjoy, as in 16:10; 27:13; 34:8,12; 49:9,19; 89:48; 90:15; 106:5 ("enjoy"); Job 9:25 ("glimpse"); 42:5; Ecc 1:16 ("experienced"); 3:13 ("find"); 6:6 ("enjoy"); Isa 53:10; La 3:1. *light.* Life in its fullness as it was created to be. For the association of light with life, see 49:19; 56:13; Job 3:20; 33:28,30; Isa 53:11.

36:10–12 The prayer: Your "love" (v. 5) and "righteousness" (v. 6), which you display in all creation—show these to all who know (acknowledge) you and are upright (the people of God). But keep the wicked, "foot" and "hand," from success against me (the king; see note on 33:16).

36:10 *love.* See article, p. 16. *those who know you.* See 9:10 and note. *righteousness.* See note on 4:1.

Ps 37 Instruction in godly wisdom. (For other "wisdom" psalms, see 34:8–22; 49; 112; others closely related are Ps 1; 73; 91; 92:6–9,12–15; 111; 119; 127–128; 133.) This psalm's dominant theme is related to the contrast between the wicked and the righteous reflected in Ps 36. The central issue addressed is: Who will "inherit the land" (vv. 9,11,22,29), i.e., live on to enjoy the blessings of the Lord in the promised land? Will the wicked, who plot (v. 12), scheme (vv. 7,32), default on debts (v. 21), use raw power to gain advantage (v. 14) and seem thereby to

do not fret when people succeed in their
    ways,
  when they carry out their wicked schemes.

8 Refrain from anger and turn from wrath;
    do not fret — it leads only to evil.
9 For those who are evil will be destroyed,
    but those who hope in the LORD will inherit
      the land.

10 A little while, and the wicked will be no more;
    though you look for them, they will not be
      found.
11 But the meek will inherit the land
    and enjoy peace and prosperity.

12 The wicked plot against the righteous
    and gnash their teeth at them;
13 but the Lord laughs at the wicked,
    for he knows their day is coming.

14 The wicked draw the sword
    and bend the bow
  to bring down the poor and needy,
    to slay those whose ways are upright.
15 But their swords will pierce their own hearts,
    and their bows will be broken.

16 Better the little that the righteous have
    than the wealth of many wicked;
17 for the power of the wicked will be broken,
    but the LORD upholds the righteous.

18 The blameless spend their days under the
    LORD's care,
  and their inheritance will endure forever.
19 In times of disaster they will not wither;
    in days of famine they will enjoy plenty.

20 But the wicked will perish:
    Though the LORD's enemies are like the
      flowers of the field,
  they will be consumed, they will go up in
      smoke.

> ## How can you refrain from anger and wrath?

flourish (vv. 7,16,35)? Or will the righteous, who trust in the Lord (vv. 3,5,7,34) and are humble (v. 11), blameless (vv. 18,37), generous (vv. 21,26), upright (v. 37) and peaceful (v. 37), and from whose mouth is heard the moral wisdom that reflects meditation on God's law (vv. 30–31)? For a similar characterization of the wicked, see 10:2–11; 73:4–12. For a similar characterization of the righteous, see Ps 112. For a similar statement concerning the transitoriness of the wicked, see Ps 49; 73:18–20.

Structurally, in this alphabetic acrostic (see Introduction: Literary Features), two verses are devoted to each letter of the alphabet, though with some irregularity. The main theme is developed in vv. 1–11, then further elaborated in the rest of the psalm. The whole is framed by statements contrasting the brief career of the wicked (vv. 1–2) and the Lord's sustaining help of the righteous (vv. 39–40).

37:1–2 See v. 7; Ps 73.
37:1 Almost identical to Pr 24:19.
37:2 See note on v. 20.
37:3 See 34:8–14 and note.
37:5 *Commit.* See 1Pe 5:7.
37:6 *your righteous reward.* That is, the prosperity and well-being that God will bestow in accordance with "your" faithful reliance on him (cf. v. 9; see Pr 8:18; 21:21 ["prosperity"] for this sense of the Hebrew word; see also Isa 48:18). *your vindication.* See 35:27 and note; see also Isa 54:17. The close Hebrew synonyms here rendered "righteous reward" and "vindication" both refer to manifestations of God's favor on those he pleases to bless or deliver, as in Isa 59:9 (where these terms are linked with "light") and 59:11 (where "justice" [or "vindication"] is linked with "deliverance"). Accordingly, "your righteous reward" and "your vindication" in this verse have direct links with "your (God's) righteousness" and "your (God's) justice" in 36:6.
37:8 *anger . . . wrath.* Evidence of fretting over the wicked's prosperity, gained to the disadvantage of and even at the expense of the righteous.
37:9 *hope in.* See v. 34. *inherit the land.* Receive from the Lord secure entitlement (for them and their children) to the promised land as the created and redeemed sphere and bountiful source of provision for the life of God's people. Those who hope in the Lord—i.e., trustfully look to him to bestow life and its blessings as a gift—will inherit the land, not those who apart from God and by evil means try to take possession of it and its wealth (see vv. 11,22,29; cf. Jos 7).
37:10 *A little while.* Shortness of time is here a figure for the certainty of an event (58:9; Job 20:5–11; Hag 2:6).
37:11 *meek.* Those who humbly acknowledge their dependence on the goodness and grace of God and betray no arrogance toward others.
37:12 *righteous.* See note on 1:5. *gnash their teeth.* See 35:16 and note.
37:13 *Lord laughs.* See 2:4. *knows their day is coming.* Strikingly, the psalmist nowhere speaks of God's active involvement in bringing the wicked down—though he hints at it in v. 22. The certainty that the life of the wicked will be "destroyed" is frequently asserted (vv. 9,22,28,34,38; cf. vv. 2,8,10,15,17,20,36,38)—and the Lord also knows it—

21 The wicked borrow and do not repay,
   but the righteous give generously;
22 those the LORD blesses will inherit the land,
   but those he curses will be destroyed.

23 The LORD makes firm the steps
   of the one who delights in him;
24 though he may stumble, he will not fall,
   for the LORD upholds him with his hand.

25 I was young and now I am old,
   yet I have never seen the righteous
     forsaken
   or their children begging bread.
26 They are always generous and lend freely;
   their children will be a blessing.*a*

27 Turn from evil and do good;
   then you will dwell in the land forever.
28 For the LORD loves the just
   and will not forsake his faithful ones.

   Wrongdoers will be completely destroyed*b*;
   the offspring of the wicked will perish.
29 The righteous will inherit the land
   and dwell in it forever.

30 The mouths of the righteous utter wisdom,
   and their tongues speak what is just.
31 The law of their God is in their hearts;
   their feet do not slip.

32 The wicked lie in wait for the righteous,
   intent on putting them to death;
33 but the LORD will not leave them in the power
     of the wicked
   or let them be condemned when brought
     to trial.

34 Hope in the LORD
   and keep his way.
   He will exalt you to inherit the land;
     when the wicked are destroyed, you will
     see it.

35 I have seen a wicked and ruthless man
   flourishing like a luxuriant native tree,
36 but he soon passed away and was no more;
   though I looked for him, he could not be
     found.

37 Consider the blameless, observe the upright;
   a future awaits those who seek peace.*c*
38 But all sinners will be destroyed;
   there will be no future*d* for the wicked.

a 26 Or *freely; / the names of their children will be used in
blessings* (see Gen. 48:20); or *freely; / others will see that their
children are blessed*   *b 28* See Septuagint; Hebrew *They will
be protected forever*   *c 37* Or *upright; / those who seek peace
will have posterity*   *d 38* Or *posterity*

but God's positive action is here reserved for his care for
and protection of the righteous. *their day.* The time when
each will be "destroyed," as in 1Sa 26:10; Job 18:20 ("his
fate").
37:14–15 *sword . . . bow . . . swords . . . bows.* See 64:3–4,7–
8; Pr 30:14 and note on Ps 5:9.
37:14 *poor and needy.* See 34:6; 35:10.
37:15 *pierce . . . hearts.* See 45:5.
37:16–17 *righteous.* See note on 1:5.
37:18 *blameless.* See v. 37; see also 15:2 and note. *under the
LORD's care.* See 1:6 ("the LORD watches over").
37:20 *like the flowers.* Cf. v. 2; 90:5–6; 92:7; 102:11; 103:15–
16; Job 14:2; Isa 40:6–7; see Jas 1:10–11.
37:21 Or "The wicked must borrow and cannot repay,/
but the righteous are able to give generously" (Dt 15:6;
28:12,44).
37:24 See Pr 24:16.
37:26 See note on v. 21.
37:27 *Turn from evil and do good.* See 34:14 and note.
37:28 *faithful ones.* See note on 4:3.
37:29 *dwell in it forever.* They and their children and children's children, in contrast to the wicked (v. 28).
37:30 *wisdom.* See 119:98,130; Dt 4:6.
37:31 *hearts.* See note on 4:7. *do not slip.* From the right
path (17:5).

> How can you continue to hope in
> face of the injustice in the world?

_____

_____

_____

_____

_____

_____

_____

_____

_____

_____

_____

³⁹ The salvation of the righteous comes from
the LORD;
he is their stronghold in time of trouble.
⁴⁰ The LORD helps them and delivers them;
he delivers them from the wicked and
saves them,
because they take refuge in him.

Psalm 38^a

A psalm of David. A petition.

¹ LORD, do not rebuke me in your anger
or discipline me in your wrath.
² Your arrows have pierced me,
and your hand has come down on me.
³ Because of your wrath there is no health in
my body;
there is no soundness in my bones because
of my sin.
⁴ My guilt has overwhelmed me
like a burden too heavy to bear.

⁵ My wounds fester and are loathsome
because of my sinful folly.
⁶ I am bowed down and brought very low;
all day long I go about mourning.
⁷ My back is filled with searing pain;
there is no health in my body.
⁸ I am feeble and utterly crushed;
I groan in anguish of heart.

⁹ All my longings lie open before you, Lord;
my sighing is not hidden from you.
¹⁰ My heart pounds, my strength fails me;
even the light has gone from my eyes.
¹¹ My friends and companions avoid me because
of my wounds;
my neighbors stay far away.
¹² Those who want to kill me set their traps,
those who would harm me talk of my ruin;
all day long they scheme and lie.

¹³ I am like the deaf, who cannot hear,
like the mute, who cannot speak;
¹⁴ I have become like one who does not hear,
whose mouth can offer no reply.
¹⁵ LORD, I wait for you;
you will answer, Lord my God.
¹⁶ For I said, "Do not let them gloat
or exalt themselves over me when my
feet slip."

¹⁷ For I am about to fall,
and my pain is ever with me.
* ¹⁸ I confess my iniquity;
I am troubled by my sin.

^a In Hebrew texts 38:1-22 is numbered 38:2-23.

37:32 *lie in wait.* See 10:8–9; see also note on 7:2. *intent on putting them to death.* Attempting to seize by false charges at court (v. 33) the very livelihood of their intended victims.
37:34 See v. 9.
37:35–36 Cf. vv. 25–26.
37:37–38 The great contrast: hope for the "upright," no hope for the "wicked."
37:39–40 *the righteous . . . them.* They are not at the mercy of the wicked: The Lord is their refuge, and in spite of all that the wicked do the Lord makes secure their inheritance in the promised land.
Ps 38–41 The final four psalms of Book I are all linked by common central themes (see introductions to these psalms). One of these themes is confession of sin, which is found elsewhere in Book I only in Ps 25; 32 (see introductions to those psalms). Significantly, following a wisdom psalm (37), the first reference to sin here characterizes it as "folly" (38:5).
Ps 38 A lament seeking relief from a severe and painful illness, God's "rebuke" (v. 1) for a sin David has committed (vv. 3–4, 18). Neither the specific occasion nor the illness can be identified. David's suffering is aggravated by the withdrawal of his friends (v. 11) and the unwarranted efforts of his enemies to seize this opportunity to bring him down (vv. 12,16,19–20). In traditional Christian usage, this is one of seven penitential psalms. Like Ps 33 (see introductory note on its structure), its length (22 verses) may be based on the number of letters in the Hebrew alphabet. The psalm is composed of five stanzas of four verses each, with a two-verse conclusion.
38 title *A petition.* Occurs elsewhere only in the title of Ps 70.
38:1–4 Plea for relief from the Lord's rebuke.
38:2 *arrows.* A vivid metaphor for God's actions against him (see Job 6:4; 34:6; La 3:12; Eze 5:16). *your hand has come down on me.* See 32:4 and note on 32:3–5.
38:3 *bones.* See note on 6:2.
38:4 *burden.* Not only a psychological "burden of guilt" but the heavy burden of suffering described in vv. 5–8.
38:5–8 The devastating physical and psychological effects of his illness.
38:8 *heart.* See note on 4:7.
38:9–12 Renewed complaint, with further elaboration of his troubles: his illness (v. 10), abandonment by his friends (v. 11) and the hostility of his enemies (v. 12).
38:11 See note on 31:11–12.
38:12 See note on 5:9. *set their traps.* See note on 9:15.
38:13–16 Let the Lord answer (v. 15) my enemies. Like a person who cannot hear or speak, David will not reply to his enemies (vv. 13–14); he waits for the Lord to act in his behalf (vv. 15–16). See 1Sa 25:32–39; 2Sa 16:10,12.
38:16 *when my feet slip.* When he experiences a personal blow to health or circumstance—here referring to his illness (66:9; 94:18; 121:3).
38:17–20 As health declines, the vigor of his many enemies increases.
38:17 *about to fall.* Death seems near. *fall.* In Hebrew, a verbal link with 35:15 ("stumbled").
38:18 See vv. 3–4; Ps 32.

¹⁹ Many have become my enemies without
  cause^a;
     those who hate me without reason are
     numerous.
²⁰ Those who repay my good with evil
     lodge accusations against me,
     though I seek only to do what is good.

²¹ LORD, do not forsake me;
     do not be far from me, my God.
²² Come quickly to help me,
     my Lord and my Savior.

Psalm 39^b

For the director of music. For Jeduthun.
A psalm of David.

¹ I said, "I will watch my ways
     and keep my tongue from sin;
  I will put a muzzle on my mouth
     while in the presence of the wicked."
² So I remained utterly silent,
     not even saying anything good.
  But my anguish increased;
³   my heart grew hot within me.
  While I meditated, the fire burned;
     then I spoke with my tongue:

⁴ "Show me, LORD, my life's end
     and the number of my days;
  let me know how fleeting my life is.
⁵ You have made my days a mere handbreadth;
     the span of my years is as nothing before you.
  Everyone is but a breath,
     even those who seem secure.^c

⁶ "Surely everyone goes around like a mere
     phantom;
  in vain they rush about, heaping up wealth
     without knowing whose it will finally be.

⁷ "But now, Lord, what do I look for?
     My hope is in you.
⁸ Save me from all my transgressions;
     do not make me the scorn of fools.
⁹ I was silent; I would not open my mouth,
     for you are the one who has done this.
¹⁰ Remove your scourge from me;
     I am overcome by the blow of your hand.
¹¹ When you rebuke and discipline anyone for
     their sin,
  you consume their wealth like a moth —
     surely everyone is but a breath.

^a 19 One Dead Sea Scrolls manuscript; Masoretic Text *my
vigorous enemies*   ^b In Hebrew texts 39:1-13 is numbered
39:2-14.   ^c 5 The Hebrew has *Selah* (a word of uncertain
meaning) here and at the end of verse 11.

38:19–20 He has sinned against the Lord, but he is innocent of any wrong against those attacking him (see note
on 35:19).
38:20 *repay my good.* See 35:12–14. *lodge accusations
against.* Accuse (falsely), as in 71:13; 109:4,20,29; Zec 3:1.
38:21–22 In conclusion, a renewed appeal.

Ps 39 David's poignant lament when deeply troubled by the fragility of human life. He is reminded of
this by the present illness through which God is rebuking
him (vv. 10–11) for his "transgressions" (v. 8). Ps 38 speaks
of silence before the enemy, Ps 39 of silence before God.
Both are laments in times of illness (God's "rebuke," v. 11;
38:1); both acknowledge sin, and both express deep trust
in God. See introduction to Ps 40. In addition, this psalm
has many links with Ps 90; see also Ps 49. The psalm's
structure is symmetrical: The first two stanzas of five and
three Hebrew poetic lines are balanced by the last two
stanzas of five and three lines. At the center (v. 6; see note
on 6:6) stands a wisdom observation that places David's
situation in the broader context of a widespread human
condition (see note on v. 6).
39 title *For the director of music.* See note on Ps 4 title.
Jeduthun. One of David's three choir leaders (1Ch 16:41–42;
25:1,6; 2Ch 5:12; called his "seer" in 2Ch 35:15). Jeduthun is
probably also the Ethan of 1Ch 6:44; 15:19; if so, he represented the family of Merari, even as Asaph did the family of Gershon and Heman the family of Kohath, the three
sons of Levi (1Ch 6:16,33,39,43–44).
39:1–3 Introduction: Having determined to keep silent,
he could finally no longer suppress his anguish.
39:1 He had kept a muzzle on his mouth for fear that rebellious words would escape in the hearing of the wicked
(see Ps 73).
39:2–3 Suppressed anguish only intensified the agony
(see Jer 20:9).

39:4–5 A prayer for understanding and patient ac-
ceptance of the brief span of human life.
39:4 *how fleeting my life is.* See 78:39 and note on 37:20.
39:5 *as nothing before you.* See 90:4. *but a breath.* See v. 11;
62:9; 144:4. For *Selah,* see NIV text note and note on 3:2.
39:6 Could almost serve as a summary of Ecclesiastes.
39:7–11 A prayer for forgiveness and rescue.
39:8 *Save me.* As from an enemy. *scorn of fools.* If the Lord
does not restore him, he will be mocked (22:7–8; 69:6–12)
by godless fools (14:1).
39:10 *blow of your hand.* See 32:4; 38:2.

Additional Insights

The contents of the superscriptions
[psalm titles] vary but fall into a few
broad categories: (1) author, (2) name
of collection, (3) type of psalm, (4) musical notation, (5) liturgical notations
and (6) brief introductions of occasion
for composition.

¹²"Hear my prayer, LORD,
    listen to my cry for help;
    do not be deaf to my weeping.
I dwell with you as a foreigner,
    a stranger, as all my ancestors were.
¹³Look away from me, that I may enjoy life
      again
    before I depart and am no more."

Psalm 40^a

For the director of music. Of David. A psalm.

¹I waited patiently for the LORD;
    he turned to me and heard my cry.
²He lifted me out of the slimy pit,
    out of the mud and mire;
    he set my feet on a rock
    and gave me a firm place to stand.
³He put a new song in my mouth,
    a hymn of praise to our God.
Many will see and fear the LORD
    and put their trust in him.

⁴Blessed is the one
    who trusts in the LORD,
who does not look to the proud,
    to those who turn aside to false gods.^b
⁵Many, LORD my God,
    are the wonders you have done,
    the things you planned for us.
None can compare with you;
    were I to speak and tell of your deeds,
    they would be too many to declare.

⁶Sacrifice and offering you did not desire —
    but my ears you have opened^c —
    burnt offerings and sin offerings^d you did
      not require.
⁷Then I said, "Here I am, I have come —
    it is written about me in the scroll.^e

^a In Hebrew texts 40:1-17 is numbered 40:2-18.   ^b 4 Or *to lies*   ^c 6 Hebrew; some Septuagint manuscripts *but a body you have prepared for me*   ^d 6 Or *purification offerings*   ^e 7 Or *come / with the scroll written for me*

Additional Insights

As for Davidic authorship, there can be little doubt that the Psalter contains psalms composed by that noted singer and musician and that there was at one time a "Davidic" psalter.

39:11 *rebuke and discipline.* See 6:1; 38:1. *but a breath.* See note on v. 5.
39:12–13 A prayer simply for a return to previous joys of life for the time he has left.
  39:12 *a foreigner, a stranger.* He lives this life before God only as a pilgrim passing through, as his ancestors were (see Abraham's words about himself in Ge 23:4; see also 1Pe 2:11; Heb 11:13).
39:13 *Look away from me.* See Job 7:17–19; 10:20–21; 14:6. *enjoy life again.* See Job 9:27; 10:20. *am no more.* Here there is no glimpse of what lies beyond the horizon of death (see note on 6:5).
  Ps 40–41 Book I of the Psalter closes with two psalms containing "Blessed are those [or "is the one"] who" statements (40:4; 41:1), thus balancing the two psalms with which the Book begins (1:1; 2:12). In this way, the whole of Book I is framed by declarations of the blessedness of those who "delight . . . in the law of the LORD" (1:2), who "take refuge in him" (2:12), who do "not look to the proud" but make the Lord their trust (40:4) and who have "regard for the weak" (41:1)—a concise instruction in godliness. See introduction to Ps 1–2.
  Ps 40 A psalm of both thanksgiving for past help and lament over current troubles. The causes of distress are not specified, but David acknowledges that they are occasioned by his sin (v. 12), as in Ps 38–39; 41 (see introductions to Ps 39; 41). They are aggravated by the gloating of his enemies, a theme also present in Ps 38–39; 41 (see introduction to Ps 38). The psalm begins with praise of God for his past mercies (vv. 1–5: two stanzas of five Hebrew poetic lines each) and a testimony to the king's own faithfulness to the Lord (vv. 6–10: two three-line stanzas). These form the grounds for his present appeal for help (vv. 11–17: two five-line stanzas and a concluding couplet; note the structural centering of vv. 6–10). For other lengthy prefaces to prayer, see Ps 44; 89. Ps 70 is a somewhat revised duplicate of vv. 13–17 of this psalm.
40:1–5 Praise of the Lord for past mercies (see introduction to Ps 9).
  40:1–3 David's experience of God's past help in time of trouble, which moved him to praise and others to faith (see notes on 7:17; 9:1).
40:2 See 30:1 and note.
40:3 *new song.* See note on 33:3. *Many will see.* As a result of David's praise (see 18:49; 22:22–31; see also note on 9:1). *fear.* See notes on 15:4; 34:8–14.
40:4–5 The Lord's benevolence to others: to all who trust in the Lord (v. 4), and to his people Israel (v. 5).
40:4 See Jer 17:7; praise of the Lord for the blessedness of those who trust in him (32:1–2; 146:5). *Blessed.* See note on 1:1. *proud.* See note on 31:23.
  40:5 *wonders.* See note on 9:1. *planned.* God's actions in behalf of Israel are according to his predetermined purpose (Isa 25:1; 46:10–11).
  40:6–8 David's commitment to God's will. Heb 10:5–10 applies these verses to Christ.
  40:6 *did not desire . . . not require.* More important is obedience (1Sa 15:22), especially to God's moral law (Isa 1:10–17; Am 5:21–24; Mic 6:6–8)—i.e., the ten basic commandments of his covenant (Ex 20:3–17; Dt 5:7–21). *ears . . . opened.* Ears made able and eager to hear God's law (Pr 28:9; Isa 48:8; 50:4–5).

8 I desire to do your will, my God;
    your law is within my heart."

9 I proclaim your saving acts in the great assembly;
    I do not seal my lips, LORD,
    as you know.
10 I do not hide your righteousness in my heart;
    I speak of your faithfulness and your saving
        help.
    I do not conceal your love and your faithfulness
        from the great assembly.

11 Do not withhold your mercy from me, LORD;
    may your love and faithfulness always
        protect me.
12 For troubles without number surround me;
    my sins have overtaken me, and I cannot see.
    They are more than the hairs of my head,
        and my heart fails within me.
13 Be pleased to save me, LORD;
    come quickly, LORD, to help me.

14 May all who want to take my life
    be put to shame and confusion;
    may all who desire my ruin
    be turned back in disgrace.
15 May those who say to me, "Aha! Aha!"
    be appalled at their own shame.
16 But may all who seek you
    rejoice and be glad in you;
    may those who long for your saving help
        always say,
    "The LORD is great!"

17 But as for me, I am poor and needy;
    may the Lord think of me.
    You are my help and my deliverer;
    you are my God, do not delay.

40:7 *Here I am, I have come.* Probably refers to David's commitment to the Lord at the time of his enthronement. *it is written about me in the scroll.* Some take this to be a reference to a prophecy, perhaps Dt 17:14–15. The context, however, strongly suggests that the "scroll" refers to the personal copy of the law that the king is to "write for himself" (Dt 17:18) at the time of his enthronement to serve as the covenant charter of his administration (see Dt 17:18–20; 2Ki 11:12; cf. 1Ki 2:3; see also NIV text note).
40:8 *I desire.* Whatever is in full accord with God's "desire" (v. 6)—a claim that frames the stanza.

40:9–10 David's life is filled with praise, proclaiming God's faithful and loving acts on behalf of his people (cf. 85:10–11). This, too, God desires more than animal sacrifices (50:7–15).
40:9 *proclaim.* See 68:11; 96:2; as good tidings (1Ki 1:42; Isa 40:9; 41:27; 52:7; 61:1). *in the great assembly.* See note on 1:5. *not seal my lips.* He is not silent about God's praise (see 38:13–16; 39:1 and notes).
40:10 *heart.* See note on 4:7. *your love and your faithfulness.* See note on 26:3.
40:11–17 The prayer for help.
40:11–13 David's plea for deliverance from his troubles.
40:11 *your love and faithfulness.* Which he has been proclaiming to all at the temple (see v. 10 and note).
40:12 *sins have overtaken me.* In the form of the "troubles without number" that burden him (see Ps 38–39 and their introductions). *more than the hairs of my head.* See Mt 10:30; Lk 12:7. *heart.* See note on 4:7.
40:14–16 Prayer for God's saving help to confound David's adversaries and move the godly to praise. For harassment by enemies in times of trouble, see 38:12; 39:8; 41:5,7 and often in the Psalms (see note on 5:9). For both form and substance, see 35:26–27.
40:14 *shame . . . confusion . . . disgrace.* David asks that those who have wished to put him to public shame be put to shame themselves (see note on 5:10).
40:15 *Aha! Aha!* See note on 3:2.
40:17 *poor and needy.* In need of God's help (see notes on 34:6; 35:10).

Spend some time confessing your sins to God and then record your response to his forgiveness.

_____

_____

_____

_____

_____

_____

▶ Why is it important to confess sin (32:1)?

_____

_____

_____

_____

▶ What do you learn about God in Psalm 33?

_____

_____

_____

_____

▶ What does unconfessed sin do to a person (Ps 38)?

_____

_____

_____

_____

▶ How did the psalmist describe his relationship with God in Psalm 40 and how does that apply to your own relationship with God?

_____

_____

_____

_____

Psalm 41[a]

For the director of music. A psalm of David.

[1] Blessed are those who have regard for the
    weak;
    the LORD delivers them in times of
    trouble.
[2] The LORD protects and preserves them —
    they are counted among the blessed in
    the land —
    he does not give them over to the desire of
    their foes.
[3] The LORD sustains them on their sickbed
    and restores them from their bed of
    illness.

[4] I said, "Have mercy on me, LORD;
    heal me, for I have sinned against you."
[5] My enemies say of me in malice,
    "When will he die and his name perish?"
[6] When one of them comes to see me,
    he speaks falsely, while his heart gathers
    slander;
    then he goes out and spreads it around.

[7] All my enemies whisper together
    against me;
    they imagine the worst for me, saying,
[8] "A vile disease has afflicted him;
    he will never get up from the place where
    he lies."
[9] Even my close friend,
    someone I trusted,
    one who shared my bread,
    has turned[b] against me.

[10] But may you have mercy on me, LORD;
    raise me up, that I may repay them.
[11] I know that you are pleased with me,
    for my enemy does not triumph
    over me.
[12] Because of my integrity you uphold me
    and set me in your presence forever.

[13] Praise be to the LORD, the God of Israel,
    from everlasting to everlasting.
            Amen and Amen.

---

[a] In Hebrew texts 41:1-13 is numbered 41:2-14.   [b] 9 Hebrew
has lifted up his heel

Ps 41 David's lament when seriously ill. He acknowledges that his illness is related to his sin (v. 4). See introductions to Ps 38–40. His enemies greet the prospect of his death with malicious glee (see note on 5:9), and even his "close friend" (v. 9) betrays his friendship (see note on 31:11–12). This psalm concludes a collection of four psalms connected by common themes and, together with Ps 40, forms the conclusion to Book I (see introduction to Ps 40–41). (Book I begins and ends with a "Blessed" psalm.) In its structure, the psalm is symmetrical, composed of four stanzas of three verses each. The first and fourth stanzas frame the psalmist's complaint with expressions of confidence; stanzas two and three elaborate the complaint itself. Verse 13 is actually not part of the psalm but the doxology that closes Book I (see note on v. 13).

41 title *For the director of music.* See note on Ps 4 title.

41:1–3 Confidence that the Lord will restore.

41:1 *Blessed are those who have regard for the weak.* True of all, but especially of a king, whose duty it is to defend the powerless (72:2,4,12–14; 82:3–4; Pr 29:14; 31:8–9; Isa 11:4; Jer 22:16). *Blessed.* See note on 1:1.

41:4–6 David prays for God to show mercy and heal him.

41:4 *sinned.* See note on 32:3–5.

41:5 *When will he die . . . ?* See note on 3:2.

41:6 *see me.* Visit me in my sickness. *speaks falsely.* Speaks as if he were my friend. *heart.* See note on 4:7.

41:7–9 His enemies and his friend.

41:9 *close friend . . . who shared my bread.* One who shared the king's table—i.e., was an honored, as well as trusted, friend (see note on 31:11–12). Reference may be to one who had sealed his friendship by a covenant (see note on 23:5). For Jesus' use of this verse in application to himself, see Jn 13:18. In fulfilling the role of his royal ancestor as God's anointed king over Israel, the greatest Son of David also experienced the hostility of others and the betrayal of a trusted associate.

41:10–12 Prayer, with confidence.

41:10 *that I may repay them.* That I (as king) may call them to account.

41:12 *my integrity.* See note on 15:2. *in your presence.* As the royal servant of Israel's heavenly King. (For the idiom, see 101:7; 1Sa 16:22, "in my service"; 1Ki 10:8, "before you"; 17:1, "whom I serve.") *forever.* Never to be rejected (2Sa 7:15–16).

41:13 The doxology with which the worshiping community is to respond to the contents of Book I (see 72:18–19; 89:52; 106:48; 150).

BOOK II

Psalms 42 – 72

Psalm 42[a,b]

*For the director of music. A maskil[c]
of the Sons of Korah.*

[1] As the deer pants for streams of water,
   so my soul pants for you, my God.
[2] My soul thirsts for God, for the living God.
   When can I go and meet with God?
[3] My tears have been my food
   day and night,
while people say to me all day long,
   "Where is your God?"
[4] These things I remember
   as I pour out my soul:
how I used to go to the house of God
   under the protection of the Mighty One[d]
with shouts of joy and praise
   among the festive throng.

[5] Why, my soul, are you downcast?
   Why so disturbed within me?
Put your hope in God,
   for I will yet praise him,
   my Savior and my God.

[6] My soul is downcast within me;
   therefore I will remember you
from the land of the Jordan,
   the heights of Hermon — from Mount
      Mizar.
[7] Deep calls to deep
   in the roar of your waterfalls;
all your waves and breakers
   have swept over me.

---

[a] In many Hebrew manuscripts Psalms 42 and 43 constitute one psalm.   [b] In Hebrew texts 42:1-11 is numbered 42:2-12.   [c] Title: Probably a literary or musical term   [d] 4 See Septuagint and Syriac; the meaning of the Hebrew for this line is uncertain.

Additional Insights

The Psalter is poetry from first to last. The psalms are impassioned, vivid and concrete; they are rich in images, in simile and metaphor.

Ps 42–45 Book II of the Psalter begins with three psalms (but see introduction to Ps 42–43) and an attached royal psalm in perfect balance with the ending of Book II (see introduction to Ps 69–72). These psalms contain certain key words found elsewhere in Book II only in Ps 69–71—and in the cluster of seven psalms placed at the center of this Book (see introduction to Ps 54–60). Although Ps 42–43 is the lament of an individual and Ps 44 a community lament, the two have much in common. Central to both is the cry, "Why, God?" (42:9; 43:2; 44:23–24)—why have you forgotten me/us (42:9; 44:24) and rejected me/us (43:2; 44:23) in the face of the oppression of our enemies (42:9; 44:24)? But that "Why?" (see note on 6:3), so expressive of the tension faith experiences in the face of such circumstances as the psalmists describe, is not the last word. Just here—and that in the first of these two introductory psalms—the psalmist speaks to his despondency with his own faithful refrain, "hope in God" (42:5,11; 43:5), because his "love" will not fail (42:8; 44:26).

Ps 42–43 A lament with a prayer for deliverance from being "oppressed by the enemy" (42:9; 43:2) and for restoration to the presence of God at his temple. That these two psalms form a single prayer (though they are counted as two psalms also in the Septuagint, the pre-Christian Greek translation of the OT [but see NIV text note]) is evident from its unique structure (see below) and the development of common themes. This psalm begins Book II of the Psalter (see introduction to Ps 42–45), a collection that is distinguished from Book I primarily by the fact that the Hebrew word for "God" (*Elohim*) predominates, whereas in the first book the Hebrew word for "the LORD" (*Yahweh*) predominates.

42 title *For the director of music.* See note on Ps 4 title. *maskil.* See note on Ps 32 title. *of the Sons of Korah.* Or "for the Sons of Korah"; see "For Jeduthun" in Ps 39 title. "Sons of Korah" refers to the Levitical choir made up of the descendants of Korah appointed by David to serve in the temple liturgy.

42:1 *deer pants for . . . water.* Because its life depends on water—especially when being pressed by hunters, as the psalmist was by his oppressors. *soul.* See note on 6:3.

42:2 *When . . . ?* Circumstances (v. 9; 43:1–2) now prevent him from being at the temple. *meet with God.* Enter his presence to commune with him (Ex 19:17; 29:42–43; 30:6,36).

42:4 *soul.* See note on 6:3.

42:5 The refrain: The psalmist speaks to his despondency by encouraging himself to trust in God (see 27:13–14 and introduction to Ps 27). *praise him.* For his saving help (see notes on 7:17; 9:1; see also 43:4).

42:6–10 The cause and depth of the trouble of his soul.

42:6 *soul is downcast.* See vv. 5,11; 43:5. *therefore I will remember you.* As he remembers (v. 4) in his exile the joy of his past intimacy with God, so now in his exile he remembers God and painfully laments (vv. 7,9–10), yet not without hope (v. 8).

42:7 *Deep calls . . . your waterfalls.* Often taken to be an allusion to the cascading waters of the upper Jordan as they rush down from Mount Hermon. It is more likely, however, that this is a literary allusion to the "waterfalls"

⁸ By day the LORD directs his love,
   at night his song is with me —
   a prayer to the God of my life.

⁹ I say to God my Rock,
   "Why have you forgotten me?
   Why must I go about mourning,
      oppressed by the enemy?"
¹⁰ My bones suffer mortal agony
      as my foes taunt me,
   saying to me all day long,
      "Where is your God?"

¹¹ Why, my soul, are you downcast?
      Why so disturbed within me?
   Put your hope in God,
      for I will yet praise him,
      my Savior and my God.

Psalm 43ᵃ

¹ Vindicate me, my God,
      and plead my cause
      against an unfaithful nation.
   Rescue me from those who are
      deceitful and wicked.
² You are God my stronghold.
      Why have you rejected me?
   Why must I go about mourning,
      oppressed by the enemy?
³ Send me your light and your faithful care,
      let them lead me;
   let them bring me to your holy mountain,
      to the place where you dwell.
⁴ Then I will go to the altar of God,
      to God, my joy and my delight.
   I will praise you with the lyre,
      O God, my God.

⁵ Why, my soul, are you downcast?
      Why so disturbed within me?
   Put your hope in God,
      for I will yet praise him,
      my Savior and my God.

Psalm 44ᵇ

*For the director of music. Of the
Sons of Korah. A maskil.ᶜ*

¹ We have heard it with our ears, O God;
      our ancestors have told us
   what you did in their days,
      in days long ago.

ᵃ In many Hebrew manuscripts Psalms 42 and 43 constitute
one psalm.   ᵇ In Hebrew texts 44:1-26 is numbered 44:2-27.
ᶜ Title: Probably a literary or musical term

by which the waters from God's storehouse of water above (see note on 36:8)—the "deep" above—pour down into the streams and rivers that empty into the seas—the "deep" below. It pictures the great distress the author suffers, and the imagery is continued in the following reference to God's "waves and breakers" sweeping over him (see 69:1–2; 88:7; Jnh 2:3,5; see also note on 32:6). God's hand is involved in the psalmist's suffering, at least to the extent that he has allowed this catastrophe. He seems to the psalmist to have "forgotten" (v. 9)—to have "rejected" (43:2)—him. But he makes no link between this and any sin in his life (Ps 44; 77).

42:8 The center: confession of hope in all the trouble. *directs his love.* Sends forth his love, like a messenger to do his will (43:3). *love.* See article, p. 16. *his song.* A song concerning him. *prayer.* Praise and prayer belong together in the thought of the psalmist.
43:1–4 Prayer for deliverance from the enemy and for restoration to God's presence.
43:2 Echoes 42:9.
43:3 *your light and your faithful care.* Personified as God's messengers who work out (1) his salvation (light; see note on 27:1) and (2) his faithful care in behalf of his own (26:3; 30:9; 40:10). *holy mountain.* See note on 2:6.
43:4 See note on 7:17. *to the altar.* See 26:6 and note.
Ps 44 Israel's lament to the Lord after suffering a devastating defeat at the hand of an enemy. The psalm probably relates to an experience of the kingdom of Judah (which as a nation did not break covenant with the Lord until late in their history), perhaps during the reign of Jehoshaphat or Hezekiah.
44 title See note on Ps 42 title.
44:1–8 Praise to God for past victories: (1) those by which Israel became established in the land (vv. 1–3) and (2) those by which Israel has been kept secure in the land (vv. 4–8).
44:1 See 78:3.

> When was a time when you were
> unfairly accused of something?
> How did you handle it?

_____

_____

_____

_____

_____

_____

2 With your hand you drove out the nations
  and planted our ancestors;
 you crushed the peoples
  and made our ancestors flourish.
3 It was not by their sword that they won
   the land,
  nor did their arm bring them victory;
 it was your right hand, your arm,
  and the light of your face, for you loved them.

4 You are my King and my God,
  who decrees[a] victories for Jacob.
5 Through you we push back our enemies;
  through your name we trample our foes.
6 I put no trust in my bow,
  my sword does not bring me victory;
7 but you give us victory over our enemies,
  you put our adversaries to shame.
8 In God we make our boast all day long,
  and we will praise your name forever.[b]

9 But now you have rejected and humbled us;
  you no longer go out with our armies.
10 You made us retreat before the enemy,
  and our adversaries have plundered us.
11 You gave us up to be devoured like sheep
  and have scattered us among the nations.
12 You sold your people for a pittance,
  gaining nothing from their sale.

13 You have made us a reproach to our neighbors,
  the scorn and derision of those around us.
14 You have made us a byword among the nations;
  the peoples shake their heads at us.
15 I live in disgrace all day long,
  and my face is covered with shame
16 at the taunts of those who reproach and
   revile me,
  because of the enemy, who is bent on revenge.

17 All this came upon us,
  though we had not forgotten you;
  we had not been false to your covenant.
18 Our hearts had not turned back;
  our feet had not strayed from your path.
19 But you crushed us and made us a haunt for
   jackals;
  you covered us over with deep darkness.

20 If we had forgotten the name of our God
  or spread out our hands to a foreign god,
21 would not God have discovered it,
  since he knows the secrets of the heart?
22 Yet for your sake we face death all day long;
  we are considered as sheep to be slaughtered.

---

a 4 Septuagint, Aquila and Syriac; Hebrew King, O God; /
command   b 8 The Hebrew has Selah (a word of uncertain
meaning) here.

44:3 *light of your face.* See notes on 4:6; 13:1.
44:4 *my.* Here and elsewhere in this psalm the first-person singular pronoun refers to the nation corporately (see note on Ps 30 title).
44:5,8 *your name.* See v. 20.
44:8 *In God we make our boast.* That is, we give God all the praise. For *Selah,* see NIV text note and note on 3:2.
44:9–16 But now you have forsaken us: (1) You have caused us to suffer defeat (vv. 9–12); (2) you have shamed us before our enemies (vv. 13–16).
44:11 *gave us up to be devoured like sheep.* Have not protected us as our Shepherd-King (see v. 4 and note on 23:1).
44:14 *byword.* An expression of disdain. *shake their heads.* In scorn (64:8).
44:17–22 And we have not been disloyal to you: (1) We have not been untrue to your covenant (vv. 17–19); (2) you are our witness that we have not turned to another god (vv. 20–22).
44:17 *your covenant.* See Ex 19–24.
44:18 *hearts.* See note on 4:7. *your path.* The way marked out in God's covenant (see note on 5:8).
44:19 *you crushed us.* But that cannot be used as evidence that we have been disloyal. *haunt for jackals.* A desolate place, uninhabited by people (Isa 13:22; Jer 9:11). *deep darkness.* The absence of all that was associated with the metaphor "light" (see notes on 30:1; 36:9).
44:20 *spread out our hands.* Prayed (see Ex 9:29).
44:22 *Yet for your sake.* From the time of Israel's stay in Egypt (Ex 1), they had suffered the hostility of the nations because of their relationship with the Lord (Mt 10:34). For Paul's application of this verse to the Christian community in the light of Christ's death and resurrection, see Ro 8:36.

> **How had God worked in the lives of your ancestors? In good or bad circumstances, how can you see God's hand at work?**

_____

_____

_____

_____

_____

_____

_____

²³ Awake, Lord! Why do you sleep?
　　Rouse yourself! Do not reject us forever.
²⁴ Why do you hide your face
　　and forget our misery and oppression?

²⁵ We are brought down to the dust;
　　our bodies cling to the ground.
²⁶ Rise up and help us;
　　rescue us because of your unfailing love.

Psalm 45^a

For the director of music. To the tune of "Lilies."
Of the Sons of Korah. A maskil.^b A wedding song.

¹ My heart is stirred by a noble theme
　　as I recite my verses for the king;
　　my tongue is the pen of a skillful writer.

² You are the most excellent of men
　　and your lips have been anointed with grace,
　　since God has blessed you forever.

³ Gird your sword on your side, you mighty one;
　　clothe yourself with splendor and majesty.
⁴ In your majesty ride forth victoriously
　　in the cause of truth, humility and justice;
　　let your right hand achieve awesome deeds.
⁵ Let your sharp arrows pierce the hearts of the
　　　king's enemies;
　　let the nations fall beneath your feet.
⁶ Your throne, O God,^c will last for ever and ever;
　　a scepter of justice will be the scepter of your
　　　kingdom.
⁷ You love righteousness and hate wickedness;
　　therefore God, your God, has set you above
　　　your companions
　　by anointing you with the oil of joy.

^a In Hebrew texts 45:1-17 is numbered 45:2-18.　　^b Title: Probably a literary or musical term　　^c 6 Here the king is addressed as God's representative.

Bronze and silver scepter-head found in the sacred area at Dan (9th century BC). Psalm 45:6 reads, "Your throne, O God, will last for ever and ever; a scepter of justice will be the scepter of your kingdom."

Z. Radovan/www.BibleLandPictures.com

44:23–26 The appeal for help: (1) awake to our need (vv. 23–24); (2) arise to our help (vv. 25–26; see introduction to Ps 16).
44:24 *hide your face.* See note on 13:1.
44:25 *brought down to the dust.* About to sink into death (see 22:29 and note; see also note on 30:1). In Hebrew there is a verbal link with the refrain, "Why, my soul, are you downcast?" in Ps 42–43.
44:26 *Rise up and help.* See 46:1,5. *unfailing love.* See article, p. 16; see also 42:8 and note.

Ps 45 A song in praise of the king on his wedding day (see title; see also introduction to Ps 42–45). He undoubtedly belonged to David's dynasty, and the song was probably used at more than one royal wedding. Since the bride is a foreign princess (see vv. 10,12), the wedding reflects the king's standing as a figure of international significance (see note on v. 9). Accordingly he is addressed as one whose reign is to be characterized by victories over the nations (vv. 3–5; cf. Ps 2; 110). As a royal son of David, he is a type (foreshadowing) of Christ. After the exile this psalm was applied to the Messiah, the promised Son of David who would sit on David's throne (for the application of vv. 6–7 to Christ, see Heb 1:8–9).
45 title *For the director of music.* See note on Ps 4 title. *Lilies.* See Ps 69 title. "Lilies" may be an abbreviated form of "The Lily (Lilies) of the Covenant" found in the titles of Ps 60; 80. *Of the Sons of Korah.* See note on Ps 42 title. *maskil.* See note on Ps 32 title. *song.* See note on Ps 30 title.
45:1 See v. 17, where the speaker pledges (perhaps by means of this song) to perpetuate the king's memory throughout the generations and awaken the praise of the nations. *heart.* See note on 4:7.
45:2 *most excellent of men.* One who is a very handsome man—but this king is so far beyond ordinary men as to be almost godlike (see note on v. 6).
45:3–5 Go forth with your sword victoriously in the service of all that is right, and clothe yourself thereby with glory—make your reign adorn you more truly than the wedding garb with which you are now arrayed (v. 8).
45:5 *nations fall beneath your feet.* See 2:8–9; 110:1–2,5–6.
45:6–9 The glory of the king's reign: justice and righteousness (Ps 72).
45:6 *O God.* Possibly the king's throne is called God's throne because he is God's appointed regent. But it is also possible that the king himself is addressed as "god." The Davidic king (the "Lord's anointed," 2Sa 19:21), because of his special relationship with God, was called at his enthronement the "son" of God (2:7; 2Sa 7:14; 1Ch 28:6; cf. Ps 89:27). In this psalm, which praises the king and especially extols his "splendor and majesty" (v. 3), it is not unthinkable that he was called "god" as a title of honor (cf. Isa 9:6). Such a description of the Davidic king attains its fullest meaning when applied to Christ, as the author of Hebrews does (Heb 1:8–9). *for ever and ever.* See vv. 2,17. Such was the language used with respect to kings (see note on 21:4). It here gains added significance in the light of God's covenant with David (89:4,29,36; 132:12; 2Sa 7:16). In Christ, the Son of David, it is fulfilled. *scepter.* See photo, this page.
45:7 *companions.* The noble guests of the king, perhaps from other lands. *oil of joy.* God has anointed him with

8 All your robes are fragrant with myrrh and
   aloes and cassia;
   from palaces adorned with ivory
   the music of the strings makes you glad.
9 Daughters of kings are among your honored
   women;
   at your right hand is the royal bride in gold
   of Ophir.

10 Listen, daughter, and pay careful attention:
   Forget your people and your father's house.
11 Let the king be enthralled by your beauty;
   honor him, for he is your lord.
12 The city of Tyre will come with a gift,[a]
   people of wealth will seek your favor.
13 All glorious is the princess within her chamber;
   her gown is interwoven with gold.
14 In embroidered garments she is led to the
   king;
   her virgin companions follow her —
   those brought to be with her.
15 Led in with joy and gladness,
   they enter the palace of the king.

16 Your sons will take the place of your fathers;
   you will make them princes throughout
   the land.

17 I will perpetuate your memory through all
   generations;
   therefore the nations will praise you for ever
   and ever.

Psalm 46[b]

*For the director of music. Of the Sons of Korah.
According to* alamoth.[c] *A song.*

1 God is our refuge and strength,
   an ever-present help in trouble.
2 Therefore we will not fear, though the earth
   give way
   and the mountains fall into the heart of
   the sea,
3 though its waters roar and foam
   and the mountains quake with their surging.[d]

4 There is a river whose streams make glad the
   city of God,
   the holy place where the Most High dwells.
5 God is within her, she will not fall;
   God will help her at break of day.
6 Nations are in uproar, kingdoms fall;
   he lifts his voice, the earth melts.

---

[a] 12 Or *A Tyrian robe is among the gifts*   [b] In Hebrew texts
46:1-11 is numbered 46:2-12.   [c] Title: Probably a musical
term   [d] 3 The Hebrew has *Selah* (a word of uncertain
meaning) here and at the end of verses 7 and 11.

a more delightful oil than the aromatic oils with which
his head and body were anointed on his wedding day—
namely, with joy (23:5; Isa 61:3).
45:9 *Daughters of kings.* Whether members of his royal
harem (1Ki 11:1–3) or guests at his wedding, they represent
international recognition of the king. *in gold of Ophir.*
Adorned with jewels of finest gold and all the finery associated with it.
45:12 *city of Tyre.* The king of Tyre was the first foreign
ruler to recognize the Davidic dynasty (2Sa 5:11), and Solomon maintained close relations with that city-state (1Ki 5;
9:10–14,26–28). As a great trading center on the Mediterranean coast, Tyre was world renowned for its wealth (Isa
23; Eze 26:1—28:19). *people of wealth.* Such as those from
your homeland. *seek your favor.* Desire to be in your good
graces as the wife of this king. These honors will be yours
if you faithfully honor your royal husband.
45:16 *Your.* The king's. *take the place of your fathers.* As
the family line continues (dynastic succession). Perhaps
it is also hinted that they will surpass the fathers in honor
(see note on v. 2). *land.* Or "earth."
Ps 46–48 Following the cluster of psalms that introduce
Book II of the Psalter (see introduction to Ps 42–45), the
next thematically related cluster of psalms all express
confidence in the security of God's people in the midst of
a threatening world.

Ps 46 A celebration of the security of Jerusalem as
the city of God (the inspiration of Martin Luther's
great hymn "A Mighty Fortress Is Our God"; see vv. 7,11).
Thematically, this psalm is closely related to Ps 48 (see
also Ps 76; 87), while Ps 47 celebrates God's victorious
reign over all the earth (see introduction to Ps 46–48). It
probably predates the exile. However, as a song concerning the "city of God" (v. 4), the royal city of his kingdom on
earth (Ps 48), it remained for Israel a song of hope celebrating the certain triumph of God's kingdom.
46 title *alamoth.* See NIV text note. Since the Hebrew
word appears to mean "young women," the phrase "According to *alamoth*" may refer to the "young women
playing the timbrels" who accompanied the singers as
the liturgical procession made its way to the temple
(68:25). *A song.* See note on Ps 30 title.

46:1–3 A triumphant confession of fearless trust in
God, though the continents break up and sink beneath the surging waters of the seas—i.e., though the creation itself may become chaotic (see Ge 1:2; Jer 4:23) and all
may appear to be going down before the onslaught of the
primeval deep. The described upheaval is probably imagery for great threats to Israel's existence (see note on 32:6),
especially from their enemies (see vv. 6,8–10; 65:5–8).
46:3 For *Selah,* see NIV text note and note on 3:2.

46:4 *river.* Jerusalem had no river, unlike Thebes (Na
3:8), Damascus (2Ki 5:12), Nineveh (Na 2:6,8) or Babylon (137:1)—yet she had a "river." Here the "river" of 36:8
(see note there) serves as a metaphor for the continual
outpouring of the sustaining and refreshing blessings of
God, which make the city of God like the Garden of Eden
(see v. 5; Ge 2:10; Isa 33:21; 51:3; cf. also Eze 31:4–9).

46:5 *at break of day.* When attacks against cities
were likely to be launched. His help brings on the
dawn of deliverance, dispelling the night of danger (cf. Isa
37:36 for an example).

7 The LORD Almighty is with us;
the God of Jacob is our fortress.

8 Come and see what the LORD has done,
the desolations he has brought on the earth.
9 He makes wars cease
to the ends of the earth.
He breaks the bow and shatters the spear;
he burns the shields[a] with fire.
10 He says, "Be still, and know that I am God;
I will be exalted among the nations,
I will be exalted in the earth."

11 The LORD Almighty is with us;
the God of Jacob is our fortress.

Psalm 47[b]

For the director of music. Of the Sons of Korah. A psalm.

1 Clap your hands, all you nations;
shout to God with cries of joy.

2 For the LORD Most High is awesome,
the great King over all the earth.
3 He subdued nations under us,
peoples under our feet.
4 He chose our inheritance for us,
the pride of Jacob, whom he loved.[c]

5 God has ascended amid shouts of joy,
the LORD amid the sounding of trumpets.
6 Sing praises to God, sing praises;
sing praises to our King, sing praises.
7 For God is the King of all the earth;
sing to him a psalm of praise.

8 God reigns over the nations;
God is seated on his holy throne.
9 The nobles of the nations assemble
as the people of the God of Abraham,
for the kings[d] of the earth belong to God;
he is greatly exalted.

Psalm 48[e]

A song. A psalm of the Sons of Korah.

1 Great is the LORD, and most worthy of praise,
in the city of our God, his holy mountain.

2 Beautiful in its loftiness,
the joy of the whole earth,
like the heights of Zaphon[f] is Mount Zion,
the city of the Great King.

---

a 9 Or *chariots*   b In Hebrew texts 47:1-9 is numbered 47:2-10.
c 4 The Hebrew has *Selah* (a word of uncertain meaning) here.   d 9 Or *shields*   e In Hebrew texts 48:1-14 is numbered 48:2-15.   f 2 *Zaphon* was the most sacred mountain of the Canaanites.

46:6 The effect of God's voice dwarfs the tumult of the nations. *lifts his voice.* See 2:5; 9:5; Jer 25:30; Am 1:2; see also 104:7. God's thunder is evoked (see introduction to Ps 29), the thunder of his wrath (18:13; Isa 2:10). *earth melts.* As though struck by lightning (97:4–5).

46:8 *Come and see.* An invitation to see God's victories in the world (see 48:8 and note). *the LORD.* Emphatic because of its rare use in Book II of the Psalter. *on the earth.* Among the hostile nations.

46:10 *He says.* God's voice breaks through as he addresses the nations (v. 6)—the climax. *Be still.* Here, the Hebrew for this phrase probably means "Stop!" or "Enough!" as in 1Sa 15:16. *know.* Acknowledge. *I will be exalted . . . in the earth.* God's mighty acts in behalf of his people will bring him universal recognition, a major theme in the Psalter (22:27; 47:9; 57:5,11; 64:9; 65:8; 66:1–7; 67:2–5,7; 77:14; 86:9; 98:2–3; 99:2–3; 102:15) and elsewhere in the OT (Ex 7:5; 14:4,18; Lev 26:45; Nu 14:15; 1Sa 17:46; 1Ki 8:41–43; 2Ki 19:19; Isa 2:2–3; 11:10; 25:3; 49:6–7; 51:5; 52:10; 60:1–14; 62:1–2; Jer 16:19; Eze 20:41; 28:25; 36:23; Hab 2:14). This has proven to be supremely true of God's climactic saving act in the birth, life, death, resurrection and glorification of Jesus Christ—yet to be brought to complete fruition at his return.

Ps 47 Celebration of the universal reign of Israel's God: a testimony to the nations. This psalm belongs to a group of hymns to the Great King found elsewhere clustered in Ps 92–100. It dates from the period of the monarchy and was composed for use in the temple liturgy on one of the high festival days. The specific setting is perhaps the Festival of Tabernacles (Lev 23:34), which was also the festival for which Solomon waited to dedicate the temple (1Ki 8:2). A liturgical procession is presupposed (v. 5), similar to that indicated in Ps 24; 68.

47 title See note on Ps 42 title.

47:1 *Clap your hands.* As at the enthronement of a king (see 2Ki 11:12; see also 98:8) or at other times of rejoicing (Isa 55:12). *cries of joy.* See 1Ki 1:40; 2Ki 11:14.

47:4 *inheritance.* The promised land (Ge 12:7; 17:8; Ex 3:8; Dt 1:8; Jer 3:18).

47:5–6 The center of the poem (see note on 6:6). These verses portray the liturgical ascension of God to the temple—perhaps represented by the processional bearing of the ark into the temple. The ark is symbolic of God's throne; the temple is the earthly symbol of his heavenly palace (Ps 24; 68).

47:7–9 The liturgical enthronement of God as world ruler.

47:8 *seated on his holy throne.* In the Most Holy Place of the temple, where he takes the reins of world rule into his hands (Jer 17:12). This verse is frequently echoed in Revelation (Rev 4:9,10; 5:1,7,13; 6:16; 7:10,15; 19:4).

Ps 48 A celebration of the security of Zion (as viewed with the eyes of faith) in that it is the city of the Great King (see introductions to Ps 46–47; see also introduction to Ps 46–48). It may have been sung by the Levitical choir on behalf of the assembled worshipers at the temple. Structure and theme are beautifully matched. The first and last verses combine to frame the whole with a comforting confession concerning Zion's God.

48:2 *Beautiful.* Its loftiness and secure position are its beauty (see note on 27:4). *loftiness.* Although not the highest ridge in its environment, in its significance as

³God is in her citadels;
  he has shown himself to be her fortress.

⁴When the kings joined forces,
  when they advanced together,
⁵they saw her and were astounded;
  they fled in terror.
⁶Trembling seized them there,
  pain like that of a woman in labor.
⁷You destroyed them like ships of Tarshish
  shattered by an east wind.

⁸As we have heard,
  so we have seen
 in the city of the LORD Almighty,
  in the city of our God:
 God makes her secure
  forever.ᵃ

⁹Within your temple, O God,
  we meditate on your unfailing love.
¹⁰Like your name, O God,
  your praise reaches to the ends of the
    earth;
  your right hand is filled with
    righteousness.
¹¹Mount Zion rejoices,
  the villages of Judah are glad
  because of your judgments.

¹²Walk about Zion, go around her,
  count her towers,
¹³consider well her ramparts,
  view her citadels,
 that you may tell of them
  to the next generation.

¹⁴For this God is our God for ever and ever;
  he will be our guide even to the end.

Psalm 49ᵇ

For the director of music. Of the Sons of Korah. A psalm.

¹Hear this, all you peoples;
  listen, all who live in this world,
²both low and high,
  rich and poor alike:
³My mouth will speak words of wisdom;
  the meditation of my heart will give you
    understanding.
⁴I will turn my ear to a proverb;
  with the harp I will expound my
    riddle:

⁵Why should I fear when evil days come,
  when wicked deceivers surround me —

ᵃ 8 The Hebrew has *Selah* (a word of uncertain meaning)
here.   ᵇ In Hebrew texts 49:1-20 is numbered 49:2-21.

---

the mountain of God it is the "highest" mountain in the
world (see 68:15–16 and note; Isa 2:2). *joy of the whole
earth.* Perhaps referring to admiration from other nations, like that expressed by the queen of Sheba (1Ki 10:1–
13). *Zaphon.* See NIV text note. Mount Zaphon in the far
north was for the Phoenicians the sacred residence of El,
the chief of their gods—as Mount Olympus was the
mountain citadel of Zeus for the Greeks.

48:3 God himself, not Zion's walls, was the city's defense, a fact on which the next stanza elaborates
(see note on vv. 12–13). *her citadels.* See v. 13.

48:4–7 The futile attacks of hostile nations—they fled in
panic when they saw that the Great King was in Zion. Such
events as the destruction of the confederacy in the days
of Jehoshaphat (2Ch 20) or the slaughter of the Assyrians
in the time of Hezekiah (2Ki 19:35–36) may have been in
the psalmist's mind.

48:8 The central verse and theme (see note on 6:6).
heard . . . seen. "Seen" is climactic, as in Job 42:5. They
had heard because "our ancestors have told us what you
did in their days" (44:1; see 78:3), but now in the liturgical
experience of God at his temple they have "seen" how
secure the city of God is.

48:9 *Within your temple.* In the temple courts. *unfailing love.* See article, p. 16. As is clear from vv. 10–11,
reference here is to God's saving acts by which he has expressed his covenant love for his people (31:21; 40:9–10).

48:11 *judgments.* God's righteous judgments, by which he
has acted in defense of Zion.

48:12–13 The people are called to contemplate Zion's
defense, viewed from the perspective of what they
have "seen" (v. 8) at the temple. The strength of Zion's
"towers," "ramparts" and "citadels" is the presence of God.

Ps 49–53 This cluster of psalms presents a striking
contrast that brings the Psalter's call for godliness
into sharp focus. On the one hand, we meet two psalms
that face each other: (1) God's summons to his people to
come before him and hear his verdict concerning their
lives (Ps 50) and (2) a penitent's humble prayer for forgiveness and cleansing (Ps 51). On the other hand, these
are bracketed by two psalms (49; 52) that denounce those
who trust in their wealth (49:6; 52:7) and make their
"boast" either in that wealth (49:6) or in the "evil" practices by which they obtained it (52:1). These descriptions
of the ungodly are found nowhere else in the Psalter. In
the first of these framing psalms, such people are characterized as "foolish" and "senseless" (49:10). So it is appropriate that this four-psalm segment of the Psalter has
appended to it in climax a somewhat revised repetition
of Ps 14 with its denunciation of the fools whose thoughts
and ways are God-less. Placed immediately after Ps 46–
48, these five psalms serve as a stern reminder that only
those who put their trust in the Lord have reason to celebrate the security of "the city of our God" (48:1,8; see
introduction to Ps 46–48).

Ps 49 A wisdom psalm concerning rich fools who
proudly rely on their great wealth and on themselves
to assure their welfare and security in the world (see Ps 52
and introduction to Ps 49–53). The Levitical author, a son
of Korah, knows what it is to be without wealth (see Nu
18:21–24; Dt 14:27–29) and has observed the attitudes of
many of the rich (vv. 5–6). He has seen through their folly,

⁶ those who trust in their wealth
and boast of their great riches?
⁷ No one can redeem the life of another
or give to God a ransom for them—
⁸ the ransom for a life is costly,
no payment is ever enough—
⁹ so that they should live on forever
and not see decay.
¹⁰ For all can see that the wise die,
that the foolish and the senseless also perish,
leaving their wealth to others.
¹¹ Their tombs will remain their houses^a forever,
their dwellings for endless generations,
though they had^b named lands after themselves.

¹² People, despite their wealth, do not endure;
they are like the beasts that perish.

¹³ This is the fate of those who trust in themselves,
and of their followers, who approve their
sayings.^c
¹⁴ They are like sheep and are destined to die;
death will be their shepherd
(but the upright will prevail over them in the
morning).
Their forms will decay in the grave,
far from their princely mansions.
¹⁵ But God will redeem me from the realm of
the dead;
he will surely take me to himself.
¹⁶ Do not be overawed when others grow rich,
when the splendor of their houses increases;
¹⁷ for they will take nothing with them when
they die,
their splendor will not descend with them.
¹⁸ Though while they live they count themselves
blessed—
and people praise you when you prosper—
¹⁹ they will join those who have gone before them,
who will never again see the light of life.

²⁰ People who have wealth but lack understanding
are like the beasts that perish.

Psalm 50

A psalm of Asaph.

¹ The Mighty One, God, the LORD,
speaks and summons the earth
from the rising of the sun to where it sets.
² From Zion, perfect in beauty,
God shines forth.
³ Our God comes
and will not be silent;

^a 11 Septuagint and Syriac; Hebrew *In their thoughts their houses will remain*   ^b 11 Or *generations, / for they have*
^c 13 The Hebrew has *Selah* (a word of uncertain meaning) here and at the end of verse 15.

however, and offers his wisdom for all to hear (vv. 1–2), so that those who are awed by the rich may be freed from their spell. Inescapable death is the destiny and undoing of such "foolish and . . . senseless" (49:10) people, and in the end the "upright will prevail over them" (v. 14).
49:3 See Mt 12:34. *heart.* See note on 4:7.
49:4 *turn my ear.* The wisdom he is about to speak first had to be "heard" by him—all true wisdom is from God (Job 28). *proverb . . . riddle.* The two Hebrew words for these nouns were used to refer to insightful pieces of instruction that were artfully crafted (78:2 ["parable," "things from of old"]; Pr 1:6; Eze 17:2 ["allegory," "parable"]).
49:7–9 Wealth cannot buy escape from death—not even one's family "redeemer" can accomplish it (cf. Ex 21:30; Lev 25:47–49). Only God himself can redeem a life from the grave (see v. 15 and note).
49:10 Any who have "eyes in their heads" (Ecc 2:14) can see that even the wise die (Ecc 7:2; 9:5) and leave their wealth to others (Ecc 2:18,21). How much more the fool (73:18–20; 92:6–7)! See also 52:5; 89:48; Job 30:23; Ecc 2:14–16.
49:14 *death will be their shepherd.* For the imagery of death (or the grave) as an insatiable monster feeding on its victims, see 69:15; 141:7; Pr 1:12; 27:20; 30:15–16; Isa 5:14; Jnh 2:2; Hab 2:5. The imagery is borrowed from Canaanite mythology, which so depicts the god Mot ("Death"). As one Canaanite document reads, "Do not approach divine Mot, or he will put you like a lamb into his mouth."
49:15 See note on vv. 7–9. *redeem . . . from the realm of the dead.* Cf. v. 11. While the psalmist may here refer to saving (for a while) from the universal prospect of death (as in Job 5:20; see 116:8), the context strongly suggests that he, as one of the upright, speaks of his final destiny. Perhaps the thought is of being conveyed into the presence of God in his heavenly temple, analogous to the later Jewish thought of being conveyed to "Abraham's side" (Lk 16:22; see notes on 6:5; 11:7; 16:9–11; 17:15). *take me to himself.* See 73:24; Ge 5:24.
Ps 50 The Lord calls his covenant people to account. For this psalm's place in the arrangement of the Psalter, see introduction to Ps 49–53. The psalm appears to have been composed for a temple liturgy in which Israel reaffirms their commitment to God's covenant. A leader of the Levitical choir addresses Israel on behalf of the Lord (see Ps 15; 24, either of which may have been spoken earlier in the same liturgy). This liturgy was possibly related to the Festival of Tabernacles (see Dt 31:9–13; see also introduction to Ps 47). In its rebuke of a false understanding of sacrifice, the psalm has affinity with the prophecies of Amos, Micah and Isaiah and so may date from the late eighth and/or early seventh centuries BC. Others find a closer relationship with the reformation of Josiah (2Ki 22:1—23:25) and the ministry of Jeremiah.
50 title A traditional ascription of the psalm to Asaph; or it may mean "for Asaph" (see "For Jeduthun" in Ps 39 title) or for the descendants of Asaph who functioned in his place.
50:1 *The Mighty One, God, the LORD.* A sequence found elsewhere only in Jos 22:22. Ps 50 is noteworthy for its use of numerous names and titles for God (seven in all: three in v. 1, four in the rest of the psalm). *the earth.* See "the heavens . . . the earth" (v. 4) and "the heavens" (v. 6).

a fire devours before him,
  and around him a tempest rages.
4 He summons the heavens above,
  and the earth, that he may judge his people:
5 "Gather to me this consecrated people,
  who made a covenant with me by sacrifice."
6 And the heavens proclaim his righteousness,
  for he is a God of justice.*a,b*

7 "Listen, my people, and I will speak;
  I will testify against you, Israel:
  I am God, your God.
8 I bring no charges against you concerning your
    sacrifices
  or concerning your burnt offerings, which
    are ever before me.
9 I have no need of a bull from your stall
  or of goats from your pens,
10 for every animal of the forest is mine,
  and the cattle on a thousand hills.
11 I know every bird in the mountains,
  and the insects in the fields are mine.
12 If I were hungry I would not tell you,
  for the world is mine, and all that is in it.
13 Do I eat the flesh of bulls
  or drink the blood of goats?

14 "Sacrifice thank offerings to God,
  fulfill your vows to the Most High,
15 and call on me in the day of trouble;
  I will deliver you, and you will honor me."

16 But to the wicked person, God says:

"What right have you to recite my laws
  or take my covenant on your lips?
17 You hate my instruction
  and cast my words behind you.
18 When you see a thief, you join with him;
  you throw in your lot with adulterers.
19 You use your mouth for evil
  and harness your tongue to deceit.
20 You sit and testify against your brother
  and slander your own mother's son.
21 When you did these things and I kept silent,
  you thought I was exactly*c* like you.
  But I now arraign you
  and set my accusations before you.

22 "Consider this, you who forget God,
  or I will tear you to pieces, with no one to
    rescue you:
23 Those who sacrifice thank offerings honor me,
  and to the blameless*d* I will show my salvation."

---

a 6 With a different word division of the Hebrew; Masoretic
Text *for God himself is judge* *b 6* The Hebrew has *Selah* (a
word of uncertain meaning) here. *c 21* Or *thought the 'I AM'*
was *d 23* Probable reading of the original Hebrew text; the
meaning of the Masoretic Text for this phrase is uncertain.

When Moses renewed the covenant between the Lord and Israel on the plains of Moab, he called upon the heavens and the earth to serve as third-party witnesses to the covenant (see Dt 4:26; 30:19; 31:28). The Lord now summons these (vv. 1–4) to testify that his present word to his people is in complete accord with that covenant (Isa 1:2).
50:2 *perfect in beauty.* Because God resides there (cf. Eze 27:3–4,11; 28:12). *shines forth.* Manifests his glory as he comes to act (see 80:1; 94:1; Dt 33:2; cf. Eze 28:7,17), now calling his people to account but not yet announcing judgment as in Isa 1 or Mic 1.
50:5 *consecrated people.* See note on 4:3. *by sacrifice.* Sacrifices were a part of the ritual that sealed the covenant (see Ex 24:4–8) and continued to be an integral part of Israel's expression of covenant commitment to the Lord.
50:7–15 The Lord corrects his people.
50:7 *my people . . . your God.* "Our God" (v. 3) and "your God" (here) reflect the covenant bond (see Zec 8:8).
50:8–13 Israel had not failed to bring enough sacrifices (v. 8), but they were ever tempted to think that sacrifices were of first importance to God, as though he were dependent on them. This notion was widespread among Israel's pagan neighbors. See note on 40:6.
50:10 *thousand.* Used here figuratively for a very large number.
50:14–15 God wants Israel to acknowledge their dependence on him by giving thank offerings for his mercies (v. 14) and by praying to him in times of need (v. 15; see 116:17–19). Those who do so may expect God's gracious answer to their prayers (stated more directly in v. 23). God also desires obedience to his moral law (see vv. 16–21 and note on 40:6).
50:15 *honor me.* With praise in the fulfillment of the vows (v. 23)—and, implicitly, with obedience to his covenant law (see following verses).
50:16–23 The Lord's rebuke of the wicked.
50:16 *recite my laws.* Apparently a part of the liturgy of covenant commitment.
50:17 *You hate my instruction.* They show their rejection of God's law by not obeying it.
50:19 *use your mouth for evil.* See note on 5:9.
50:21 God's merciful and patient silence is distorted by the wicked into bad and self-serving theology (Ecc 8:11; Isa 42:14; 57:11).
50:22 *God.* A relatively rare word for "God" (Hebrew *Eloah*), though common in Job. See note on v. 1.

Additional Insights

The Psalter is for the most part a book of the laments and praises of God's people. But there are also psalms that are explicitly instructional in form and purpose, teaching the way of godliness.

▶ How were the Israelites false to their covenant with God (44:17)?

_____

_____

_____

_____

_____

▶ In what ways does God help his people (Ps 46)?

_____

_____

_____

_____

_____

▶ Why is God's Word important to a believer (49:3–4)?

_____

_____

_____

_____

_____

▶ What do you learn about God's mercy and judgment in Psalm 50?

_____

_____

_____

_____

_____

Psalm 51[a]

For the director of music. A psalm of David. When the prophet Nathan came to him after David had committed adultery with Bathsheba.

[1] Have mercy on me, O God,
  according to your unfailing love;
according to your great compassion
  blot out my transgressions.
[2] Wash away all my iniquity
  and cleanse me from my sin.

[3] For I know my transgressions,
  and my sin is always before me.
[4] Against you, you only, have I sinned
  and done what is evil in your sight;
so you are right in your verdict
  and justified when you judge.
[5] Surely I was sinful at birth,
  sinful from the time my mother conceived me.
[6] Yet you desired faithfulness even in the
    womb;
  you taught me wisdom in that secret
    place.

[7] Cleanse me with hyssop, and I will be clean;
  wash me, and I will be whiter than snow.
[8] Let me hear joy and gladness;
  let the bones you have crushed rejoice.
[9] Hide your face from my sins
  and blot out all my iniquity.

[10] Create in me a pure heart, O God,
  and renew a steadfast spirit within me.
[11] Do not cast me from your presence
  or take your Holy Spirit from me.
[12] Restore to me the joy of your salvation
  and grant me a willing spirit, to
    sustain me.

[a] In Hebrew texts 51:1-19 is numbered 51:3-21.

Additional Insights

Hebrew poetry lacks rhyme and regular meter. Its most distinctive and pervasive feature is parallelism.

Ps 51 David's humble prayer for forgiveness and cleansing. As the lament of a contrite sinner, it represents a proper response to the Lord's confrontation of his people in Ps 50 (compare v. 16 with 50:8-15; see also introduction to Ps 49–53). This psalm has many points of contact with Ps 25. In traditional Christian usage it is one of seven penitential psalms.

51:1–2 Opening prayer for pardon (see Lk 18:13). Note the piling up of synonyms: mercy, unfailing love, great compassion; blot out, wash, cleanse; transgressions, iniquity, sin (for this last triad, see note on 32:5).

51:1 *unfailing love.* See article, p. 16. *blot out.* See v. 9. The image is that of a papyrus scroll on which God had recorded David's deeds. The blotting out of sins pictures full forgiveness (Jer 18:23; see Isa 43:25). For the imagery of God's keeping records of the events in his realm in the way that earthly kings do, see 56:8 and note; 87:6; 130:3; 139:16 and note; Ne 13:14; Da 7:10; see also Ex 32:32–33.

51:2 See v. 7. *cleanse me.* Make me clean in your sight (Lev 11:32).

51:3 *before me.* On my mind.

51:4 *Against you . . . only.* David acknowledges that his sin was preeminently against God (see 2Sa 12:13; cf. Ge 20:6; 39:9; Lk 15:18). He had violated specific covenant stipulations (Ex 20:13–14,17). *when you judge.* As the Lord did through Nathan the prophet (2Sa 12:7–12).

51:5 He cannot plead that this sin was a rare aberration in his life; it sprang from what he is and has been from birth (see 58:3; Ge 8:21; 1Ki 8:46; cf. Jn 9:34; Eph 2:3). The apparently similar statements in Job 14:4; 15:14; 25:4–6 rise from a different motivation.

51:6 The great contrast: He has acted absolutely contrary to what God desires and to what God has been teaching him. But it is just this "desire" of God and this teaching of God that are his hope—what he pleads for in vv. 7,10. *wisdom.* Those who give themselves over to sin are fools; those who have God's law in their hearts are wise (37:30–31).

51:7–9 Renewed prayer for pardon (see note on vv. 1–2).

51:7 *hyssop.* Often used to refer to cleansing from ritual impurity (see Ex 12:22; Lev 14:4,6; see also photo, p. 72). *be clean.* See v. 2. *whiter than snow.* Like a filthy garment, he needs washing (see note on v. 2); but if God washes him, he will be exceedingly pure (Isa 1:18; Da 7:9; Rev 7:14; 19:14).

51:10–12 Prayer for a pure heart, a steadfast spirit of faithfulness and a willing spirit of service. These can be his only if God does not reject him and take his Holy Spirit from him. If granted, the joy of God's salvation will return to gladden his troubled soul.

51:10 *Create.* As something new, which cannot emerge from what now is (v. 5) and which only God can fashion (see Ge 1:1; Isa 65:17; Jer 31:22). *heart.* See note on 4:7.

51:11 The two requests are essentially one (139:7; Eze 39:29). David's prayer recalls the rejection of Saul

Hyssop plant. "Cleanse me with hyssop, and I will be clean; wash me, and I will be whiter than snow" (Ps 51:7).

¹³Then I will teach transgressors your ways,
　　so that sinners will turn back to you.
¹⁴Deliver me from the guilt of bloodshed,
　　O God,
　　you who are God my Savior,
　　and my tongue will sing of your
　　　righteousness.
¹⁵Open my lips, Lord,
　　and my mouth will declare your praise.
¹⁶You do not delight in sacrifice, or I would
　　bring it;
　　you do not take pleasure in burnt
　　offerings.
¹⁷My sacrifice, O God, is*a* a broken spirit;
　　a broken and contrite heart
　　you, God, will not despise.

¹⁸May it please you to prosper Zion,
　　to build up the walls of Jerusalem.
¹⁹Then you will delight in the sacrifices of the
　　righteous,
　　in burnt offerings offered whole;
　　then bulls will be offered on your altar.

a 17 Or *The sacrifices of God are*

(1Sa 16:1,14; 2Sa 7:15) and pleads for God not to take away his Spirit, by which he had equipped and qualified him for his royal office (1Sa 16:13; cf. 2Sa 23:1–2). *Holy Spirit.* The phrase is found elsewhere in the OT only in Isa 63:10–11. By his Spirit, God effected his purposes in creation (104:30; Ge 1:2; Job 33:4) and redemption (Isa 32:15; 44:3; 63:11,14; Hag 2:5), equipped his servants for their appointed tasks (Ex 31:3; Nu 11:29; Jdg 3:10; 1Sa 10:6; 16:13; Isa 11:2; 42:1), inspired his prophets (Nu 24:2–3; 2Sa 23:2; Ne 9:30; Isa 59:21; 61:1; Eze 11:5; Mic 3:8; Zec 7:12) and directed their ministries (1Ki 18:12; 2Ki 2:16; Isa 48:16; Eze 2:2; 3:14). And it is by his Spirit that God gives his people a "new heart and . . . a new spirit" to live by his will (see Eze 36:26–27; see also Jer 24:7; 32:39; Eze 11:19; 18:31).
51:13–17 The vow to praise God (see note on 7:17).
51:14 If God will only forgive, praise will follow. *righteousness.* See note on 4:1.
51:16 See note on 40:6.

51:17 *broken spirit; a broken and contrite heart.* What pleases God more than sacrifices is a humble heart that looks to him when troubles crush and penitently pleads for mercy when sin has been committed (see 50:7–15 and notes; see also 34:17–18).
51:19 *sacrifices of the righteous.* Such as are pleasing to God; here, sacrifices accompanied by praise for God's mercies (see 50:14–15 and notes).

Psalm 52[a]

For the director of music. A maskil[b] of David. When Doeg the Edomite had gone to Saul and told him: "David has gone to the house of Ahimelek."

1 Why do you boast of evil, you mighty hero?
  Why do you boast all day long,
    you who are a disgrace in the eyes of God?
2 You who practice deceit,
    your tongue plots destruction;
    it is like a sharpened razor.
3 You love evil rather than good,
    falsehood rather than speaking the truth.[c]
4 You love every harmful word,
    you deceitful tongue!

5 Surely God will bring you down to everlasting ruin:
    He will snatch you up and pluck you from your tent;
    he will uproot you from the land of the living.
6 The righteous will see and fear;
    they will laugh at you, saying,
7 "Here now is the man
    who did not make God his stronghold
  but trusted in his great wealth
    and grew strong by destroying others!"

8 But I am like an olive tree
    flourishing in the house of God;
  I trust in God's unfailing love
    for ever and ever.
9 For what you have done I will always praise you
    in the presence of your faithful people.
  And I will hope in your name,
    for your name is good.

Psalm 53[d]

For the director of music. According to mahalath.[e] *A maskil[b] of David.*

1 The fool says in his heart,
    "There is no God."
  They are corrupt, and their ways are vile;
    there is no one who does good.

2 God looks down from heaven
    on all mankind
  to see if there are any who understand,
    any who seek God.

---

[a] In Hebrew texts 52:1-9 is numbered 52:3-11.   [b] Title: Probably a literary or musical term   [c] 3 The Hebrew has *Selah* (a word of uncertain meaning) here and at the end of verse 5.   [d] In Hebrew texts 53:1-6 is numbered 53:2-7.   [e] Title: Probably a musical term

Ps 52 Fearless confidence in God when under attack by an arrogant and evil enemy. David stands in the presence of God and from the high tower of that refuge hurls his denunciation (much like the prophetic denunciation in Isa 22:15–19) into the face of his attacker. Though not a wisdom psalm, it has much in common with Ps 49 (see introduction to Ps 49–53; see also introduction to Ps 49). The extended depiction of David's enemy forms a sharp contrast with the spirit of Ps 51. See also David's denunciation of Goliath (1Sa 17:45–47).
52:3 Your whole moral sense is perverted. *love.* Prefer. For *Selah,* see NIV text note and note on 3:2.
52:5 Note the triple imagery: "bring you down," "snatch you up," "uproot you." The arrogant enemy will meet the same end as the rich fools of Ps 49. *from your tent.* See Job 18:14. *uproot you.* Contrast v. 8.
52:6 *righteous.* See note on 1:5. *fear.* Learn from your downfall.
52:8 *like an olive tree.* Which lives for hundreds of years. *flourishing.* See 1:3. It will not be uprooted (v. 5). *in the house of God.* Olive trees were not planted in the temple courts, but David had access to God's temple as his refuge (see 15:1; 23:6; 27:4; 61:4 and note), where he was kept safe. *unfailing love.* See article, p. 16.
52:9 A vow to praise God (see note on 7:17). *faithful people.* See note on 4:3.
Ps 53 A testimony concerning the folly of the wicked, a somewhat revised version of Ps 14; see introduction there. (The main difference between the two psalms is that here the word "God" is used instead of "the Lord"; see also note on v. 5.) The original psalm may have been revised in the light of an event such as is narrated in 2Ch 20. Here it also serves as a further commentary on the kind of arrogant fool denounced in Ps 49; 52 (see introduction to Ps 49–53).
53 title *For the director of music.* See note on Ps 4 title. *mahalath.* Possibly the name of a tune. The Hebrew appears to be the word for "suffering" or "sickness" (see Ps 88 title and NIV text note there). Perhaps the Hebrew phrase indicates here that the psalm is to be used in a time of affliction, when the godless mock (see Ps 102; see also note on 5:9). *maskil.* See note on Ps 32 title.
53:1–4 See notes on 14:1–4.

Additional Insights

As the good and faithful Judge, [God] delivers those who are oppressed or wrongfully attacked and redresses the wrongs committed again them.

³Everyone has turned away, all have become
    corrupt;
  there is no one who does good,
    not even one.

⁴Do all these evildoers know nothing?

  They devour my people as though eating bread;
    they never call on God.
⁵But there they are, overwhelmed with dread,
    where there was nothing to dread.
  God scattered the bones of those who
    attacked you;
  you put them to shame, for God despised them.

⁶Oh, that salvation for Israel would come out
    of Zion!
  When God restores his people,
    let Jacob rejoice and Israel be glad!

Psalm 54ᵃ

*For the director of music. With stringed instruments.
A maskilᵇ of David. When the Ziphites had gone
to Saul and said, "Is not David hiding among us?"*

¹Save me, O God, by your name;
    vindicate me by your might.
²Hear my prayer, O God;
    listen to the words of my mouth.

³Arrogant foes are attacking me;
    ruthless people are trying to kill me —
    people without regard for God.ᶜ

⁴Surely God is my help;
    the Lord is the one who sustains me.

⁵Let evil recoil on those who slander me;
    in your faithfulness destroy them.

⁶I will sacrifice a freewill offering to you;
    I will praise your name, LORD, for it is good.
⁷You have delivered me from all my troubles,
    and my eyes have looked in triumph on
    my foes.

Psalm 55ᵈ

*For the director of music. With stringed
instruments. A maskilᵇ of David.*

¹Listen to my prayer, O God,
    do not ignore my plea;
²   hear me and answer me.
  My thoughts trouble me and I am distraught

53:5 Differs considerably from 14:5–6, though the basic thought remains the same: God overwhelms the godless who attack his people. Here the verbs are in the past tense (perhaps to express the certainty of their downfall). *where there was nothing to dread.* They fell victim to fear when, humanly speaking, they were not even threatened. God's curse fell on them rather than on Israel (see Lev 26:36–37; see also Jdg 7:21; 2Ki 3:22–23; 7:6–7; Pr 28:1). *scattered the bones.* Over the battlefield of their defeat, their bodies left unburied like something loathsome and a source of shame (see Isa 14:18–20; Jer 8:2). *God despised them.* As they had despised him.

Ps 54–60 A cluster of seven laments framed by an individual lament (Ps 54) and a community lament (Ps 60; see introduction to Ps 42–45). The psalm that introduces this cluster (Ps 54) is a lament that is paradigmatic in its structure (see introduction to this psalm below). The psalm that concludes it echoes the key complaint of Ps 44, namely, that God has "rejected" his people and no longer goes out "with our armies" (44:9; 60:10).

Ps 54 A lament in response to enemies who want to have David killed. The psalm is short, like those of Ps 3; 4; 13; yet it is one of the most typical laments of the Psalter, containing the main speech functions found in these laments (see Introduction: Psalm Types). Completely symmetrical, the psalm is framed by David's cry for vindication (v. 1) and his statement of assurance that he will look in triumph on his foes (v. 7). A confession of confidence (v. 4) centers the psalm (see 42:8 and note on 6:6).

54 title *For the director of music.* See note on Ps 4 title. *maskil.* See note on Ps 32 title. *When.* For the event referred to, see 1Sa 23:19; see also note on Ps 3 title.
54:1–2 Prayer for God to judge his case (Ps 17).
54:1 *name.* See v. 6.
54:3 A complaint against his enemies. *without regard for God.* Like those of Ps 53. For *Selah,* see NIV text note and note on 3:2.
54:4 A confession of confidence at the center of the prayer (see 42:8 and note).
54:5 The call for redress (see note on 5:10).
54:6 The vow to praise God (see note on 7:17). *name.* See v. 1.
54:7 Assurance of being heard (see note on 3:8).

Ps 55 A lament seeking God's help when threatened by a powerful conspiracy in Jerusalem under the leadership of a former friend. The situation described is like that of Absalom's conspiracy against the king (25:15–17): The city is in turmoil; danger is everywhere; there is uncertainty as to who can be trusted; rumors, false reports and slander are circulating freely. Under such circumstances David longs for a secure refuge (vv. 6–8). That being out of the question, he casts his cares on the Lord, whom he knows he can trust. In its structure, the psalm is framed by a plea for help (v. 1) and a simple confession of faith: "I trust in you" (v. 23); at the center (v. 15) stands the heart of the lament.
55:1–3 Initial appeal for God to hear.

ᵃ In Hebrew texts 54:1-7 is numbered 54:3-9.   ᵇ Title: Probably a literary or musical term   ᶜ 3 The Hebrew has *Selah* (a word of uncertain meaning) here.   ᵈ In Hebrew texts 55:1-23 is numbered 55:2-24.

³   because of what my enemy is saying,
        because of the threats of the wicked;
     for they bring down suffering on me
        and assail me in their anger.

⁴ My heart is in anguish within me;
        the terrors of death have fallen on me.
⁵ Fear and trembling have beset me;
        horror has overwhelmed me.
⁶ I said, "Oh, that I had the wings of a dove!
        I would fly away and be at rest.
⁷ I would flee far away
        and stay in the desert;ᵃ
⁸ I would hurry to my place of shelter,
        far from the tempest and storm."

⁹ Lord, confuse the wicked, confound their words,
        for I see violence and strife in the city.
¹⁰ Day and night they prowl about on its walls;
        malice and abuse are within it.
¹¹ Destructive forces are at work in the city;
        threats and lies never leave its streets.

¹² If an enemy were insulting me,
        I could endure it;
     if a foe were rising against me,
        I could hide.
¹³ But it is you, a man like myself,
        my companion, my close friend,
¹⁴ with whom I once enjoyed sweet fellowship
        at the house of God,
     as we walked about
        among the worshipers.

¹⁵ Let death take my enemies by surprise;
        let them go down alive to the realm of the dead,
        for evil finds lodging among them.

¹⁶ As for me, I call to God,
        and the LORD saves me.
¹⁷ Evening, morning and noon
        I cry out in distress,
        and he hears my voice.
¹⁸ He rescues me unharmed
        from the battle waged against me,
        even though many oppose me.
¹⁹ God, who is enthroned from of old,
        who does not change —
     he will hear them and humble them,
        because they have no fear of God.

²⁰ My companion attacks his friends;
        he violates his covenant.
²¹ His talk is smooth as butter,
        yet war is in his heart;
     his words are more soothing than oil,
        yet they are drawn swords.

ᵃ 7 The Hebrew has *Selah* (a word of uncertain meaning) here
and in the middle of verse 19.

55:4–8 His heart's anguish.
55:4–5 Danger is everywhere (31:13), a danger so great that it is as if death itself were stalking him (18:4–5; 116:3).
55:4 *heart.* See note on 4:7. *terrors of death.* See 1Sa 5:11; 15:32; 28:5; Job 18:14.
55:6–8 He longs to escape to a secure place, away from treacherous and conniving people (see similarly Jer 9:2–6).
55:7 For *Selah*, see NIV text note and note on 3:2.
55:9–11 Prayer for God to foil the plots of his enemies.
55:9 *confuse . . . confound their words.* Paralyze the conspirators with conflicting designs, as at Babel (Ge 11:5–9; see 2Sa 17:1–14). *the city.* See v. 11; Jerusalem.
55:10 *malice and abuse.* Like watchmen on the walls (see 127:1; 130:6; SS 5:7).
55:11 *threats and lies.* Like watchmen who patrol the city streets (SS 3:3).
55:12–14 The insults and plots of an enemy can be endured—but those of a treacherous friend are unbearable.
55:13 *my companion, my close friend.* See v. 20; see also 41:9 and note.
55:14 *at the house of God.* Their ties of friendship had been a bond hallowed by common commitment to the Lord and sealed by its public display in the presence of God and the worshipers at the temple.
55:15 The centered (see note on 6:6) prayer for redress (see article, p. 15). *Let death take my enemies.* The conspirators were seeking his death. *alive to the realm of the dead.* May they go to the grave before life has run its normal course (v. 23; Nu 16:29–33; Pr 1:12; Isa 5:14).
55:16–19 Assurance of being heard (see note on 3:8).
55:17 *Evening, morning and noon I cry out.* Cf. Da 6:10.
55:18 *rescues.* See Isa 50:2; Jer 31:11.
55:19 He who is the eternal King will deal with those who never change in their ways and show "no fear of God" (see 36:1 and note; see also Ps 14; 53).
55:20–21 Further sorrowful (or angry) reflection over the treachery of his former friend.
55:21 See 28:3; Pr 5:3–4; see also note on 5:9. *heart.* See note on 4:7.

> **Is there something that causes you anguish? Pour out a prayer to God about it.**

_____

_____

_____

_____

_____

_____

²²Cast your cares on the LORD
    and he will sustain you;
he will never let
    the righteous be shaken.
²³But you, God, will bring down the wicked
    into the pit of decay;
the bloodthirsty and deceitful
    will not live out half their days.

But as for me, I trust in you.

Psalm 56[a]

For the director of music. To the tune of "A Dove on Distant Oaks." Of David. A miktam.[b] When the Philistines had seized him in Gath.

¹Be merciful to me, my God,
    for my enemies are in hot pursuit;
    all day long they press their attack.
²My adversaries pursue me all day long;
    in their pride many are attacking me.

³When I am afraid, I put my trust in you.
⁴ In God, whose word I praise —
  in God I trust and am not afraid.
    What can mere mortals do to me?

⁵All day long they twist my words;
    all their schemes are for my ruin.
⁶They conspire, they lurk,
    they watch my steps,
    hoping to take my life.
⁷Because of their wickedness do not[c] let them
        escape;
    in your anger, God, bring the nations down.

⁸Record my misery;
    list my tears on your scroll[d] —
    are they not in your record?
⁹Then my enemies will turn back
    when I call for help.
    By this I will know that God is for me.

¹⁰In God, whose word I praise,
    in the LORD, whose word I praise —
¹¹in God I trust and am not afraid.
    What can man do to me?

¹²I am under vows to you, my God;
    I will present my thank offerings to you.
¹³For you have delivered me from death
    and my feet from stumbling,
    that I may walk before God
    in the light of life.

ᵃ In Hebrew texts 56:1-13 is numbered 56:2-14.   ᵇ Title: Probably a literary or musical term   ᶜ 7 Probable reading of the original Hebrew text; Masoretic Text does not have do not.   ᵈ 8 Or misery; / put my tears in your wineskin

55:22–23 Once more, assurance of being heard.

🍃 **55:22** A testimony to all who are assembled at the temple. 1Pe 5:7 echoes this assurance. *righteous.* See note on 1:5.

55:23 *pit of decay.* The grave (see note on 30:1). *not live out half their days.* See note on v. 15.

🍃 **Ps 56** A plea to God for help when the psalmist is attacked by enemies and his very life is threatened. It is marked by consoling trust in the face of unsettling fear.

56 title *For the director of music.* See note on Ps 4 title. *miktam.* See note on Ps 16 title. *When.* See note on Ps 3 title. For the event referred to, see 1Sa 21:10–15; see also Ps 34 title and note. *had seized.* Or "were about to seize."

56:1–2 Initial appeal for God's help.

56:2 *their pride.* Confident in their position of strength, David's enemies take no account of his God (see notes on 3:2; 5:9; 10:11).

56:3–4 See vv. 10–11; confession of trust in the face of fear.

🍃 **56:4** *word.* God's reassuring promise that he will be the God of his people and will come to their aid when they appeal to him (see 50:15; 91:15; see also 119:74,81; 130:5). *mortals.* Human feebleness compared with God's power (see note on 10:18).

56:5–7 Accusation and call for redress (see note on 5:9–10).

56:5 *twist my words.* See notes on 3:2; 5:9; 10:11.

56:7 See note on 5:10.

56:8–9 Appeal for God to take special note of the psalmist's troubles.

56:8 *Record . . . list . . . on your scroll.* Record my troubles in your heavenly royal records as matters calling for your action (see note on 51:1).

56:9 If God takes such note of his tears that he records them in his book, he will surely respond to David's call for help.

56:10–11 Renewed confession of trust in the face of fear (vv. 3–4).

56:12–13 Assurance of being heard (see note on 3:8).

🍃 **56:12** *I am under vows.* Speaking as if his prayer has already been heard, David acknowledges that now he must keep the vows he made to God when he was in trouble (see 66:14 and note on 7:17).

56:13 *stumbling.* See note on 35:15. *before God.* See note on 11:7. *light of life.* The full blessedness of life (see note on 36:9).

Additional Insights

If God takes such note of [David's] tears that he records them in his book, he will surely respond to David's call for help.

Psalm 57[a]

*For the director of music. To the tune of "Do
Not Destroy." Of David. A miktam.[b] When
he had fled from Saul into the cave.*

[1] Have mercy on me, my God, have mercy on me,
for in you I take refuge.
I will take refuge in the shadow of your wings
until the disaster has passed.

[2] I cry out to God Most High,
to God, who vindicates me.
[3] He sends from heaven and saves me,
rebuking those who hotly pursue me — [c]
God sends forth his love and his faithfulness.

[4] I am in the midst of lions;
I am forced to dwell among ravenous
beasts —
men whose teeth are spears and arrows,
whose tongues are sharp swords.

[5] Be exalted, O God, above the heavens;
let your glory be over all the earth.

[6] They spread a net for my feet —
I was bowed down in distress.
They dug a pit in my path —
but they have fallen into it themselves.

[7] My heart, O God, is steadfast,
my heart is steadfast;
I will sing and make music.
[8] Awake, my soul!
Awake, harp and lyre!
I will awaken the dawn.

[9] I will praise you, Lord, among the nations;
I will sing of you among the peoples.
[10] For great is your love, reaching to the
heavens;
your faithfulness reaches to the skies.

[11] Be exalted, O God, above the heavens;
let your glory be over all the earth.

[a] In Hebrew texts 57:1-11 is numbered 57:2-12.   [b] Title:
Probably a literary or musical term   [c] 3 The Hebrew has
Selah (a word of uncertain meaning) here and at the end of
verse 6.

Additional Insights

Literary features [in the psalms] include assonance, alliteration, wordplays, repetition and the piling up of
synonyms.

Ps 57 A lament when threatened by fierce enemies
(it has many links with Ps 56). The psalm appears to
reflect the imagery of the night of danger followed by the
morning of salvation (v. 8: "I will awaken the dawn"). For
other instances of these associations, see 30:5; 46:5;
59:6,14,16; 63:1,6; 90:14. Verses 7–11 are used again in
108:1–5. Structurally, the psalm is made up of two balanced halves, each having seven Hebrew lines and each
composed of three couplets and a refrain. For the placement of this psalm in the arrangement of Book II of the
Psalter, see introduction to Ps 42–45; see also introduction to Ps 54–60.

57 title See note on Ps 56 title. *Do Not Destroy.* See Ps 58;
59; 75 titles. *When.* For the event referred to, see 1Sa 24:1–
3; see also Ps 142 title.
57:1–5 The prayer.
57:1 Initial cry for God's merciful help. *shadow of your
wings.* See note on 17:8.
57:2–3 Confidence of being heard.
57:2 *who vindicates me.* See 138:8. Or the Hebrew can be
translated "who makes an end of troubles for me" (cf.
7:9).
57:3 *He sends.* God sends his love and faithfulness (here
personified) as his messengers from heaven to save his
servant (see note on 43:3). *his love and his faithfulness.*
See note on 26:3. *love.* See article, p. 16.
57:4 The threatening situation. *I am forced to dwell.* Like a
sheep among lions. *ravenous beasts.* The psalmists often
compare their enemies to ferocious beasts (see note on
7:2). *tongues.* See note on 5:9.
57:5 A prayer for God to show his exalted power and glory
throughout his creation by coming to his servant's rescue, repeated in v. 11 (see 7:6–7; 21:13; 46:10; 59:5,8; 113:4–
9; cf. Ex 14:4; Isa 26:15; 44:23; 59:19; see also note on Ps
46:10).
57:6–11 Praise for God's saving help—confidently
anticipating the desired deliverance. For such a
sudden transition from prayer to assurance, see note
on 3:8.
57:6 The threat and its outcome: The enemies suffer the
calamity they plotted. *net . . . pit.* They hunted him as if
he were a wild beast, but the "lions" (v. 4) themselves
were caught (see 7:15; 9:15; Pr 26:27).
57:7 All cause for fear has been removed. *heart.* See note
on 4:7. *is steadfast.* Feels secure (112:7).
57:8 *Awake . . . Awake.* Greet with joy the dawn of the
day of deliverance (Isa 51:9,17; 52:1). *soul.* Or "glory."
harp and lyre. Instruments (here personified) to accompany the praise of the Lord at his temple in celebration of
deliverance (see 71:22; 81:2 and note on Ps 4 title). *awaken
the dawn.* With joyful cries proclaiming God's saving act.
(Dawn, too, is here personified—the Canaanites even dei-
fied it.)
57:9–10 The vow to praise God (see notes on 7:17; 9:1).
57:10 *love.* See article, p. 16, and note on 6:4. *reaching to
the heavens . . . to the skies.* See note on 36:5.
57:11 The refrain (see v. 5), but now as praise (18:46; 30:1;
34:3; 35:27; 40:16; 70:4; 92:8; 97:9; 99:2; 113:4; 148:13).

Psalm 58[a]

For the director of music. To the tune of "Do Not Destroy." Of David. A miktam.[b]

1 Do you rulers indeed speak justly?
    Do you judge people with equity?
2 No, in your heart you devise injustice,
    and your hands mete out violence on the earth.

3 Even from birth the wicked go astray;
    from the womb they are wayward,
        spreading lies.
4 Their venom is like the venom of a snake,
    like that of a cobra that has stopped its ears,
5 that will not heed the tune of the charmer,
    however skillful the enchanter may be.

6 Break the teeth in their mouths, O God;
    LORD, tear out the fangs of those lions!
7 Let them vanish like water that flows away;
    when they draw the bow, let their arrows fall
        short.
8 May they be like a slug that melts away as it
        moves along,
    like a stillborn child that never sees the sun.

9 Before your pots can feel the heat of the thorns—
    whether they be green or dry—the wicked
        will be swept away.[c]
10 The righteous will be glad when they are avenged,
    when they dip their feet in the blood of the
        wicked.
11 Then people will say,
    "Surely the righteous still are rewarded;
    surely there is a God who judges the earth."

Psalm 59[d]

For the director of music. To the tune of "Do Not Destroy." Of David. A miktam.[b] When Saul had sent men to watch David's house in order to kill him.

1 Deliver me from my enemies, O God;
    be my fortress against those who are
        attacking me.
2 Deliver me from evildoers
    and save me from those who are after my blood.

3 See how they lie in wait for me!
    Fierce men conspire against me
    for no offense or sin of mine, LORD.
4 I have done no wrong, yet they are ready to
        attack me.
    Arise to help me; look on my plight!

---

a In Hebrew texts 58:1-11 is numbered 58:2-12.   *b* Title: Probably a literary or musical term   *c* 9 The meaning of the Hebrew for this verse is uncertain.   *d* In Hebrew texts 59:1-17 is numbered 59:2-18.

Ps 58 A communal lament asking God, the supreme Judge, to set right human affairs, judging those rulers who corrupt justice and championing the cause of the righteous. (The psalm was applied by the early church to Jesus' trial before the Sanhedrin; see Mt 26:57–68 and parallels.) Concern for the just use of judicial power is pervasive throughout the OT. This was the primary agency in the administrative structures of the ancient Near East for the protection of the innocent (usually the poor and powerless) against the assaults of unscrupulous people (usually the rich and powerful). Israelite society was troubled with the corruption of this judicial power from the days of Samuel to the end of the monarchy (1Sa 8:3; Isa 1:23; 5:23; 10:1–2; Eze 22:6,12; Am 5:7,10–13; Mic 3:1–3,9–11; 7:2). Even in David's time all was not well (2Sa 15:1–4).

58:1 *rulers.* Or "gods" (see Ps 82:1 and note; see also introduction to Ps 82), a title applied to those whose administrative positions called upon them to act as earthly representatives of God's heavenly court (see Dt 1:17; 2Ch 19:6 and note on Ps 45:6). *speak justly.* Make fair judicial pronouncements.

58:3 *from birth . . . from the womb.* Their corrupt ways are not sporadic; they act in accordance with their nature (51:5). Here reference is to "the wicked"; the author does not make a general statement about all people, as is the case in Ge 6:5; 8:21; Job 14:4; 15:14–16; 25:4–6. *the wicked.* Most probably a characterization of the rulers. For a description of the wicked in general, see Ps 10.

58:6–8 Appeal for God to defang the wicked rulers and purge the land of such perverse judges. The author uses imagery drawn from conventional curses of the ancient Near East (see note on 5:10).

58:7 *water that flows away.* And is absorbed by the ground. *arrows.* Malicious pronouncements (57:4—but the Hebrew of the whole clause is obscure).

58:9 See NIV text note. The verse may be speaking picturesquely of the speed of God's judgment—speed probably signifying here the inescapable certainty of his judgment (see note on 37:10; see also Lk 18:7–8). *thorns.* Twigs from wild thornbushes were used as fuel for quick heat (118:12; Ecc 7:6). *swept away.* As by a storm—God's storm (Job 27:21).

58:10 *righteous.* Here a judicial term for those who are in the right but who have been wronged (see note on 1:5). *when they are avenged.* When the wrongs committed against them are redressed. *dip their feet in the blood.* Vivid imagery borrowed from the literary conventions of the ancient Near East (68:23). Its origin is the exaggerated language of triumphant reports of victory on the battlefield.

58:11 The climax: When God has judged the unjust rulers (see v. 1 and note), all people will see that right ultimately triumphs under God's just rule (see note on 46:10; see also Ps 93; 96–99). No more will people despair, like those in Mal 3:15.

Ps 59 A lament to God when endangered by enemy attacks (for links with Ps 55, see introduction to that psalm; see also introduction to Ps 54–60). If originally composed by David under the circumstances noted in the superscription, it must have been revised for use by one of David's royal sons when Jerusalem was under siege by a hostile force made up of troops from many nations—as

⁵You, LORD God Almighty,
    you who are the God of Israel,
    rouse yourself to punish all the nations;
    show no mercy to wicked traitors.ᵃ

⁶They return at evening,
    snarling like dogs,
    and prowl about the city.
⁷See what they spew from their mouths —
    the words from their lips are sharp as swords,
    and they think, "Who can hear us?"
⁸But you laugh at them, LORD;
    you scoff at all those nations.

⁹You are my strength, I watch for you;
    you, God, are my fortress,
10   my God on whom I can rely.

God will go before me
    and will let me gloat over those who slander me.
¹¹But do not kill them, Lord our shield,ᵇ
    or my people will forget.
In your might uproot them
    and bring them down.
¹²For the sins of their mouths,
    for the words of their lips,
    let them be caught in their pride.
For the curses and lies they utter,
13   consume them in your wrath,
    consume them till they are no more.
Then it will be known to the ends of the earth
    that God rules over Jacob.

¹⁴They return at evening,
    snarling like dogs,
    and prowl about the city.
¹⁵They wander about for food
    and howl if not satisfied.
¹⁶But I will sing of your strength,
    in the morning I will sing of your love;
for you are my fortress,
    my refuge in times of trouble.

¹⁷You are my strength, I sing praise to you;
    you, God, are my fortress,
    my God on whom I can rely.

ᵃ 5 The Hebrew has *Selah* (a word of uncertain meaning) here and at the end of verse 13.   ᵇ 11 Or *sovereign*

Additional Insights

The Psalter is theologically rich. Its theology is, however, not abstract or systematic but doxological, confessional and practical.

when Hezekiah was besieged by the Assyrians (2Ki 18:19). (Some, however, ascribe it to Nehemiah; see Ne 4.) The enemy weapon most prominent is the tongue, attacking with slander and curses (see note on 5:9). In this psalm, too, the imagery of the night of danger (vv. 6,14), followed by the morning of deliverance (v. 16), is evoked (see introduction to Ps 57).

59:1 *be my fortress.* Or "raise me to a high, secure place."

59:2 *evildoers . . . those who are after my blood.* Common characterizations of those who attack the psalmists out of malice.

59:3–5 By slander (v. 10) and lies (v. 12) the enemies seek to justify their attacks, but the psalmist protests his innocence and pleads with God to judge those who wrong him (58:11).
59:5 *rouse yourself.* See note on 7:6. *punish . . . show no mercy.* See note on 5:10. *traitors.* Whether Israelites had joined in the attack is not clear; the Hebrew indicates only that the enemies were treacherous. For *Selah*, see NIV text note and note on 3:2.
59:7 *words from their lips are sharp as swords.* Their "curses and lies" (v. 12). For the imagery, see 57:4; see also note on 5:9. *they think.* See note on 3:2.
59:9 *watch.* Hebrew *shamar* (see note on v. 17). This verb is used similarly in 31:6; Jnh 2:8 ("cling to"); the basic idea appears to be to "look to expectantly" for help. The psalmist watches as one who longingly waits for the morning (of salvation); see 130:6.
59:10–13 The prayer renewed. Confident that the Lord will hear his prayer (v. 10) and will punish the nations (v. 5), the psalmist prays that God will not sweep them away suddenly but will prolong their punishment so that Israel ("my people," v. 11) will not forget God's acts of salvation, as they had done so often before (78:11; 106:13). Nevertheless, the psalmist asks God not to allow the enemies to escape the full consequences of their malice (vv. 12–13).
59:12 See note on v. 7. *caught in their pride.* Let the pride with which they treacherously attack the Lord's servant and his people be the trap that catches them.
59:14–16 Assurance of being heard (see note on 3:8). Just as God mocks the defiant pack of "dogs" (vv. 6–8), so the psalmist will sing for joy at God's triumph over them.
59:17 The vow to praise God (see note on 7:17). *sing.* Hebrew *zamar* (see note on v. 9). The play on words in the refrain marks an advance from looking to God for help in the night of danger to singing in the morning of salvation (cf. 57:8 and note; cf. also 30:5).

> ## How do the psalms confirm God's sovereignty over creation?

_____

_____

_____

_____

Psalm 60[a]

For the director of music. To the tune of "The Lily of the Covenant." A miktam[b] of David. For teaching. When he fought Aram Naharaim[c] and Aram Zobah,[d] and when Joab returned and struck down twelve thousand Edomites in the Valley of Salt.

¹ You have rejected us, God, and burst upon us;
    you have been angry — now restore us!
² You have shaken the land and torn it open;
    mend its fractures, for it is quaking.
³ You have shown your people desperate times;
    you have given us wine that makes us stagger.
⁴ But for those who fear you, you have raised a banner
    to be unfurled against the bow.[e]

⁵ Save us and help us with your right hand,
    that those you love may be delivered.

[a] In Hebrew texts 60:1-12 is numbered 60:3-14.   [b] Title: Probably a literary or musical term   [c] Title: That is, Arameans of Northwest Mesopotamia   [d] Title: That is, Arameans of central Syria   [e] 4 The Hebrew has *Selah* (a word of uncertain meaning) here.

CITIES AND REGIONS IN PSALM 60

Ps 60 A national lament requesting God's help after suffering a severe blow by a foreign nation, presumably Edom (v. 9). The prayer leader may have been the king (the "me" in v. 9), as in 2Ch 20. The lament that God has "rejected" (vv. 1,10) his people and no longer goes out "with our armies" (v. 10) links the psalm with Ps 44 (see 44:9; see also introduction to Ps 54–60).

60 title See note on Ps 56 title. *The Lily of the Covenant.* See Ps 80 title and note on Ps 45 title. *For teaching.* Only here in the psalm titles. For other songs that Israel was to learn, see Dt 31:19,21; 2Sa 1:18. That it was intended for a variety of uses, especially to convey confidence in times of national threat, is illustrated by its use in Ps 108. *When.* For the events referred to, see 2Sa 8; 1Ch 18 (perhaps also 2Sa 10).

60:1–3 Lament over God's rejection of his people (44:9–16; 89:38–45) and prayer for restoration.

60:1 *rejected us.* At least momentarily (30:5). Defeat by the enemy is interpreted as a sign of God's anger (though no reason for that anger is noted, and the bond between Israel and God is not broken). *burst upon.* Like a flood (2Sa 5:20).

60:2 *shaken the land.* As by a devastating earthquake—such as was occasionally experienced in ancient Canaan.

60:3 *wine that makes us stagger.* A lament that God has made them drink from the cup of his wrath rather than from his cup of blessing and salvation (see note on 16:5).

60:4–8 A plea for help, grounded in reasons for confidence. The petition (v. 5) is followed by a reassuring message from the Lord (vv. 6–8)—perhaps recalling an already ancient word from the time of the conquest. In any event, the Lord is depicted as Israel's triumphant Warrior-King (Ex 15:3,13–18).

> **What word pictures stand out to you in this section of the psalms?**
>
> _____
> _____
> _____
> _____
> _____
> _____
> _____
> _____
> _____

⁶God has spoken from his sanctuary:
  "In triumph I will parcel out Shechem
    and measure off the Valley of Sukkoth.
⁷Gilead is mine, and Manasseh is mine;
    Ephraim is my helmet,
    Judah is my scepter.
⁸Moab is my washbasin,
    on Edom I toss my sandal;
    over Philistia I shout in triumph."

⁹Who will bring me to the fortified city?
    Who will lead me to Edom?
¹⁰Is it not you, God, you who have now rejected us
    and no longer go out with our armies?
¹¹Give us aid against the enemy,
    for human help is worthless.
¹²With God we will gain the victory,
    and he will trample down our enemies.

Additional Insights

God rules over all. At the core of the theology of the Psalter is the conviction that the gravitational center of life . . . is God.

60:6 *parcel out . . . measure off.* Divide his conquered territory among his servant people who were with him in the battles. *Shechem . . . Sukkoth.* Representative of the territory west and east of the Jordan taken over by the Lord and Israel (Ge 33:17–18; 1Ki 12:25). See map, p. 80.

60:7 Israel is the Lord's kingdom—the land conquered and his people established within it. *Gilead . . . Manasseh.* Half of Manasseh was established in Gilead, east of the Jordan, and half of it west of the Jordan, just north of Ephraim (Jos 13:29–31; 17:5–11). This once again showed that the Lord's kingdom included territory both east and west of the Jordan. *Ephraim . . . Judah.* The two leading tribes of Israel, the one representative of the Rachel tribes (Ephraim) in the north, the other of the Leah tribes (Judah) in the south; see Ge 48:13–20; 49:8–12; Nu 2:3,18; Jos 15–16. Together they represented all Israel (Isa 11:13; Zec 9:13). *helmet.* As a powerful and aggressive tribe (Dt 33:17; Jdg 7:24—8:3; 12:1), Ephraim figuratively represents the Lord's helmet. *scepter.* Called such because from Judah would come (Ge 49:10)—and had now come (1Sa 16:1–13)—the Lord's chosen earthly regent over his people (2Sa 7).

60:8 *Moab . . . Edom . . . Philistia.* Perpetual enemies on Israel's eastern, southern and western borders, respectively (see Ex 15:14–15; see also Ex 13:17; Nu 20:14–21; 22–24).

60:9 *me . . . me.* Possibly referring to the king (see introduction), though the praying community may be referring to itself collectively (see note on Ps 30 title). *lead me.* As God went before his people into battle in the wilderness (Ex 13:21) and during the conquest (Ex 23:27–28; 33:2; Dt 9:3; 31:8).

> Praise God for his power in a song or poem.

QUESTIONS FOR REFLECTION

▶ How does God give people a pure heart (51:10)?

_____

_____

_____

_____

▶ Psalm 55 may have been composed by David when his son Absalom tried to overthrow David's reign. How might this psalm help you look to God the next time you feel overwhelmed?

_____

_____

_____

_____

_____

▶ Can your heart be steadfast when facing troubles (57:7)? How?

_____

_____

_____

_____

▶ What do you learn about the importance of expressing emotions from the psalms?

_____

_____

_____

_____

_____

Psalm 61[a]

For the director of music. With stringed instruments. Of David.

[1] Hear my cry, O God;
　　listen to my prayer.

[2] From the ends of the earth I call to you,
　　I call as my heart grows faint;
　　lead me to the rock that is higher
　　　than I.
[3] For you have been my refuge,
　　a strong tower against the foe.

[4] I long to dwell in your tent forever
　　and take refuge in the shelter of your
　　　wings.[b]
[5] For you, God, have heard my vows;
　　you have given me the heritage of those
　　　who fear your name.

[6] Increase the days of the king's life,
　　his years for many generations.
[7] May he be enthroned in God's presence
　　　forever;
　　appoint your love and faithfulness to
　　　protect him.

[8] Then I will ever sing in praise of your
　　　name
　　and fulfill my vows day after day.

Psalm 62[c]

*For the director of music. For Jeduthun.
A psalm of David.*

[1] Truly my soul finds rest in God;
　　my salvation comes from him.
[2] Truly he is my rock and my salvation;
　　he is my fortress, I will never be shaken.

[3] How long will you assault me?
　　Would all of you throw me down—
　　this leaning wall, this tottering fence?
[4] Surely they intend to topple me
　　from my lofty place;
　　they take delight in lies.

[a] In Hebrew texts 61:1-8 is numbered 61:2-9.　　[b] 4 The Hebrew has *Selah* (a word of uncertain meaning) here.　　[c] In Hebrew texts 62:1-12 is numbered 62:2-13.

Ps 61–64 A series of four psalms linked together by the common theme of strong reliance on God for deliverance in the face of great—perhaps mortal—danger.

Ps 61 A lament with a prayer for restoration to God's presence. The circumstances appear to be similar to those referred to in Ps 42–43. Here, however, a king is involved (v. 6), and if the author was David, he may have composed this psalm at the time of his flight from Absalom (2Sa 17:21–29).

61:2 *ends of the earth.* So it seemed (42:6). Possibly the phrase here refers to the brink of the netherworld, i.e., the grave (63:9); the psalmist feels himself near death. *heart.* See note on 4:7. *lead me.* See 23:2. *rock.* Secure place (27:5; 40:2). *higher than I.* The place of security that he seeks is beyond his reach; only God can bring him to it. Since God is often confessed by the psalmists to be their "rock of refuge" (31:2; see also 18:2; 62:2,6–7; 71:3; 94:22), it may be that God himself is that higher "rock" (the secure refuge) that the psalmist pleads for (v. 3). Or it may be the secure refuge of God's sanctuary (see v. 4; see also 27:5).

61:3 The reason he appeals to God: God has never failed him as a refuge.

61:4 *dwell in.* See note on 15:1. *tent.* Likely the tabernacle as representative of God's presence (2Sa 6:17; 7:2; 1Ki 1:39; 2:28–30). *shelter of your wings.* See note on 17:8. For *Selah*, see NIV text note and note on 3:2.

61:5 *my vows.* The vows that accompanied his prayers (see 50:14; 66:14; see also note on 7:17). *heritage.* A place with God's people in the promised land, together with all that the Lord had promised to give and to be to his people (16:6; 37:18; 135:12; 136:21–22).

61:6–7 Prayer for the king's long life. The king himself may have made this prayer—such transitions to the third person are known from the literature of the ancient Near East—or it may be the prayer of the people, perhaps voiced by a priest or Levite. Later Jewish interpretations applied these verses to the Messiah. They are fulfilled in Christ, David's greatest Son.

Ps 62 The psalmist commits himself to God when threatened by the assaults of conspirators who wish to "topple me from my lofty place" (v. 4). The author may have been a king. If it was David, the circumstances could well have been the efforts of the family of Saul to topple him. Verse 3 suggests a time of weakness and may indicate advanced age. Implicitly the psalm is an appeal to God to uphold him. No psalm surpasses it in its expression of simple trust in God (see Ps 31).

62:1–2 Profession of complete trust in God for protection.

62:3–4 The threatening activities of the enemies.

62:3 Question to the assailants: Will you never give up? *leaning wall . . . tottering fence.* Metaphors for the psalmist's fragile condition: either (1) a confession that he has no strength in himself, (2) an acknowledgment that he is

With their mouths they bless,
 but in their hearts they curse.^a

5 Yes, my soul, find rest in God;
 my hope comes from him.
6 Truly he is my rock and my salvation;
 he is my fortress, I will not be shaken.
7 My salvation and my honor depend on God^b;
 he is my mighty rock, my refuge.
8 Trust in him at all times, you people;
 pour out your hearts to him,
 for God is our refuge.

9 Surely the lowborn are but a breath,
 the highborn are but a lie.
 If weighed on a balance, they are nothing;
 together they are only a breath.
10 Do not trust in extortion
 or put vain hope in stolen goods;
 though your riches increase,
 do not set your heart on them.

11 One thing God has spoken,
 two things I have heard:
 "Power belongs to you, God,
12 and with you, Lord, is unfailing love";
 and, "You reward everyone
 according to what they have done."

Psalm 63^c

A psalm of David. When he was in the Desert of Judah.

1 You, God, are my God,
 earnestly I seek you;
 I thirst for you,
 my whole being longs for you,
 in a dry and parched land
 where there is no water.

2 I have seen you in the sanctuary
 and beheld your power and your glory.
3 Because your love is better than life,
 my lips will glorify you.
4 I will praise you as long as I live,
 and in your name I will lift up my hands.
5 I will be fully satisfied as with the richest of
 foods;
 with singing lips my mouth will praise you.

6 On my bed I remember you;
 I think of you through the watches of the
 night.
7 Because you are my help,
 I sing in the shadow of your wings.

^a 4 The Hebrew has *Selah* (a word of uncertain meaning) here
and at the end of verse 8.   ^b 7 Or / *God Most High is my
salvation and my honor*   ^c In Hebrew texts 63:1-11 is
numbered 63:2-12.

in a weakened condition or, perhaps, (3) a reflection on how his enemies perceive him, as a "pushover."
62:4 *lofty place.* Possibly the throne. *lies.* See note on 10:7. *bless.* For example, "Long live the king" (1Sa 10:24; 2Sa 16:16; see also 1Ki 1:25,34,39). *curse.* Invoke harm on the psalmist. For *Selah,* see NIV text note and note on 3:2.

🌿 **62:5** *find rest.* The psalmist speaks a word of self-encouragement to find in God what he already has (rest, v. 1; see also 27:13–14; 42:5,11; 43:5).
62:9–10 Humans, as a threat, are nothing (see note on 10:18).
62:9 *breath . . . lie.* People appear to be much more than they really are (see 37:2,20; 39:5 and notes), especially the rich and powerful.

🌿 **62:10** A warning to those (including those conspiring against him) who trust in their own devices to get what they want (by fair means or foul) rather than trusting in God to sustain them—a virtual summary of Ps 49. *heart.* See note on 4:7.

🌿 **62:11–12** The climax: recollection of God's reassuring word to his people. *Power . . . unfailing love.* He is able to do all that he has promised and is committed to his people's salvation and blessedness.
62:12 *unfailing love.* See article, p. 16.

🌿 **Ps 63** A confession of longing for God and for the security his presence offers when deadly enemies threaten. This lament is vividly described by the metaphor of thirst (v. 1) and hunger (v. 5; see 42:1–2). Like Ps 62 this psalm is an implicit prayer. It is linked to that psalm also by the advancement from hearing (62:11) to seeing (v. 2; see 48:8 and note). The imagery of the night of danger (v. 6) and the morning of salvation (see note on v. 1) once more occurs (see introduction to Ps 57). In the early church this psalm was prescribed for daily public prayers. In its structure, the initial expression of lament and longing (v. 1) gives way at the end to the expectation of joy (v. 11)—the literary frame of the psalm. Verse 6 provides the key thematic link connecting vv. 1 and 11. It stands at the center between two precisely balanced stanzas (vv. 2–5,7–10), each having four verses and each made up of 27 Hebrew words. The psalmist's night meditations (v. 6) nurture his longing for God (v. 1; cf. 143:5–6) and reinforce his expectations (v. 11).

🌿 **63:1** Intense longing for God in a time of need. *dry and parched land.* A metaphor (143:6; Isa 32:2) for his situation of need, in which he does not taste "the richest of foods" (v. 5) supplied by the "river whose streams make glad the city of God" (46:4; see note there).
63:2–5 Comforting reflection on what he had seen in the sanctuary; it awakens joyful expectations.
63:2 See 27:4; 48:8 and notes.
63:3 *love.* See article, p. 16.
63:4 *lift up my hands.* While lifting the hands to God usually signifies prayer, it also—though rarely in biblical reference—accompanied praise (134:2).
63:6 *On my bed.* At night as he expectantly awaits the dawning of the morning of deliverance. *watches of the night.* See 119:148; La 2:19.
63:7 *shadow of your wings.* See note on 17:8. God's saving help brings the psalmist back to the sanctuary (v. 2) with songs of praise.

⁸ I cling to you;
  your right hand upholds me.

⁹ Those who want to kill me will be destroyed;
  they will go down to the depths of the earth.
¹⁰ They will be given over to the sword
  and become food for jackals.

¹¹ But the king will rejoice in God;
  all who swear by God will glory in him,
  while the mouths of liars will be silenced.

Psalm 64^a

For the director of music. A psalm of David.

¹ Hear me, my God, as I voice my complaint;
  protect my life from the threat of the enemy.

² Hide me from the conspiracy of the wicked,
  from the plots of evildoers.
³ They sharpen their tongues like swords
  and aim cruel words like deadly arrows.
⁴ They shoot from ambush at the innocent;
  they shoot suddenly, without fear.

⁵ They encourage each other in evil plans,
  they talk about hiding their snares;
  they say, "Who will see it^b?"
⁶ They plot injustice and say,
  "We have devised a perfect plan!"
  Surely the human mind and heart are
    cunning.

⁷ But God will shoot them with his arrows;
  they will suddenly be struck down.
⁸ He will turn their own tongues against them
  and bring them to ruin;
  all who see them will shake their heads in
    scorn.
⁹ All people will fear;
  they will proclaim the works of God
  and ponder what he has done.

¹⁰ The righteous will rejoice in the LORD
  and take refuge in him;
  all the upright in heart will glory in him!

Psalm 65^c

For the director of music. A psalm of David. A song.

¹ Praise awaits^d you, our God, in Zion;
  to you our vows will be fulfilled.
² You who answer prayer,
  to you all people will come.

---

^a In Hebrew texts 64:1-10 is numbered 64:2-11.   ^b 5 Or *us*
^c In Hebrew texts 65:1-13 is numbered 65:2-14.   ^d 1 Or *befits*;
the meaning of the Hebrew for this word is uncertain.

63:8 He has experienced God's "love," which is "better than life" (v. 3).
63:9 His enemies will get what they deserve; in wanting to kill him they forfeit their own lives (see Ge 9:5; Ex 21:23; Dt 19:21; see also note on Ps 5:10). The final end of the enemies stands in sharp contrast with the psalmist's prospects, as anticipated in vv. 7–8—but also as voiced in v. 4: "I will praise," but "they will go down" to the place of silence (v. 11). *depths of the earth.* See note on 30:1; here, the netherworld or grave (see also note on 61:2).
63:10 *food for jackals.* Like bodies of enemies left unburied on the battlefield to add to their disgrace (see note on 53:5). Note the vivid portrayal of the contrast between the two prospects: "I will be fully satisfied as with the richest of foods" (v. 5); "they will . . . become food for jackals."
Ps 64 A lament to God when threatened by a conspiracy (see introduction to Ps 61–64). The circumstances may be similar to those reflected in Ps 62 (see introduction to that psalm), but here there is no allusion to the king's weakened condition, and it is not clear whether the conspirators come from within or outside Israel. As so often in the laments of the Psalter, the enemy's tongue is his main weapon (see note on 5:9).
64:4 *without fear.* They feel themselves secure from exposure and retaliation (see Ps 10 and notes on 10:6,11), but see vv. 7–8.
64:5–6 The enemies' contemptuous self-confidence.
64:5 *hiding their snares.* See note on 9:15.
64:7–9 Confidence in God's righteous judgment—he will do to the adversaries what they had intended to do to David (vv. 3–4)—and its effect on those who hear about it.
64:8 *shake their heads.* In scorn (44:14).
64:9 All people will fear, proclaim and ponder how God's "works" undo and judge the doings of the "evildoers" (v. 2; see note on 46:10; see also 40:3; 58:11; 65:8).
64:10 Concluding statement that the righteous will rejoice in the Lord and praise him. *righteous.* See note on 1:5, here corresponding to "the innocent" (v.4).
Ps 65–68 Four thanksgiving psalms dominated by the theme of praise and linked by the shared recognition that God's "awesome" deeds evoke the wonder of "all the ends of the earth" and move (or should move) "all the earth" to join Israel in singing the praise of their God (see note on 46:10).
Ps 65 A thanksgiving psalm praising God's goodness to his people. In answer to their prayers (1) he pardons their sins so that they continue to enjoy the "good things" that accompany their fellowship with him at his temple (vv. 1–4); (2) as the One who established the secure order of the creation, he also orders the affairs of the world so that international turbulence is put to rest and Israel is secure in their land (vv. 5–8); and (3) he turns the promised land into a veritable Garden of Eden (vv. 9–13).
65:2 *all people.* Perhaps referring to all God's people, as in Joel 2:, though most interpreters believe (in light of vv. 5,8) that the reference is more universal, as in 64:9; 66:1,4,8; 67:3–5 and elsewhere. *will come.* To praise God as the (only) God who hears and graciously answers prayers.

³When we were overwhelmed by sins,
you forgave*a* our transgressions.
⁴Blessed are those you choose
and bring near to live in your courts!
We are filled with the good things of your
house,
of your holy temple.

⁵You answer us with awesome and righteous
deeds,
God our Savior,
the hope of all the ends of the earth
and of the farthest seas,
⁶who formed the mountains by your power,
having armed yourself with strength,
⁷who stilled the roaring of the seas,
the roaring of their waves,
and the turmoil of the nations.
⁸The whole earth is filled with awe at your
wonders;
where morning dawns, where evening fades,
you call forth songs of joy.

⁹You care for the land and water it;
you enrich it abundantly.
The streams of God are filled with water
to provide the people with grain,
for so you have ordained it.*b*
¹⁰You drench its furrows and level its ridges;
you soften it with showers and bless its crops.
¹¹You crown the year with your bounty,
and your carts overflow with abundance.
¹²The grasslands of the wilderness overflow;
the hills are clothed with gladness.
¹³The meadows are covered with flocks
and the valleys are mantled with grain;
they shout for joy and sing.

Psalm 66

For the director of music. A song. A psalm.

¹Shout for joy to God, all the earth!
²   Sing the glory of his name;
make his praise glorious.
³Say to God, "How awesome are your deeds!
So great is your power
that your enemies cringe before you.
⁴All the earth bows down to you;
they sing praise to you,
they sing the praises of your name."*c*

⁵Come and see what God has done,
his awesome deeds for mankind!

---

*a 3 Or made atonement for   b 9 Or for that is how you
prepare the land   c 4 The Hebrew has Selah (a word of
uncertain meaning) here and at the end of verses 7 and 15.*

65:3–4 The crucial act of divine mercy that opens the way for the benefits spelled out in the two remaining stanzas.

65:3 *forgave our transgressions.* Accepted the atonement sacrifices you appointed and so forgave our sins (see NIV text note; see also 32:1–2; 78:38; 79:9).

65:5 *awesome . . . deeds.* Acts of God such as were associated with his deliverance of Israel from Egypt and the conquest of Canaan, acts of power that made Israel's enemies cringe (see 66:3; see also 106:22; 145:6; Dt 10:21; 2Sa 7:23; Isa 64:3). *righteous deeds.* Saving acts by which God kept his covenanted promises to Israel (see note on 4:1).

65:6–7 The God of creation, who by his power brought order to the world out of the earlier chaos (Ge 1), similarly in the redemption of his people establishes a peaceful order among nations (Isa 2:4; 11:6–9; Mic 4:3–4) so that Israel may be at rest in the promised land (Ps 33; 46). God's mighty acts in redemption are often compared by OT poets with his mighty acts in creation (74:12–17; 89:9–18; Isa 27:1; 40:6–14,21–31; 51:9–11), since his power as Creator guaranteed his power as Redeemer. *formed the mountains . . . stilled . . . the seas.* Gave order to the whole creation (95:4–5).

65:7 *turmoil of the nations.* God's stilling the turbulence of the nations—which often threatened Israel—is compared to his taming the turbulence of the primeval waters of chaos (see note on 32:6).

65:8 All peoples will (ultimately) see God's saving acts in behalf of his people and will be moved to awe (see note on 46:10). And all creation will rejoice (v. 13). *wonders.* Or "signs," referring to God's great saving acts, such as those he performed when he delivered Israel out of Egypt (Dt 4:34; see Ps 78:43; 105:27; 135:9).

65:9–13 God blesses the promised land with all good things in answer to Israel's prayers.

65:9 *streams of God.* See note on 36:8.

65:13 *they shout for joy and sing.* In the exuberant language of the psalmists, all creation—even its inanimate elements—joins the human chorus to celebrate the goodness of God in creation, blessing and redemption (see 89:12; 96:11–13; 98:8–9; 103:22; 145:10; 148:3–4,7–10; see also Job 38:7; Isa 44:23; 49:13; 55:12).

Ps 66 A psalm of thanksgiving for God's answer to prayer—probably delivering the psalmist from an enemy threat. He has set his personal experience of God's saving help as one of God's people in the larger context of God's help of Israel in the exodus. The thanks is offered at the temple in fulfillment of a vow (vv. 13–14; see note on 7:17). Such praise was often climaxed by a call for others to take up the praise (see note on 9:1). Here the psalmist exuberantly begins with that call and, as often elsewhere (e.g., 67:3–5; 68:32; 98:4; 99:1–3; 100:1; 117:1), addresses it even to the far corners of the earth.

66:1–4 Calling all the earth to joyful praise.

66:4 See note on 46:10. For *Selah,* see NIV text note and note on 3:2.

66:5–7 Recollection of God's deliverance of Israel at the Red Sea as a sign of his power to rule over the nations. The psalmist portrays his deliverance (see introduction above) both as similar to this Red Sea rescue in its manifestation of God's saving power (see 65:5–7 for a comparison of God's mighty saving acts with his mighty

⁶He turned the sea into dry land,
    they passed through the waters on foot —
    come, let us rejoice in him.
⁷He rules forever by his power,
    his eyes watch the nations —
    let not the rebellious rise up against him.

⁸Praise our God, all peoples,
    let the sound of his praise be heard;
⁹he has preserved our lives
    and kept our feet from slipping.
¹⁰For you, God, tested us;
    you refined us like silver.
¹¹You brought us into prison
    and laid burdens on our backs.
¹²You let people ride over our heads;
    we went through fire and water,
    but you brought us to a place of abundance.

¹³I will come to your temple with burnt offerings
    and fulfill my vows to you —
¹⁴vows my lips promised and my mouth spoke
    when I was in trouble.
¹⁵I will sacrifice fat animals to you
    and an offering of rams;
    I will offer bulls and goats.

¹⁶Come and hear, all you who fear God;
    let me tell you what he has done for me.
¹⁷I cried out to him with my mouth;
    his praise was on my tongue.
¹⁸If I had cherished sin in my heart,
    the Lord would not have listened;
¹⁹but God has surely listened
    and has heard my prayer.
²⁰Praise be to God,
    who has not rejected my prayer
    or withheld his love from me!

Psalm 67ᵃ

*For the director of music. With stringed
instruments. A psalm. A song.*

¹May God be gracious to us and bless us
    and make his face shine on us — ᵇ
²so that your ways may be known on earth,
    your salvation among all nations.

³May the peoples praise you, God;
    may all the peoples praise you.
⁴May the nations be glad and sing for joy,
    for you rule the peoples with equity
    and guide the nations of the earth.
⁵May the peoples praise you, God;
    may all the peoples praise you.

ᵃ In Hebrew texts 67:1-7 is numbered 67:2-8.   ᵇ 1 The
Hebrew has *Selah* (a word of uncertain meaning) here and at
the end of verse 4.

acts of creation) and as a continuation of God's same saving purposes.
66:6 *waters.* Possibly the Jordan, but more likely a parallel reference to the "Red Sea."
66:8–12 Praise of God's deliverance of his people.
66:9 *from slipping.* See note on 38:16.

66:10 *tested . . . refined.* From one point of view, times of distress constitute a testing of God's people as to their trust in and loyalty to God. The metaphor is borrowed from the technology of refining precious metals, which included heating the metals in a crucible to see if all impurities had been removed (see 12:6 and note; 17:3; 1Pe 1:7).

66:11–12 *You . . . You.* God's rule is all-pervasive; even when enemies maliciously oppress his people, God is not a mere passive observer but has his own holy purposes in it (Isa 45:7; Am 3:6). *prison . . . burdens . . . ride over.* Probably recalling the Egyptian oppression from which the exodus brought relief.
66:12 *fire and water.* Conventional metaphors for severe trials (Isa 43:2). *to a place of abundance.* God's people were brought out of a situation of distress into a situation of overflowing blessings (23:5): the promised land.

66:16–20 Proclamation of what God has done for the psalmist—in praise of God and addressed to the worshiping congregation (cf. 34:1–7).
66:20 *Praise be to God.* See v. 8. *love.* See article, p. 16.
Ps 67 Communal thanksgiving for God's blessing. Its content, form and brevity suggest that it served as a liturgical prayer of the people at the conclusion of worship, perhaps just prior to (or immediately after) the priestly benediction (see note on v. 1). God's blessing of his people (as well as his saving acts in their behalf) will catch the attention of the nations and move them to praise him (65:2).
67:1 The heart of the prayer, echoing the priestly benediction (see Nu 6:24–26). *make his face shine.* See notes on 4:6; 13:1. For *Selah*, see NIV text note and note on 3:2.

67:2 May God's favors to his people be so obvious that all the world takes notice (see note on 46:10).

67:3–5 The motivation. Elaborating on v. 2, the people speak of the worldwide praise that will resound to God when he graciously blesses his people. Their wish is twofold: (1) that God's blessings may be so abundant that the people will be moved to praise him, and (2) that the nations may indeed add their praise to that of Israel—an appropriate expression at this climax of the liturgy of worship.

67:4 May the nations rejoice in the Lord when they see how benevolent the rule of God is (65:7–8; 98:4–6; 100:1).

Additional Insights

God's rule is all-pervasive; even when enemies maliciously oppress his people, God is not a mere passive observer but has his own holy purposes in it.

⁶The land yields its harvest;
  God, our God, blesses us.
⁷May God bless us still,
  so that all the ends of the earth will fear him.

Psalm 68 ᵃ

For the director of music. Of David. A psalm. A song.

¹May God arise, may his enemies be scattered;
  may his foes flee before him.
²May you blow them away like smoke —
  as wax melts before the fire,
  may the wicked perish before God.
³But may the righteous be glad
  and rejoice before God;
  may they be happy and joyful.

⁴Sing to God, sing in praise of his name,
  extol him who rides on the clouds ᵇ;
  rejoice before him — his name is the LORD.
⁵A father to the fatherless, a defender of
    widows,
  is God in his holy dwelling.
⁶God sets the lonely in families, ᶜ
  he leads out the prisoners with singing;
  but the rebellious live in a sun-scorched land.

⁷When you, God, went out before your people,
  when you marched through the wilderness, ᵈ
⁸the earth shook, the heavens poured down
    rain,
  before God, the One of Sinai,
  before God, the God of Israel.
⁹You gave abundant showers, O God;
  you refreshed your weary inheritance.
¹⁰Your people settled in it,
  and from your bounty, God, you provided for
    the poor.

¹¹The Lord announces the word,
  and the women who proclaim it are a mighty
    throng:
¹²"Kings and armies flee in haste;
  the women at home divide the plunder.
¹³Even while you sleep among the sheep pens, ᵉ
  the wings of my dove are sheathed with
    silver,
  its feathers with shining gold."
¹⁴When the Almighty ᶠ scattered the kings in
    the land,
  it was like snow fallen on Mount Zalmon.

ᵃ In Hebrew texts 68:1-35 is numbered 68:2-36.   ᵇ 4 Or
name, / prepare the way for him who rides through the deserts
ᶜ 6 Or *the desolate in a homeland*   ᵈ 7 The Hebrew has
Selah (a word of uncertain meaning) here and at the end of
verses 19 and 32.   ᵉ 13 Or *the campfires; or the saddlebags*
ᶠ 14 Hebrew *Shaddai*

67:6–7 The effects of God's blessing his people.
67:6 The promised land will yield its abundance (65:9–13).
Ps 68 A hymn celebrating the triumphal march of Israel's God from Mount Sinai to Mount Zion. Interwoven in it is a prayer that this mighty display of God's power will be continued until all God's people are rescued and secure and all kingdoms of the earth bring tribute to and sing the praises of the God of Israel. The voice heard here is that of the worshiping community, and the psalm may originally have accompanied a liturgical procession of the people up to the temple in Jerusalem (see introductions to Ps 24; 47; 118; 132). The first half of the psalm (vv. 1–18 have 19 Hebrew poetic lines) contains many clear references to God's triumphal march from Mount Sinai (in the days of Moses) to Mount Zion (in the days of David). The second half of the psalm (vv. 19–35 also have 19 Hebrew poetic lines) is framed by the cry "Praise be to the Lord/God" and looks forward with expectations of God's continuing triumphs until the redemption of his people is complete and his kingly rule is universally acknowledged with songs of thanksgiving. The early church, taking its cue from Eph 4:8–13, understood this psalm to foreshadow the resurrection, ascension and present rule of Christ and the final triumph of his church over the hostile world. Ps 68 is the last in a series of four (see introduction to Ps 65–68).
68:1–3 The start of the procession, liturgically recalling the beginning of God's march with his people in army formation from Sinai (Nu 10:33–35).
68:3 *righteous.* Israel as the committed people of God in distinction from those opposed to the coming of God's kingdom (the "wicked" of v. 2); see 1:5 and note.
68:4 *who rides on the clouds.* An epithet of Baal found in Canaanite literature is used to make the point that the Lord (Yahweh, not Baal) is the exalted One who truly makes the storm cloud his chariot (v. 33; 18:9; 104:3; Dt 33:26; Isa 19:1; Mt 26:64).
68:5–6 God is the defender of the powerless (see 9:12 and note; 10:14; 146:7–9; 147:6; Dt 10:18).
68:6 *sets the lonely in families.* Brings them into the community of faith (see Ex 1:21; Ru 4:14–17; 1Sa 2:5). *leads out the prisoners.* As he led Israel out of Egypt (see 69:33; 107:10,14). *sun-scorched land.* A place utterly barren, lacking even soil for vegetation (Eze 26:4,14).
68:7–10 Recollection of God's march through the wilderness from Sinai into the promised land (Jdg 5:4–5; Hab 3:3–6).
68:8 *earth shook.* A reference to the quaking of Mount Sinai (Ex 19:18). *heavens poured down rain.* Here and in Jdg 5:4 rain is closely associated with the quaking of the earth as a manifestation of the majesty of God. Verse 9 suggests rain that refreshed the people on their journey.
68:10 *it.* Probably refers to the promised land. *bounty.* See 31:19 and note. *provided.* From the produce of Canaan (Jos 5:11–12). *poor.* Israel as a people dependent on God.
68:11–14 Recollection of God's victories over the kings of Canaan.
68:11 *announces the word.* God declares beforehand that he will be victorious over the Canaanite kings (Ex 23:22–23,27–28,31; Dt 7:10–24; 11:23–25; Jos 1:2–6). *women who proclaim it.* It seems that women were primarily

¹⁵Mount Bashan, majestic mountain,
  Mount Bashan, rugged mountain,
¹⁶why gaze in envy, you rugged mountain,
  at the mountain where God chooses to reign,
  where the LORD himself will dwell forever?
¹⁷The chariots of God are tens of thousands
  and thousands of thousands;
  the Lord has come from Sinai into his
    sanctuary.^a
¹⁸When you ascended on high,
  you took many captives;
  you received gifts from people,
  even from^b the rebellious —
  that you,^c LORD God, might dwell there.

¹⁹Praise be to the Lord, to God our Savior,
  who daily bears our burdens.
²⁰Our God is a God who saves;
  from the Sovereign LORD comes escape from
    death.
²¹Surely God will crush the heads of his enemies,
  the hairy crowns of those who go on in their
    sins.
²²The Lord says, "I will bring them from Bashan;
  I will bring them from the depths of the sea,
²³that your feet may wade in the blood of your foes,
  while the tongues of your dogs have their
    share."

²⁴Your procession, God, has come into view,
  the procession of my God and King into the
    sanctuary.
²⁵In front are the singers, after them the musicians;
  with them are the young women playing the
    timbrels.
²⁶Praise God in the great congregation;
  praise the LORD in the assembly of Israel.
²⁷There is the little tribe of Benjamin, leading
    them,
  there the great throng of Judah's princes,
  and there the princes of Zebulun and of Naphtali.

²⁸Summon your power, God^d;
  show us your strength, our God, as you have
    done before.
²⁹Because of your temple at Jerusalem
  kings will bring you gifts.
³⁰Rebuke the beast among the reeds,
  the herd of bulls among the calves of the
    nations.
  Humbled, may the beast bring bars of silver.
  Scatter the nations who delight in war.

---

^a 17 Probable reading of the original Hebrew text; Masoretic Text *Lord is among them at Sinai in holiness*   ^b 18 Or *gifts for people, / even*   ^c 18 Or *they*   ^d 28 Many Hebrew manuscripts, Septuagint and Syriac; most Hebrew manuscripts *Your God has summoned power for you*

responsible for singing Israel's songs of victory (see 40:9 and note; Ex 15:1–21; Jdg 5; 1Sa 18:6–7).

68:14 *Almighty.* See NIV text note. *like snow fallen on Mount Zalmon.* A mountain near Shechem bore this name (Jdg 9:46–48), but some identify the mountain referred to here as Jebel Druze, a dark volcanic mountain east of Bashan. Its name appears to mean "the dark one"—in distinction from the Lebanon ("the white one") range, composed of limestone—and the figure may involve the contrast of white snow scattered on "Dark Mountain." The reference may then be to abandoned weapons littering the field from which the kings have fled headlong (2Ki 7:15).

68:15–18 Celebration of God's ascent to Mount Zion.

68:15–16 The mountains surrounding Bashan, including the towering Mount Hermon, are portrayed as being jealous because God has chosen Mount Zion as the seat of his rule, making it the "highest" of mountains (see 48:2 and note).

68:17 *chariots of God.* God's great heavenly host, here likened to a vast chariot force (2Ki 6:17; Hab 3:8,15). In the time of the Roman Empire Jesus referred to God's host in terms of "legions" (Mt 26:53).

68:18 *that you . . . might dwell there.* Grammatically completes the clause, "When you ascended on high." Paul applies this verse (as translated in the Septuagint, the pre-Christian Greek translation of the OT) to the ascended Christ (see Eph 4:8–13), thereby implying that Christ's ascension was a continuation of, and a fulfillment of, God's establishment of his kingdom in his royal city, Jerusalem (see introduction to this psalm).

68:19–23 Joyous confession of hope that God's victorious campaigns will continue until the salvation of his people is complete.

68:19 *bears our burdens.* Releases us from bearing the burdens that enslavement to our enemies would impose on us (81:6; Isa 9:4; 10:27). But some associate this line with such passages as 55:22; Isa 46:4.

68:22 *them.* The enemies who fled at the victorious onward march of God and his host (vv. 12,17). *Bashan . . . depths of the sea.* The former (see also v. 15) was the high plateau east of the Jordan, the latter the Mediterranean Sea—none of the enemies will escape (Am 9:1–4).

68:27 All Israel is represented, from little Benjamin to powerful Judah, and tribes from the north as well as the south. *Benjamin, leading.* Perhaps reflecting the fact that from the tribe of Benjamin came the first king (Saul), who began the royal victories over Israel's enemies (1Sa 11:11; 14:20–23).

68:28–31 Prayer for God to continue his conquest of the threatening powers.

68:29 *Because of your temple.* Because God's earthly royal house has been established in Jerusalem in which his power and presence are evident. *bring you gifts.* Acknowledge you by bringing tribute, as subjected kings brought tribute to their conquerors (2Sa 8:2,6,10; 2Ki 3:4).

68:30 *beast among the reeds.* The pharaoh (Eze 29:3). *herd of bulls among the calves.* Powerful princes supporting the pharaoh, and the lesser princes of other nations. Egypt is singled out here as representative of the hostile nations—because of Israel's past experiences with that world power. It may also be that at the time the psalm

³¹Envoys will come from Egypt;
    Cush^a will submit herself to God.

³²Sing to God, you kingdoms of the earth,
    sing praise to the Lord,
³³to him who rides across the highest heavens,
    the ancient heavens,
    who thunders with mighty voice.
³⁴Proclaim the power of God,
    whose majesty is over Israel,
    whose power is in the heavens.
³⁵You, God, are awesome in your sanctuary;
    the God of Israel gives power and strength to
        his people.

Praise be to God!

Psalm 69^b

*For the director of music. To the
tune of "Lilies." Of David.*

¹Save me, O God,
    for the waters have come up to my
        neck.
²I sink in the miry depths,
    where there is no foothold.
I have come into the deep waters;
    the floods engulf me.
³I am worn out calling for help;
    my throat is parched.
My eyes fail,
    looking for my God.
⁴Those who hate me without reason
    outnumber the hairs of my head;
many are my enemies without cause,
    those who seek to destroy me.
I am forced to restore
    what I did not steal.

⁵You, God, know my folly;
    my guilt is not hidden from you.

⁶Lord, the LORD Almighty,
    may those who hope in you
    not be disgraced because of me;
God of Israel,
    may those who seek you
    not be put to shame because of me.
⁷For I endure scorn for your sake,
    and shame covers my face.
⁸I am a foreigner to my own family,
    a stranger to my own mother's children;
⁹for zeal for your house consumes me,
    and the insults of those who insult you fall
        on me.

---

^a *31* That is, the upper Nile region   ^b In Hebrew texts 69:1-36
is numbered 69:2-37.

---

was composed Egypt was the one great empire on Israel's immediate horizons. *Scatter the nations.* See v. 1; so that Israel may have peace (46:9; 48:4–7; 65:7; 76:3).

68:33 See v. 4 and note.

🌿 **68:35** *gives power and strength to his people.* The Lord of all has made Israel his people (his "kingdom"; see Ex 19:5–6), and his rule among them makes them participants in his victorious power (see 29:10–11; cf. Eph 1:17–23).

Ps 69–72 Book II of the Psalter closes with a cluster of three laments and an attached royal psalm—in perfect balance with its beginning (see note on Ps 42–45). These three lament psalms were originally all pleas of a king in Israel for deliverance from enemies (apparently internal) determined to do away with him. The attached prayer for the king (Ps 72) stands in similar relationship to Ps 69–71 as Ps 45 stands to Ps 42–44 and brings Book II to its conclusion.

🌿 **Ps 69** A lament psalm that appeals to God to have mercy and to save from a host of enemies: the prayer of a godly king when under vicious attack by a widespread conspiracy at a time when God had wounded him (v. 26) for some sin in his life (v. 5). If, as tradition claims, David authored the original psalm (see title), the occasion is unknown. The authors of the NT viewed this cry of a godly sufferer as foreshadowing the sufferings of Christ; no other psalm, except Ps 22, is quoted more frequently in the NT.

69 title *For the director of music.* See note on Ps 4 title. *Lilies.* See note on Ps 45 title.

69:1–4 Description of the dire distress that evokes the psalmist's complaint.

69:1–2 *waters . . . miry depths . . . deep waters . . . floods.* Conventional imagery for great distress (see notes on 30:1; 32:6)—here the results of God's wounding (v. 26), but especially of the attacks of the enemies (vv. 14–15,29).

69:3 *throat is parched.* See 22:15.

69:4 *without reason . . . without cause.* Those whom he has not wronged are pitted against him. *outnumber the hairs of my head.* See note on 40:12. *I am forced.* An illustrative way of saying that his enemies are spreading false accusations about him (see 5:9 and note).

69:5 A confession of personal guilt—the reason why God has wounded him (v. 26) and why he is "afflicted and in pain" (v. 29). *folly.* See NIV text note on 14:1.

69:6–12 Prayer that God's discipline of his godly servant may not bring disgrace on all those who trustingly look to the Lord. The author acknowledges that God's wounding of him has been occasioned by some sin in his life (but he has not sinned against those who have become his enemies). Because of his present suffering, his enemies mock his deep commitment to the Lord (22:6–8; 42:3; 79:10; 115:2; Job 2:9). Implicitly he prays that God will restore him again and vindicate his trust in him.

69:8 Even those nearest him dissociate themselves from him (see 31:11–12 and note).

🌿 **69:9** *zeal for your house.* The psalmist's concern for God's honor also characterized Jesus (Jn 2:17). *insults of those who insult you.* Those who mock God also mock his servant who trusts in him (74:18,22–23; 2Ki 18:31–35), as Christ experienced (Ro 15:3).

¹⁰When I weep and fast,
    I must endure scorn;
¹¹when I put on sackcloth,
    people make sport of me.
¹²Those who sit at the gate mock me,
    and I am the song of the drunkards.

¹³But I pray to you, LORD,
    in the time of your favor;
in your great love, O God,
    answer me with your sure salvation.
¹⁴Rescue me from the mire,
    do not let me sink;
deliver me from those who hate me,
    from the deep waters.
¹⁵Do not let the floodwaters engulf me
    or the depths swallow me up
    or the pit close its mouth over me.

¹⁶Answer me, LORD, out of the goodness of your
    love;
    in your great mercy turn to me.
¹⁷Do not hide your face from your servant;
    answer me quickly, for I am in trouble.
¹⁸Come near and rescue me;
    deliver me because of my foes.

¹⁹You know how I am scorned, disgraced and
    shamed;
    all my enemies are before you.
²⁰Scorn has broken my heart
    and has left me helpless;
I looked for sympathy, but there was none,
    for comforters, but I found none.
²¹They put gall in my food
    and gave me vinegar for my thirst.

²²May the table set before them become a snare;
    may it become retribution and^a a trap.
²³May their eyes be darkened so they cannot see,
    and their backs be bent forever.
²⁴Pour out your wrath on them;
    let your fierce anger overtake them.
²⁵May their place be deserted;
    let there be no one to dwell in their tents.
²⁶For they persecute those you wound
    and talk about the pain of those you hurt.
²⁷Charge them with crime upon crime;
    do not let them share in your salvation.
²⁸May they be blotted out of the book of life
    and not be listed with the righteous.

²⁹But as for me, afflicted and in pain —
    may your salvation, God, protect me.

³⁰I will praise God's name in song
    and glorify him with thanksgiving.

^a 22 Or snare / and their fellowship become

69:10–11 *weep and fast . . . put on sackcloth.* As tokens of humbling himself before the Lord in repentance as he prays for God to have mercy and restore him (see 35:13 and note; see also Ge 37:34; 2Sa 12:16–17; Joel 1:13–14; 2:15–17; Jnh 3:5).
69:12 *Those who sit at the gate . . . drunkards.* Everyone, from the elders of the city to the town drunks.
69:13–15 Though they mock, I pray to you.
69:13 *time of your favor.* When God is near to save (see 32:6 and note; see also Isa 49:8; 61:2; 2Co 6:2). *great love.* See article, p. 16.
69:14–15 *mire . . . deep waters . . . floodwaters . . . depths.* See note on vv. 1–2. The psalmists' petitions commonly echo their earlier descriptions of the distress that occasions the prayer. Here the return to the beginning marks the end of the first half of the psalmist's appeal to God.
69:15 *swallow me.* See note on 49:14. *pit.* See note on 30:1.
69:16–18 An appeal for God to hear—such as commonly begins the prayers brought together in the Psalter.
69:16 *love.* See article, p. 16.
69:17 *hide your face.* See note on 13:1.
69:19–21 In my trouble they heaped on scorn instead of bringing comfort (see 35:11–16; see also 142:4; Job 13:4; 16:2; 21:34).
69:20 *heart.* See note on 4:7.
🌿 **69:21** *gall in my food . . . vinegar for my thirst.* Vivid metaphors for the bitter scorn they made him eat and drink when his whole being craved the nourishment and refreshment of comfort. The authors of the Gospels, especially Matthew, suggest that the suffering expressed in this verse foreshadowed Christ's suffering on the cross (Mt 27:34,48; Mk 15:23,36; Lk 23:36; Jn 19:29).
69:22–23 For Paul's application of these verses to the Jews who rejected the Christ, see Ro 11:9–10.
69:22 They had set his table with "gall" and "vinegar" (v. 21). *table set before them.* Reference may be to the meal accompanying the sealing of a covenant (see note on 23:5). In that case, this verse alludes to a pact uniting the enemies and calls on God to turn it against them. *become a snare . . . a trap.* Note the unusual use of this imagery (see note on 9:15).
69:23 They mocked him for his "wound" (v. 26); now may they experience the same failing of the eyes (see v. 3) and bending of the back (from weakness and pain; see 38:5–8).
69:24 *overtake them.* Like a flash flood.
69:25 They sought to remove him from his place; may they be removed. Cf. Peter's application of this judgment to Judas (Ac 1:20).
69:26 The great wrong committed by his enemies against him and to which reference has repeatedly been made.
69:27 They have falsely charged him with crimes (v. 4); may their real crimes all be charged against them.
69:28 They had plotted his death; may death be their destiny. *book of life.* God's royal list of the righteous, whom he blesses with life (1:3; 7:9; 11:7; 34:12; 37:17,29; 55:22; 75:10; 92:12–14; 140:13). For other references to God's books see note on 51:1. In the NT the "book of life" refers to God's list of those destined for eternal life (see Php 4:3; Rev 3:5; 13:8; 17:8; 20:12,15; 21:27; cf. Lk 10:20; Heb 12:23).
69:29 A summary renewal of the prayer just prior to the

³¹ This will please the LORD more than an ox,
  more than a bull with its horns and hooves.
³² The poor will see and be glad—
  you who seek God, may your hearts live!
³³ The LORD hears the needy
  and does not despise his captive people.

³⁴ Let heaven and earth praise him,
  the seas and all that move in them,
³⁵ for God will save Zion
  and rebuild the cities of Judah.
Then people will settle there and possess it;
³⁶   the children of his servants will inherit it,
  and those who love his name will dwell there.

Psalm 70ᵃ

For the director of music. Of David. A petition.

¹ Hasten, O God, to save me;
  come quickly, LORD, to help me.

² May those who want to take my life
  be put to shame and confusion;
may all who desire my ruin
  be turned back in disgrace.
³ May those who say to me, "Aha! Aha!"
  turn back because of their shame.
⁴ But may all who seek you
  rejoice and be glad in you;
may those who long for your saving help
    always say,
  "The LORD is great!"

⁵ But as for me, I am poor and needy;
  come quickly to me, O God.
You are my help and my deliverer;
  LORD, do not delay.

ᵃ In Hebrew texts 70:1-5 is numbered 70:2-6.

vow to praise God (see note on v. 5). *pain.* An echo of v. 26. *your salvation.* Cf. vv. 13,27. *protect me.* See note on Ps 59:1.

69:30–33 A vow to praise God (see note on 7:17) out of assurance that the prayer will be heard (see note on 3:8).

69:32 *poor.* See note on 34:6. *see and be glad.* See 22:26 and note. *hearts.* See note on 4:7. *live.* Overflow with the joy of life, because the Lord does hear the prayers of his people in need—contrary to the mocking of scoffers.

69:34–36 A call for all creation to take up the praise of the Lord (see note on 9:1), a call that confidently anticipates that God will restore Judah and assure his people's inheritance in the promised land.

69:34 See 148:1–13; Isa 49:13.

69:35–36 *people . . . children.* God's people and their children through the generations, specifically "those who love his name."

69:35 *Zion.* See note on 9:11.

Ps 70 A lament when threatened by enemies—a somewhat revised duplicate of 40:13–17. This is the second in a series of three such laments; its language has many links with that of Ps 71. For this psalm's placement in the Psalter, see introduction to Ps 69–72; for its special relationship to Ps 71, see introduction to that psalm. The psalm is framed by pleas for God to "come quickly" with his help (vv. 1,5). The rest of the psalm focuses on the effects of God's saving help: (1) upon those "who want to take my life" (vv. 2–3) and (2) for those "who seek you" (v. 4).

70 title See note on Ps 4 title. *A petition.* See note on Ps 38 title.

70:4 God's deliverance of his servant will give joy to all who trust in the Lord, because they see in it the assurance of their own salvation. *The LORD is great!* Because his saving help is sure and effective (contrast v. 3).

70:5 The language of this verse forms a frame with v. 1: "God," "LORD," "come quickly," "(my) help (me)." *poor and needy.* See note on 35:10.

List some of your favorite verses from the psalms.

_____

_____

_____

_____

_____

_____

_____

▶ What does Psalm 63 teach you about continuing to pray to God throughout the day?

_____

_____

_____

_____

_____

▶ Psalm 65 describes God's blessings as the abundance in nature. What metaphors would you use to describe God's blessings in your life?

_____

_____

_____

_____

_____

▶ What biblical events does Psalm 66 point to?

_____

_____

_____

_____

_____

▶ How does the psalmist envision God in Psalm 68?

_____

_____

_____

_____

_____

Psalm 71

¹ In you, LORD, I have taken refuge;
　　let me never be put to shame.
² In your righteousness, rescue me and deliver me;
　　turn your ear to me and save me.
³ Be my rock of refuge,
　　to which I can always go;
　give the command to save me,
　　for you are my rock and my fortress.
⁴ Deliver me, my God, from the hand of the
　　wicked,
　　from the grasp of those who are evil and
　　　cruel.

⁵ For you have been my hope, Sovereign LORD,
　　my confidence since my youth.
⁶ From birth I have relied on you;
　　you brought me forth from my mother's
　　　womb.
　I will ever praise you.
⁷ I have become a sign to many;
　　you are my strong refuge.
⁸ My mouth is filled with your praise,
　　declaring your splendor all day long.

⁹ Do not cast me away when I am old;
　　do not forsake me when my strength
　　　is gone.
¹⁰ For my enemies speak against me;
　　those who wait to kill me conspire
　　　together.
¹¹ They say, "God has forsaken him;
　　pursue him and seize him,
　　　for no one will rescue him."
¹² Do not be far from me, my God;
　　come quickly, God, to help me.
¹³ May my accusers perish in shame;
　　may those who want to harm me
　　　be covered with scorn and disgrace.

¹⁴ As for me, I will always have hope;
　　I will praise you more and more.

¹⁵ My mouth will tell of your righteous deeds,
　　of your saving acts all day long—
　　　though I know not how to relate them all.
¹⁶ I will come and proclaim your mighty acts,
　　Sovereign LORD;
　　I will proclaim your righteous deeds, yours
　　　alone.

Ps 71 A lament in old age when enemies threaten because they see that the king's strength is waning (see note on 5:9). The psalm bears no title, but it may well be that Ps 70 was viewed by the editors of the Psalms as the introduction to Ps 71 (compare vv. 1,12–13 with 70:1–2,5), in which case the psalm is ascribed to David (in his old age; see vv. 9,18). This suggestion gains support from the fact that Ps 72 is identified as written by or for King Solomon (see introduction to that psalm). This is the third in a series of three laments (see introduction to Ps 69–72); its dominant theme is hope (v. 14). Formally symmetrical, the psalm is composed of six stanzas, having a five-four-five, five-four-five line pattern (in Hebrew): vv. 1–4 (five lines), vv. 5–8 (four lines), vv. 9–13 (five lines), vv. 15–18 (five lines), vv. 19–21 (four lines), vv. 22–24 (five lines). Thus each half is made up of 14 lines. At the center (v. 14; see note on 6:6) stands a confident confession of hope. The whole is framed by an appeal for help (vv. 1–4) and a vow to praise God in anticipation of deliverance (vv. 22–24). The second and fifth stanzas are linked by references to the troubles the king has experienced; stanzas three and four are linked by references to old age.
71:1–4 The initial appeal for God's help. Verses 1–3 differ only a little from 31:1–3a.
71:2 *your righteousness.* See vv. 15–16,19,24; see also note on 4:1.
71:3 *give the command to save.* In Hebrew a noteworthy verbal link with 44:4 ("who decrees victories"). The Hebrew phraseology occurs only in these two places in the OT.
71:5–8 A confession that the Lord has always been his hope (vv. 14,19–21).
71:5–6 Cf. 22:10–11.
71:7 *sign to many.* The troubles of his life (v. 20) have been viewed by others as holding some special significance—especially since the Lord has been his "strong refuge" through them all.
71:8 *My mouth is filled with your praise . . . your splendor.* Because of the Lord's faithful care, the psalmist has been moved to fulfill in his life the high purpose of God in saving and blessing his people (Jer 13:11; 33:9).
71:9–13 A prayer for God's continuing help in the waning years of the psalmist's life.
71:10 *enemies speak against me.* See notes on 3:2; 5:9.
71:12 *Do not be far from me.* Cf. 22:11,19; 35:22; 38:21. *come quickly . . . to help me.* Cf. 22:19; 38:22; 40:13; 70:1; cf. also 70:5; 141:1.
71:13 A plea for redress (see note on 5:10). Key words in this closing verse of the first half of the psalm are echoed in the last verse of the second half. Similar language is found in 35:4,26; 40:14–15; 70:2–3; 83:17; 109:28–29.
71:14 A centered confession of unfaltering hope—providing a striking link with Ps 42–43 (see 42:8 and note; see also note on 6:6).

¹⁷ Since my youth, God, you have taught me,
    and to this day I declare your marvelous
      deeds.
¹⁸ Even when I am old and gray,
    do not forsake me, my God,
  till I declare your power to the next
      generation,
    your mighty acts to all who are to come.

¹⁹ Your righteousness, God, reaches to the
      heavens,
    you who have done great things.
    Who is like you, God?
²⁰ Though you have made me see troubles,
    many and bitter,
    you will restore my life again;
  from the depths of the earth
    you will again bring me up.
²¹ You will increase my honor
    and comfort me once more.

²² I will praise you with the harp
    for your faithfulness, my God;
  I will sing praise to you with the lyre,
    Holy One of Israel.
²³ My lips will shout for joy
    when I sing praise to you —
    I whom you have delivered.
²⁴ My tongue will tell of your righteous acts
    all day long,
  for those who wanted to harm me
    have been put to shame and confusion.

Psalm 72

Of Solomon.

¹ Endow the king with your justice, O God,
    the royal son with your righteousness.
² May he judge your people in
      righteousness,
    your afflicted ones with justice.

³ May the mountains bring prosperity to the
      people,
    the hills the fruit of righteousness.
⁴ May he defend the afflicted among the
      people
    and save the children of the needy;
    may he crush the oppressor.
⁵ May he endure^a as long as the sun,
    as long as the moon, through all
      generations.
⁶ May he be like rain falling on a mown
      field,
    like showers watering the earth.

^a 5 Septuagint; Hebrew *You will be feared*

71:15–18 A vow to praise God, accompanying the renewal of his prayer (v. 18); see note on 7:17.
71:15 *tell . . . righteous deeds . . . saving acts.* Here one of the "righteous deeds" the psalmist vows to "tell" is God's act of deliverance in answer to the psalmist's prayer (see notes on vv. 16–17; 4:1).
71:16–17 *mighty acts . . . righteous deeds . . . marvelous deeds.* God's "mighty (marvelous) acts" in behalf of his people are expressions of his righteousness; see also his "righteous acts" (v. 24).
71:16 *come.* To the place where God's people assemble for worship.
71:19–21 A confession that the Lord is still his hope, in the face of all his troubles (vv. 5–8,14).
71:19 *reaches to the heavens.* Is as expansive as all space above the earth (see also 36:5 and note). *Who is like you, God?* See Mic 7:18.
71:20 *you have made me see troubles.* The "troubles" referred to are not specified. That God is somehow involved the psalmist does not question; he shares the mature and robust faith that all things are in the hands of the one sovereign God (see Dt 6:4), the God to whom he turns in prayer (cf. 1Sa 16:11–12; Isa 45:5–7; Am 3:6). *restore my life again.* He who gave him life (v. 6) will renew his life. *depths of the earth.* The realm of the dead, of which the grave is the portal (see note on 30:1).
71:22–24 A vow to praise in confident anticipation of God's saving help (see notes on 3:8; 7:17).
71:22 *harp . . . lyre.* See note on 57:8. *Holy One of Israel.* See 78:41; 89:18; see also 2Ki 19:22.
71:24 *righteous acts.* God's saving acts in behalf of his people according to his covenant promises (see 88:12; Jdg 5:11; 1Sa 12:7; Da 9:16; Mic 6:5; Rev 15:4).
Ps 72 A prayer for the king, a son of David who rules on David's throne as God's earthly regent over his people. It may have been used at the time of the king's coronation (as were Ps 2; 110). These verses express the desire of the nation that the king's reign will, as a consequence of God's endowment of his servant, be characterized by justice and righteousness, the supreme virtues of kingship. The prayer reflects the ideal concept of the king and the glorious effects of his reign. See Jeremiah's indictment of some of the last Davidic kings (e.g., Jer 22:2–3,13,15) and the prophetic announcement of the Messiah's righteous rule (Isa 9:7; 11:4–5; Jer 23:5–6; 33:15–16; Zec 9:9). Later Jewish tradition saw in this psalm a description of the Messiah, as did the early church. The last three verses do not belong to the prayer (see notes there). For this psalm's function within Book II of the Psalter, see introduction to Ps 69–72.
72 title *Of Solomon.* Either by him or for him—of course, both may be true. This psalm was probably also used by Israel (Judah) as a prayer for later Davidic kings.
72:1 The basic prayer. *justice . . . righteousness.* May the king be endowed with the gift for and the love of justice and righteousness so that his reign reflects the rule of God himself. Solomon asked for the necessary wisdom so he could govern God's people justly (see 1Ki 3:9,11–12; see also Pr 16:12). *righteousness.* See note on 4:1.
72:2–7 A prayer for the quality of his reign: May it be righteous, prosperous and enduring.

⁷In his days may the righteous flourish
  and prosperity abound till the moon is
    no more.

⁸May he rule from sea to sea
  and from the River*ᵃ* to the ends of the earth.
⁹May the desert tribes bow before him
  and his enemies lick the dust.
¹⁰May the kings of Tarshish and of distant shores
    bring tribute to him.
  May the kings of Sheba and Seba
    present him gifts.
¹¹May all kings bow down to him
  and all nations serve him.

¹²For he will deliver the needy who cry out,
  the afflicted who have no one to help.
¹³He will take pity on the weak and the needy
  and save the needy from death.
¹⁴He will rescue them from oppression and
    violence,
  for precious is their blood in his sight.

¹⁵Long may he live!
  May gold from Sheba be given him.
  May people ever pray for him
  and bless him all day long.
¹⁶May grain abound throughout the land;
  on the tops of the hills may it sway.
  May the crops flourish like Lebanon
  and thrive*ᵇ* like the grass of the field.
¹⁷May his name endure forever;
  may it continue as long as the sun.

  Then all nations will be blessed through him,*ᶜ*
  and they will call him blessed.

¹⁸Praise be to the LORD God, the God of Israel,
  who alone does marvelous deeds.
¹⁹Praise be to his glorious name forever;
  may the whole earth be filled with his glory.
    Amen and Amen.

²⁰This concludes the prayers of David son of Jesse.

BOOK III

Psalms 73 – 89

Psalm 73

A psalm of Asaph.

¹Surely God is good to Israel,
  to those who are pure in heart.

ᵃ 8 That is, the Euphrates   *ᵇ 16* Probable reading of the
original Hebrew text; Masoretic Text *Lebanon, / from the city*
ᶜ 17 Or *will use his name in blessings* (see Gen. 48:20)

72:3 Righteousness in the realm will be like fertilizing rain on the land, for then the Lord will bless his people with abundance (vv. 6–7; 5:12; 65:9–13; 133:3; Lev 25:19; Dt 28:8).
72:5 *endure as long as the sun.* See 21:4 and note.
72:6 See v. 3 and note; see also v. 7.
72:7 *righteous.* See note on 1:5. *flourish.* Because the king supports and protects them and uses all his royal power to suppress the wicked (Ps 101).
72:8–14 The extent of his domain (vv. 8–11) as the result of his righteous rule (vv. 12–14).
72:8 May his kingdom and authority extend to all the world (see vv. 9–11; cf. 110:2 and note). Ideally and potentially, as God's earthly regent, he possesses royal authority that extends on earth as far as God's—an expectation that is fulfilled in Christ. See Zec 9:10.
72:9 May the tribes of the Arabian Desert to the east yield to him. *lick the dust.* See Mic 7:17.
72:10 May the kings whose lands border the Mediterranean Sea to the west acknowledge him as lord, as well as those who rule in south Arabia and along the eastern African coast. *Tarshish.* A distant Mediterranean seaport, perhaps as far west as modern Spain. *Seba.* Elsewhere in the OT associated with Cush (Ge 10:7; Isa 43:3); it may refer to a region in modern Sudan, south of Egypt.
72:15–17 Concluding summation: May the king enjoy a long, prosperous, world-renowned reign—one that blesses all the nations.
72:17 *all nations.* The language recalls the promise to Abraham (Ge 12:3; 22:18) and suggests that it will be fulfilled through the royal son of David—ultimately the Messiah.
72:18–19 A doxology at the conclusion of Book II of the Psalter (see 41:13 and note). It is the people's response, their "Amen," to the contents of Book II.
72:19 *filled with his glory.* See note on 85:9.
72:20 An editorial notation. *prayers of David.* See titles of Ps 86; 142.
Ps 73–78 Book III consists of three groupings of psalms, having an overall symmetrical pattern (six psalms [73–78], five psalms [79–83], six psalms [84–89]) and at its center (Ps 81) an urgent exhortation to fundamental covenant loyalty to the Lord (see introduction to Ps 79–83, introduction to Ps 84–89 and introduction to Ps 81).
Ps 73 A word of godly wisdom concerning the destinies of the righteous and the wicked. Placed at the beginning of Book III, this psalm voices the faith (confessed [v. 1], tested [vv. 2–26] and reaffirmed [vv. 27–28]) that undergirds the following collection. It serves in Book III as Ps 1–2 serve in Book I (see introduction to Ps 1–2). Here the psalmist addresses one of the most disturbing problems of the OT people of God: How is it that the wicked so often prosper while the godly suffer so much? Thematically the psalm has many links with Ps 49 (see introduction to that psalm; see also Ps 37).
73 title The psalm is ascribed to Asaph, leader of one of David's three Levitical choirs (the other two leaders were Heman and Jeduthun/Ethan; these three represented the families and descendants of the three sons of Levi; see notes on Ps 39; 42; 50 titles). It begins a collection of 11 Asaphite psalms (Ps 73–83), to which Ps 50 at one time probably belonged. In view of the fact that the collection

² But as for me, my feet had almost slipped;
  I had nearly lost my foothold.
³ For I envied the arrogant
  when I saw the prosperity of the wicked.

⁴ They have no struggles;
  their bodies are healthy and strong.*a*
⁵ They are free from common human burdens;
  they are not plagued by human ills.
⁶ Therefore pride is their necklace;
  they clothe themselves with violence.
⁷ From their callous hearts comes iniquity*b*;
  their evil imaginations have no limits.
⁸ They scoff, and speak with malice;
  with arrogance they threaten oppression.
⁹ Their mouths lay claim to heaven,
  and their tongues take possession of the earth.
¹⁰ Therefore their people turn to them
  and drink up waters in abundance.*c*
¹¹ They say, "How would God know?
  Does the Most High know anything?"

¹² This is what the wicked are like —
  always free of care, they go on amassing
    wealth.

¹³ Surely in vain I have kept my heart pure
  and have washed my hands in innocence.
¹⁴ All day long I have been afflicted,
  and every morning brings new
    punishments.

¹⁵ If I had spoken out like that,
  I would have betrayed your children.
¹⁶ When I tried to understand all this,
  it troubled me deeply
¹⁷ till I entered the sanctuary of God;
  then I understood their final destiny.

¹⁸ Surely you place them on slippery ground;
  you cast them down to ruin.
¹⁹ How suddenly are they destroyed,
  completely swept away by terrors!
²⁰ They are like a dream when one awakes;
  when you arise, Lord,
  you will despise them as fantasies.

²¹ When my heart was grieved
  and my spirit embittered,
²² I was senseless and ignorant;
  I was a brute beast before you.

²³ Yet I am always with you;
  you hold me by my right hand.

---

a 4 With a different word division of the Hebrew; Masoretic
Text *struggles at their death; / their bodies are healthy*
b 7 Syriac (see also Septuagint); Hebrew *Their eyes bulge with
fat*   *c* 10 The meaning of the Hebrew for this verse is
uncertain.

clearly contains prayers from a later date (e.g., Ps 74; 79; 83), references to Asaph in these titles must sometimes include descendants of Asaph who functioned in his place (see note on Ps 50 title; see also 1Ch 25:1-2,6-9; 2Ch 29:30). The Asaphite psalms are dominated by the theme of God's rule over his people and the nations.

73:1 *God is good to Israel.* The goodness of God to his people is a recurring theme in Scripture (1Ch 16:34; Ps 13:6; 106:1; 107:1; 118:1,29; 136:1; cf. also Ro 8:28; Eph 1:9; Php 2:13; 1Ti 4:4; 1Pe 2:3; 2Pe 1:3). *pure in heart.* See v. 13; see also note on 24:4. *heart.* See note on 4:7.

73:4–12 A description of the prosperous state of the wicked and the haughty self-reliance such prosperity engenders. It is the exaggerated picture that envious and troubled eyes perceived (see the description of the wicked in 10:2–11; cf. Job's anguished portrayal of the prosperity of the wicked in Job 21).

73:13–14 The thoughts that plagued the psalmist when he compared the state of the wicked with his own troubled lot.

73:15–28 The renewal of faith: In the temple, where God's ways are celebrated and taught, the psalmist sees the destiny God has appointed for the wicked (v. 17).

73:15 *If I had spoken out like that.* If the psalmist had given public expression to his thoughts as embodying true insight. *your children.* Those characterized by a humble reliance on and commitment to God.

73:17 *till I entered the sanctuary of God.* The crucial turning point (see note on vv. 15–28). Communion with God solves many problems.

73:18–20 Though the wicked seem to prosper, God has made their position precarious; without warning they are swept away. The psalmist does not reflect on their state after death but leaves it as his final word that the wicked fall utterly and inevitably from their state of proud prosperity (see Ps 49; cf. the final state of the godly in v. 24).

> Was there a time in your faith journey when your faith wavered? What did you do?

_____

_____

_____

_____

_____

_____

_____

_____

²⁴You guide me with your counsel,
and afterward you will take me into glory.
²⁵Whom have I in heaven but you?
And earth has nothing I desire besides you.
²⁶My flesh and my heart may fail,
but God is the strength of my heart
and my portion forever.

²⁷Those who are far from you will perish;
you destroy all who are unfaithful to you.
²⁸But as for me, it is good to be near God.
I have made the Sovereign LORD my refuge;
I will tell of all your deeds.

Psalm 74

A maskil^a of Asaph.

¹O God, why have you rejected us forever?
Why does your anger smolder against the
sheep of your pasture?
²Remember the nation you purchased long ago,
the people of your inheritance, whom you
redeemed —
Mount Zion, where you dwelt.
³Turn your steps toward these everlasting ruins,
all this destruction the enemy has brought
on the sanctuary.

⁴Your foes roared in the place where you met
with us;
they set up their standards as signs.
⁵They behaved like men wielding axes
to cut through a thicket of trees.
⁶They smashed all the carved paneling
with their axes and hatchets.
⁷They burned your sanctuary to the ground;
they defiled the dwelling place of your Name.
⁸They said in their hearts, "We will crush them
completely!"
They burned every place where God was
worshiped in the land.

⁹We are given no signs from God;
no prophets are left,
and none of us knows how long this will be.
¹⁰How long will the enemy mock you, God?
Will the foe revile your name forever?
¹¹Why do you hold back your hand, your right hand?
Take it from the folds of your garment and
destroy them!

¹²But God is my King from long ago;
he brings salvation on the earth.

¹³It was you who split open the sea by your power;
you broke the heads of the monster in the
waters.

^a Title: Probably a literary or musical term

73:20 When God arouses himself as from sleep (see note on 7:6) and deals with the wicked, they vanish like the shadowy characters of a dream.

73:23–26 Although the psalmist had (almost) fallen to the level of beastly ignorance, God has not, will not, let him go—ever!

73:24 God's counsel has overcome the psalmist's folly and will guide him through all the pitfalls of life (16:7; 32:8; 107:11). *take me into glory.* At the end of the believer's pilgrimage on earth (see 49:15 and note).

73:25 Though he has envied the prosperity of the wicked, he now confesses that nothing in heaven or earth is more desirable than God.

73:26 *My flesh . . . heart.* My whole being (see 84:2). *strength.* Or "rock" (cf. 18:2 and note; 19:14). *portion.* Since the psalmist was a Levite, the Lord was his portion in the promised land in that he lived by the people's tithes dedicated to the Lord (Nu 18:21–24; Dt 10:9; 18:1–2). But here he confesses more—what every godly Israelite could confess: The Lord himself is the sustainer and pre- server of the life of those who put their trust in him (see note on 16:5–6).

73:27 *all who are unfaithful.* Or "all who commit (spiritual) prostitution/adultery" Although this expression else- where refers to blatant idolatry (as, e.g., in Dt 31:16; Jer 2:20; Hos 2:5) or to political alliance with any world power rather than relying on the Lord for security (as, e.g., in Eze 16:26–29), here it refers to the reliance of the wicked on their predatory economic and political practices, the "violence" with which they accumulated their wealth at the expense of others (vv. 6–11).

Ps 74 A lament asking God to come to the aid of his peo- ple and defend his cause in the face of the mocking of the enemies—the Lord's relation to his people is like that of a king to his nation. The psalm dates from the time of the exile, when Israel had been destroyed as a nation, the promised land devastated and the temple reduced to ruins (Ps 79; La 2). Its relationship to the ministries of Jeremiah and Ezekiel is uncertain.

74:2 *purchased.* Or "acquired" or "created" (see Ex 15:16). *your inheritance.* See Dt 9:29. *redeemed.* Here, as often, a synonym for "delivered." *Mount Zion.* See note on 9:11. This verse recalls the victory song of Ex 15 (see especially vv. 13–17, and compare the center verse of this psalm, v. 12, with the last verse of the song, Ex 15:18) and thus sets the stage for the other exodus recollections that follow. The Babylonian destruction of Zion seems to be the undoing of God's great victory over Egypt when he redeemed his people.

74:3 *Turn your steps toward.* Hurry to restore.

74:4 *standards.* Probably troop standards (Nu 1:52; Isa 31:9; Jer 4:21). See photo, p. 99. *as signs.* Signifying their triumph.

74:7 The NIV capitalizes "Name" when it stands for God's presence at the sanctuary (Dt 12:5).

74:9–11 The complaint and prayer renewed (vv. 1–2).

74:12 The center verse (center line in the Hebrew text; see note on 6:6). The whole psalm presupposes the truth confessed here: God is Israel's King, their hope and Savior; Israel is God's people (kingdom). This ac- counts for both the complaint and the prayer, and why the destruction of Israel brings with it the mocking of

Standards held and raised by Egyptian soldiers on the wall of the temple of Hatshepsut, Egypt. Ps 74:4 says "they set up their standards as signs."

© 2018 by Zondervan

¹⁴ It was you who crushed the heads of
　　Leviathan
　　and gave it as food to the creatures of the
　　　desert.
¹⁵ It was you who opened up springs and
　　streams;
　　you dried up the ever-flowing rivers.
¹⁶ The day is yours, and yours also the night;
　　you established the sun and moon.
¹⁷ It was you who set all the boundaries of the
　　earth;
　　you made both summer and winter.

¹⁸ Remember how the enemy has mocked you,
　　Lord,
　　how foolish people have reviled your
　　　name.
¹⁹ Do not hand over the life of your dove to wild
　　beasts;
　　do not forget the lives of your afflicted
　　　people forever.

God. *my.* Communal use of the singular pronoun (see note on Ps 30 title). *from long ago.* From the days of the exodus (Ex 3:7; 19:5–6).

🌿 **74:13–17** The Lord is the mighty God of salvation and creation (see 65:6–7 and note).

🛡🌿 **74:13–14** Recollection of God's mighty acts when he delivered his people from Egypt. The imagery is borrowed from ancient Near Eastern creation myths, in which the primeval chaotic waters were depicted as a many-headed monster that the creator-god overcame, after which he established the world order (see note on 32:6). The poet here interweaves creation and salvation themes to celebrate the fact that the God of Israel has shown by his saving acts (his opening of the Red Sea for his people and his destruction of the Egyptians) that he is able to overcome all hostile powers to redeem his people and establish his new order in the world. For poetic use of this imagery (1) to celebrate God's creation works, see 89:10; Job 9:13; 26:12–13; (2) to celebrate the deliverance from Egypt, see Isa 51:9; (3) to announce a future deliverance of Israel, see Isa 27:1. Echoes of the same imagery are present in the judgment announced against Egypt in Eze 29:3–5; 32:2–6.

20 Have regard for your covenant,
    because haunts of violence fill the dark
        places of the land.
21 Do not let the oppressed retreat in disgrace;
    may the poor and needy praise your name.
22 Rise up, O God, and defend your cause;
    remember how fools mock you all day long.
23 Do not ignore the clamor of your adversaries,
    the uproar of your enemies, which rises
        continually.

Psalm 75[a]

*For the director of music. To the tune of "Do
Not Destroy." A psalm of Asaph. A song.*

1 We praise you, God,
    we praise you, for your Name is near;
    people tell of your wonderful deeds.

2 You say, "I choose the appointed time;
    it is I who judge with equity.
3 When the earth and all its people quake,
    it is I who hold its pillars firm.[b]
4 To the arrogant I say, 'Boast no more,'
    and to the wicked, 'Do not lift up your
        horns.[c]
5 Do not lift your horns against heaven;
    do not speak so defiantly.'"

6 No one from the east or the west
    or from the desert can exalt themselves.
7 It is God who judges:
    He brings one down, he exalts another.
8 In the hand of the LORD is a cup
    full of foaming wine mixed with spices;
    he pours it out, and all the wicked of the earth
        drink it down to its very dregs.

9 As for me, I will declare this forever;
    I will sing praise to the God of Jacob,
10 who says, "I will cut off the horns of all the
        wicked,
    but the horns of the righteous will be lifted up."

Psalm 76[d]

*For the director of music. With stringed
instruments. A psalm of Asaph. A song.*

1 God is renowned in Judah;
    in Israel his name is great.
2 His tent is in Salem,
    his dwelling place in Zion.

---

[a] In Hebrew texts 75:1-10 is numbered 75:2-11.   [b] 3 The
Hebrew has *Selah* (a word of uncertain meaning) here.
[c] 4 *Horns* here symbolize strength; also in verses 5 and 10.
[d] In Hebrew texts 76:1-12 is numbered 76:2-13.

74:15 Recollection of God's water miracles at the "Red Sea," in the wilderness and at the Jordan.

74:16–17 God is the One who established the orders of creation; he (alone) is able to effect redemption and establish his kingdom in the world against all creaturely opposition.

74:18–23 A prayer for God to defend his cause and restore his people.

74:20 *your covenant.* God's covenant to be the God of Israel, the one who makes his people secure and richly blessed in the promised land (see Ex 19:5–6; 23:27–31; 34:10–11; Lev 26:11–12,42,44–45; Dt 28:1–14; see also Ps 105:8–11; 106:45; 111:5,9; Isa 54:10; Jer 14:21; Eze 16:60).

Ps 75 A hymn expressing confidence in God when arrogant worldly powers threaten Israel's security. The psalm may date from the time of the Assyrian menace (see 2Ki 18:13—19:37). See also Ps 11; 76. Thematic parallels to the song of Hannah (1Sa 2:1–10) are numerous. The worshiping congregation speaks (v. 1), perhaps led in its praise by one of the descendants of Asaph (v. 9).

75:2–5 A reassuring word from above: God will not fail to call the arrogant to account. It is not clear whether a new word from the Lord is heard or whether these verses recall (and perhaps summarize) earlier prophetic words (such as those of Isaiah in 2Ki 19:21–34).

75:2 God will not fail to judge (see Ps 96; 98)—but in his own time.

75:3 When, because of the upsurge of evil powers, the whole moral order of the world seems to have crumbled, God still guarantees its stability (see note on 11:3). *pillars.* A figure for that which stabilizes the world order (see note on 24:2). For *Selah*, see NIV text note and note on 3:2.

75:4 *arrogant . . . wicked.* To the psalmists the wicked are both arrogant (see especially Ps 10 and note on 10:2–11; 73:4–12 and note; 94:4; see also note on 31:23) and foolish (see introduction to Ps 14 and note on 14:1; 74:18,22; 92:6; 94:8 and note on 94:8–11). *lift up your horns.* A figure here for defiant opposition, based on the action of attacking bulls. "Horn" (see also v. 10) is a common biblical metaphor for vigor or strength (see NIV text notes here and on 18:2).

75:6–8 Triumphant echo from earth: perhaps spoken by the Levitical song leader in elaboration of the comforting word from God.

75:8 *cup.* See note on 16:5. *mixed with spices.* The spices used increased the intoxicating effect (see Pr 9:2,5; 23:29–30; SS 8:2; Isa 65:11). *drink it down.* Because God pours it out, they have no choice.

75:9 Concluding vow to praise God forever (see note on 7:17) for his righteous judgments. *me.* Probably the Levitical song leader speaking representatively for the people, but the pronoun may be a communal use of the singular, as in 74:12 (see note on Ps 30 title). *Jacob.* A synonym for Israel (see Ge 32:28).

75:10 *righteous.* See note on 1:5. *lifted up.* See v. 7; see also note on v. 4.

Ps 76 A hymn celebrating the Lord's invincible power in defense of Jerusalem, his royal city. The psalm is thematically related to Ps 46; 48; 87 (see introduction to Ps 46). The ancient tradition may well be correct that the psalm was composed after the Lord's destruction of Sennacherib's army when it threatened Jerusalem (2Ki 19:35).

³There he broke the flashing arrows,
  the shields and the swords, the weapons
    of war.ª

⁴You are radiant with light,
  more majestic than mountains rich with game.
⁵The valiant lie plundered,
  they sleep their last sleep;
 not one of the warriors
  can lift his hands.
⁶At your rebuke, God of Jacob,
  both horse and chariot lie still.

⁷It is you alone who are to be feared.
  Who can stand before you when you are
    angry?
⁸From heaven you pronounced judgment,
  and the land feared and was quiet —
⁹when you, God, rose up to judge,
  to save all the afflicted of the land.
¹⁰Surely your wrath against mankind brings you
    praise,
  and the survivors of your wrath are restrained.ᵇ

¹¹Make vows to the LORD your God and fulfill
    them;
  let all the neighboring lands
  bring gifts to the One to be feared.
¹²He breaks the spirit of rulers;
  he is feared by the kings of the earth.

Psalm 77ᶜ

*For the director of music. For Jeduthun.
Of Asaph. A psalm.*

¹I cried out to God for help;
  I cried out to God to hear me.
²When I was in distress, I sought the Lord;
  at night I stretched out untiring hands,
  and I would not be comforted.

³I remembered you, God, and I groaned;
  I meditated, and my spirit grew faint.ᵈ
⁴You kept my eyes from closing;
  I was too troubled to speak.
⁵I thought about the former days,
  the years of long ago;
⁶I remembered my songs in the night.
  My heart meditated and my spirit asked:

⁷"Will the Lord reject forever?
  Will he never show his favor again?

ª *3* The Hebrew has *Selah* (a word of uncertain meaning) here and at the end of verse 9.   ᵇ *10* Or *Surely the wrath of mankind brings you praise, / and with the remainder of wrath you arm yourself*   ᶜ In Hebrew texts 77:1-20 is numbered 77:2-21.   ᵈ *3* The Hebrew has *Selah* (a word of uncertain meaning) here and at the end of verses 9 and 15.

76:1–3 God's crushing defeat of the enemy in defense of Zion.

76:1 *is renowned.* Now especially—as a result of his marvelous act. *Israel.* Probably refers to the whole of God's covenant people. As a result of the Assyrian invasions, many displaced Israelites from the northern kingdom now resided in Judah (see introduction to Ps 80).

76:2 *tent . . . dwelling place.* Since the two Hebrew words for these nouns frequently refer to a lion's den, covert or lair (10:9; 104:22; Job 38:40; Jer 25:38; Am 3:4), it may be that the psalmist is here depicting Israel's God as a lion overpowering its prey. In that case, an alternative rendering of v. 4 should be considered. *Salem.* Jerusalem, as the parallelism makes clear. *Zion.* See note on 9:11.

76:3 For *Selah,* see NIV text note and note on 3:2.

76:4–10 Praise of the awesome majesty of God, whose mighty judgment evokes fearful reverence (see introduction).

76:5–6 Perhaps echoes also God's victory over the Egyptians at the Red Sea (Ex 14:28,30; 15:4–5,10).

76:7 *you alone . . . you.* This first line of the second four-line stanza echoes the emphatic "you" with which the first four-line stanza begins (v. 4).

76:8 *From heaven.* Though God is present in Zion (v. 2), he sovereignly rules from heaven.

76:10 *brings you praise.* When his judgments bring deliverance, those rescued praise him. If the alternative translation in the NIV text note is taken, "the wrath of mankind brings you praise" would mean that when people rise up against God's kingdom he crushes them in wrath, to his own praise as Victor and Deliverer. And "the remainder of wrath" would indicate that particular judgments do not exhaust his wrath; a remainder is left to deal with other hostile powers.

76:11–12 Let Israel acknowledge God's help with grateful vows; let the nations acknowledge his sovereign rule with tribute.

76:12 *spirit of rulers.* Their bold rebelliousness.

Ps 77 Comforting reflections in a time of great distress. For the relationship of this psalm to Ps 74, see introduction to Ps 73–78. The interplay of verb forms in vv. 1–6 makes it uncertain whether the psalm is a lament in the face of a current threat (in which case the verbs of these verses would have to be rendered in the present tense) or the recollection of a past experience (as the NIV understands it). The "distress" (v. 2) appears to be personal rather than national.

77:1–9 Anguished perplexity over God's apparent inaction, when he seemingly fails to respond to unceasing and urgent prayers.

Additional Insights

God is the Great King over all, the One to whom all things are subject.

⁸Has his unfailing love vanished forever?
  Has his promise failed for all time?
⁹Has God forgotten to be merciful?
  Has he in anger withheld his compassion?"

¹⁰Then I thought, "To this I will appeal:
  the years when the Most High stretched out
    his right hand.
¹¹I will remember the deeds of the LORD;
  yes, I will remember your miracles of
    long ago.
¹²I will consider all your works
  and meditate on all your mighty deeds."

¹³Your ways, God, are holy.
  What god is as great as our God?
¹⁴You are the God who performs miracles;
  you display your power among the peoples.
¹⁵With your mighty arm you redeemed your
    people,
  the descendants of Jacob and Joseph.

¹⁶The waters saw you, God,
  the waters saw you and writhed;
    the very depths were convulsed.
¹⁷The clouds poured down water,
  the heavens resounded with thunder;
    your arrows flashed back and forth.
¹⁸Your thunder was heard in the whirlwind,
  your lightning lit up the world;
    the earth trembled and quaked.
¹⁹Your path led through the sea,
  your way through the mighty waters,
    though your footprints were not seen.

²⁰You led your people like a flock
  by the hand of Moses and Aaron.

Psalm 78

A maskil[a] of Asaph.

¹My people, hear my teaching;
  listen to the words of my mouth.
²I will open my mouth with a parable;
  I will utter hidden things, things from
    of old —
³things we have heard and known,
  things our ancestors have told us.
⁴We will not hide them from their descendants;
  we will tell the next generation
  the praiseworthy deeds of the LORD,
    his power, and the wonders he has done.
⁵He decreed statutes for Jacob
  and established the law in Israel,
  which he commanded our ancestors
    to teach their children,

---

[a] Title: Probably a literary or musical term

77:3–6 Remembrance of God's past mercies intensifies the present perplexity (as also in 22:1–11). God's failure to act now is so troubling that the psalmist cannot sleep (cf. 3:5; 4:8) and words fail (but see vv. 10–20).
77:3 For *Selah*, see NIV text note and note on 3:2.
77:6 *heart.* See note on 4:7.
77:7–9 Though words fail (v. 4), troubled thoughts will not go away.
77:8 *unfailing love.* See article, p. 16.
77:10–20 Reassuring recollection of God's mighty acts in behalf of Israel in the exodus.
  77:10–12 Faith's decision to look beyond the present troubles—and God's bewildering inactivity—to draw hope anew from God's saving acts of old.
77:13–20 God's mighty acts in the exodus recalled.
77:15 *redeemed.* Here, as often, a synonym for "delivered." *Joseph.* OT authors sometimes refer to the northern kingdom as "Joseph" (or "Ephraim," Joseph's son) in distinction from the southern kingdom of Judah (78:67; 2Sa 19:20; 1Ki 11:28; Eze 37:16,19; Am 5:6,15; 6:6; Zec 10:6). However, here and elsewhere (80:1; 81:5; Ob 18) Joseph—the one elevated to the position of firstborn (see Ge 48:5; Jos 16:1–4; 1Ch 5:2; Eze 47:13)—represents the whole of his generation and thus also all the descendants of Jacob.
  77:16–19 A poetically heightened description of the majesty of God displayed when he opened a way through the Red Sea (74:13–15). Verses 16,19 speak expressly of that event; the intervening verses (vv. 17–18) evoke the majesty of God displayed in the thunderstorm and earthquake. Ex 14:19 speaks only of God's cloud, not of a thunderstorm or earthquake, but the Hebrew poets often associated either or both with the Lord's coming to effect redemption or judgment—no doubt because these were the two most fearsome displays of power known to them (18:12–14; 68:8; Jdg 5:4–5; Hab 3:6,10). For Christians, the display of God's power in behalf of his people now includes the resurrection of Jesus Christ from the dead (see Mt 28:2; cf. Eph 1:18–23).
77:20 Completes the thought of v. 15. *led your people.* Through the Desert of Sinai. *like a flock.* See 23:1 and note.
  Ps 78 A salvation-history psalm, warning Israel not to repeat their sins of the past but to remember God's saving acts and marvelously persistent grace and, remembering, to keep faith with him and his covenant. Here, as elsewhere (pervasively in the OT), trust in and loyalty to God on the part of God's people are covenant matters. They do not spring from abstract principles (such as the formal structure of the God-human relationship) or from general human consciousness (such as feelings of dependence on "God" or a sense of awe in the presence of the "holy"), but they result from remembering God's mighty saving acts. Correspondingly, unfaithfulness is the more blameworthy because it contemptuously disregards all God's wonderful acts in his people's behalf (Ps 105–106).
  78:1–8 Our children must hear what our fathers have told us, so that they may be faithful to the Lord.
78:1–2 This introduction is written in the style of a wisdom writer (see Ps 49:1–4).
78:2 *parable . . . hidden things.* While both terms had specialized uses, they apparently also became conventionalized more generally for instruction in a wide variety of

⁶ so the next generation would know them,
  even the children yet to be born,
  and they in turn would tell their children.
⁷ Then they would put their trust in God
  and would not forget his deeds
  but would keep his commands.
⁸ They would not be like their ancestors —
  a stubborn and rebellious generation,
  whose hearts were not loyal to God,
  whose spirits were not faithful to him.

⁹ The men of Ephraim, though armed with bows,
  turned back on the day of battle;
¹⁰ they did not keep God's covenant
  and refused to live by his law.
¹¹ They forgot what he had done,
  the wonders he had shown them.
¹² He did miracles in the sight of their ancestors
  in the land of Egypt, in the region of Zoan.
¹³ He divided the sea and led them through;
  he made the water stand up like a wall.
¹⁴ He guided them with the cloud by day
  and with light from the fire all night.
¹⁵ He split the rocks in the wilderness
  and gave them water as abundant as the seas;
¹⁶ he brought streams out of a rocky crag
  and made water flow down like rivers.

¹⁷ But they continued to sin against him,
  rebelling in the wilderness against the
    Most High.
¹⁸ They willfully put God to the test
  by demanding the food they craved.
¹⁹ They spoke against God;
  they said, "Can God really
  spread a table in the wilderness?
²⁰ True, he struck the rock,
  and water gushed out,
  streams flowed abundantly,
  but can he also give us bread?
  Can he supply meat for his people?"
²¹ When the Lord heard them, he was furious;
  his fire broke out against Jacob,
  and his wrath rose against Israel,
²² for they did not believe in God
  or trust in his deliverance.
²³ Yet he gave a command to the skies above
  and opened the doors of the heavens;
²⁴ he rained down manna for the people to eat,
  he gave them the grain of heaven.
²⁵ Human beings ate the bread of angels;
  he sent them all the food they could eat.
²⁶ He let loose the east wind from the heavens
  and by his power made the south wind blow.
²⁷ He rained meat down on them like dust,
  birds like sand on the seashore.

forms (see note on 49:4). Mt 13:35 refers to this verse as a prophecy of Jesus' parabolic teaching. Matthew apparently perceived in this psalm a recitation of God's mighty acts that required spiritual discernment to understand their full meaning, just as Jesus' parables did.

78:4–5 The Lord's saving acts and his covenant statutes—both must be taught, and in relationship, for together they remain the focal point for faith and obedience down through the generations (vv. 7–8).

78:4 *not hide them.* See Job 15:18.

78:5 *teach their children.* See, e.g., Ex 10:2; 12:26–27; 13:8,14; Dt 4:9; 6:7,20–21.

78:9–16 The northern kingdom has violated God's covenant, not remembering his saving acts (a message emphasized by the prophets Amos and Hosea). Israel's history with God has been a long series of rebellions on their part (vv. 9–16,32–39,56–64), beginning already in the wilderness (vv. 17–31,40–55).

78:9 *men of Ephraim.* The northern kingdom, dominated by the tribe of Ephraim. *turned back.* Neither the tribe of Ephraim nor the northern kingdom had a reputation for cowardice or ineffectiveness in battle (see, e.g., Dt 33:17). So this verse is best understood as a metaphor for Israel's betrayal of God's covenant (v. 10), related to the figure of the "faulty bow" (v. 57).

78:12–16 A summary reference to the plagues in Egypt and to the water miracles at the Red Sea and in the wilderness. In the two cycles that follow (vv. 17–39,40–64), further elaboration intensifies the indictment.

78:12 See Ex 7–12. *Zoan.* A city in the northeast part of the Nile delta (see v. 43; see also Nu 13:22).

78:13 See Ex 14:1—15:21.

78:17–31 Israel's rebelliousness in the wilderness; God's marvelous provision of food—and his anger.

78:17 *continued.* Although no sin in the wilderness has yet been mentioned, the poet probably expected his readers to recall (in conjunction with the miraculous provisions of water just mentioned) how the people grumbled at Marah because of lack of water (Ex 15:24). *Most High.* See vv. 35,56; see also Ge 14:19.

78:20 *bread . . . meat.* The poet is probably combining and compressing two episodes (Ex 16:2–3; Nu 11:4).

78:23 *opened the doors of the heavens.* For this imagery, see Ge 7:11; 2Ki 7:2; Mal 3:10.

78:25 *bread of angels.* So called because it came down from heaven. *angels.* Or "mighty ones." The Hebrew word is used only here of the angels, but reference is clearly to heavenly beings (103:20).

Additional Insights

[God] created all things and preserves them. Because he ordered them, they have a well-defined and true identity.

²⁸ He made them come down inside their camp,
  all around their tents.
²⁹ They ate till they were gorged —
  he had given them what they craved.
³⁰ But before they turned from what they craved,
  even while the food was still in their mouths,
³¹ God's anger rose against them;
  he put to death the sturdiest among them,
  cutting down the young men of Israel.

³² In spite of all this, they kept on sinning;
  in spite of his wonders, they did not believe.
³³ So he ended their days in futility
  and their years in terror.
³⁴ Whenever God slew them, they would seek him;
  they eagerly turned to him again.
³⁵ They remembered that God was their Rock,
  that God Most High was their Redeemer.
³⁶ But then they would flatter him with their
  mouths,
  lying to him with their tongues;
³⁷ their hearts were not loyal to him,
  they were not faithful to his covenant.
³⁸ Yet he was merciful;
  he forgave their iniquities
  and did not destroy them.
  Time after time he restrained his anger
  and did not stir up his full wrath.
³⁹ He remembered that they were but flesh,
  a passing breeze that does not return.

⁴⁰ How often they rebelled against him in the
  wilderness
  and grieved him in the wasteland!
⁴¹ Again and again they put God to the test;
  they vexed the Holy One of Israel.
⁴² They did not remember his power —
  the day he redeemed them from the oppressor,
⁴³ the day he displayed his signs in Egypt,
  his wonders in the region of Zoan.
⁴⁴ He turned their river into blood;
  they could not drink from their streams.
⁴⁵ He sent swarms of flies that devoured them,
  and frogs that devastated them.
⁴⁶ He gave their crops to the grasshopper,
  their produce to the locust.
⁴⁷ He destroyed their vines with hail
  and their sycamore-figs with sleet.
⁴⁸ He gave over their cattle to the hail,
  their livestock to bolts of lightning.
⁴⁹ He unleashed against them his hot anger,
  his wrath, indignation and hostility —
  a band of destroying angels.
⁵⁰ He prepared a path for his anger;
  he did not spare them from death
  but gave them over to the plague.

78:26–28 See Ex 16:13; Nu 11:31.
78:26 *east wind . . . south wind.* Since the quail were migrating from Egypt at this time, the south wind may have carried them north and the east wind may have diverted them to the wilderness area occupied by the Israelites (the book of Numbers does not provide wind directions).
78:27 *like dust . . . like sand.* Similes for a huge number.
78:30–31 See Nu 11:33.
78:32–39 Rebelliousness, which became Israel's way of life, showed itself early in the wilderness wandering (vv. 17–31) and continued throughout that journey.
78:32 *did not believe.* That God could give them victory over the Canaanites (Nu 14:11).
78:33 The exodus generation was condemned to die in the wilderness (see Nu 14:22–23,28–35; cf. Heb 3:16–19).
78:34–37 A cycle repeated frequently during the period of the judges.
78:35 *Rock.* See note on 18:2.
78:36 See Isa 29:13.
78:37 *hearts.* See note on 4:7.
78:40–64 The second cycle (the first is vv. 17–39).
78:40–55 Israel's rebelliousness began in the wilderness; they did not remember how they had been delivered from oppression by God's plagues upon Egypt (v. 12). Yet he brought his people through the sea and the wilderness and established them in the promised land.
78:44–51 The plagues upon Egypt (Ex 7–12): The sequence in Exodus is followed only in the first and last; the third, fifth, sixth and ninth plagues are not mentioned.

> **What do you think the next generation needs to know about God?**

_____

_____

_____

_____

_____

_____

_____

_____

_____

_____

51 He struck down all the firstborn of Egypt,
   the firstfruits of manhood in the tents
      of Ham.
52 But he brought his people out like a flock;
   he led them like sheep through the
      wilderness.
53 He guided them safely, so they were unafraid;
   but the sea engulfed their enemies.
54 And so he brought them to the border of his
      holy land,
   to the hill country his right hand had taken.
55 He drove out nations before them
   and allotted their lands to them as an
      inheritance;
   he settled the tribes of Israel in their homes.

56 But they put God to the test
   and rebelled against the Most High;
   they did not keep his statutes.
57 Like their ancestors they were disloyal and
      faithless,
   as unreliable as a faulty bow.
58 They angered him with their high places;
   they aroused his jealousy with their idols.
59 When God heard them, he was furious;
   he rejected Israel completely.
60 He abandoned the tabernacle of Shiloh,
   the tent he had set up among humans.
61 He sent the ark of his might into captivity,
   his splendor into the hands of the enemy.
62 He gave his people over to the sword;
   he was furious with his inheritance.
63 Fire consumed their young men,
   and their young women had no wedding
      songs;
64 their priests were put to the sword,
   and their widows could not weep.

65 Then the Lord awoke as from sleep,
   as a warrior wakes from the stupor of wine.
66 He beat back his enemies;
   he put them to everlasting shame.
67 Then he rejected the tents of Joseph,
   he did not choose the tribe of Ephraim;
68 but he chose the tribe of Judah,
   Mount Zion, which he loved.
69 He built his sanctuary like the heights,
   like the earth that he established forever.
70 He chose David his servant
   and took him from the sheep pens;
71 from tending the sheep he brought him
   to be the shepherd of his people Jacob,
   of Israel his inheritance.
72 And David shepherded them with integrity
      of heart;
   with skillful hands he led them.

78:49 *destroying angels.* The poet personifies God's wrath, indignation and hostility as agents of his anger.
78:51 *tents.* Dwellings. *Ham.* For the association of Ham with Egypt, see 105:23,27; 106:21–22; Ge 10:6.
78:52 *like a flock.* See 77:20 and note.
78:53 *sea.* Red Sea (see Ex 15:1–21).
78:55 Summarizes the story told in Joshua.
78:56–64 Rebelliousness continued to be Israel's way of life in the promised land (a recurring theme of Judges; see also 1Sa 2:12—7:2), so God rejected Israel (v. 59; see Jer 7:15).
78:57 *faulty bow.* See note on v. 9.
78:59 *rejected Israel completely.* Abandoned the people to their enemies. The psalmist does not speak of a permanent casting off of Israel, not even of the ten northern tribes.
78:60 *Shiloh.* The center of worship since the time of Joshua (Jos 18:1,8; 21:1–2; Jdg 18:31; 1Sa 1:3; Jer 7:12), it was located in Ephraim between Bethel and Shechem (see Jdg 21:19). Apparently it was destroyed by the Philistines when they captured the ark or shortly afterward.
78:61 *his might . . . his splendor.* The ark is here so called because it was the sign of God's kingship in Israel and the focal point for the display of his power and glory (26:8; 63:2; 1Sa 4:3,21–22).
78:63 *Fire.* Often associated with the sword (vv. 62,64) as the two primary instruments of destruction in ancient warfare. *no wedding songs.* So great was the catastrophe that both the wedding songs of the brides and the wailing of the widows (v. 64) were silenced in the land.
78:64 *priests were put to the sword.* See 1Sa 4:11.
78:65–72 The Lord's election of Judah (instead of Ephraim) as the leading tribe in Israel (anticipated in Jacob's deathbed blessing of his sons, Ge 49:8–12), of Mount Zion (instead of Shiloh) as the place of his sanctuary (royal seat) and of David as his regent to shepherd his people.
78:66–72 The saving events noted have two focal points: (1) God's decisive victory over his enemies (thus securing his realm) and the establishment of Zion as his royal city, and (2) the appointment of David to be the shepherd of his people.
78:68,70 *he chose . . . Mount Zion . . . He chose David.* See Ps 132.
78:69 *heights . . . earth.* The verse is subject to two interpretations: (1) The Lord built his sanctuary as impregnable as a mountain fortress and as enduring and immovable as the age-old earth, or (2) the Lord built his sanctuary as secure and enduring as the heavens and the earth (see note on 24:2) and there manifests himself as the Lord of glory (24:7–10; 26:8; 63:2; 96:6), even as he does in the creation (19:1; 29:9; 97:6).
78:70–71 See 1Sa 16:11–13; 2Sa 7:8.
78:70 *his servant.* Here an official title marking David as a member of God's royal administration. For David as God's "servant," see also 89:3,20,39; 132:10.
78:71 *shepherd.* See v. 72; see also note on 23:1.
78:72 Israel under the care of the Lord's royal shepherd from the house of David was for the prophets the hope of God's people (see Eze 34:23; 37:24; Mic 5:4—fulfilled in Jesus Christ, Mt 2:6; Jn 10:11; Rev 7:17). *shepherded.* See note on 23:1.

Psalm 79

A psalm of Asaph.

¹O God, the nations have invaded your
  inheritance;
  they have defiled your holy temple,
  they have reduced Jerusalem to rubble.
²They have left the dead bodies of your
    servants
  as food for the birds of the sky,
  the flesh of your own people for the animals
    of the wild.
³They have poured out blood like water
  all around Jerusalem,
  and there is no one to bury the dead.
⁴We are objects of contempt to our
    neighbors,
  of scorn and derision to those around us.

⁵How long, LORD? Will you be angry forever?
  How long will your jealousy burn like fire?

Ps 79–83 A group of five psalms at the center of Book III
that are framed by two anguished laments of the community when the nation has been invaded by powerful
enemies (for the different events alluded to, see introductions to Ps 79; 83). In the center of this group (Ps 81)—
thus also at the center of Book III—stands an urgent ad-
monition to wayward Israel, reminding God's people that
only if they are faithful to the Lord, who brought them
out of Egypt, will he preserve them or rescue them from
the ravaging of their enemies.

Ps 79 Israel's lament to God asking for forgiveness and
help and for his judgment on the nations that have so
cruelly destroyed them, showing utter contempt for both
the Lord and his people. The poignancy of its appeal is
heightened by its juxtaposition to Ps 77 (recalling God's
saving acts under Moses) and Ps 78 (recalling God's saving acts under David), two psalms with which it is significantly linked by the shepherd-sheep figure and other
thematic elements. Israel acknowledges that the Lord
has used the nations to punish them for their sins, so
they plead for pardon. But they know too that the nations
have acted out of their hostility to and disdain for God
and his people; that warrants Israel's plea for God's judg-

Ancient street in Jerusalem that used to run under Robinson's Arch. The rubble in the background is
from the desctruction of Jerusalem in AD 70 by the Romans. "O God, the nations have invaded your
inheritance; they have defiled your holy temple, they have reduced Jerusalem to rubble" (Ps 79:1).

6 Pour out your wrath on the nations
    that do not acknowledge you,
  on the kingdoms
    that do not call on your name;
7 for they have devoured Jacob
    and devastated his homeland.

8 Do not hold against us the sins of past
        generations;
  may your mercy come quickly to meet us,
    for we are in desperate need.
9 Help us, God our Savior,
    for the glory of your name;
  deliver us and forgive our sins
    for your name's sake.
10 Why should the nations say,
    "Where is their God?"

  Before our eyes, make known among the nations
    that you avenge the outpoured blood of your
        servants.
11 May the groans of the prisoners come before
        you;
    with your strong arm preserve those
        condemned to die.
12 Pay back into the laps of our neighbors seven
        times
    the contempt they have hurled at you, Lord.
13 Then we your people, the sheep of your pasture,
    will praise you forever;
  from generation to generation
    we will proclaim your praise.

Psalm 80[a]

For the director of music. To the tune of "The Lilies of the Covenant." Of Asaph. A psalm.

1 Hear us, Shepherd of Israel,
    you who lead Joseph like a flock.
  You who sit enthroned between the cherubim,
    shine forth 2before Ephraim, Benjamin and
        Manasseh.
  Awaken your might;
    come and save us.

[a] In Hebrew texts 80:1-19 is numbered 80:2-20.

Additional Insights

God tolerates no rivals. As the Great King by right of creation and his enduring, absolute sovereignty, God ultimately will not tolerate any worldly power that opposes, denies or ignores him.

ment on the nations (Isa 10:5–11; 47:6–7). Daniel's prayer (Da 9:4–19) contains much that is similar to the elements of penitence in this psalm.

79 title *Asaph.* See note on Ps 73 title.

79:1–4 What the nations have done: They have attacked God's own special domain, violated his temple, destroyed his royal city, slaughtered his people, degraded them in death (by withholding burial—see note on 53:5—and leaving their bodies as carrion for birds and beasts) and reduced them to the scorn of the world.

79:1 *rubble.* See photo, p. 106.

79:2 *your servants.* Though banished from the Lord's land for sins that cannot be denied, the exiles plead their special covenant relationship with God (see "your own people," here, and "your people, the sheep of your pasture," v. 13). *your own people.* See note on 4:3.

79:5–8 A prayer for God to relent and deal with the nations who do not acknowledge him.

79:6–7 See Jer 10:25. Perhaps the psalmist is quoting Jeremiah here.

79:6 *Pour out your wrath.* As they "poured out" (v. 3) the blood of your people. The exiles plead with God to redress the wrongs committed against them (see note on 5:10).

79:7 *devoured.* Like wild beasts (see 44:11; 74:19 and note on 7:2). *Jacob.* A synonym for Israel (Ge 32:28).

79:8 *sins of past generations.* Israel suffered exile because of the accumulated sins of the nation (2Ki 17:7–23; 23:26–27; 24:3–4; Da 9:4–14), of which they did not repent until the judgment of God had fallen on them. The exiles here pray that God will take notice of their penitence and not continue to hold the sins of past generations against his now repentant people. *mercy.* Here personified as God's agent sent to bring relief (see notes on 23:6; 43:3).

79:9–11 A prayer for God to help and forgive his people and to redress the violent acts of the enemies.

79:9 *for the glory of your name.* As the desolation of God's people brings reproach to God (v. 10), so their salvation and prosperity bring him glory (see note on 23:3). *forgive.* See note on 65:3.

79:11 *prisoners . . . those condemned to die.* The exiles, as imperial captives in Babylonia (102:20)—not actually in prisons, but under threat of death if they should seek to return to their homeland.

79:12–13 Concluding prayer and vow to praise God.

79:12 *seven times.* In full measure; the number seven symbolized completeness. *contempt . . . at you.* The enemies' violent action against Israel was above all a high-handed reviling of God (vv. 1,10; 2Ki 19:10–12,22–23; Isa 52:5).

Ps 80 Israel's lament to God asking for restoration when they had been ravaged by a foreign power. For the relationship of this psalm to the others in its group, see introduction to Ps 79–83. It seems likely that "Ephraim, Benjamin and Manasseh" (v. 2) here represent the northern kingdom. Recent archaeological surveys of the Holy Land have shown that Jerusalem and the surrounding countryside experienced a dramatic increase in population at this time, no doubt the result of a massive influx of displaced persons from the north fleeing the Assyrian threat. This could account for the presence of "Ephraim, Benjamin and Manasseh" at the Jerusalem

³Restore us, O God;
    make your face shine on us,
    that we may be saved.

⁴How long, LORD God Almighty,
    will your anger smolder
    against the prayers of your people?
⁵You have fed them with the bread of tears;
    you have made them drink tears by the bowlful.
⁶You have made us an object of derision[a] to our
        neighbors,
    and our enemies mock us.

⁷Restore us, God Almighty;
    make your face shine on us,
    that we may be saved.

⁸You transplanted a vine from Egypt;
    you drove out the nations and planted it.
⁹You cleared the ground for it,
    and it took root and filled the land.
¹⁰The mountains were covered with its shade,
    the mighty cedars with its branches.
¹¹Its branches reached as far as the Sea,[b]
    its shoots as far as the River.[c]

¹²Why have you broken down its walls
    so that all who pass by pick its grapes?
¹³Boars from the forest ravage it,
    and insects from the fields feed on it.
¹⁴Return to us, God Almighty!
    Look down from heaven and see!
  Watch over this vine,
15   the root your right hand has planted,
    the son[d] you have raised up for yourself.

¹⁶Your vine is cut down, it is burned with fire;
    at your rebuke your people perish.
¹⁷Let your hand rest on the man at your right hand,
    the son of man you have raised up for yourself.
¹⁸Then we will not turn away from you;
    revive us, and we will call on your name.

¹⁹Restore us, LORD God Almighty;
    make your face shine on us,
    that we may be saved.

---

a 6 Probable reading of the original Hebrew text; Masoretic
Text *contention*   *b 11* Probably the Mediterranean
c 11 That is, the Euphrates   *d 15* Or *branch*

Additional Insights

Restore us, LORD God Almighty; make
your face shine on us, that we may
be saved.

sanctuary, and for a national prayer for restoration with
special focus on these tribes (see notes below).
80:1–3 An appeal for God to arouse himself and go before
his people again with all his glory and might as he did of
old in the wilderness.
80:1 See the shepherd-flock motif in 74:1; 77:20; 78:52,71–
72; 79:13; see also 23:1–2 and notes. *shine forth.* Let your
glory be seen again, as in the wilderness journey (Ex
24:16–17; 40:34–35), but now especially through your new
saving act (102:15–16; Ex 14:4,17–18; Nu 14:22; Isa 40:5;
44:23; 60:1–2).
80:2 *before Ephraim, Benjamin and Manasseh.* March
against the nations as you marched in the midst of your
army from Sinai into the promised land (in that march
the ark of the covenant advanced in front of the troops
of these three tribes; see Nu 10:21–24; see also introduction to Ps 68). *Awaken.* See note on 7:6.
80:3 *make your face shine.* See vv. 7,19; an echo of the
priestly benediction (see Nu 6:25; see also notes on 4:6;
13:1).
80:4–7 A lament over the Lord's severe punishment of his
people.
80:5 God has now given them tears to eat and tears to
drink rather than "the bread of angels" and water from
the rock (78:20,25).
80:8–16 This use of the vine-vineyard metaphor (here
to describe Israel's changed condition) is found also in
the Prophets (see Isa 3:14; 5:1–7; 27:2; Jer 2:21; 12:10; Eze
17:6–8; 19:10–14; Hos 10:1; 14:7; Mic 7:1; see also Ge 49:22;
Mt 20:1–16; Mk 12:1–9; Lk 20:9–16; Jn 15:1–5).
80:8–11 Israel was once God's flourishing, transplanted
vine.
80:12–15 A prayer for God to renew his care for his ravaged
vine.
80:12 *Why . . . ?* Israel's anguished perplexity over God's
apparent abandonment (see note on 6:3). *broken down
its walls.* Taken away its defenses.
80:14 *Watch over.* See Ex 3:16. But the Hebrew for this
phrase may have the sense here that it has in Ru 1:6:
"Come to the aid of."
80:15 *son.* Israel (Ex 4:22–23; Hos 11:1). But "son" may
sometimes be used also to refer to a vine branch (see
NIV text note). That may be the case here, thus yielding
the conventional pair "root and branch," a figure for the
whole vine (see Job 18:16; 29:19; Eze 17:7; Mal 4:1; see also
Isa 5:24; 27:6; 37:31; Eze 17:9; 31:7; Hos 9:16; Am 2:9; Ro
11:16).
80:16–19 Concluding prayer for restoration.
80:17 *Let your hand rest on.* Show your favor to (Ezr
7:6,9,28; 8:18,22,31; Ne 2:8,18). *your right hand.* Reference
may be to the Davidic king as the Lord's anointed, seated
in the place of honor in God's presence (110:1) and the one
in whom the hope of the nation rested (2:7–9; 72:8–11;
89:21–25).
80:18 A vow to be loyal to God and to trust in him alone. It
occurs in a place where it would be more common to find
a vow to praise God (see note on 7:17).

▶ In what do you place your hope (71:5)?

_____

_____

_____

_____

▶ Can you relate to the psalmist's envy in Psalm 73? In what ways?

_____

_____

_____

_____

▶ How would you describe God's power (74:13–17)?

_____

_____

_____

_____

▶ What do you learn about the story of God's plan of salvation from the history relayed in Psalm 78?

_____

_____

_____

_____

Psalm 81[a]

For the director of music. According to gittith.[b] *Of Asaph.*

[1] Sing for joy to God our strength;
   shout aloud to the God of Jacob!
[2] Begin the music, strike the timbrel,
   play the melodious harp and lyre.

[3] Sound the ram's horn at the New Moon,
   and when the moon is full, on the day of our
      festival;
[4] this is a decree for Israel,
   an ordinance of the God of Jacob.
[5] When God went out against Egypt,
   he established it as a statute for Joseph.

   I heard an unknown voice say:

[6] "I removed the burden from their shoulders;
   their hands were set free from the basket.
[7] In your distress you called and I rescued you,
   I answered you out of a thundercloud;
   I tested you at the waters of Meribah.[c]
[8] Hear me, my people, and I will warn you —
   if you would only listen to me, Israel!
[9] You shall have no foreign god among you;
   you shall not worship any god other
      than me.
[10] I am the LORD your God,
   who brought you up out of Egypt.
   Open wide your mouth and I will fill it.

[11] "But my people would not listen to me;
   Israel would not submit to me.
[12] So I gave them over to their stubborn hearts
   to follow their own devices.

[13] "If my people would only listen to me,
   if Israel would only follow my ways,
[14] how quickly I would subdue their enemies
   and turn my hand against their foes!
[15] Those who hate the LORD would cringe
      before him,
   and their punishment would last forever.
[16] But you would be fed with the finest of wheat;
   with honey from the rock I would
      satisfy you."

---

[a] In Hebrew texts 81:1-16 is numbered 81:2-17.   [b] Title: Probably a musical term   [c] 7 The Hebrew has *Selah* (a word of uncertain meaning) here.

Ps 81 A festival hymn. It was probably composed for use at both the New Year festival (the first day of the month, "New Moon") and the beginning of Tabernacles (the 15th day of the month, full moon); see notes below. As memorials of God's saving acts, Israel's annual religious festivals called the nation to celebration, remembrance and recommitment.

81:1–5 A summons to celebrate the appointed sacred festival.

81:1 *Jacob.* A synonym for Israel (Ge 32:28).

81:2 *harp and lyre.* See note on 57:8.

81:3 *ram's horn.* The ram's horn trumpet (Ex 19:13). *our festival.* Probably the Festival of Tabernacles often called simply "the festival" (see, e.g., 1Ki 8:2,65).

81:5 *When God went out against Egypt.* Some believe this indicates that the festival referred to is Passover and Unleavened Bread (Ex 12:14,42). More likely it serves as a reference to the whole exodus period, while highlighting especially God's triumph over Egypt by which he had set his people free (vv. 6–7). *Joseph.* See note on 77:15. *heard an unknown voice.* The "voice" is the thunder of God's judgment against Egypt (v. 7), which the Levitical author then proceeds to interpret as to its present reference for the celebrating congregation (vv. 6–16).

81:6–10 God heard and delivered and now summons his people to loyalty.

81:6 *burden . . . basket.* The forced labor to which the Israelites were subjected in Egypt (Ex 1:11–14).

81:8–10 God heard his people in their distress (vv. 6–7); now they must listen to him.

81:10 *Open wide your mouth.* Trust in the Lord alone for all of life's needs. *I will fill it.* See v. 16; as he did in the wilderness (see 78:23–29; see also 37:3–4; Dt 11:13–15; 28:1–4).

81:11–16 Israel has not listened—if only God's people would! See Eze 18:23,32; 33:11.

81:12 It is God who circumcises the heart (see Dt 30:6; see also 1Ki 8:58; Jer 31:33; Eze 11:19; 36:26). Thus for God to abandon his people to their sins is the most fearful of

Additional Insights

God has delivered [Israel] by mighty acts out of the hands of the world powers, has given them a land of their own and has united them with himself in covenant as the initial embodiment of his redeemed kingdom.

Psalm 82

A psalm of Asaph.

[1] God presides in the great assembly;
  he renders judgment among the "gods":

[2] "How long will you[a] defend the unjust
  and show partiality to the wicked?[b]
[3] Defend the weak and the fatherless;
  uphold the cause of the poor and the
    oppressed.
[4] Rescue the weak and the needy;
  deliver them from the hand of the
    wicked.

[5] "The 'gods' know nothing, they understand
    nothing.
  They walk about in darkness;
  all the foundations of the earth are
    shaken.

[6] "I said, 'You are "gods";
  you are all sons of the Most High.'
[7] But you will die like mere mortals;
  you will fall like every other ruler."

[8] Rise up, O God, judge the earth,
  for all the nations are your inheritance.

Psalm 83[c]

A song. A psalm of Asaph.

[1] O God, do not remain silent;
  do not turn a deaf ear,
  do not stand aloof, O God.
[2] See how your enemies growl,
  how your foes rear their heads.
[3] With cunning they conspire against your
    people;
  they plot against those you cherish.
[4] "Come," they say, "let us destroy them as
    a nation,
  so that Israel's name is remembered
    no more."

[5] With one mind they plot together;
  they form an alliance against you —
[6] the tents of Edom and the Ishmaelites,
  of Moab and the Hagrites,
[7] Byblos, Ammon and Amalek,
  Philistia, with the people of Tyre.
[8] Even Assyria has joined them
  to reinforce Lot's descendants.[b]

---

[a] 2 The Hebrew is plural.   [b] 2,8 The Hebrew has *Selah* (a word of uncertain meaning) here.   [c] In Hebrew texts 83:1-18 is numbered 83:2-19.

---

punishments (see 78:29; Isa 6:9–10; 29:10; 63:17; cf. Ro 1:24,26,28).

81:13–16 See the promised covenant blessings outlined in Ex 23:22–27; Lev 26:3–13; Dt 7:12–26; 28:1–14.

Ps 82 A word of judgment on unjust rulers and judges. The author of this psalm evokes a vision of God presiding over his heavenly court—analogous to the experiences of the prophets (see 1Ki 22:19–22; Isa 6:1–7; Jer 23:18,22; see also Job 15:8). As the Great King (see introduction to Ps 47) and the Judge of all the earth (94:2; Ge 18:25; 1Sa 2:10) who "loves justice" (99:4) and judges the nations in righteousness (9:8; 96:13; 98:9), he is seen calling to account those responsible for defending the weak and oppressed on earth. These rulers and judges here are confronted by their King and Judge (Ps 58).

82 title See note on Ps 73 title.

82:1 *great assembly.* The assembly in the great Hall of Justice (cf. 1Ki 7:7) in heaven (89:5; 1Ki 22:19; Job 1:6; 2:1; Isa 6:1–4). As if in a vision, the psalmist sees the rulers and judges gathered before the Great King to give account of their administration of justice. *gods.* See v. 6. In the language of the OT—and in accordance with the conceptual world of the ancient Near East—rulers and judges, as deputies of the heavenly King, could be given the honorific title "god" (see note on 45:6) or be called "son of God" (see 2:7 and note).

82:3–4 In the OT a first-order task of kings and judges was to protect the powerless against all who would exploit or oppress them (72:2,4,12–14; Pr 31:8–9; Isa 11:4; Jer 22:3,16).

82:5 *The 'gods' know . . . nothing.* The center of the poem (see note on 6:6). They ought to have shared in the wisdom of God (1Ki 3:9; Pr 8:14–16; Isa 11:2), but they are utterly devoid of true understanding of moral issues or of the moral order that God's rule sustains (Isa 44:18; Jer 3:15; 9:24). *foundations . . . are shaken.* When such people are the wardens of justice, the whole world order crumbles (see 11:3; 75:3 and notes).

82:7 However exalted their position, these corrupt "gods" will be brought low by the same judgment as other human beings.

Ps 83 Israel's lament asking God to crush his enemies when the whole world—or so it seemed—was arrayed against his people. For this psalm's relationship to those around it, see introduction to Ps 79–83. The occasion may have been that reported in 2Ch 20, when Moab, Ammon, Edom and their allies were invading Judah. In any event, the psalm must date from sometime after the reign of Solomon and before the great thrust of Assyria in the time of King Menahem (2Ki 15:19).

83:1–4 An appeal to God to act in the face of Israel's imminent danger.

83:2 *growl.* In Hebrew the same verb as for "are in uproar" in 46:6 and for "snarling" in 59:6,14.

83:5–8 The array of nations allied against Israel—threat from every quarter.

83:6 *Hagrites.* Either Ishmaelites (descendants of Hagar) or a group mentioned in Assyrian inscriptions as an Aramean confederacy (1Ch 5:10,18–22; 27:31).

83:8 *Assyria.* Since it is mentioned only as an ally of Moab and Ammon (the descendants of Lot), Assyria, though

⁹ Do to them as you did to Midian,
  as you did to Sisera and Jabin at the river
    Kishon,
¹⁰ who perished at Endor
  and became like dung on the ground.
¹¹ Make their nobles like Oreb and Zeeb,
  all their princes like Zebah and Zalmunna,
¹² who said, "Let us take possession
  of the pasturelands of God."

¹³ Make them like tumbleweed, my God,
  like chaff before the wind.
¹⁴ As fire consumes the forest
  or a flame sets the mountains ablaze,
¹⁵ so pursue them with your tempest
  and terrify them with your storm.
¹⁶ Cover their faces with shame, LORD,
  so that they will seek your name.

¹⁷ May they ever be ashamed and dismayed;
  may they perish in disgrace.
¹⁸ Let them know that you, whose name is the
    LORD —
  that you alone are the Most High over all the
    earth.

Psalm 84ᵃ

For the director of music. According to gittith.ᵇ
Of the Sons of Korah. A psalm.

¹ How lovely is your dwelling place,
  LORD Almighty!
² My soul yearns, even faints,
  for the courts of the LORD;
my heart and my flesh cry out
  for the living God.
³ Even the sparrow has found a home,
  and the swallow a nest for herself,
  where she may have her young —
a place near your altar,
  LORD Almighty, my King and my God.
⁴ Blessed are those who dwell in your house;
  they are ever praising you.ᶜ

⁵ Blessed are those whose strength is in you,
  whose hearts are set on pilgrimage.
⁶ As they pass through the Valley of Baka,
  they make it a place of springs;
  the autumn rains also cover it with pools.ᵈ
⁷ They go from strength to strength,
  till each appears before God in Zion.

⁸ Hear my prayer, LORD God Almighty;
  listen to me, God of Jacob.

ᵃ In Hebrew texts 84:1-12 is numbered 84:2-13.   ᵇ Title:
Probably a musical term   ᶜ 4 The Hebrew has *Selah* (a word
of uncertain meaning) here and at the end of verse 8.
ᵈ 6 Or *blessings*

distantly active in the region, must not yet have become a major threat in its own right. For *Selah*, see NIV text note and note on 3:2.

83:9–12 A plea for God to destroy his enemies as he did of old in the time of the judges. Those who hurl themselves against the kingdom of God to destroy it from the earth—so that the godless powers are left to shape the destiny of the world as they will—must be crushed if God's kingdom of righteousness and peace is to come and be at rest (see note on 5:10).
83:9 *as you did to Midian.* In Gideon's great victory (Jdg 7). *as you did to Sisera and Jabin.* In Barak's defeat of the Canaanite coalition (Jdg 4).
83:10 *Endor.* Northeast of where the main battle was fought—apparently where much of the fleeing army was overtaken and decimated.
83:11 *Oreb and Zeeb . . . Zebah and Zalmunna.* Leaders of the Midianite host destroyed by Gideon (Jdg 7:25—8:21).
83:12 See v. 4.
83:13–16 The plea renewed, with vivid imagery of fleeing armies and of God's fearsome power.
83:15 Imagery of the heavenly Warrior attacking his enemies out of the thunderstorm (18:7–15; 68:33; 77:17–18; Ex 15:7–10; Jos 10:11; Jdg 5:4,20–21; 1Sa 2:10; 7:10; Isa 29:5–6; 33:3). For the storm cloud as God's chariot, see 68:4 and note.
83:16 *will seek.* See note on v. 18.
83:17–18 The prayer's climactic conclusion.
83:18 The ultimate goal of God's warfare is not merely the security of Israel and the destruction of Israel's (and God's) enemies but the worldwide acknowledgment of the true God and of his rule, even to the point of seeking him as his people do (see v. 16; see also 40:9; 58:11 and notes).
Ps 84–89 The first of the six psalms that make up the final group of Book III (see introduction to Ps 73–78) expresses yearning for fellowship with God, who dwells in his temple in Zion and from whom alone come security and blessing. References to God as "LORD Almighty" and a prayer for "our shield," the Lord's "anointed," form distinctive links with the final psalm of the group (for the former, see 84:1,3,8,12 and 89:8; for the latter, see 84:9 and 89:18,38,51). The five psalms thus introduced are four cries out of distress arranged around a central song (Ps 87) that celebrates God's special love for Zion and the care he has for all its citizens.
Ps 84 A lament of longing for the house of the Lord. The author (presumably a Levite who normally functioned in the temple service), now barred from access to God's house (perhaps when Sennacherib was ravaging Judah; see 2Ki 18:13–16), gives voice to his longing for the sweet nearness to God in his temple that he had known in the past. Reference to God and his temple and to the blessedness (vv. 4–5,12) of those having free access to both dominates the prayer and highlights its central themes.
84:1 *lovely.* The traditional rendering of the Hebrew here; could also be translated "beloved" or "loved." *LORD Almighty.* See vv. 3,8,12; see also 1Sa 1:3.
84:3 The psalmist envies the small birds that have such unhindered access to the temple and the altar. They are able even to build their nests for their young there—the place where Israel was to have communion with God.

⁹ Look on our shield,[a] O God;
  look with favor on your anointed one.

• ¹⁰ Better is one day in your courts
  than a thousand elsewhere;
  I would rather be a doorkeeper in the house of
    my God
  than dwell in the tents of the wicked.
¹¹ For the LORD God is a sun and shield;
  the LORD bestows favor and honor;
  no good thing does he withhold
  from those whose walk is blameless.

¹² LORD Almighty,
  blessed is the one who trusts in you.

Psalm 85[b]

*For the director of music. Of the Sons
of Korah. A psalm.*

¹ You, LORD, showed favor to your land;
  you restored the fortunes of Jacob.
² You forgave the iniquity of your people
  and covered all their sins.[c]
³ You set aside all your wrath
  and turned from your fierce anger.

⁴ Restore us again, God our Savior,
  and put away your displeasure toward us.
⁵ Will you be angry with us forever?
  Will you prolong your anger through all
    generations?
⁶ Will you not revive us again,
  that your people may rejoice in you?
⁷ Show us your unfailing love, LORD,
  and grant us your salvation.

⁸ I will listen to what God the LORD says;
  he promises peace to his people, his faithful
    servants —
  but let them not turn to folly.
⁹ Surely his salvation is near those who
    fear him,
  that his glory may dwell in our land.

¹⁰ Love and faithfulness meet together;
  righteousness and peace kiss each other.
¹¹ Faithfulness springs forth from the earth,
  and righteousness looks down from
    heaven.
¹² The LORD will indeed give what is good,
  and our land will yield its harvest.
¹³ Righteousness goes before him
  and prepares the way for his steps.

---

[a] 9 Or *sovereign*   [b] In Hebrew texts 85:1-13 is numbered
85:2-14.   [c] 2 The Hebrew has *Selah* (a word of uncertain
meaning) here.

84:5–7 The joyful blessedness of those who are free to
make pilgrimage to Zion—them too the psalmist envies.
  84:5 *those whose strength is in you.* Those who have
come to know the Lord as their deliverer and the sustainer of their lives. *whose hearts are set on pilgrimage.*
Joyful anticipation of the pilgrimages the Israelites took
to observe the religious festivals at Jerusalem (Zion, v. 7).
  84:6 *As they pass.* On their way to the temple. *Baka.*
Means either "weeping" or "balsam trees" (common
in arid valleys). *place of springs.* The joyful expectations of
the pilgrims transform the difficult ways into places of
refreshment. *autumn rains.* Reference to these rains suggests that the psalmist had in mind especially the pilgrimage to observe the Festival of Tabernacles.
84:8–11 A prayer for the king and its motivation: Only as
God blesses the king in Jerusalem will the psalmist once
more realize his great desire to return to his accustomed
service in the temple (see introduction).
84:8 *Jacob.* A synonym for Israel (Ge 32:28).
84:10 *doorkeeper.* Perhaps the psalmist's normal (and
humble) service at the temple (2Ki 22:4). *dwell in the tents
of the wicked.* Share in the life of those who do not hon-
or the God of Zion. Perhaps reference is to the peoples
imported by Sargon II (2Ki 17:24–33), among whom the
psalmist was forced at the time to live.
84:11 *sun.* The glorious source of the light of life (see note
on 27:1). *shield.* See note on 3:3.
  Ps 85 A communal lament to God asking for the renewal of his mercies to his people at a time when
they are once more suffering distress. Verse 12 suggests
that a drought has ravaged the land and may reflect the
drought with which the Lord chastened his people in the
time of Haggai (Hag 1:5–11). For this lament's placement in
the Psalter and its relationship to the psalms of its group,
see introduction to Ps 84–89. Christian liturgical usage
has often employed this psalm in the Christmas season.
85:1–7 The plea for the renewal of God's favor.
  85:1–3 Israel begins this prayer by appealing to the
Lord's past mercies, recalling how he has forgiven
and restored his people before (perhaps a reference to
the restoration from exile).
85:4–7 The plea acknowledges that the present troubles
are indicative of God's displeasure. No confession of sin
is expressed, but in the light of v. 3 (and possibly v. 8; see
below) it is probably implicit.
85:7 *unfailing love.* See v. 10; see also article, p. 16.
85:8–13 God's reassuring answer to the plea, conveyed
through a priest or Levite, perhaps one of the Korahites
(see note on 12:5–6; see also 2Ch 20:14).
85:8 *I will listen.* The speaker awaits the word from the
Lord. *promises peace.* The word from the Lord perhaps
takes the form of the priestly benediction (Nu 6:22–26).
  85:9 *glory.* Wherever God's saving power is displayed,
his glory is revealed (see 57:5 and note; 72:18–19; Ex
14:4,17–18; Nu 14:22; Isa 6:3; 40:5; 44:23; 66:19; Eze 39:21).
  85:10–13 God's sure mercies to his people spring
from his covenant love, to which in his faithfulness
and righteousness he remains true, and that assures his
people's welfare (peace). Cf. 40:9–10.
  85:10 *Love and faithfulness . . . righteousness and
peace.* These expressions of God's favor toward his

Psalm 86

A prayer of David.

[1] Hear me, LORD, and answer me,
　　for I am poor and needy.
[2] Guard my life, for I am faithful to you;
　　save your servant who trusts in you.
　You are my God; [3] have mercy on me, Lord,
　　for I call to you all day long.
[4] Bring joy to your servant, Lord,
　　for I put my trust in you.

[5] You, Lord, are forgiving and good,
　　abounding in love to all who call to you.
[6] Hear my prayer, LORD;
　　listen to my cry for mercy.
[7] When I am in distress, I call to you,
　　because you answer me.

[8] Among the gods there is none like you,
　　Lord;
　　no deeds can compare with yours.
[9] All the nations you have made
　　will come and worship before you, Lord;
　　they will bring glory to your name.
[10] For you are great and do marvelous
　　deeds;
　　you alone are God.

[11] Teach me your way, LORD,
　　that I may rely on your faithfulness;
　give me an undivided heart,
　　that I may fear your name.
[12] I will praise you, Lord my God, with all my
　　heart;
　　I will glorify your name forever.
[13] For great is your love toward me;
　　you have delivered me from the depths,
　　from the realm of the dead.

[14] Arrogant foes are attacking me, O God;
　　ruthless people are trying to kill me —
　　they have no regard for you.
[15] But you, Lord, are a compassionate and
　　gracious God,
　　slow to anger, abounding in love and
　　faithfulness.
[16] Turn to me and have mercy on me;
　　show your strength in behalf of your
　　　servant;
　save me, because I serve you
　　just as my mother did.
[17] Give me a sign of your goodness,
　　that my enemies may see it and be put to
　　　shame,
　　for you, LORD, have helped me and
　　　comforted me.

people are here personified (see note on 23:6), and the vivid portrayal of their meeting and embracing offers one of the most beautiful images in all Scripture of God's gracious dealings with his covenant people. *righteousness.* See vv. 11,13; see also note on 4:1.

85:11 *Faithfulness springs forth.* As new growth springs from the earth to bless all living things with plenty. *righteousness looks down.* It shines down benevolently. (With "disaster" as subject, the Hebrew for "looks down" indicates the opposite effect: Jer 6:1, "looms.") From heaven and from earth God's covenant blessings will abound till Israel's cup overflows.

85:13 *Righteousness goes before.* As in v. 10, again the psalmist uses personification. Acting either as herald or guide, righteousness leads the way and marks the course for God's engagement in his people's behalf—and righteousness is God's perfect faithfulness to all his covenant commitments (see note on 4:1).

Ps 86 The lament of an individual requesting God's help when attacked by enemies, whose fierce onslaughts betray their disdain for the Lord. Whether or not David was the author (see Introduction: Authorship and Titles [or Superscriptions]), the psalmist's identification of himself as God's "servant" (v. 2) suggests his royal status and thus his special relationship with the Lord (see 2Sa 7:5,8 and note on Ps 18 title).

86 title *prayer.* See note on Ps 17 title. *of David.* This is the only psalm in Book III (Ps 73–89) that is ascribed to David. Perhaps its placement among the Korahite psalms is in part because those who arranged the Psalter perceived a thematic link between v. 9 and 87:4.

86:1–4 Initial plea for God to have mercy and protect the life of his servant.

86:1 *poor and needy.* See 35:10; see also 34:6 and note.

86:2 *faithful to you.* The Hebrew for this phrase is *ḥasid* (see note on 4:3). *your servant.* See vv. 4,16; see also introduction. *You are my God.* Not that David has chosen him, but that he has chosen David to be his servant (1Sa 13:14; 15:28; 16:12; 2Sa 7:8). David's faithfulness to God and God's commitment to him are deliberately juxtaposed.

86:5 *love.* See vv. 13,15; see also article, p. 16.

86:8–10 At the center of his lament David gives expression to his fundamental belief (see also 115:3–7; 135:13–17) and makes clear why he appeals to Yahweh in the surrounding stanzas.

86:9 *All the nations.* See note on 46:10. This is the center verse of the psalm (see note on 6:6) and contains the psalm's most exalted confession of faith concerning God's sovereign and universal rule. *they will bring glory.* As David vows to do (v. 12). *your name.* See vv. 11–12.

86:10 *marvelous deeds.* See note on 9:1.

86:11–13 A prayer for godliness and a vow to praise God.

86:11 *Teach me . . . give me.* What would be the benefit if God were to save him from his enemies but abandon him to his own waywardness? David's dependence on God is complete, and so is his devotion to God—save me from the enemy outside but also from my frailty within (see 25:5; 51:7,10). Only one who is thus devoted to God may expect God's help and will truly fulfill the vow (v. 12). *undivided heart.* See Eze 11:19; see also 1Ch 12:33; 1Co 7:35. *heart.* See note on 4:7.

Psalm 87

Of the Sons of Korah. A psalm. A song.

[1] He has founded his city on the holy mountain.
[2] The LORD loves the gates of Zion
   more than all the other dwellings of Jacob.

[3] Glorious things are said of you,
   city of God:[a]
[4] "I will record Rahab[b] and Babylon
   among those who acknowledge me —
 Philistia too, and Tyre, along with Cush[c] —
   and will say, 'This one was born in Zion.'"[d]
[5] Indeed, of Zion it will be said,
   "This one and that one were born in her,
   and the Most High himself will establish her."
[6] The LORD will write in the register of the
         peoples:
   "This one was born in Zion."

[7] As they make music they will sing,
   "All my fountains are in you."

Psalm 88[e]

A song. A psalm of the Sons of Korah.
For the director of music. According to mahalath
leannoth.[f] *A maskil[g] of Heman the Ezrahite.*

[1] LORD, you are the God who saves me;
   day and night I cry out to you.
[2] May my prayer come before you;
   turn your ear to my cry.

[3] I am overwhelmed with troubles
   and my life draws near to death.
[4] I am counted among those who go down to
         the pit;
   I am like one without strength.
[5] I am set apart with the dead,
   like the slain who lie in the grave,
 whom you remember no more,
   who are cut off from your care.

[6] You have put me in the lowest pit,
   in the darkest depths.
[7] Your wrath lies heavily on me;
   you have overwhelmed me with all your
         waves.[h]

---

[a] 3 The Hebrew has *Selah* (a word of uncertain meaning) here
and at the end of verse 6.   [b] 4 A poetic name for Egypt
[c] 4 That is, the upper Nile region   [d] 4 Or *"I will record*
concerning those who acknowledge me: / 'This one was born in
Zion.' / Hear this, Rahab and Babylon, / and you too, Philistia,
Tyre and Cush."   [e] In Hebrew texts 88:1-18 is numbered
88:2-19.   [f] Title: Possibly a tune, "The Suffering of
Affliction"   [g] Title: Probably a literary or musical
term   [h] 7 The Hebrew has *Selah* (a word of uncertain
meaning) here and at the end of verse 10.

86:14–17 Conclusion: the lament renewed.
86:14 *ruthless.* The Hebrew for this word suggests also fe-
rocity. *they have no regard for you.* In their arrogance they
dismiss the heavenly Warrior, who is David's defender
(see note on 10:11; see also Jer 20:11).
86:15 Echoes v. 5, but is even more similar to Ex 34:6.
86:16 *show your strength.* Exert your power in my behalf.
I serve you just as my mother did. See 116:16.
86:17 *goodness.* Covenanted favors. *may see it.* May see
that you stand with me and help me.

Ps 87 A hymn celebrating Zion (Jerusalem) as the
"city of God" (v. 3), the special object of his love and
the royal city of his kingdom (see introductions to Ps 46;
48; 76). According to the ancient and consistent interpretation of Jewish and Christian interpreters alike, this
psalm stands alone in the Psalter in that it foresees the
ingathering of the nations into Zion as fellow citizens
with Israel in the kingdom of God (but see 47:9)—after
the manner of such prophetic visions as Isa 2:2–4; 19:19–
25; 25:6; 45:14,22–24; 56:6–8; 60:3; 66:23; Da 7:14; Mic
4:1–3; Zec 8:23; 14:16. So interpreted, this psalm stands in
sharpest possible contrast to the other Zion songs of the
Psalter (Ps 46; 48; 76; 125; 129; 137).
87:1 *He has founded his city.* The Lord himself has laid the
foundations of Zion (Isa 14:32) and of the temple as his
royal house. *mountain.* The Hebrew for this word is plural,
emphasizing the majesty of the holy mountain on which
God's throne has been set (see 48:2 and note).
87:2 *loves . . . more than.* As the city of his founding, his
chosen seat of rule over his people, Zion is the Lord's
most cherished city, even among the towns of Israel (see
9:11 and note; 78:68; 132:13–14). *Jacob.* A synonym for Israel (Ge 32:28).
87:4 *I will record . . . 'This one was born in Zion.'* God will
list them in his royal register (see note on 51:1) as those
who are native (born) citizens of his royal city, having all
the privileges and enjoying all the benefits and security
of such citizenship. *Rahab.* A reference to Egypt (see NIV
text note), perhaps portrayed as the mythical monster of
the deep (see 89:10). The nations listed are representative
of all Gentile peoples. As usually interpreted, the psalm
here foresees a widespread conversion to the Lord from
the peoples who from time immemorial had been hostile
to him and to his kingdom (see Isa 19:21; 26:18). But see
third NIV text note.
87:7 *All my fountains.* All that refreshes them is found in
the city of God, a possible allusion to God's "river of delights" (36:8) "whose streams make glad the city of God"
(46:4); see notes on those passages. Alternatively, "fountains" may be a metaphor for sources; the sense of the
line would then be: We all spring from you. *my.* Communal use of the singular pronoun (see note on Ps 30 title).

Ps 88 A cry out of the depths, the lament of one on
the edge of death, whose whole life has been lived,
as it were, in the near vicinity of the grave (see also Ps 90).
So troubled have been his years that he seems to have
known only the back of God's hand (God's "wrath," v. 7),
and even those nearest him have withdrawn themselves
as from one with a defiling skin disease (v. 8). No expressions of hopeful expectation (as in most laments of the
Psalter; but see Ps 44; 89) burst from these lips; the last

⁸ You have taken from me my closest friends
    and have made me repulsive to them.
I am confined and cannot escape;
⁹   my eyes are dim with grief.

I call to you, LORD, every day;
    I spread out my hands to you.
¹⁰ Do you show your wonders to the dead?
    Do their spirits rise up and praise you?
¹¹ Is your love declared in the grave,
    your faithfulness in Destruction*^a*?
¹² Are your wonders known in the place of darkness,
    or your righteous deeds in the land of oblivion?

¹³ But I cry to you for help, LORD;
    in the morning my prayer comes before you.
¹⁴ Why, LORD, do you reject me
    and hide your face from me?

¹⁵ From my youth I have suffered and been close
    to death;
    I have borne your terrors and am in despair.
¹⁶ Your wrath has swept over me;
    your terrors have destroyed me.
¹⁷ All day long they surround me like a flood;
    they have completely engulfed me.
¹⁸ You have taken from me friend and neighbor—
    darkness is my closest friend.

Psalm 89*^b*

A maskil^c of Ethan the Ezrahite.

¹ I will sing of the LORD's great love forever;
    with my mouth I will make your faithfulness
    known
    through all generations.
² I will declare that your love stands firm forever,
    that you have established your faithfulness
    in heaven itself.
³ You said, "I have made a covenant with my
    chosen one,
    I have sworn to David my servant,
⁴ 'I will establish your line forever
    and make your throne firm through all
    generations.' "*^d*

⁵ The heavens praise your wonders, LORD,
    your faithfulness too, in the assembly of the
    holy ones.
⁶ For who in the skies above can compare with
    the LORD?
    Who is like the LORD among the heavenly
    beings?

---

^a 11 Hebrew *Abaddon*   *^b* In Hebrew texts 89:1-52 is
numbered 89:2-53.   *^c* Title: Probably a literary or musical
term   *^d 4* The Hebrew has *Selah* (a word of uncertain
meaning) here and at the end of verses 37, 45 and 48.

word speaks of darkness as "my closest friend." And yet the lament begins, "LORD, you are the God who saves me." The psalm recalls the fact that although sometimes godly persons live lives of unremitting trouble (73:14), they can still grasp the hope that God is Savior (see also Ps 87 and introduction to Ps 84–89). Many early church leaders interpreted this psalm as a lament of the suffering Christ (as they did Ps 22); for that reason it became part of the Good Friday liturgy.

88:1–2 Opening appeal to the Lord as "the God who saves me."

88:3–5 Living on the brink of death. Whether the psalmist lies mortally ill or experiences some analogous trouble or peril cannot be known.

88:4 *pit.* See 28:1; 30:3,9; 143:7.

88:5 *remember no more.* From the perspective of this life, death cuts off from God's care; there is no remembering by God of the needy sufferer to rescue and restore (25:7; 74:2; 106:4). In his dark mood the author portrays his situation in bleakest colors (cf. Job's experiences).

88:6–9a You, God, have done this! The psalmist knows no reason for it (see v. 14; cf. Ps 44), but he knows God's hand is in it (Ru 1:20–21; Am 3:6). That his Savior-God shows him the face of wrath deepens his anguish and helplessness. But he does not try to resolve the dark enigma; he simply pleads his case—and it is to his Savior-God that he can appeal (v. 1).

88:8 *my closest friends.* See v. 18 and note on 31:11–12.

88:9b–12 Appeal to God to help before the psalmist sinks into "the land of oblivion" (see note on v. 5).

88:10,12 *wonders.* God's saving acts in behalf of his people (see note on 9:1).

88:10 *rise up.* In the realm of the dead (not in the resurrection); see Isa 14:9. *praise you.* See 6:5; 30:9; 115:17 and notes.

88:11 *love.* See article, p. 16.

88:13 *in the morning.* See 101:8 and note.

88:14 *Why . . . ?* See note on 6:3. *hide your face.* See note on 13:1.

88:15–18 The psalmist has been no stranger to trouble; all his life he has suffered the terrors of God (cf. Ps 90).

88:17 *like a flood.* See v. 7; see also note on 32:6.

Ps 89 A lament that mourns the downfall of the Davidic dynasty and pleads for its restoration. The bitter shock of that event (reflected in the sudden transition at v. 38) is almost unbearable—that God, the faithful and almighty One, has abandoned his anointed and made him the mockery of the nations, in seeming violation of his firm covenant with David—and it evokes from the psalmist a lament that borders on reproach. The event was probably the destruction of Jerusalem by Nebuchadnezzar in 586 BC (vv. 38–45). As with Ps 44 (see introduction to that psalm), a massive foundation is laid for the prayer with which the psalm concludes. An introduction (vv. 1–4) sings of God's love and faithfulness (vv. 1–2) and his covenant with David (vv. 3–4). These two themes are then jubilantly expanded in order: vv. 5–18, God's love and faithfulness; vv. 19–37, his covenant with David. Suddenly jubilation turns to lament, and the psalmist recounts in detail how God has rejected his anointed (vv. 38–45). Thus he comes to his plea, impatient and urgent, that God will remember once

⁷In the council of the holy ones God is greatly feared;
he is more awesome than all who surround him.
⁸Who is like you, LORD God Almighty?
You, LORD, are mighty, and your faithfulness
surrounds you.

⁹You rule over the surging sea;
when its waves mount up, you still them.
¹⁰You crushed Rahab like one of the slain;
with your strong arm you scattered your
enemies.
¹¹The heavens are yours, and yours also the earth;
you founded the world and all that is in it.
¹²You created the north and the south;
Tabor and Hermon sing for joy at your name.
¹³Your arm is endowed with power;
your hand is strong, your right hand exalted.

¹⁴Righteousness and justice are the foundation
of your throne;
love and faithfulness go before you.
¹⁵Blessed are those who have learned to acclaim you,
who walk in the light of your presence, LORD.
¹⁶They rejoice in your name all day long;
they celebrate your righteousness.
¹⁷For you are their glory and strength,
and by your favor you exalt our horn.^a
¹⁸Indeed, our shield^b belongs to the LORD,
our king to the Holy One of Israel.

¹⁹Once you spoke in a vision,
to your faithful people you said:
"I have bestowed strength on a warrior;
I have raised up a young man from among
the people.
²⁰I have found David my servant;
with my sacred oil I have anointed him.
²¹My hand will sustain him;
surely my arm will strengthen him.
²²The enemy will not get the better of him;
the wicked will not oppress him.
²³I will crush his foes before him
and strike down his adversaries.
²⁴My faithful love will be with him,
and through my name his horn^c will be exalted.
²⁵I will set his hand over the sea,
his right hand over the rivers.
²⁶He will call out to me, 'You are my Father,
my God, the Rock my Savior.'
²⁷And I will appoint him to be my firstborn,
the most exalted of the kings of the earth.
²⁸I will maintain my love to him forever,
and my covenant with him will never fail.
²⁹I will establish his line forever,
his throne as long as the heavens endure.

^a 17 Horn here symbolizes strong one.   ^b 18 Or sovereign
^c 24 Horn here symbolizes strength.

more his covenant with David (vv. 46–51). (Verse 52 concludes not the psalm but Book III of the Psalter.)
89 title *maskil.* See note on Ps 32 title. *Ethan.* Jeduthun (see note on Ps 39 title). The author was probably a Levite (perhaps a descendant of Jeduthun) who voiced this agonizing lament as spokesman for the nation.
89:1–2 God's love and faithfulness celebrated.
89:1 *love.* See vv. 2,14,24,28,33,49; see also article, p. 16. It is God's love and faithfulness that appear to have failed in his rejection (see vv. 38–45) of the Davidic king. The author repeats each of these words precisely seven times, the number of completeness (in v. 14 the Hebrew uses a different—but related—word for "faithfulness").
89:2 *in heaven itself.* God's love and faithfulness have been made sure in the highest seat of power and authority (vv. 5–8).
89:3–4 God's covenant with David celebrated (2Sa 7:8–16).
89:5–8 The Lord's faithfulness and awesome power set him apart among all the powers in the heavenly realm, and they acknowledge him with praise and reverence.
89:5 *The heavens.* All beings belonging to the divine realm in the heavens. *wonders.* God's mighty acts in creation and redemption (see note on 9:1). *assembly of the holy ones.* The divine council in heaven (see v. 7; see also note on 82:1).
89:6 *heavenly beings.* Or "sons of god(s)" (see 29:1 and note).
89:8 *your faithfulness surrounds you.* It also surrounds this stanza (v. 5).
89:9–13 The Lord's power as Creator—and creation's joy in him.
89:9–10 Poetic imagery borrowed from ancient Near Eastern myths of creation, here celebrating God's sovereign power over the primeval chaotic waters so that the creation order could be established (see Ge 1:6–10; see also notes on 65:6–7; 74:13–14).
89:10 *Rahab.* Mythical monster of the deep (see note on 87:4), probably another name for Leviathan (74:14; 104:26). The last half of this verse is probably echoed in Lk 1:51.
89:14–18 The Lord's righteousness and faithfulness in his rule in behalf of his people—and their joy in him.
89:14 Righteousness and justice are the foundation stones of God's throne (cf. Pr 16:12; 25:5; 29:14). Love and faithfulness are personified as throne attendants that herald his royal movements (see note on 23:6). *Righteousness.* See v. 16; see also note on 4:1.
89:17 *horn.* King (see NIV text note; see also v. 18).
89:18 *Holy One of Israel.* See 71:22; 78:41; 2Ki 19:22.
89:19–29 The Lord's election of David to be his regent over his people, and his everlasting covenant

Additional Insights

God chose David as king. As the Great King, Israel's covenant Lord, God chose David to be his royal representative on earth.

³⁰ "If his sons forsake my law
   and do not follow my statutes,
³¹ if they violate my decrees
   and fail to keep my commands,
³² I will punish their sin with the rod,
   their iniquity with flogging;
³³ but I will not take my love from him,
   nor will I ever betray my faithfulness.
³⁴ I will not violate my covenant
   or alter what my lips have uttered.
³⁵ Once for all, I have sworn by my holiness —
   and I will not lie to David —
³⁶ that his line will continue forever
   and his throne endure before me like the sun;
³⁷ it will be established forever like the moon,
   the faithful witness in the sky."

³⁸ But you have rejected, you have spurned,
   you have been very angry with your
      anointed one.
³⁹ You have renounced the covenant with your
      servant
   and have defiled his crown in the dust.
⁴⁰ You have broken through all his walls
   and reduced his strongholds to ruins.
⁴¹ All who pass by have plundered him;
   he has become the scorn of his neighbors.
⁴² You have exalted the right hand of his foes;
   you have made all his enemies rejoice.
⁴³ Indeed, you have turned back the edge of his
      sword
   and have not supported him in battle.
⁴⁴ You have put an end to his splendor
   and cast his throne to the ground.
⁴⁵ You have cut short the days of his youth;
   you have covered him with a mantle of shame.

⁴⁶ How long, LORD? Will you hide yourself forever?
   How long will your wrath burn like fire?
⁴⁷ Remember how fleeting is my life.
   For what futility you have created all humanity!
⁴⁸ Who can live and not see death,
   or who can escape the power of the grave?
⁴⁹ Lord, where is your former great love,
   which in your faithfulness you swore to David?
⁵⁰ Remember, Lord, how your servant has[a] been
      mocked,
   how I bear in my heart the taunts of all the
      nations,
⁵¹ the taunts with which your enemies, LORD,
      have mocked,
   with which they have mocked every step of
      your anointed one.

⁵² Praise be to the LORD forever!
      Amen and Amen.

^a 50 Or *your servants have*

---

with him. The thought is developed by couplets: (1) introduction (v. 19); (2) I have anointed David as my servant and will sustain him (vv. 20–21); (3) I will crush all his foes (vv. 22–23); (4) I will extend his realm (vv. 24–25); (5) I will make him first among the kings (vv. 26–27); (6) I will cause his dynasty to endure forever (vv. 28–29)—a promise fulfilled in the eternal reign of Jesus Christ (Jn 12:34).

89:19 *vision.* Reference is to the revelation to Samuel (1Sa 16:12) and/or to Nathan (2Sa 7:4–16). *faithful people.* See note on 4:3.

89:25 *sea . . . rivers.* David's rule will reach from the Mediterranean Sea to the Euphrates River (see 72:8; 80:11). But the author uses imagery that underscores the fact that, as his royal "son" (v. 26) and regent, David's rule will be a reflection of God's (see vv. 9–10; also compare v. 23 with v. 10).

89:27 *firstborn.* The royal son of highest privilege and position in the kingdom of God (2:7–12; 45:6–9; 72:8–11; 110), thus "the most exalted of the kings of the earth" (Rev 1:5). So the words may speak of universal rule—ultimately fulfilled in Christ.

89:30–37 The Lord's covenant with David and his dynasty was everlasting (vv. 28–29) and unconditional—though if any of his royal descendants is unfaithful he will individually suffer God's discipline (to the detriment of the entire nation).

89:38–45 God's present rejection of David's son, and all its fearful consequences—the undoing of all that had been promised and assured by covenant (see especially vv. 19–29). To fully appreciate the poignancy of this lament, cf. Ps 18.

89:46–51 An appeal—in spite of all—to God's faithfulness to his covenant with David. In this dark hour, that remains the psalmist's hope.

89:46 *How long . . . ?* See note on 6:3.

89:47 *how fleeting is my life.* See 37:20; 39:4 and notes. The shortness of human life adds urgency to the plea. *futility.* Because humans have limited powers and are subject to death, they are dependent on God's involvement in the world (see 60:11; 90:5–6 and note; 108:12; 127:1–2; see also Job 7:1–3; Ecc 1:2).

89:49 *former great love.* The love referred to in v. 1.

89:50 *Remember.* See v. 47.

89:52 A brief doxology with which the final editors concluded Book III of the Psalter (see note on 41:13).

Ps 90–100 A series of 11 psalms arranged within the frame "you have been our dwelling place throughout all generations" (90:1) and "his faithfulness continues through all generations" (100:5)—a series that begins with lament and ends with praise. The first two of these psalms (90–91) are thematically connected (point and counterpoint); the next three (92–94) form a trilogy that serves as a transition to the final thematic cluster (95–99). At the very middle, Ps 95 anticipates the four following psalms and adds a warning for the celebrants of Yahweh's reign that echoes the warning of Moses in Dt 6:13–18. Evidently the editors of the Psalter intended readers of this group of psalms to hear echoes of the voice of Moses as interceder (Ps 90) and as admonisher (95:8–11), through which ministries (shared also by Aaron and Samuel) Israel had been blessed under the reign of the Great King, Yahweh (99:6–8).

BOOK IV

Psalms 90 – 106

Psalm 90

A prayer of Moses the man of God.

¹ Lord, you have been our dwelling place
  throughout all generations.
² Before the mountains were born
  or you brought forth the whole world,
  from everlasting to everlasting you are God.

³ You turn people back to dust,
  saying, "Return to dust, you mortals."
⁴ A thousand years in your sight
  are like a day that has just gone by,
  or like a watch in the night.
⁵ Yet you sweep people away in the sleep of
    death —
  they are like the new grass of the morning:
⁶ In the morning it springs up new,
  but by evening it is dry and withered.

⁷ We are consumed by your anger
  and terrified by your indignation.
⁸ You have set our iniquities before you,
  our secret sins in the light of your presence.
⁹ All our days pass away under your wrath;
  we finish our years with a moan.
¹⁰ Our days may come to seventy years,
  or eighty, if our strength endures;
  yet the best of them are but trouble and
    sorrow,
  for they quickly pass, and we fly away.
¹¹ If only we knew the power of your anger!
  Your wrath is as great as the fear that is
    your due.
¹² Teach us to number our days,
  that we may gain a heart of wisdom.

¹³ Relent, LORD! How long will it be?
  Have compassion on your servants.
¹⁴ Satisfy us in the morning with your unfailing
    love,
  that we may sing for joy and be glad all our
    days.
¹⁵ Make us glad for as many days as you have
    afflicted us,
  for as many years as we have seen trouble.
¹⁶ May your deeds be shown to your servants,
  your splendor to their children.

¹⁷ May the favor[a] of the Lord our God rest on us;
  establish the work of our hands for us —
  yes, establish the work of our hands.

---

a 17 Or *beauty*

Ps 90 A lament to the everlasting God asking for compassion on his servants, who through the ages have known him to be their safe haven (v. 1; see also 91:9) but who also painfully experience his wrath because of their sin and his sentence of death that cuts short their lives—a plea that through this long night of his displeasure God will teach them true wisdom (see v. 12 and note) and, in the morning after, bless them in equal measure with expressions of his love so that joy may yet fill their days and the days of their children and their daily labors may be blessed. This psalm has many links with Ps 39.

90 title *A prayer.* See note on Ps 17 title. *Moses.* Tradition has assigned this psalm to Moses—perhaps because (1) it shares some language with Dt 32–33; (2) as an intercessory prayer it fits well on the lips of Moses, the great interceder for Israel (see Ex 32:11–13; 34:9; Nu 14:13–19; Dt 9:25–29; Ps 106:23; Jer 15:1; see also Ps 99:6); and (3) elsewhere only Moses asks God directly to "relent" from his anger toward Israel (v. 13; see Ex 32:12). *man of God.* A phrase normally applied in the OT to prophets, including Moses (see, e.g., Jos 14:6).

90:1 *dwelling place.* See 91:9. The Hebrew for this phrase is translated "refuge" in 71:3. Here and in 91:9 it has the connotation of "home" or "safe haven."

90:3–6 Human beings live under God's sentence of death—"Dust . . . to dust" (Ge 3:19).

90:4–5 *A . . . Yet.* Though for God 1,000 years are like a mere watch in the night (three–four hours), he cuts human life short like new grass that shows itself at dawn's light but is withered away by the hot Canaanite sun before evening falls.

90:5–6 The shortness of human life frequently occupied the thoughts of biblical writers (37:2,20,36; 39:5,11; 62:9; 78:39; 89:47; 102:3,11; 103:15–16; 109:23; 144:4; Job 8:9; 14:1–2; Ecc 6:12; Isa 40:6–8; Jas 1:10–11; 1Pe 1:24–25).

90:7–10 Even life's short span is filled with trouble, as God ferrets out every sin and makes the sinner feel his righteous anger.

90:10 *if our strength endures.* If God gives us the strength to live that long. *the best of them.* Reference is either to the best of the days or to what people prize most in their years—these are all soured by trouble and sorrow (or disappointment).

90:11–12 *If only we knew . . . Teach us.* No one can measure the extent of God's anger. But everyone ought to know the measure of their (few) days or they will play the arrogant fool, with no thought of their mortality or of their accountability to God (see Ps 10; 30:6; 49; 73:4–12; see also Dt 8).

90:13 *Relent.* Or "Turn" (cf. v. 3). *How long . . . ?* See note on 6:3.

90:14 *in the morning.* Let there be for us a dawning of your love to relieve this long, dark night of your anger (see introduction to Ps 57). The final answer to this prayer comes with the resurrection (Ro 5:2–5; 8:18; 2Co 4:16–18). *unfailing love.* See article, p. 16.

90:16 *deeds.* For a fuller description of such deeds, see the whole of Ps 111. *to their children.* As to past generations (v. 1).

90:17 *favor.* See NIV text note; see also 27:4 and note. *establish.* As you only have been our security in the world (v. 1), so also make our labors to be effective and enduring—though we are so transient.

▶ Why is music important in the worship of God (81:1–3)?

_____

_____

_____

_____

_____

▶ Where does God dwell (84:1)?

_____

_____

_____

_____

_____

▶ What emotions does God display in the psalms?

_____

_____

_____

_____

_____

▶ How does Psalm 89 apply to both David and Jesus?

_____

_____

_____

_____

_____

Psalm 91

[1] Whoever dwells in the shelter of the
   Most High
   will rest in the shadow of the Almighty.[a]
[2] I will say of the LORD, "He is my refuge and my
   fortress,
   my God, in whom I trust."

[3] Surely he will save you
   from the fowler's snare
   and from the deadly pestilence.
[4] He will cover you with his feathers,
   and under his wings you will find refuge;
   his faithfulness will be your shield and
   rampart.
[5] You will not fear the terror of night,
   nor the arrow that flies by day,
[6] nor the pestilence that stalks in the darkness,
   nor the plague that destroys at midday.
[7] A thousand may fall at your side,
   ten thousand at your right hand,
   but it will not come near you.
[8] You will only observe with your eyes
   and see the punishment of the wicked.

[9] If you say, "The LORD is my refuge,"
   and you make the Most High your dwelling,
[10] no harm will overtake you,
   no disaster will come near your tent.
[11] For he will command his angels concerning
   you
   to guard you in all your ways;
[12] they will lift you up in their hands,
   so that you will not strike your foot against a
   stone.
[13] You will tread on the lion and the cobra;
   you will trample the great lion and the
   serpent.

[14] "Because he[b] loves me," says the LORD, "I will
   rescue him;
   I will protect him, for he acknowledges my
   name.
[15] He will call on me, and I will answer him;
   I will be with him in trouble,
   I will deliver him and honor him.
[16] With long life I will satisfy him
   and show him my salvation."

[a] 1 Hebrew *Shaddai*   [b] 14 That is, probably the king

Ps 91 A glowing testimony to the security of those who trust in God—set beside Ps 90 as a counterpoint to the dismal depiction of the human condition found there (see introduction to that psalm). It was probably written by one of the temple personnel (a priest or Levite) as a word of assurance to godly worshipers. Because the "you" of vv. 3–13 applies to any who "make the Most High your dwelling" (v. 9; see 90:1), the devil applied vv. 11–12 to Jesus (Mt 4:6; Lk 4:10–11).

91:1 *shelter.* The temple (as in 27:5; 31:20; see also 23:6; 27:4), where the godly find safety under the protective wings of the Lord (v. 4; 61:4).

91:3 *fowler's snare.* Metaphor for danger from human enemies (see 124:7; see also note on 9:15). See photo, p. 122. *pestilence.* Danger to life from disease. These two threats are further elaborated in vv. 5–6.

91:4 *with his feathers . . . wings.* See note on 17:8; cf. Mt 23:37; Lk 13:34.

91:5 *terror.* As in 64:1 ("threat"), reference is to attack by enemies; thus it is paired with "arrow." These two references to threats from war are arrayed alongside "pestilence" and "plague" (v. 6), two references to mortal diseases that often reached epidemic proportions. *night . . . day.* At whatever time of day or night the threat may come, you will be kept safe—the time references are not specific to their respective phrases (see also v. 6).

91:7 *ten thousand.* Hebrew poetic convention called for 10,000 following 1,000 in parallel construction.

91:11–12 Quoted but misapplied by Satan in Mt 4:6; Lk 4:10–11.

91:12 *against a stone.* On the stony trails of Canaan (Pr 3:23).

91:13 *lion . . . cobra . . . great lion . . . serpent.* These double references to lions and to poisonous snakes balance the double references of vv. 5–6 and complete the illustrative roster of mortal threats (Am 5:19).

91:14–16 Employing the form of a prophetic message, the author supports his testimony by assuring the godly that it is confirmed by all the promises of God to those who truly love and trust him.

91:16 *With long life.* The climactic counterpoint to Ps 90.

Additional Insights

Of the 150 psalms, only 34 lack superscriptions of any kind (only 17 in the Septuagint, the pre-Christian Greek translation of the OT).

Egyptian men hunting and capturing birds with a net (Thebes, 1420–1411 BC). The psalmist declares that God will protect his people from their enemies: "Surely he will save you from the fowler's snare" (Ps 91:3).

Z. Radovan/www.BibleLandPictures.com

Psalm 92[a]

A psalm. A song. For the Sabbath day.

¹It is good to praise the LORD
    and make music to your name,
      O Most High,
²proclaiming your love in the morning
    and your faithfulness at night,
³to the music of the ten-stringed lyre
    and the melody of the harp.

⁴For you make me glad by your deeds,
    LORD;
    I sing for joy at what your hands
      have done.
⁵How great are your works, LORD,
    how profound your thoughts!
⁶Senseless people do not know,
    fools do not understand,

---

[a] In Hebrew texts 92:1-15 is numbered 92:2-16.

Ps 92 A hymn celebrating the righteous rule of God. Its testimony to the prosperity of the righteous, "planted in the house of the LORD" (v. 13), links it thematically with Ps 91 (see introduction to that psalm), while its joy over God's righteous reign relates it to the cluster of psalms that follow (Ps 93–100; see especially Ps 94). There are, in fact, reasons to believe that the editors of the Psalter brought together Ps 92–94 as a trilogy that serves as a bridge between Ps 90–91 and 95–99 (see introductions to Ps 93; 94). Notably, God's name Yahweh ("LORD") occurs seven times in this psalm. Verses 10–11 suggest that the author may have been one of Israel's kings.

92 title *A song.* See note on Ps 30 title. *For the Sabbath day.* In the postexilic liturgy of the temple, this psalm came to be sung at the time of the morning sacrifice on the Sabbath. (The rest of the weekly schedule was: first day, Ps 24; second day, Ps 48; third day, Ps 82; fourth day, Ps 94; fifth day, Ps 81; sixth day, Ps 93.)

92:1–3 Hymnic introduction.

92:2 *love.* See article, p. 16. *morning . . . night.* Continuously.

92:3 *lyre . . . harp.* See note on 57:8.

92:4–5 Joy over God's saving acts (vv. 10–11).

⁷that though the wicked spring up like
 grass
  and all evildoers flourish,
  they will be destroyed forever.

⁸But you, LORD, are forever exalted.

⁹For surely your enemies, LORD,
  surely your enemies will perish;
  all evildoers will be scattered.
¹⁰You have exalted my horn^a like that of
  a wild ox;
  fine oils have been poured on me.
¹¹My eyes have seen the defeat of my
  adversaries;
  my ears have heard the rout of my
  wicked foes.

¹²The righteous will flourish like a palm
  tree,
  they will grow like a cedar of Lebanon;
¹³planted in the house of the LORD,
  they will flourish in the courts of
  our God.
¹⁴They will still bear fruit in old age,
  they will stay fresh and green,
¹⁵proclaiming, "The LORD is upright;
  he is my Rock, and there is no wickedness
  in him."

Psalm 93

¹The LORD reigns, he is robed in majesty;
  the LORD is robed in majesty and armed
  with strength;
  indeed, the world is established, firm
  and secure.
²Your throne was established long ago;
  you are from all eternity.

³The seas have lifted up, LORD,
  the seas have lifted up their voice;
  the seas have lifted up their pounding
  waves.
⁴Mightier than the thunder of the great
  waters,
  mightier than the breakers of the
  sea —
  the LORD on high is mighty.

⁵Your statutes, LORD, stand firm;
  holiness adorns your house
  for endless days.

^a 10 Horn here symbolizes strength.

92:5 *your thoughts.* As shown by your deeds.
92:6–9 The fatal folly of evildoers (contrast vv. 12–15).
92:6 *Senseless . . . fools.* See NIV text note on 14:1; see also 49:10—and note especially 94:8–11. They do not know that the Lord rules righteously. They see the wicked flourishing but do not see the Lord or foresee the end he has appointed for them. The author thus characterizes his "wicked foes" (v. 11), whom the Lord has routed.
92:8 *forever exalted.* God's eternal exaltation assures the destruction of his enemies.
92:9 *enemies.* Here the evildoers, referred to also in v. 7.
92:10–11 Joy over God's favors (vv. 4–5): God has made him triumphant (89:24) and anointed him with "the oil of joy" (45:7; see also 23:5) by giving him victory over all his enemies.
92:12–15 The secure prosperity of the righteous (contrast vv. 6–9).
92:13 *planted in the house of the LORD.* Though the wicked may "spring up like grass," their end is sure (v. 7). But the righteous are planted in a secure place (Ps 91) and so retain the vigor of youth into old age, rejoicing in God's just discrimination (v. 15). *courts.* Of the temple (84:2,10; 2Ki 21:5; 23:11–12).
Ps 93 A hymn to the eternal, universal and invincible reign of the Lord, a theme it shares with Ps 47; 95–99. Together these hymns offer a majestic confession of faith in and hope for the kingdom of God on earth. They may all have been composed by temple personnel and spoken by them in the liturgy. Ps 93 celebrates Yahweh's secure cosmic rule that grounds his righteous and effective rule over human affairs—which is the joy (Ps 92) and the hope (Ps 94) of those who rely on him for protection against the assaults of the godless fools who live by violence. Structurally, the psalm has two short stanzas (vv. 1–2,3–4) and a conclusion (v. 5).
93:1–2 The Lord's reign, by which the creation order has been and will be secure throughout the ages, is from eternity (Ge 1:1). Though Israel as a nation has come late on the scene, their God has been King since before the creation of the world.
93:1 *The LORD reigns.* The ultimate truth, and first article, in Israel's creed (see 96:10; 97:1; 99:1; see also Zec 14:9, as well as Introduction to Psalms: Theology: Major Themes).
93:3–4 Both at and since his founding of the world, the Lord has shown himself to be mightier than all the forces of disorder that threaten his kingdom.
93:4 The thunder of the chaotic waters is no match for the thunder of the Lord's ordering word (104:7).
93:5 *statutes.* He whose indisputable rule has made the world secure has given his people life directives that are stable and reliable (19:7)—and that they must honor (95:8–11).

¹The LORD is a God who avenges.
  O God who avenges, shine forth.
²Rise up, Judge of the earth;
  pay back to the proud what they deserve.
³How long, LORD, will the wicked,
  how long will the wicked be jubilant?

⁴They pour out arrogant words;
  all the evildoers are full of boasting.
⁵They crush your people, LORD;
  they oppress your inheritance.
⁶They slay the widow and the foreigner;
  they murder the fatherless.
⁷They say, "The LORD does not see;
  the God of Jacob takes no notice."

⁸Take notice, you senseless ones among the
    people;
  you fools, when will you become wise?
⁹Does he who fashioned the ear not hear?
  Does he who formed the eye not see?
¹⁰Does he who disciplines nations not punish?
  Does he who teaches mankind lack
    knowledge?
¹¹The LORD knows all human plans;
  he knows that they are futile.

¹²Blessed is the one you discipline, LORD,
  the one you teach from your law;
¹³you grant them relief from days of trouble,
  till a pit is dug for the wicked.
¹⁴For the LORD will not reject his people;
  he will never forsake his inheritance.
¹⁵Judgment will again be founded on
    righteousness,
  and all the upright in heart will follow it.

¹⁶Who will rise up for me against the wicked?
  Who will take a stand for me against
    evildoers?
¹⁷Unless the LORD had given me help,
  I would soon have dwelt in the silence of
    death.
¹⁸When I said, "My foot is slipping,"
  your unfailing love, LORD, supported me.
¹⁹When anxiety was great within me,
  your consolation brought me joy.

²⁰Can a corrupt throne be allied with you —
  a throne that brings on misery by its
    decrees?
²¹The wicked band together against the
    righteous
  and condemn the innocent to death.
²²But the LORD has become my fortress,
  and my God the rock in whom I take refuge.

Ps 94 An appeal to the Lord, as "Judge of the earth" (v. 2), to redress the wrongs perpetrated against the weak by arrogant and wicked persons who occupy seats of power. The psalm has links with Ps 92 (see introductions to Ps 92; 93) but is the voice of the oppressed within Israel, seeking redress at God's throne for injustices done to them by the "fools" smugly established in the power structures of the nation. Thus it is unique within the Ps 90–100 group of psalms and stands here as representative of the many cries of the oppressed found in Books I–III of the Psalter.
94:1–3 Initial appeal to God, the Judge.
94:1 *avenges.* Redresses wrongs (see note on 5:10; see also Dt 32:35,41). To avenge is the function of a king in his role as chief executive of the realm. Thus a direct conceptual link with Ps 47; 93; 95–99 is established at the outset.
94:2 *the proud.* See vv. 4–7 for a description of them.
94:4–7 Indictment of the wicked.
94:4 *arrogant words . . . boasting.* For similar expressions of the arrogance of the wicked, see 10:2–11 and notes.
94:7 *They say.* See note on 3:2. *Jacob.* A synonym for Israel (Ge 32:28).
94:8–11 Warning to the wicked—those "senseless . . . fools" (see 92:6–9; see also NIV text note on 14:1).
94:10 *disciplines.* Keeps them in line by means of punishment (Lev 26:18; Jer 31:18). *teaches.* Gives human beings some knowledge of the creation order (Isa 28:26).
94:12–15 Here the focus shifts from the arrogance and folly of the wicked to the happy state of those who count themselves among the Lord's people and who live under his discipline and rely on his royal protection.
94:12 *Blessed.* See note on 1:1. *discipline . . . teach.* See v. 10 and note. Here the author speaks of God's correcting and teaching his people in the ways of his law.
94:14 *people . . . inheritance.* See v. 5. The Lord will not abandon the powerless among his people to the injustice of their oppressors. Paul may be echoing this verse in Ro 11:1–2.
94:15 However this difficult verse is to be translated, the author appears to say that God's righteous rule will restore justice for those who have been wrongfully treated while being themselves innocent—described as "the upright in heart" (v. 21).
94:16–19 The Lord is the only sure court of appeal.
94:17 *silence of death.* See note on 30:1. Without God's help the wicked would have silenced the psalmist in the grave, but now it is the wicked for whom the pit will be dug (v. 13).
94:20–23 Confidence that the Lord's justice will prevail. Cf. notes on 89:14; Zec 8:16.
94:20 *corrupt throne.* A seat of authority that works mischief. The author speaks of injustice at the center of power.
Ps 95 A hymn calling for worship of the Lord, spoken by a priest or Levite to the assembled Israelites at the temple. (See introduction to Ps 93.) Placed at the center of its group (Ps 90–100) and at the beginning of a series of psalms celebrating the universal reign of Israel's God (Ps 95–99), Ps 95 contains a sharp reminder that Israel's sense of security under Yahweh's rule—from which spring both their lament (as in Ps 90; 94) and their praise (as in Ps 91–93; 95–100)—is warranted only if Israel proves to be Yah-

²³He will repay them for their sins
    and destroy them for their wickedness;
    the LORD our God will destroy them.

Psalm 95

¹Come, let us sing for joy to the LORD;
    let us shout aloud to the Rock of our
        salvation.
²Let us come before him with thanksgiving
    and extol him with music and song.

³For the LORD is the great God,
    the great King above all gods.
⁴In his hand are the depths of the earth,
    and the mountain peaks belong to him.
⁵The sea is his, for he made it,
    and his hands formed the dry land.

⁶Come, let us bow down in worship,
    let us kneel before the LORD our Maker;
⁷for he is our God
    and we are the people of his pasture,
    the flock under his care.

Today, if only you would hear his voice,
⁸"Do not harden your hearts as you did at
        Meribah,^a
    as you did that day at Massah^b in the
        wilderness,
⁹where your ancestors tested me;
    they tried me, though they had seen what
        I did.
¹⁰For forty years I was angry with that generation;
    I said, 'They are a people whose hearts go
        astray,
    and they have not known my ways.'
¹¹So I declared on oath in my anger,
    'They shall never enter my rest.'"

Psalm 96

¹Sing to the LORD a new song;
    sing to the LORD, all the earth.
²Sing to the LORD, praise his name;
    proclaim his salvation day after day.
³Declare his glory among the nations,
    his marvelous deeds among all peoples.

⁴For great is the LORD and most worthy of
        praise;
    he is to be feared above all gods.
⁵For all the gods of the nations are idols,
    but the LORD made the heavens.
⁶Splendor and majesty are before him;
    strength and glory are in his sanctuary.

^a 8 *Meribah* means *quarreling.*   ^b 8 *Massah* means *testing.*

weh's loyal and obedient servant. Its function in context is similar to that of Ps 81 (see introduction to Ps 79–83).

95:3–5 Why Israel is to praise the Lord—because he is above all gods, and there is no corner of the universe that is not in his hand. The ancient pagan world had different gods for different peoples, different geographic areas, different cosmic regions (heaven, earth, netherworld) and different aspects of life (e.g., war, fertility, crafts).

95:6–11 The exhortation to submit to the Lord with obedient hearts—a bent knee is not enough. For a NT reflection on these verses in the light of the advent of Christ, see Heb 3:7—4:13.

95:6 *our Maker.* Both as Creator of all things (Ge 1) and as Israel's Redeemer, he has made them what they are: the people of the Lord in the earth (Isa 45:9–13; 51:12–16).

95:7 *people of his pasture.* See 100:3; Jer 23:1; Eze 34:17–23. Since kings were commonly called the shepherds of their people (see note on 23:1), their realms could be referred to as their pastures (23:2; Jer 25:36; 49:20; 50:45). *if only you would hear his voice.* In the liturgy of the religious festival, possibly in some such manner as Ps 50 and/or 78. The concern expressed in what follows echoes that of Moses in Dt 6:16–19.

95:10 *forty years.* The climax of Israel's rebellion came when God's people faithlessly refused to undertake the conquest of Canaan and considered returning to Egypt (Nu 14:1–4). It was then that God condemned them to a 40-year stay in the wilderness (Nu 14:34).

95:11 *on oath.* See Nu 14:28; Dt 1:34–35. *never enter my rest.* The language of Nu 14:30 is "not one of you will enter the land," but since the promised land was also called the place where God will give his people "rest" (Jos 1:13,15; see Ex 33:14; Dt 12:10; 25:19), the two statements are equivalent. *rest.* A rich concept indicating the Israelites' possession of a place with God in the earth where they are secure from all external threats and internal calamities.

Ps 96 A hymn calling for all nations to praise the Lord as the only God and to proclaim the glory of his reign throughout the world—an OT anticipation of the world mission of the NT people of God (Mt 28:16–20). (See introductions to Ps 93; 95.) This psalm appears in slightly altered form in 1Ch 16:23–33.

96:1–3 The call to all the earth to sing the praise of the Lord among the nations. Triple repetition for emphasis ("Sing . . . sing . . . Sing") was a common feature in OT liturgical calls to worship (see vv. 7–9; see also 103:20–22; 118:2–4; 135:1; 136:1–3; cf. Isa 6:3).

96:1 *all the earth.* See v. 9; or "all the land," in which case the call is addressed to all Israel. However, the worldwide perspective of this psalm (see especially v. 7) suggests that here the psalmist has in view broader horizons (see 97:1; 100:1 and note; 117:1; see also note on 9:1).

96:4–6 Why "all the earth" (v. 1) is to praise the Lord: He alone is God (Ps 115).

96:5 *made the heavens.* As the Maker of the heavenly realm, in pagan eyes the abode of the gods, the Lord is greater than all the gods (97:7).

96:6 *Splendor and majesty . . . strength and glory.* Two pairs of divine attributes personified as throne attendants

⁷Ascribe to the Lᴏʀᴅ, all you families of nations,
    ascribe to the Lᴏʀᴅ glory and strength.
⁸Ascribe to the Lᴏʀᴅ the glory due his name;
    bring an offering and come into his courts.
⁹Worship the Lᴏʀᴅ in the splendor of his*ᵃ*
        holiness;
    tremble before him, all the earth.
¹⁰Say among the nations, "The Lᴏʀᴅ reigns."
    The world is firmly established, it cannot be
        moved;
    he will judge the peoples with equity.

¹¹Let the heavens rejoice, let the earth be glad;
    let the sea resound, and all that is in it.
¹²Let the fields be jubilant, and everything in them;
    let all the trees of the forest sing for joy.
¹³Let all creation rejoice before the Lᴏʀᴅ, for he
        comes,
    he comes to judge the earth.
He will judge the world in righteousness
    and the peoples in his faithfulness.

Psalm 97

¹The Lᴏʀᴅ reigns, let the earth be glad;
    let the distant shores rejoice.
²Clouds and thick darkness surround him;
    righteousness and justice are the foundation
        of his throne.
³Fire goes before him
    and consumes his foes on every side.
⁴His lightning lights up the world;
    the earth sees and trembles.
⁵The mountains melt like wax before the Lᴏʀᴅ,
    before the Lord of all the earth.
⁶The heavens proclaim his righteousness,
    and all peoples see his glory.

⁷All who worship images are put to shame,
    those who boast in idols —
    worship him, all you gods!

⁸Zion hears and rejoices
    and the villages of Judah are glad
    because of your judgments, Lᴏʀᴅ.
⁹For you, Lᴏʀᴅ, are the Most High over all the
        earth;
    you are exalted far above all gods.
¹⁰Let those who love the Lᴏʀᴅ hate evil,
    for he guards the lives of his faithful ones
    and delivers them from the hand of the
        wicked.
¹¹Light shines*ᵇ* on the righteous
    and joy on the upright in heart.

whose presence before the Lord heralds the exalted nature of the one, universal King. For similar personifica-
tions, see 23:6 and note. *glory.* The Hebrew for this word
here connotes radiant beauty.

96:9 *splendor of his holiness.* See note on 29:2. *tremble.* In
reverent awe, equivalent to "fear" (v. 4).

96:10 *The Lᴏʀᴅ reigns.* See 93:1 and note. *The
world . . . with equity.* In OT perspective, the world
order is one, embracing both its physical and moral aspects because both have been established by God as aspects of his one kingdom and both are upheld by his one
rule. Therefore God's rule over creation and over human
affairs (also his acts of creation and redemption) is often
spoken of in one breath, and righteousness, faithfulness
and love are equally ascribable to both. And since the creation order can still testify to God's goodness (Ge 1), it
often serves in OT poetry (as it does here) as a manifest
assurance that God's rule over human affairs will also be
"with equity," "in righteousness" and "in . . . faithfulness"
(vv. 10,13; see 9:7–8; 11:3; 33:4–11; 36:5–9; 57:10; 58:11; 65:6–
7; 71:19; 74:13–14,16–17; 75:2; 82:5; 93:3–4; 98:9; 99:4;
119:89–91).

96:11–12 Because God's kingdom is one (see v. 10 and
note), all his creatures will rejoice when God's rule
over humankind brings righteousness to full expression
in his cosmic kingdom (see note on 65:13; see also 97:7–9).
For the present state of the creation as it awaits the fullness of redemption, see Ro 8:21–22.

Ps 97 A hymn of joyful celebration of the Lord's righteous
reign over all the earth (see introductions to Ps 93; 95),
with special attention to the benefits of the Lord's reign
enjoyed by Israel (see introduction to Ps 96). The psalm's
two main divisions (vv. 1–6,8–12—closely balanced, having 42 and 43 Hebrew words, respectively) are joined by
a centered verse (v. 7; see note on 6:6) that serves as a
counterpoint to the main theme.

97:2–6 The Lord's majestic glory revealed in the sky's
awesome displays, especially in the thunderstorm (see
18:7–15 and note; see also introduction to Ps 29).

97:2 *Clouds and thick darkness.* The dark storm
clouds that hide the sun and cast a veil across the
sky are dramatic visual reminders that the fierce heat and
brilliance (also metaphors) of God's naked glory must be
veiled from creaturely eyes (Ex 19:9; 1Ki 8:12). Thus also a
curtain closed off the Most Holy Place in the tabernacle
and temple (Ex 26:33; 2Ch 3:14), veiling it in darkness.

97:6 *proclaim his righteousness.* The stable order of the
heavens' vast array "speaks" (19:1–4); it declares that
God's reign similarly upholds the moral order (see note
on 96:10). *all peoples see.* Verses 2–6 have spoken of general revelation (cf. 19:1–6).

97:7 The center verse (see note on 6:6) and counterpoint of the psalm: joy to all who acknowledge the
Lord; shame and disgrace to those who trust in false
gods. *worship him.* With biting irony the psalm calls on all
the gods that people foolishly worship as if they were real
to bow in worship before the Lord (see v. 9; see also 29:1
and note).

97:8–12 A declaration of Zion's joy that the Lord
reigns (vv. 8–9), and a reminder that only those who
hate evil have real cause to rejoice in his righteous rule
(vv. 10–12).

¹²Rejoice in the LORD, you who are righteous,
  and praise his holy name.

Psalm 98

A psalm.

¹Sing to the LORD a new song,
  for he has done marvelous things;
 his right hand and his holy arm
  have worked salvation for him.
²The LORD has made his salvation known
  and revealed his righteousness to the nations.
³He has remembered his love
  and his faithfulness to Israel;
 all the ends of the earth have seen
  the salvation of our God.

⁴Shout for joy to the LORD, all the earth,
  burst into jubilant song with music;
⁵make music to the LORD with the harp,
  with the harp and the sound of singing,
⁶with trumpets and the blast of the ram's
      horn—
  shout for joy before the LORD, the King.

⁷Let the sea resound, and everything in it,
  the world, and all who live in it.
⁸Let the rivers clap their hands,
  let the mountains sing together for joy;
⁹let them sing before the LORD,
  for he comes to judge the earth.
 He will judge the world in righteousness
  and the peoples with equity.

Psalm 99

¹The LORD reigns,
  let the nations tremble;
 he sits enthroned between the cherubim,
  let the earth shake.
²Great is the LORD in Zion;
  he is exalted over all the nations.
³Let them praise your great and awesome
      name —
  he is holy.

⁴The King is mighty, he loves justice —
  you have established equity;
 in Jacob you have done
  what is just and right.
⁵Exalt the LORD our God
  and worship at his footstool;
  he is holy.

⁶Moses and Aaron were among his priests,
  Samuel was among those who called on his
      name;

Ps 98 A hymn calling for joyful celebration of the Lord's righteous reign (see introductions to Ps 93; 95). Its beginning and end echo Ps 96, with which it has been paired (see introduction to Ps 96). The three stanzas progressively extend the call to ever wider circles: (1) the worshiping congregation at the temple (vv. 1–3); (2) all the peoples of the earth (vv. 4–6); (3) the whole creation (vv. 7–9). The first stanza recalls God's revelation of his righteousness (v. 2) in the past; the last stanza speaks confidently of his coming rule "in righteousness" (v. 9); the middle stanza is enclosed by the jubilant cry "Shout for joy" (vv. 4,6).

98:1–3 The call to celebrate in song God's saving acts in behalf of his people.

98:2 *made . . . known . . . revealed . . . to the nations.* God's saving acts in behalf of his people are also his self-revelation to the nations; in this sense God is his own evangelist (see 77:14 and note on 46:10; see also Isa 52:10). *salvation . . . righteousness.* God's saving acts reveal his righteousness (see notes on 4:1; 71:24).

98:4–6 The call to all the earth to join in the celebration.

98:6 *trumpets.* The special long, straight trumpets of the sanctuary (referred to only here in Psalms). *ram's horn.* The more common trumpet (referred to also in 47:5; 81:3; 150:3).

98:7–9 The call to the whole creation to celebrate (see note on 96:11–12).

Ps 99 A hymn celebrating the Lord as the great and holy King in Zion—with special emphasis on the benefits of the Lord's reign for Israel, a feature it shares with Ps 97 (see introduction to Ps 96). In developing his theme, the poet makes striking use of the symbolic significance (completeness) of the number seven: Seven times he speaks of the "LORD," and seven times he refers to him by means of independent personal pronouns (Hebrew). (See introduction to Ps 93.)

99:1–3 The God enthroned in Zion is ruler over all the nations—let them acknowledge him.

99:1 *The LORD reigns.* See 93:1 and note. *tremble . . . shake.* In reverent awe before God. *cherubim.* See 80:1; see also Ex 25:18; Eze 1:5 and photo, p. 128.

99:4 *is mighty . . . loves justice.* Two chief characteristics of God's reign. *established equity.* That is, created conditions in the world that embody equity—especially for Israel (see 96:10 and note). *Jacob.* A synonym for Israel (Ge 32:28). *just and right.* Justice and righteousness, as in 97:2 (cf. 119:121; Eze 18:5). Though even the heavens proclaim God's righteousness (see 97:6 and note), it is in the whole complex of his saving acts in and for Israel that the righteousness of God's reign is especially disclosed (see 98:2 and note).

99:5 See also v. 9. For other refrains in the Psalms, see introduction to Ps 42–43. *footstool.* God's royal footstool (2Ch 9:18), here a metaphor linking the heavenly throne with the earthly; when God sits on his heavenly throne, his earthly throne is his footstool (here "his holy mountain," v. 9; see 132:7; 1Ch 28:2; La 2:1; see also photo, p., 128).

99:6 *Moses . . . Aaron . . . Samuel.* These three no doubt serve here as representatives of all those the Lord used as intermediaries with his people in times of great crises.

An ivory plaque from Megiddo (13th–12th century BC) depicts a ruler on his cherub-flanked throne with his attendants inspecting prisoners. Psalm 99:1 describes the Lord as "enthroned between the cherubim." Verse five also says we are to "Exalt the LORD our God and worship at his footstool"—a footstool can also be seen on the ivory plaque.

Z. Radovan/www.BibleLandPictures.com

they called on the LORD
and he answered them.
⁷He spoke to them from the pillar of cloud;
they kept his statutes and the decrees he
gave them.

⁸LORD our God,
you answered them;
you were to Israel a forgiving God,
though you punished their misdeeds.ᵃ
⁹Exalt the LORD our God
and worship at his holy mountain,
for the LORD our God is holy.

Psalm 100

A psalm. For giving grateful praise.

¹Shout for joy to the LORD, all the earth.
² Worship the LORD with gladness;
come before him with joyful songs.
³Know that the LORD is God.
It is he who made us, and we are hisᵇ;
we are his people, the sheep of his pasture.

⁴Enter his gates with thanksgiving
and his courts with praise;
give thanks to him and praise his name.
⁵For the LORD is good and his love endures
forever;
his faithfulness continues through all
generations.

ᵃ 8 Or *God, / an avenger of the wrongs done to them*
ᵇ 3 Or *and not we ourselves*

99:7 *spoke to them from the pillar of cloud.* Though reference may be to all Israel ("them"), more likely the hymn recalls God's speaking with Moses (Ex 33:9) and Aaron (Nu 12:5–6). But that special mode of revelation in the wilderness may also be generalized here to include God's revelations to Samuel, who was called to his prophetic ministry at the sanctuary, "where the ark of God was" (1Sa 3:3; see also 1Sa 12:23).

Ps 100 A hymn calling for praise to the Lord. This psalm closes the series that begins with Ps 90. It has special affinity with 95:1–2,6–7; see also Ps 117. (See introduction to Ps 93.) The second main division (vv. 4–5) parallels the structure of the first (vv. 1–3), namely, a call to praise followed by a declaration of why the Lord is worthy of praise.

100 title *grateful praise.* See v. 4. Perhaps it indicates that the psalm was to accompany a thank offering (see note on 7:17; see also Lev 7:12).

100:1 *all the earth.* Though vv. 3,5 clearly speak of God's special relationship with Israel, the call to worship goes out to the whole world, which ought to acknowledge the Lord because of what he has done for his people (see also Ps 98–99; 117).

100:3 *Know.* Acknowledge. *made us.* See 95:6 and note. *sheep of his pasture.* See 95:7 and note; see also note on 23:1.

Additional Insights

Shout for joy to the LORD, all the earth.
Worship the LORD with gladness;
come before him with joyful songs.

▶ Who are the enemies of God (92:9)?

_____

_____

_____

_____

_____

▶ How does Psalm 94 reveal God's power and sovereignty over nations and world politics?

_____

_____

_____

_____

_____

▶ What are you tempted to worship in your life instead of God (97:7)?

_____

_____

_____

_____

_____

▶ How can nature worship God (Ps 98)?

_____

_____

_____

_____

_____

Psalm 101

Of David. A psalm.

[1] I will sing of your love and justice;
　to you, LORD, I will sing praise.
[2] I will be careful to lead a blameless life —
　when will you come to me?

I will conduct the affairs of my house
　with a blameless heart.
[3] I will not look with approval
　on anything that is vile.

I hate what faithless people do;
　I will have no part in it.
[4] The perverse of heart shall be far from me;
　I will have nothing to do with what is evil.

[5] Whoever slanders their neighbor in secret,
　I will put to silence;
whoever has haughty eyes and a proud heart,
　I will not tolerate.

[6] My eyes will be on the faithful in the land,
　that they may dwell with me;
the one whose walk is blameless
　will minister to me.

[7] No one who practices deceit
　will dwell in my house;
no one who speaks falsely
　will stand in my presence.

[8] Every morning I will put to silence
　all the wicked in the land;
I will cut off every evildoer
　from the city of the LORD.

Psalm 102[a]

*A prayer of an afflicted person who has grown
weak and pours out a lament before the LORD.*

[1] Hear my prayer, LORD;
　let my cry for help come to you.
[2] Do not hide your face from me
　when I am in distress.
Turn your ear to me;
　when I call, answer me quickly.

[3] For my days vanish like smoke;
　my bones burn like glowing embers.

[a] In Hebrew texts 102:1-28 is numbered 102:2-29.

Ps 101–110 A collection of ten psalms located between two other groups (see introductions to Ps 90–100; 111–119) and framed by two psalms that pertain to the king (the first the king's vow to pattern his reign after God's righteous rule; the last God's commitment to maintain the king—his anointed—and give him victories over all his enemies).

Ps 101 A king's pledge to reign righteously (2Ki 23:3), after the pattern of God's rule. If authored by David (see title), it may have been composed before the ark of God was successfully brought into Jerusalem (see note on v. 2a; see also 2Sa 6). Only Christ, the great Son of David, has perfectly fulfilled these commitments.

101:1 *love and justice.* Two of the chief qualities of God's rule (see 6:4; 99:4 and notes). For this particular combination, see Hos 12:6; Mic 6:8; cf. Zec 7:9.

101:2a *blameless.* See vv. 2b,6. *when . . . ?* Perhaps expressive of David's yearning for the presence of the ark of the Lord in his royal city as the sign of God's readiness to be with him and sustain him in his pledge to reign as he ought. For later kings it would be a plea for divine enablement relative to the pledge given in vv. 1–2 (cf. Ps 72; 1Ki 3:7–9).

101:2b–3a The essential commitment. *heart . . . look.* In OT understanding, a person follows the dictates of the heart—the inmost being (see note on 4:7)—and/or the attractions of the eye—external influences (119:37; Jdg 14:1–2; 2Sa 11:2; 2Ki 16:10; Job 31:1; Pr 4:25; 17:24). For the combination of heart and eyes, see v. 5; Nu 15:39; Job 31:7; Pr 21:4; Ecc 2:10; Jer 22:17.

101:3b–4 A repudiation of evil deeds and those who promote them (v. 7).

101:3b *faithless.* Those who rebel against what is right (see Hos 5:2, "rebels").

101:4 *perverse.* The opposite of "blameless" (see 18:26, "devious"; see also Pr 11:20; 19:1; 28:6). A perverse heart and a deceitful tongue (v. 7) are root and fruit (Pr 17:20).

101:5 A pledge to remove from his presence all slanderous and all arrogant persons (v. 8). *put to silence.* Destroy (as in 54:5; 94:23). See v. 8. *haughty eyes . . . proud heart.* See vv. 2b–3a and note; called "the unplowed field of the wicked" in Pr 21:4; cf. Ps 131:1; Isa 10:12. The arrogant tend to be ruthless (Isa 10:12) and are a law to themselves (see note on 31:23).

101:6 A pledge to surround himself in his reign with the faithful and blameless. *My eyes will be on.* I will look with favor on (see 33:18; 34:15). *the faithful.* Those who maintain moral integrity. *minister to me.* Serve as my aide (Ex 24:13), attendant (Ge 39:4; 1Ki 19:21), personal servant (2Ki 4:43), commander and official (1 Ch 27:1; 2Ch 17:19; Pr 29:12).

101:8 A pledge to remove all the wicked from the Lord's kingdom (v. 5). *Every morning.* With diligence and persistence (Jer 21:12; Zep 3:5). It appears to have been custom-

⁴My heart is blighted and withered like grass;
    I forget to eat my food.
⁵In my distress I groan aloud
    and am reduced to skin and bones.
⁶I am like a desert owl,
    like an owl among the ruins.
⁷I lie awake; I have become
    like a bird alone on a roof.
⁸All day long my enemies taunt me;
    those who rail against me use my name as
        a curse.
⁹For I eat ashes as my food
    and mingle my drink with tears
¹⁰because of your great wrath,
    for you have taken me up and thrown me aside.
¹¹My days are like the evening shadow;
    I wither away like grass.

¹²But you, LORD, sit enthroned forever;
    your renown endures through all generations.
¹³You will arise and have compassion on Zion,
    for it is time to show favor to her;
        the appointed time has come.
¹⁴For her stones are dear to your servants;
    her very dust moves them to pity.
¹⁵The nations will fear the name of the LORD,
    all the kings of the earth will revere your
        glory.
¹⁶For the LORD will rebuild Zion
    and appear in his glory.
¹⁷He will respond to the prayer of the destitute;
    he will not despise their plea.

¹⁸Let this be written for a future generation,
    that a people not yet created may praise
        the LORD:

Additional Insights

Laments (perhaps surprisingly the most common type of psalm in the Psalter) are at the opposite end of the emotional spectrum from hymns. Laments are identified by several distinct characteristics, though not all of these are present in every lament: (1) an introductory call to God for help; (2) a description of the problem; (3) a confession of sin or an assertion of trust or innocence; (4) a call to God to deal with the problem; and (5) a declaration of confidence in God's response and/or commitment to praise him.

ary for kings to hear judicial cases in the morning—when the mind is fresh and the air cool. That is when victims looked for deliverance from those oppressing them (cf. 88:13; 143:8; Isa 33:2).

Ps 102 The lament of an unnamed individual in a time of great distress. In early Christian worship this psalm came to be used as a penitential prayer, even though it contains no explicit confession of sin.

102 title Unique in the Psalter (no author named and no liturgical or historical notes), the title identifies only the life situation in which the prayer is to be used, and in accordance with vv. 1–11,23–24 it designates the prayer as that of an individual. In addition, vv. 12–22,28 clearly indicate national involvement in the calamity.

102:1–2 Initial appeal for God to hear.

102:3–11 The description of distress—a suffering so great that it withers body and spirit—brought on by a visitation of God's wrath (v. 10) and making him the mockery of his enemies (v. 8). For the framing imagery that binds this section together, see vv. 3–4 and v. 11.

102:4 *heart.* Here "heart" is used in combination with "bones" (v. 3) to refer to the whole person (body and spirit); see note on 4:7; see also 22:14; Pr 14:30; 15:30; Isa 66:14 ("and you" represents the Hebrew for "and your bones"); Jer 20:9; 23:9. *blighted.* Or "scorched" (by the hot sun); see 121:6. *withered like grass.* See v. 11; see also note on 90:5–6.

102:6 *owl.* Associated with desert areas and ruins (Isa 34:11,15; Jer 50:39; Zep 2:14).

102:9 *drink . . . tears.* For tears as food and drink, see 42:3; 80:5.

102:11 An echo of vv. 3–4. *shadow.* See 109:23; 144:4; Job 8:9; 14:2; Ecc 6:12. *grass.* See 37:20; 90:5–6 and notes.

102:12–17 Assurance that heaven's eternal King will surely hear the prayer of the destitute (v. 17) and restore Zion. For such expressions of assurance in the laments of the Psalter, see note on 3:8. This six-verse stanza weaves its themes in a balanced *a-b-c/a-b-c* pattern.

102:12 *sit enthroned forever.* A central theme of the preceding collection (Ps 90–100). Because God reigns forever and remains the same (v. 27), his mercies to those who look to him for salvation will not fail. *renown.* See note on 30:4 ("name"). For elaborate celebrations of the Lord's renown, see Ps 111; 135; 145.

102:13 This verse and v. 16 (see also v. 14) suggest that the psalmist's distress was occasioned by the Babylonian exile. *appointed time.* The time set by God for judgment and deliverance (75:2; Ex 9:5; 2Sa 24:15; Da 11:27,35). Perhaps the psalmist is referring to a time announced by a prophet.

102:14 *dear to your servants.* If Zion, the city of God (46:4; 48:1–2,8; 87:3; 101:8; 132:13), is so loved by the Lord's servants (Ps 126; 137), how much more is she cherished by the Lord!

102:16 *will rebuild Zion.* Yahweh will "have compassion" on Zion (v. 13) by rebuilding her. *and appear in his glory.* Or "and thus appear in his glory" (see v. 15 and note on 46:10; see also Isa 40:1–5). This hope will find its fullest expression in the "new Jerusalem" (Rev 21).

102:17 *the destitute.* Reference is to "your servants" (v. 14). *their plea.* Expressive of the pity they feel for their beloved Zion now lying in ruins (v. 14).

19 "The Lord looked down from his sanctuary
   on high,
   from heaven he viewed the earth,
20 to hear the groans of the prisoners
   and release those condemned to death."
21 So the name of the Lord will be declared
   in Zion
   and his praise in Jerusalem
22 when the peoples and the kingdoms
   assemble to worship the Lord.

23 In the course of my life[a] he broke my strength;
   he cut short my days.
24 So I said:
   "Do not take me away, my God, in the midst of
   my days;
   your years go on through all generations.
25 In the beginning you laid the foundations of
   the earth,
   and the heavens are the work of your hands.
26 They will perish, but you remain;
   they will all wear out like a garment.
   Like clothing you will change them
   and they will be discarded.
27 But you remain the same,
   and your years will never end.
28 The children of your servants will live in your
   presence;
   their descendants will be established
   before you."

Psalm 103

Of David.

1 Praise the Lord, my soul;
   all my inmost being, praise his holy name.
2 Praise the Lord, my soul,
   and forget not all his benefits —
3 who forgives all your sins
   and heals all your diseases,
4 who redeems your life from the pit
   and crowns you with love and compassion,
5 who satisfies your desires with good things
   so that your youth is renewed like the
   eagle's.

6 The Lord works righteousness
   and justice for all the oppressed.

7 He made known his ways to Moses,
   his deeds to the people of Israel:
8 The Lord is compassionate and gracious,
   slow to anger, abounding in love.
9 He will not always accuse,
   nor will he harbor his anger forever;

102:18–22 Let God's certain deliverance of his people be recorded for his continual praise (v. 8)—until that great day when the worshiping community celebrating Zion's redemption has expanded to include representatives of the "peoples" and "kingdoms" of the world (v. 22). See introduction to Ps 117; see also Rev 15:4; 21:24,26.
102:18 *written.* Only here does a psalmist call for memory to be sustained by a written record of God's saving act; usually oral transmission suffices (22:30; 44:1; 78:1–4). *created.* Brought into being by God's sovereign act (51:10; 104:30; 139:13).
102:20 *prisoners . . . those condemned to death.* Perhaps prisoners of war, but more likely the exiles in Babylon (see 79:11 and note).
102:21 *praise.* See note on 9:1.
102:22 See note on 46:10; 96; 98; 100. The expectation here expressed may also be influenced by such prophecies as Isa 2:2–4; Mic 4:1–3.
102:23–28 Concluding recapitulation. The stanza is framed by the radical contrast expressed in vv. 23,28. That human life is cut short (v. 23) by the One whose own being spans all ages (vv. 25–27) adds to the psalmist's sense of loss on the one hand but also to his hope on the other (v. 28) and thus to the urgency of his prayer—as in 90:1–6 (see note on 90:4–5).
102:23–24a See vv. 3–11.
102:26 *Like clothing.* With his first creation God clothed himself with the manifestation of his glory (see 8:1,3–4; 19:1; 29:3–9; 104:1,31; Isa 6:3; see also Job 38–41, especially 40:10). But he is more enduring than what he has made— and the first creation will give way to a new creation (Isa 65:17; 66:22).
102:28 Because the Lord does not change (v. 27), Israel's future is secure (Mal 3:6). *live in your presence.* Or "dwell in the (promised) land" (see 37:3,29; see also 69:36; Isa 65:9). *established before you.* See 2Sa 7:24.
Ps 103 A salvation-history hymn, celebrating God's love and compassion toward his people. Calls to praise (vv. 1–2,20–22) frame the body of the hymn (vv. 3–19) and set its tone. The recital of praise falls into two unequal parts: (1) a three-verse celebration of personal benefits received (vv. 3–5) and (2) a 14-verse recollection of God's mercies to his people Israel (vv. 6–19).
103:1–2 Call to praise God, directed inward (cf. vv. 20–22).
103:1–2,22 *my soul.* A conventional Hebrew way of addressing oneself (104:1,35; 116:7; see also note on 6:3).
103:3–5 Recital of personal blessings received.
103:4 *redeems.* A synonym for "delivers." *pit.* A metaphor for the grave (see note on 30:1). *love and compassion.* The key words of the hymn (see vv. 8,11,13,17). *love.* See vv. 8,11,17; see also article, p. 16.
103:5 *like the eagle's.* The vigor of youth is restored to match the proverbial, unflagging strength of the eagle (see Isa 40:30–31).
103:6–19 God's love and compassion toward his people.
103:6 Verses 6 and 19 form a literary frame characterizing the reign of God, under which Israel has been so graciously blessed. *righteousness.* See v. 17; see also note on 4:1.
103:7 *his ways.* See 25:10 and note.

---

[a] 23 Or *By his power*

¹⁰ he does not treat us as our sins deserve
　　or repay us according to our iniquities.
¹¹ For as high as the heavens are above the
　　earth,
　　so great is his love for those who fear him;
¹² as far as the east is from the west,
　　so far has he removed our transgressions
　　　from us.

¹³ As a father has compassion on his children,
　　so the Lord has compassion on those who
　　　fear him;
¹⁴ for he knows how we are formed,
　　he remembers that we are dust.
¹⁵ The life of mortals is like grass,
　　they flourish like a flower of the field;
¹⁶ the wind blows over it and it is gone,
　　and its place remembers it no more.
¹⁷ But from everlasting to everlasting
　　the Lord's love is with those who fear him,
　　and his righteousness with their children's
　　　children—
¹⁸ with those who keep his covenant
　　and remember to obey his precepts.

¹⁹ The Lord has established his throne in
　　heaven,
　　and his kingdom rules over all.

²⁰ Praise the Lord, you his angels,
　　you mighty ones who do his bidding,
　　who obey his word.
²¹ Praise the Lord, all his heavenly hosts,
　　you his servants who do his will.
²² Praise the Lord, all his works
　　everywhere in his dominion.

　　Praise the Lord, my soul.

Psalm 104

¹ Praise the Lord, my soul.

Lord my God, you are very great;
　　you are clothed with splendor and majesty.

² The Lord wraps himself in light as with a
　　garment;
　　he stretches out the heavens like a tent
³　　and lays the beams of his upper chambers on
　　　their waters.
He makes the clouds his chariot
　　and rides on the wings of the wind.
⁴ He makes winds his messengers,^a
　　flames of fire his servants.

⁵ He set the earth on its foundations;
　　it can never be moved.

---

^a 4 Or *angels*

 103:11–12 The vastness of God's love (note the spatial imagery) is supremely shown in his forgiving Israel's sins.
103:11 See 36:5–9. *so great is.* So prevails. *those who fear him.* See vv. 13,17–18.
103:12 See Isa 1:18; 38:17; 43:25; Jer 31:34; 50:20; Mic 7:18–19.
103:13–18 God's compassion on his people as frail mortals (78:39).
103:13–14 In Hebrew the initial words of these two verses strikingly echo the sounds of the initial words of vv. 11–12, thereby effecting a tight literary bond between vv. 13–18 and vv. 7–12.
103:14 *we are dust.* See Ge 2:7; 3:19.
103:15–16 See note on 90:5–6.
103:17–18 The infinite temporal span of God's love (cf. the spatial imagery in vv. 11–12).
103:17 *everlasting to everlasting . . . their children's children.* God's love outlasts anyone's little time in this life (cf. note on 109:12).
103:19 See v. 6 and note; see also 9:4,7; 11:4; 47:2,7–8; 123:1.
103:20–22 Concluding call to praise, directed to all creatures—from the psalmist's inner self (vv. 1–2) to the creatures who serve God in heaven. A call to praise God is often the climax of praise in the Psalter (as also of the whole collection; see Ps 148–150). See note on 9:1. *Praise . . . Praise . . . Praise.* See note on 96:1–3. (The final line was probably added by the editors of the Psalter; see 104:1,35.)
103:20 *who do his bidding.* See 91:11; Heb 1:14.
103:21 *servants.* Translates the participle of the Hebrew verb for "minister" in 101:6 (see note there).
103:22 *all his works.* See 65:13; 96:11–12 and notes.
Ps 104 A hymn to the Creator. The preexilic author has adapted Ge 1 to his own quite different purpose and has subordinated its sequence somewhat to his own design. Ge 1 recounts God's acts of creation as his first work at the beginning, but the poet views the created world displayed before his eyes and sings the glory of its Maker and Sustainer. The psalmist's theme is the visible creation, which he views as the radiant and stately robe with which the invisible Creator has clothed himself to display his glory.
104:2–4 The celestial realm above.
104:2 *light.* Cf. the first day of creation (Ge 1:3–5). *heavens.* Cf. the second day of creation (Ge 1:6–8). *like a tent.* Over the earth and the luminaries that give it light.
104:3 *upper chambers.* Vivid imagery for the heavenly abode of God (see v. 13). In the singular, the Hebrew for this phrase usually refers to the upper-level room of a house (as in 1Ki 17:19; 2Ki 1:2). *their waters.* The waters above the "tent" (v. 2; see Ge 1:7), from which, in the imagery of the OT, God gives the rain (see v. 13; see also 36:8 and note). *clouds his chariot.* See 18:7–15; 68:4; 77:16–19 and notes.
104:4 *winds . . . flames of fire.* The winds and lightning bolts of the thunderstorm, here personified as the agents of God's purposes (see 148:8; cf. 103:21; see also Heb 1:7).
104:5–9 God establishes an orderly earth. Verses 5,9 frame the stanza, highlighting its two main themes.
104:5 *earth.* Land in distinction from sky and seas, not the earth as a planet (Ge 1:10). *foundations.* See 24:2 and note. *can never be moved.* Firmly founded (93:1; 96:10), it will not give way (cf. v. 9).

⁶You covered it with the watery depths as with a garment;
 the waters stood above the mountains.
⁷But at your rebuke the waters fled,
 at the sound of your thunder they took to flight;
⁸they flowed over the mountains,
 they went down into the valleys,
 to the place you assigned for them.
⁹You set a boundary they cannot cross;
 never again will they cover the earth.

¹⁰He makes springs pour water into the ravines;
 it flows between the mountains.
¹¹They give water to all the beasts of the field;
 the wild donkeys quench their thirst.
¹²The birds of the sky nest by the waters;
 they sing among the branches.
¹³He waters the mountains from his upper chambers;
 the land is satisfied by the fruit of his work.
¹⁴He makes grass grow for the cattle,
 and plants for people to cultivate —
 bringing forth food from the earth:
¹⁵wine that gladdens human hearts,
 oil to make their faces shine,
 and bread that sustains their hearts.
¹⁶The trees of the LORD are well watered,
 the cedars of Lebanon that he planted.
¹⁷There the birds make their nests;
 the stork has its home in the junipers.
¹⁸The high mountains belong to the wild goats;
 the crags are a refuge for the hyrax.

¹⁹He made the moon to mark the seasons,
 and the sun knows when to go down.
²⁰You bring darkness, it becomes night,
 and all the beasts of the forest prowl.
²¹The lions roar for their prey
 and seek their food from God.
²²The sun rises, and they steal away;
 they return and lie down in their dens.
²³Then people go out to their work,
 to their labor until evening.

²⁴How many are your works, LORD!
 In wisdom you made them all;
 the earth is full of your creatures.
²⁵There is the sea, vast and spacious,
 teeming with creatures beyond number —
 living things both large and small.
²⁶There the ships go to and fro,
 and Leviathan, which you formed to frolic there.

²⁷All creatures look to you
 to give them their food at the proper time.

104:9 *set a boundary.* So that the land ("earth") will never be overwhelmed by the sea (cf. v. 5; see also Ge 9:15).
104:10–18 God makes the earth a flourishing garden of life—the center of the psalm and the focal point of the author's contemplation of the creation (the earth, bounded by sky, vv. 2–4, and sea, vv. 24–26). Cf. the third and sixth days of creation (Ge 1:9–13,24–31).
104:10–12 The gift of water from below—watering the ravines of the Negev, south of Israel's heartland.
104:13–15 The gift of water from above—watering the uplands of Israel's heartland with its cultivated fields.
104:13 *upper chambers.* See v. 3 and note.
104:15 *hearts . . . hearts.* See note on 4:7. *oil.* Olive oil. *make their faces shine.* As food (1Ki 17:12), causing a person's face to glow with health, and/or as cosmetic (Est 2:12).
104:16–18 Well-watered Lebanon (north of Israel's heartland), with its great trees, its hordes of birds and its alpine animals, the very epitome of God's earthly parkland (72:16; 2Ki 14:9; 19:23; Isa 10:34; 35:2; 40:16; 60:13; Jer 22:6; Hos 14:7).
104:19–23 The orderly cycles of life (the temporal element; see notes on vv. 2–4,5–9; see also introduction) on earth, governed by the moon and sun. Cf. the fourth day of creation (Ge 1:14–19).
104:24–26 The nautical realm below. Cf. the fifth day of creation (Ge 1:20–23). The realm of the sea is structurally balanced with the celestial realm (vv. 2–4) as the other boundary to the realm of earth.
104:26 *Leviathan.* That fearsome mythological monster of the deep (see Job 3:8) is here portrayed as nothing more than God's harmless pet playing in the ocean.
104:27–30 By God's benevolent care this zoological garden flourishes. Cf. the sixth day of creation (Ge 1:24–31).

How does the natural world inspire your faith?

_____

_____

_____

_____

_____

_____

_____

_____

²⁸When you give it to them,
    they gather it up;
  when you open your hand,
    they are satisfied with good things.
²⁹When you hide your face,
    they are terrified;
  when you take away their breath,
    they die and return to the dust.
³⁰When you send your Spirit,
    they are created,
  and you renew the face of the ground.

³¹May the glory of the LORD endure forever;
    may the LORD rejoice in his works —
³²he who looks at the earth, and it trembles,
    who touches the mountains, and they smoke.

³³I will sing to the LORD all my life;
    I will sing praise to my God as long as I live.
³⁴May my meditation be pleasing to him,
    as I rejoice in the LORD.
³⁵But may sinners vanish from the earth
    and the wicked be no more.

Praise the LORD, my soul.

Praise the LORD.^a

Psalm 105

¹Give praise to the LORD, proclaim his name;
    make known among the nations what he
      has done.
²Sing to him, sing praise to him;
    tell of all his wonderful acts.
³Glory in his holy name;
    let the hearts of those who seek the LORD
      rejoice.
⁴Look to the LORD and his strength;
    seek his face always.

⁵Remember the wonders he has done,
    his miracles, and the judgments he
      pronounced,
⁶you his servants, the descendants of Abraham,
    his chosen ones, the children of Jacob.
⁷He is the LORD our God;
    his judgments are in all the earth.

⁸He remembers his covenant forever,
    the promise he made, for a thousand
      generations,
⁹the covenant he made with Abraham,
    the oath he swore to Isaac.
¹⁰He confirmed it to Jacob as a decree,
    to Israel as an everlasting covenant:

^a *35* Hebrew *Hallelu Yah*; in the Septuagint this line stands at the beginning of Psalm 105.

104:29 *hide your face.* See note on 13:1.
104:30 *your Spirit.* See note on 51:11. *created.* See note on 102:18.
104:31 *glory of the LORD.* Such as is displayed in his creation (see 19:1–4a and note).
104:32 He is so much greater than his creation that with a look or a touch or a word (33:6,9) he could undo it.
104:33–35 A concluding expression of the psalmist's devotion to Yahweh (cf. NIV text note on v. 35).
104:33 A vow to praise God—here attached to a hymn of praise (see note on 7:17).
104:34 *my meditation.* The preceding hymn.
104:35 *Praise the LORD* (last occurrence). Probably belonged originally to Ps 105 (see NIV text note and 105:45; 106:1,48).

Ps 105 A salvation-history hymn, exhorting Israel to worship and trust in the Lord because of all his saving acts in fulfillment of his covenant with Abraham to give his descendants the land of Canaan. It was composed to be addressed to Israel by a Levite (see 1Ch 16:7 and compare vv. 1–15 with 1Ch 16:8–22) on one of Israel's annual religious festivals, possibly the Festival of Tabernacles (Lev 23:34) but more likely the Festival of Weeks or Pentecost (see Ex 23:16; Lev 23:15–21; Nu 28:26; Dt 16:9–12; see also Dt 26:1–11). For other recitals of the same history (but for different purposes), see Ps 78; 106; Jos 24:2–13; Ne 9:7–25.

The introduction is composed of seven verses in two parts: (1) an exhortation (with ten imperatives) to worship the Lord (vv. 1–4); (2) a call to remember what the Lord has done (vv. 5–7). The main body that follows is framed by two four-verse stanzas (vv. 8–11, 42–45) that summarize—as introduction and conclusion—its main theme: The Lord has remembered his covenant with Abraham. The editors of the Psalter have added an outer frame of "Praise the LORD" (Hebrew "Hallelujah"; see NIV text note on 104:35).
105:1–4 The exhortation to worship Yahweh and trust in him.

105:1 *Give praise.* See note on Ps 100 title. *his name.* See v. 3. *make known among the nations.* As an integral part of praise (see note on 9:1).
105:2 *wonderful acts.* See v. 5 ("wonders"); see also note on 9:1.
105:3,25 *hearts.* See note on 4:7.
105:5–7 Exhortation to remember God's saving acts.

105:5 *Remember.* As a motivation for and focus of worship and the basis for trust—remember how the Lord has remembered (vv. 8–11). *judgments.* See v. 7; see also note on 48:11. *pronounced.* As Lord, he commands and it is done (7:6 ["decree justice"]; 33:9; 71:3; 78:23; 147:15,18; 148:5; Isa 5:6; 55:11; Jer 1:12; Am 9:3–4).
105:6,9 *Abraham . . . Jacob . . . Isaac.* While "Jacob" occurs 34 times in the Psalter, Abraham is recalled by name in Psalms only here (see also v. 42) and in 47:9. Reference to Isaac occurs in Psalms only here.
105:8–11 The Lord remembers his covenant with Abraham (vv. 42–45).
105:8 *covenant.* The promissory covenant of Ge 15:9–21. This verse and v. 9 may be echoed in Lk 1:72–73. *thousand generations.* See Ex 20:6; Dt 7:9; 1Ch 16:15.
105:10 *as a decree.* As a fixed policy governing his future actions (see note on v. 45).

¹¹ "To you I will give the land of Canaan
　　as the portion you will inherit."

¹² When they were but few in number,
　　few indeed, and strangers in it,
¹³ they wandered from nation to nation,
　　from one kingdom to another.
¹⁴ He allowed no one to oppress them;
　　for their sake he rebuked kings:
¹⁵ "Do not touch my anointed ones;
　　do my prophets no harm."

¹⁶ He called down famine on the land
　　and destroyed all their supplies of food;
¹⁷ and he sent a man before them —
　　Joseph, sold as a slave.
¹⁸ They bruised his feet with shackles,
　　his neck was put in irons,
¹⁹ till what he foretold came to pass,
　　till the word of the LORD proved him true.
²⁰ The king sent and released him,
　　the ruler of peoples set him free.

105:12–41 A recital of God's saving acts in Israel's behalf from the granting of the covenant (v. 11; Ge 15:9–21) to its fulfillment (v. 44; Jos 21:43). Cf. the recital prescribed by Moses in conjunction with the offering of firstfruits (Dt 26:1–11).
105:14–15 See Ge 20:2–7.

Additional Insights

By God's covenant, Israel was to live among the nations, loyal only to their heavenly King. They were to trust solely in his protection, hope in his promises, live in accordance with his will and worship him exclusively.

Illustration of the plague of frogs from a 14th-century Hebrew manuscript. Ps 105 recounts the plagues in Egypt.

Z. Radovan/www.BibleLandPictures.com

²¹He made him master of his household,
    ruler over all he possessed,
²²to instruct his princes as he pleased
    and teach his elders wisdom.

²³Then Israel entered Egypt;
    Jacob resided as a foreigner in the land of Ham.
²⁴The LORD made his people very fruitful;
    he made them too numerous for their foes,
²⁵whose hearts he turned to hate his people,
    to conspire against his servants.
²⁶He sent Moses his servant,
    and Aaron, whom he had chosen.
²⁷They performed his signs among them,
    his wonders in the land of Ham.
²⁸He sent darkness and made the land dark—
    for had they not rebelled against his words?
²⁹He turned their waters into blood,
    causing their fish to die.
³⁰Their land teemed with frogs,
    which went up into the bedrooms of their
      rulers.
³¹He spoke, and there came swarms of flies,
    and gnats throughout their country.
³²He turned their rain into hail,
    with lightning throughout their land;
³³he struck down their vines and fig trees
    and shattered the trees of their country.
³⁴He spoke, and the locusts came,
    grasshoppers without number;
³⁵they ate up every green thing in their land,
    ate up the produce of their soil.
³⁶Then he struck down all the firstborn in their land,
    the firstfruits of all their manhood.
³⁷He brought out Israel, laden with silver and gold,
    and from among their tribes no one faltered.
³⁸Egypt was glad when they left,
    because dread of Israel had fallen on them.

³⁹He spread out a cloud as a covering,
    and a fire to give light at night.
⁴⁰They asked, and he brought them quail;
    he fed them well with the bread of heaven.
⁴¹He opened the rock, and water gushed out;
    it flowed like a river in the desert.

⁴²For he remembered his holy promise
    given to his servant Abraham.
⁴³He brought out his people with rejoicing,
    his chosen ones with shouts of joy;
⁴⁴he gave them the lands of the nations,
    and they fell heir to what others had toiled
      for—
⁴⁵that they might keep his precepts
    and observe his laws.

    Praise the LORD.[a]

[a] 45 Hebrew *Hallelu Yah*

105:22 *instruct.* Or "bind," i.e., govern or control. He whose "neck" (v. 18; Hebrew *nephesh*) had been shackled was given authority to "bind" the pharaoh's princes "as he pleased" (Hebrew "with his *nephesh*"—here meaning his will). *elders.* The pharaoh's counselors, conventionally older men of wide experience and learning.
105:23,27 *land of Ham.* See 78:51 and note.
105:25 *turned.* In OT perspective God's sovereign control over Israel's destiny is so complete that it governs—mysteriously—even the evil that others commit against them; hence the bold language used here (Ex 4:21; 7:3; Jos 11:20; 2Sa 24:1; Isa 10:5–7; 37:26–27; Jer 34:22).
105:26,42 *servant.* See 78:70 and note.
105:28–36 Recital of the plagues against Egypt. In this poetic recollection seven plagues (symbolizing completeness) represent the ten plagues of Ex 7–11. Apart from omissions (the plagues of livestock disease and boils) the poet follows the order of Exodus, except that he combines the third and fourth plagues (gnats and flies)—in reverse order—to stay within the number seven. He also places the ninth plague (darkness) first in order to frame his recital with mention of the two plagues that climaxed the series.
105:30 *frogs.* See photo, p. 136.
105:37 *laden with silver and gold.* See Ex 3:22; 12:35–36.
105:39 *as a covering.* Elsewhere it is said that the cloud (symbolic of God's presence) served (1) as a guide for Israel in their wilderness journeys (78:14; Ex 13:21; Nu 9:17; Ne 9:12,19), (2) as a shield of darkness to protect Israel from the pursuing Egyptians (Ex 14:19–20) and (3) as a covering for the fiery manifestations of God's glorious presence (Ex 16:10; 24:16; 34:5; 40:34–35,38; Nu 11:25; 12:5; 16:42; Dt 31:15; 1Ki 8:11). The psalmist appears to highlight yet another function: God's protective cover over his people in the wilderness, perhaps as his shading "wings" (17:8; see note there), so that the sun would not harm them by day (121:5–6).
105:40 *bread of heaven.* See 78:24–25 and note on 78:25; see also Jn 6:31–32.
105:41 *like a river.* Poetically heightened imagery to evoke due wonder for the event. This miracle of the wilderness wanderings concludes the recital and has been placed in climactic position as one of the most striking manifestations of God's redeeming power and benevolence (see 114:8; Isa 43:19–20; cf. Isa 50:2).
105:42–45 Concluding summary (balancing the introduction to the recital: vv. 8–11).
105:44 *gave them the lands.* See v. 11.
105:45 *precepts.* God has kept his "decree" (v. 10) so that Israel might keep his "precepts"—the Hebrew word is the same (see note on v. 5: "remember"). God's redemptive working in fulfillment of his covenant promise has as its goal the creating of a people in the earth who conform their lives to his holy will (Isa 5:1–7).

1 Praise the Lord.[a]

Give thanks to the Lord, for he is good;
  his love endures forever.

2 Who can proclaim the mighty acts of the Lord
  or fully declare his praise?
3 Blessed are those who act justly,
  who always do what is right.

4 Remember me, Lord, when you show favor to
    your people,
  come to my aid when you save them,
5 that I may enjoy the prosperity of your chosen
    ones,
  that I may share in the joy of your nation
  and join your inheritance in giving praise.

6 We have sinned, even as our ancestors did;
  we have done wrong and acted wickedly.
7 When our ancestors were in Egypt,
  they gave no thought to your miracles;
  they did not remember your many kindnesses,
  and they rebelled by the sea, the Red Sea.[b]
8 Yet he saved them for his name's sake,
  to make his mighty power known.
9 He rebuked the Red Sea, and it dried up;
  he led them through the depths as through a
    desert.
10 He saved them from the hand of the foe;
  from the hand of the enemy he redeemed
    them.
11 The waters covered their adversaries;
  not one of them survived.
12 Then they believed his promises
  and sang his praise.

13 But they soon forgot what he had done
  and did not wait for his plan to unfold.
14 In the desert they gave in to their craving;
  in the wilderness they put God to the test.
15 So he gave them what they asked for,
  but sent a wasting disease among them.

16 In the camp they grew envious of Moses
  and of Aaron, who was consecrated to the
    Lord.
17 The earth opened up and swallowed Dathan;
  it buried the company of Abiram.
18 Fire blazed among their followers;
  a flame consumed the wicked.
19 At Horeb they made a calf
  and worshiped an idol cast from metal.
20 They exchanged their glorious God
  for an image of a bull, which eats grass.

---

[a] 1 Hebrew *Hallelu Yah*; also in verse 48   [b] 7 Or *the Sea of Reeds*; also in verses 9 and 22

Ps 106 A salvation-history hymn, stressing Israel's long history of rebellion and a prayer for God to once again save his people. In length, poetic style and shared themes it has much affinity with Ps 105, even while it contrasts with it by reciting the past as a history of rebellion (Ps 78; Ne 9:5–37). See further the introduction to Ps 101–110.

In the final edited form of the Psalter, the psalm is set between two liturgical calls to praise ("Hallelujah!"). Within this outer frame stands another, also drawn from the liturgical language of praise (vv. 1b,48a). And still a third frame (formed by two couplets devoted to prayer [vv. 4–5,47; see notes there]) encloses the main body of the psalm. Verses 2–3 are transitional. While the recital character of the central theme (as in Ps 105; see also Ps 78) controls the basic outline, attention to symmetry brings to light the carefully designed pattern of thematic development. The recital begins with 14 Hebrew poetic lines devoted to the period of the exodus and the wilderness wanderings (vv. 6–18) and ends with 14 Hebrew lines devoted to Israel's time in the promised land (vv. 34–46). The intervening verses (vv. 19–33) make up three stanzas with a six-four-six line pattern. In the two six-line stanzas, instances of Israel's engagement in idolatry in the wilderness period are recalled (the golden calf at Horeb [vv. 19–23]; the Baal of Peor in the plains of Moab [vv. 28–33]). These stanzas each end with a word about Moses: In the first, Moses intercedes for Israel and wards off God's wrath; in the second, Israel so vexes Moses that he acts rashly and loses his opportunity to enter the promised land—a most poignant contrast. At the center, a four-line stanza recalls Israel's refusal to take over the promised land and Yahweh's condemnation of that generation to die in the wilderness (see Nu 14:1–23; cf. Heb 3:16–19).

106:1–5 Introduction.
106:1 *Give thanks to the Lord.* With praise (see note on Ps 100 title); a conventional, liturgical call to praise God (107:1; 118:1,29; 136:1). *love.* See article, p. 16.
106:2–3 Transition to the main body of the psalm—question and answer.
106:2 *Who can . . . declare his praise?* A rhetorical question. No one can fully declare his praise. *his praise.* See note on 9:1.
106:3 *Blessed.* See note on 1:1. *act justly . . . do what is right.* See note on 119:121. This verse answers the question posed in v. 2.
106:4–5 A poetic couplet, voicing the prayer of an individual (cf. v. 47).
106:4 *Remember me.* As one committed to the way of life described in v. 3. *when you show favor.* Or "with the favor you show" (vv. 44–46). *when you save them.* Or "with your salvation." The psalmist prays that God will include him in all the mercies of his "great love" (v. 45), which he shows to his people. Thus the inner logic of the prayer seems to be completed at v. 46.
106:5 *prosperity . . . joy . . . praise.* A progressive sequence of cause and effect. *your inheritance.* See v. 40.
106:6–12 Israel's rebelliousness and the Lord's mercy in the exodus event.
106:6 A general confession of sin introducing the recital. *We.* The author identifies himself with Israel in their rebellion, even as he prays for inclusion in God's mercies toward his people (Ezr 9:6–7).

²¹ They forgot the God who saved them,
    who had done great things in Egypt,
²² miracles in the land of Ham
    and awesome deeds by the Red Sea.
²³ So he said he would destroy them —
    had not Moses, his chosen one,
   stood in the breach before him
    to keep his wrath from destroying them.

²⁴ Then they despised the pleasant land;
    they did not believe his promise.
²⁵ They grumbled in their tents
    and did not obey the LORD.
²⁶ So he swore to them with uplifted hand
    that he would make them fall in the wilderness,
²⁷ make their descendants fall among the nations
    and scatter them throughout the lands.

²⁸ They yoked themselves to the Baal of Peor
    and ate sacrifices offered to lifeless gods;
²⁹ they aroused the LORD's anger by their wicked
    deeds,
    and a plague broke out among them.
³⁰ But Phinehas stood up and intervened,
    and the plague was checked.
³¹ This was credited to him as righteousness
    for endless generations to come.
³² By the waters of Meribah they angered the LORD,
    and trouble came to Moses because of them;
³³ for they rebelled against the Spirit of God,
    and rash words came from Moses' lips.^a

³⁴ They did not destroy the peoples
    as the LORD had commanded them,
³⁵ but they mingled with the nations
    and adopted their customs.
³⁶ They worshiped their idols,
    which became a snare to them.
³⁷ They sacrificed their sons
    and their daughters to false gods.
³⁸ They shed innocent blood,
    the blood of their sons and daughters,
   whom they sacrificed to the idols of Canaan,
    and the land was desecrated by their blood.
³⁹ They defiled themselves by what they did;
    by their deeds they prostituted themselves.

⁴⁰ Therefore the LORD was angry with his people
    and abhorred his inheritance.
⁴¹ He gave them into the hands of the nations,
    and their foes ruled over them.
⁴² Their enemies oppressed them
    and subjected them to their power.
⁴³ Many times he delivered them,
    but they were bent on rebellion
    and they wasted away in their sin.

^a 33 Or *against his spirit, / and rash words came from his lips*

106:7,22 *miracles.* For example, the plagues against Egypt (see note on 9:1, "wonderful deeds").

106:10 *redeemed.* Here, as often, a synonym for "delivered."

106:12 *sang his praise.* See Ex 15:1–21.

106:13–18 Israel's discontent and the Lord's judgments.

106:13–15 Discontent with the Lord's provisions (Ex 16; Nu 11).

106:16–18 Discontent with the Lord's leadership arrangements (Nu 16:1–35).

106:19–23 Idolatry at Horeb and Moses' intercession.

106:20 *glorious God.* See 1Sa 15:29; Jer 2:11; Hos 4:7.

106:22 *land of Ham.* See 78:51 and note.

106:23 *stood in the breach.* See Ex 32:11–14,31–32.

106:24–27 Israel's lack of faith at the border of the promised land and the Lord's judgment (Nu 14:1–23).

106:24 *pleasant land.* So described in Jer 3:19; 12:10; Zec 7:14; see also Dt 8:7–9; Eze 20:6.

106:27 *scatter them throughout the lands.* See Lev 26:33; Dt 28:36–37,64; Eze 20:23.

106:28–33 Idolatry at Peor (vv. 28–31), and Moses barred from entering the land (vv. 32–33).

106:28 *yoked themselves to.* See Nu 25:3,5.

106:31 *credited to him as righteousness.* As Abram's faith was "credited . . . to him as righteousness" (Ge 15:6), so, says the psalmist, was Phinehas's priestly zeal for the Lord (Nu 25:7–8). *for endless generations.* The psalmist refers to the "covenant of a lasting priesthood" (Nu 25:13) that the Lord granted Phinehas as a gracious reward for his zealous act. It was the granting of this promissory covenant that warranted the statement about crediting righteousness, for God's granting of a promissory covenant to Abram had followed upon his crediting Abram's faith to him as righteousness (Ge 15:9–21). Similarly, God's promissory covenants with Noah (Ge 9:9–17) and with David (2Sa 7:5–16) followed upon God's testimony to their righteousness (Ge 7:1; 1Sa 13:14).

106:33 *against the Spirit of God.* For an alternative rendering of the Hebrew, see NIV text note. The interpretation embodied in the NIV text appears warranted by Isa 63:10 (see also Ps 78:40). For the Spirit of God present and at work in the wilderness wanderings, see Ex 31:3; Nu 11:17; 24:2; Ne 9:20; Isa 63:10–14. See also note on 51:11.

106:34–39 A general description of Israel's rebelliousness in the promised land, applicable from the time of the judges to the Babylonian exile.

106:36 *became a snare to them.* See Ex 23:33; Dt 7:16; Jdg 2:3; 8:27; cf. Ex 10:7; 34:12; 1Sa 18:21; cf. also note on 9:15.

106:37 *false gods.* The Hebrew word for this phrase occurs elsewhere in the OT only in Dt 32:17.

106:38 Cf. Jer 19:4–5. *innocent blood.* The blood of anyone not guilty of a capital crime. *desecrated.* The very land itself is defiled by the slaughter of innocents (Nu 35:33; Jer 3:2,9).

106:39 *defiled.* See Lev 18:24; Jer 2:23; Eze 20:30–31; 22:3–4. *prostituted themselves.* See Ex 34:15.

106:40–46 God's stern measures against his rebellious people (vv. 40–43), but at the same time his gracious remembering of his covenant (vv. 44–46). The judgments here recalled focus particularly on God's most severe covenant sanctions (Lev 26:25–26,33,38–39; Dt 28:25,36–37,48–57,64–68).

106:40 *abhorred.* See 5:6.

44 Yet he took note of their distress
  when he heard their cry;
45 for their sake he remembered his covenant
  and out of his great love he relented.
46 He caused all who held them captive
  to show them mercy.

47 Save us, LORD our God,
  and gather us from the nations,
that we may give thanks to your holy name
  and glory in your praise.

48 Praise be to the LORD, the God of Israel,
  from everlasting to everlasting.

Let all the people say, "Amen!"

Praise the LORD.

BOOK V

Psalms 107 – 150

Psalm 107

1 Give thanks to the LORD, for he is good;
  his love endures forever.

2 Let the redeemed of the LORD tell their story —
  those he redeemed from the hand of the foe,
3 those he gathered from the lands,
  from east and west, from north and south.*a*

4 Some wandered in desert wastelands,
  finding no way to a city where they could
    settle.
5 They were hungry and thirsty,
  and their lives ebbed away.
6 Then they cried out to the LORD in their
    trouble,
  and he delivered them from their distress.
7 He led them by a straight way
  to a city where they could settle.
8 Let them give thanks to the LORD for his
    unfailing love
  and his wonderful deeds for mankind,
9 for he satisfies the thirsty
  and fills the hungry with good things.

10 Some sat in darkness, in utter darkness,
  prisoners suffering in iron chains,
11 because they rebelled against God's commands
  and despised the plans of the Most High.
12 So he subjected them to bitter labor;
  they stumbled, and there was no one to help.
13 Then they cried to the LORD in their trouble,
  and he saved them from their distress.

a 3 Hebrew north and the sea

106:44 *heard their cry.* See Ex 2:23; 3:7–9; Nu 20:16; Jdg 3:9,15; 4:3; 6:6–7; 10:10; 1Sa 9:16; 2Ch 20:6–12; Ne 9:27–28.
106:45 *remembered his covenant.* See 105:8,42; Ex 2:24; Lev 26:42,45. *love.* See article, p. 16.
106:46 Makes clear that the author's recital includes the Babylonian captivity (1Ki 8:50; 2Ch 30:9; Ezr 9:9; Jer 42:12). Although there were earlier captivities of Israelite communities, no other captive group was said to have been shown "mercy."
106:47 A communal prayer for deliverance and restoration from dispersion (see introduction and note on v. 4). *glory in.* Triumphantly celebrate. The Hebrew for this phrase is found elsewhere only in the parallel in 1Ch 16:35. *praise.* See note on 9:1.
106:48a A conventional word of praise, serving as the doxology to close the psalm and Book IV (see 41:13 and note; see also introduction to this psalm and note on v. 1).
106:48b *Let all the people say.* 1Ch 16:36 sets off the closing exclamations somewhat differently. *Amen!* See Dt 27:15; 1Ch 16:36; Ne 5:13; Jer 11:5; Ro 1:25; 1Co 14:16.

Ps 107 A salvation-history hymn, exhorting Israel to praise the Lord for his unfailing love in that he hears the prayers of those in need and saves them. It was composed for liturgical use at one of Israel's annual religious festivals. Interpretations vary widely, but the following is most likely: Having experienced anew God's mercies in their return from Babylonian exile (v. 3; see Jer 33:11), Israel is led by a Levite in celebrating God's unfailing benevolence toward those who have cried out to him in the crises of their lives. In its recitative style the psalm is closely related to Ps 104–106, and in its language to Ps 105–106. See introduction to Ps 101–110.
107:1–3 Introductory call to praise Yahweh.
107:1 A conventional, liturgical call to praise the Lord (see 106:1; 118:1,29; 136:1; Jer 33:11). *Give thanks.* See vv. 8,15,21,31; see also note on Ps 100 title. *he is good.* See note on 73:1. *love.* See vv. 8,15,21,31,43; see also article, p. 16.
107:2 *redeemed.* Here, as often, a synonym for "delivered."
107:3 *from the lands.* From the dispersion resulting from the Assyrian (2Ki 17:6) and Babylonian captivities (see 2Ki 24:14,16; 25:11,26; Jer 52:28–30; see also Ne 1:8; Est 8:5,9,13; Isa 11:12; 43:5–6; Eze 11:17; 20:34). *south.* See NIV text note. The NIV translation assumes that the last two letters of the Hebrew word have been lost, which if supplied yield "south."
107:4–9 Deliverance for those lost in the "desert wastelands." No reference is made to rebellion (as in the third and fourth stanzas), but since Israel had journeyed through the desert on their way to Canaan, they had first-hand experience of the terrors of the desert. They were, moreover, bounded on the east by the great Arabian Desert (as on the west by the Mediterranean Sea; see vv. 23–32), across which their merchant caravans traveled.
107:6 *they cried out.* The author uses the same Hebrew verb in v. 28, thus linking the fifth stanza with the second. In vv. 13,19 he uses a different (but similar-sounding) Hebrew verb, linking the third and fourth stanzas. Just as Israel's history was a history of divine deliverance (Ps 105) and a history of rebellion (Ps 106), so also it was a history of crying out to the Lord in distress (see references in note on 106:44).

¹⁴He brought them out of darkness, the utter
darkness,
and broke away their chains.
¹⁵Let them give thanks to the LORD for his
unfailing love
and his wonderful deeds for mankind,
¹⁶for he breaks down gates of bronze
and cuts through bars of iron.

¹⁷Some became fools through their rebellious
ways
and suffered affliction because of their
iniquities.
¹⁸They loathed all food
and drew near the gates of death.
¹⁹Then they cried to the LORD in their trouble,
and he saved them from their distress.
²⁰He sent out his word and healed them;
he rescued them from the grave.
²¹Let them give thanks to the LORD for his
unfailing love
and his wonderful deeds for mankind.
²²Let them sacrifice thank offerings
and tell of his works with songs of joy.

²³Some went out on the sea in ships;
they were merchants on the mighty waters.
²⁴They saw the works of the LORD,
his wonderful deeds in the deep.
²⁵For he spoke and stirred up a tempest
that lifted high the waves.
²⁶They mounted up to the heavens and went
down to the depths;
in their peril their courage melted away.
²⁷They reeled and staggered like drunkards;
they were at their wits' end.
²⁸Then they cried out to the LORD in their trouble,
and he brought them out of their distress.
²⁹He stilled the storm to a whisper;
the waves of the sea*ᵃ* were hushed.
³⁰They were glad when it grew calm,
and he guided them to their desired haven.
³¹Let them give thanks to the LORD for his
unfailing love
and his wonderful deeds for mankind.
³²Let them exalt him in the assembly of the people
and praise him in the council of the elders.

³³He turned rivers into a desert,
flowing springs into thirsty ground,
³⁴and fruitful land into a salt waste,
because of the wickedness of those who lived
there.
³⁵He turned the desert into pools of water
and the parched ground into flowing
springs;

ᵃ 29 Dead Sea Scrolls; Masoretic Text / *their waves*

107:8 For other refrains, see introduction to Ps 42–43. *wonderful deeds.* See vv. 15,21,24,31; see also note on 9:1.
107:10–16 Deliverance from the punishment of foreign bondage. God even delivers those who cry out to him when their distress is a result of his discipline for their sins (vv. 17–20, 33–41).
107:10 *sat in darkness . . . utter darkness.* Vivid imagery for distress (see 18:28; Isa 5:30; 8:22; 59:9; see also note on 44:19). *prisoners.* While the reference is no doubt to foreign bondage, the imagery of being bound was also used by OT poets to refer to other forms of distress (Job 36:8; Isa 28:22; La 3:7); so the reference may be deliberately ambiguous.
107:11 *plans.* God's wise directives embodied in his words (see 73:24 and note).
107:12 *subjected them to bitter labor.* A labor so burdensome it broke their spirit. *stumbled.* Their strength failed (31:10; 109:24; Ne 4:10; Isa 40:30; Zec 12:8).
107:13 *cried to.* See note on v. 6.
107:16 Either this verse is quoted from Isa 45:2 or both verses quote an established saying. *gates of bronze.* City gates—normally of wood; here proverbially of bronze, the strongest gates then imaginable (see 1Ki 4:13; cf. Jer 1:18). *bars of iron.* Bars that secured city gates (Dt 3:5; Jer 51:30). "Can a man break iron . . . or bronze?" was a proverb of the time (Jer 15:12).
107:17–22 Deliverance from the punishment of a wasting disease (see note on vv. 10–16).
107:17 *fools.* See Jer 4:22; see also NIV text note on 14:1. "Fools despise wisdom and instruction" (Pr 1:7; see v. 43). *affliction because of their iniquities.* See Lev 26:16,25; Dt 28:20–22,35,58–61.
107:18 *gates of death.* The realm of the dead was sometimes depicted as a netherworld city with a series of concentric walls and gates (seven, each inside the other, according to ancient Near Eastern mythology) to keep those descending there from returning to the land of the living (see 9:13; see also Mt 16:18).
107:19 *cried to.* See note on v. 6. *saved.* See v. 13 (another link between the second and third stanzas); cf. vv. 6,28.
107:20 *his word.* His command, here personified as the agent of his purpose (see 147:15,18; see also note on 23:6).
107:22 *thank offerings.* See Lev 7:12–15; 22:29–30. *tell of his works.* See note on 7:17. In their concluding lines, stanzas four and five are linked, as are stanzas two and three. *songs of joy.* See, e.g., Ps 116.
107:23–32 Deliverance from the perils of the sea (see note on vv. 4–9). Israel's merchants also braved the sea in pursuit of trade (Ge 49:13; Jdg 5:17; 1Ki 9:26–28; 10:22).
107:23 *mighty waters.* See 29:3.
107:24 *wonderful deeds in the deep.* Since the peoples of the eastern Mediterranean coastlands associated the "mighty waters" (v. 23) of the sea with the primeval chaotic waters (see note on 32:6), the Lord's total control of them was always for Israel a cause of wonder and a sense of security. Therefore the terrifying storms that sometimes swept the Mediterranean (Jnh 1; Ac 27) are here included among his wonderful deeds.
107:33–42 A twofold instructive supplement recalling how the Lord sometimes disciplined his people by turning the fruitful land (v. 34) into a virtual desert (1Ki 17:1–7;

³⁶ there he brought the hungry to live,
and they founded a city where they could settle.
³⁷ They sowed fields and planted vineyards
that yielded a fruitful harvest;
³⁸ he blessed them, and their numbers greatly increased,
and he did not let their herds diminish.

³⁹ Then their numbers decreased, and they were humbled
by oppression, calamity and sorrow;
⁴⁰ he who pours contempt on nobles
made them wander in a trackless waste.
⁴¹ But he lifted the needy out of their affliction
and increased their families like flocks.
⁴² The upright see and rejoice,
but all the wicked shut their mouths.

⁴³ Let the one who is wise heed these things
and ponder the loving deeds of the LORD.

Psalm 108ᵃ

A song. A psalm of David.

¹ My heart, O God, is steadfast;
I will sing and make music with all my soul.
² Awake, harp and lyre!
I will awaken the dawn.
³ I will praise you, LORD, among the nations;
I will sing of you among the peoples.
⁴ For great is your love, higher than the heavens;
your faithfulness reaches to the skies.
⁵ Be exalted, O God, above the heavens;
let your glory be over all the earth.

⁶ Save us and help us with your right hand,
that those you love may be delivered.
⁷ God has spoken from his sanctuary:
"In triumph I will parcel out Shechem
and measure off the Valley of Sukkoth.
⁸ Gilead is mine, Manasseh is mine;
Ephraim is my helmet,
Judah is my scepter.
⁹ Moab is my washbasin,
on Edom I toss my sandal;
over Philistia I shout in triumph."

¹⁰ Who will bring me to the fortified city?
Who will lead me to Edom?
¹¹ Is it not you, God, you who have rejected us
and no longer go out with our armies?
¹² Give us aid against the enemy,
for human help is worthless.
¹³ With God we will gain the victory,
and he will trample down our enemies.

ᵃ In Hebrew texts 108:1-13 is numbered 108:2-14.

2Ki 8:1) but then restored the land again (Ru 1:6; 1Ki 18:44–45), so that the hungry (v. 36) could live there and prosper in the midst of plenty. But then he sent powerful armies against them (such as the Assyrians, 2Ki 17:3–6, and the Babylonians, 2Ki 24:10–17; 25:1–26) that devastated the land once more and deported its people; yet afterward he restored the needy (v. 41). But the poet generalizes upon these experiences in the manner of the wisdom teachers.

107:40 Perhaps quoted from Job 12:21,24. In their prosperity the people, led by their nobles, grow proud and turn their backs on the God who has blessed them (Dt 31:20; 32:15), so he returns them to the desert (Dt 32:10; Hos 2:3,14).

107:41 *needy.* Those in need of help (see v. 39; see also 9:18 and note).

107:42 Conclusion to the instruction (vv. 33–41); perhaps an echo of Job 5:16. *upright . . . wicked.* A frequent contrast in OT wisdom literature (Pr 2:21–22; 11:6–7; 12:6; 14:11; 15:8; 21:18,29; 29:27—but the Hebrew for "wicked" here is shared more often with Job).

107:43 Conclusion to the psalm. *one who is wise.* See Dt 32:29; Hos 14:9. *these things.* The instruction in vv. 33–42. *ponder the loving deeds of the LORD.* The theme of vv. 4–32, emphatically reiterated.

Ps 108 A hymn of praise for God's love and a prayer for his help against the enemies—a combination (with very slight modifications) of 57:7–11 and 60:5–12. For a similar composition of a new psalm by combination of portions from several psalms, see 1Ch 16:8–36. The celebration of the greatness of God's love (v. 4) links this psalm thematically with Ps 103 (103:11). See introduction to Ps 101–110.

108 title *song.* See note on Ps 30 title. *of David.* Both sources (Ps 57; 60) were credited to him.

108:1–5 Praise of God's love, possibly intended to function here as an expression of trust in God (the God of vv. 7–9,11), to whom appeal is to be made (vv. 6,12).

108:1 *soul.* Or "glory" (see note on 7:5).

108:6–13 Prayer for God's help against enemies (see 60:5–12).

> List some things you have learned about God through your church.

_____

_____

_____

_____

_____

_____

Psalm 109

For the director of music. Of David. A psalm.

¹My God, whom I praise,
  do not remain silent,
²for people who are wicked and deceitful
  have opened their mouths against me;
  they have spoken against me with lying
    tongues.
³With words of hatred they surround me;
  they attack me without cause.
⁴In return for my friendship they accuse me,
  but I am a man of prayer.
⁵They repay me evil for good,
  and hatred for my friendship.

⁶Appoint someone evil to oppose my enemy;
  let an accuser stand at his right hand.
⁷When he is tried, let him be found guilty,
  and may his prayers condemn him.
⁸May his days be few;
  may another take his place of leadership.
⁹May his children be fatherless
  and his wife a widow.
¹⁰May his children be wandering beggars;
  may they be driven*ᵃ* from their ruined
    homes.
¹¹May a creditor seize all he has;
  may strangers plunder the fruits of his
    labor.
¹²May no one extend kindness to him
  or take pity on his fatherless children.
¹³May his descendants be cut off,
  their names blotted out from the next
    generation.
¹⁴May the iniquity of his fathers be remembered
    before the Lord;
  may the sin of his mother never be
    blotted out.
¹⁵May their sins always remain before the Lord,
  that he may blot out their name from the
    earth.

¹⁶For he never thought of doing a kindness,
  but hounded to death the poor
  and the needy and the brokenhearted.
¹⁷He loved to pronounce a curse —
  may it come back on him.
  He found no pleasure in blessing —
  may it be far from him.
¹⁸He wore cursing as his garment;
  it entered into his body like water,
  into his bones like oil.
¹⁹May it be like a cloak wrapped about him,
  like a belt tied forever around him.

ᵃ 10 Septuagint; Hebrew *sought*

Ps 109 A lament to God requesting deliverance from false accusers. The author speaks of his enemies in the singular in vv. 6–19 but in the plural elsewhere. Either (1) the author shifts here to a collective mode of speaking, or (2) the enemies are united under a leader whose personal animosity toward the psalmist has fired the antagonism of others and so is singled out for special attention (see article, p. 15). Thematically, this prayer has much affinity with Ps 35. Within the cluster in which it stands, its affinity is with Ps 102—and it is only one line longer than that psalm.

109 title See note on Ps 4 title.

109:1–5 Appeal to God to deliver David from false accusers.

109:2–5 The particulars of his case, which he presents before the heavenly bar of justice (35:11–16).

109:2 *opened their mouths against me.* See note on 5:9.

109:4 *but I am a man of prayer.* In contrast to the enemy (vv. 16–18). The intent may be: But I have prayed for them (as in 35:13–14; see note there).

109:6–15 Appeal for judicial redress—that the Lord will deal with them in accordance with their malicious intent against him, matching punishment with crime (see note on 5:10; see also 35:7–10 and note).

109:6 *someone evil . . . accuser.* The psalmist's enemy falsely accused him in order to bring him down; now let the enemy be confronted by an accuser.

109:8 *days be few.* The false accuser was no doubt seeking to effect David's death (1Ki 21:8–15). *another take his place of leadership.* The enemy held some official position and was perhaps plotting a coup. For a NT application of these words to Judas, see Ac 1:20.

109:10–11 May he also be deprived of all his property so that he has no inheritance to pass on to his children.

109:12 *no one extend kindness.* See v. 16. *his . . . children.* The close identity of a man with his children and of children with their parents, resulting from the tightly bonded unity of the three-or four-generation households of that ancient society, is alien to the modern reader, whose sense of self is highly individualistic. But that deep, profoundly human bond accounts for the ancient legal principle of "punishing the children for the sin of the parents to the third and fourth generation" (see Ex 20:5; but see also 103:17; Ge 18:19).

109:13 Since a man lived on in his children (see previous note), the focus of judgment remains on the false accuser (21:10; 37:28).

109:14–15 *iniquity of his fathers . . . sin of his mother . . . their sins.* These verses return to the theme of vv. 7–8 (and thus form a frame around the stanza): May the indictment the accuser lodges against him include the sins of his parents (see note on v. 12).

109:15 *blot out their name.* May this slanderer be the last of his family line.

109:16–20 The ruthless character of the enemy—may he be made to suffer the due consequences (10:2–15; 59:12–13). Accusation of the adversary is a common feature in psalms that are appeals to the heavenly Judge (see, e.g., 5:9–10; 10:2–11; 17:10–12).

109:18 *into his body like water, into his bones like oil.* Pronouncing curses on others was his food and drink, as well as his clothing; he lived by such cursing (cf. Pr 4:17).

²⁰ May this be the LORD's payment to my
accusers,
to those who speak evil of me.

²¹ But you, Sovereign LORD,
help me for your name's sake;
out of the goodness of your love,
deliver me.
²² For I am poor and needy,
and my heart is wounded within me.
²³ I fade away like an evening shadow;
I am shaken off like a locust.
²⁴ My knees give way from fasting;
my body is thin and gaunt.
²⁵ I am an object of scorn to my accusers;
when they see me, they shake their heads.

²⁶ Help me, LORD my God;
save me according to your unfailing love.
²⁷ Let them know that it is your hand,
that you, LORD, have done it.
²⁸ While they curse, may you bless;
may those who attack me be put to shame,
but may your servant rejoice.
²⁹ May my accusers be clothed with disgrace
and wrapped in shame as in a cloak.

³⁰ With my mouth I will greatly extol the LORD;
in the great throng of worshipers I will
praise him.
³¹ For he stands at the right hand of the needy,
to save their lives from those who would
condemn them.

Psalm 110

Of David. A psalm.

¹ The LORD says to my lord:[a]

"Sit at my right hand
until I make your enemies
a footstool for your feet."

² The LORD will extend your mighty scepter from
Zion, saying,
"Rule in the midst of your enemies!"
³ Your troops will be willing
on your day of battle.
Arrayed in holy splendor,
your young men will come to you
like dew from the morning's womb.[b]

⁴ The LORD has sworn
and will not change his mind:
"You are a priest forever,
in the order of Melchizedek."

---

[a] 1 Or *Lord*   [b] 3 The meaning of the Hebrew for this
sentence is uncertain.

109:21–25 The intensity of "my" suffering—Lord, deliver me!

109:21 *for your name's sake.* See note on 23:3. *love.* See v. 26; see also article, p. 16.

109:22 The psalmist's description of his situation echoes the words of v. 16. *poor and needy.* Dependent on the Lord (see notes on 34:6, 35:10). *heart.* See note on 4:7. *is wounded.* The Hebrew for this phrase sounds like the Hebrew for "curse" in vv. 17–18, a deliberate wordplay—while he lives by cursing, I live with deep inward pain.

109:23 *I fade away.* Apparently the psalmist suffers a life-sapping affliction, which is the occasion for his enemies to turn on him (see vv. 24–25; see also note on 5:9). *like an evening shadow.* See 102:11. *shaken off.* See Ne 5:13; Job 38:13.

109:26–29 Concluding petition, with many echoes of preceding themes.

109:28 *servant.* Perhaps identifies the psalmist as the Lord's anointed (see title; see also 78:70 and note).

109:30–31 A vow to praise the Lord for his deliverance (see note on 7:17).

Ps 110 Prophecies concerning the Messianic King-Priest. This psalm (specifically its two brief prophecies, vv. 1,4) is frequently referred to in the NT testimony to Christ. Like Ps 2, it has the marks of a coronation psalm, composed for use at the enthronement of a new Davidic king. Before the Christian era, Jews already viewed it as Messianic. Because of the manner in which it has been interpreted in the NT—especially by Jesus (see Mt 22:43–45 and parallels, where Jesus attributes Ps 110 to David) but also by Peter (Ac 2:34–36) and the author of Hebrews (see especially Heb 1:13; 5:6–10; 7:11–28)—Christians have generally held that this is the most directly "prophetic" of all the psalms. If so, David, speaking prophetically (2Sa 23:2), composed a coronation psalm for his great future Son, of whom the prophets did not speak until later. It may be, however, that David composed the psalm for the coronation of his son Solomon, that he called him "my lord" (v. 1; but see NIV text note) in view of his new status, which placed him above the aged David, and that in so doing he spoke a word that had far larger meaning than he knew at the time. This would seem to be more in accord with what we know of David from Samuel, Kings and Chronicles.

110:1 The first prophecy (see note on v. 4). *my lord.* My sovereign, therefore superior to David (see Mt 22:44–45; Mk 12:36–37; Lk 20:42–44; Ac 2:34–35; Heb 1:13 and their contexts). *right hand.* The place of honor beside a king (45:9; 1Ki 2:19); thus he is made second in authority to God himself. NT references to Jesus' exaltation to this position are many (Mt 26:64; Mk 14:62; 16:19; Lk 22:69; Ac 2:33; 5:31; 7:55–56; Ro 8:34; Eph 1:20; Col 3:1; Heb 1:3; 8:1; 10:12; 12:2). *footstool for your feet.* See Heb 10:12–13. Ancient kings often had themselves portrayed as placing their feet on vanquished enemies (Jos 10:24). For a royal footstool as part of the throne, see 2Ch 9:18. For the thought here, see 1Ki 5:3. Paul applies this word to Christ in 1Co 15:25; Eph 1:22.

110:2 *Zion.* David's royal city (2Sa 5:7,9), but also God's (see 9:11 and note), where he rules as the Great King (Ps 46; 48; 132:13–18). The Lord's anointed is his regent over his emerging kingdom in the world.

"A Priest . . . in the Order of Melchizedek" Ps 110:4

David and his royal sons, as chief representatives of the rule of God, performed many worship-focused activities, such as overseeing the ark of the covenant (see 2Sa 6:1–15, especially v. 14; 1Ki 8:1), building and overseeing the temple (1Ki 5–7; 2Ki 12:4–7; 22:3–7; 23:4–7; 2Ch 15:8; 24:4–12; 29:3–11; 34:8) and overseeing the work of the priests and Levites and the temple liturgy (1Ch 6:31; 15:11–16; 16:4–42; 23:3–31; 25:1; 2Ch 17:7–9; 19:8–11; 29:25,30; 31:2; 35:15–16; Ezr 3:10; 8:20; Ne 12:24,36,45). In all these duties they exercised authority over even the high priest. But they could not engage in those specifically priestly functions that had been assigned to the Aaronic priesthood (2Ch 26:16–18).

In the present message the son of David is installed by God as king-priest in Zion after the manner of Melchizedek, the king-priest of God Most High at Jerusalem in the days of Abraham (see Ge 14:18,20). As such a king-priest, he was appointed to a higher order of priesthood than that of Aaron and his sons. (For the union of king and priest in one person, see Zec 6:13.) What this means for Christ's priesthood is the main theme of Heb 7.

▶ How was Jesus Christ like Melchizedek?

_____

_____

_____

_____

⁵ The Lord is at your right hand[a];
    he will crush kings on the day of his wrath.
⁶ He will judge the nations, heaping up
      the dead
    and crushing the rulers of the whole
      earth.
⁷ He will drink from a brook along the way,[b]
    and so he will lift his head high.

[a] 5 Or *My lord is at your right hand,* Lord   [b] 7 The meaning of the Hebrew for this clause is uncertain.

110:3 *willing.* Or "freewill offerings," i.e., they will offer themselves as dedicated warriors to support you on the battlefield (Jdg 5:2)—as the Israelites offered their treasures for the building of the tabernacle in the wilderness (see Ex 35:29; 36:3; see also Ezr 1:4; 2:68). Accordingly, Paul speaks of Christ's followers offering their bodies "as a living sacrifice" (Ro 12:1) and of himself as a "drink offering" (Php 2:17); see also 2Co 8:5.

110:4 The second prophecy (see note on v. 1). *has sworn.* In accordance also with his sworn covenant to maintain David's royal line forever (89:35–37). The force of this oath is elaborated by the author of Hebrews (Heb 6:16–18; 7:20–22). *priest . . . in the order of Melchizedek.* See article, above. *forever.* Permanently and irrevocably; perhaps alluded to in Jn 12:34.

Additional Insights

God is the righteous Judge. Because God is the Great King, he is the ultimate Executor of justice among humans.

Additional Insights

The Lord is at your right hand; he will crush kings on the day of his wrath.

▶ How can you have a blameless heart in your family relationships (101:2)?

_____

_____

_____

_____

_____

▶ For what things does the psalmist praise God (Ps 103)?

_____

_____

_____

_____

_____

▶ How can you remember what God has done for you (105:5)?

_____

_____

_____

_____

_____

▶ What prophecies regarding Jesus do you see in Psalm 110?

_____

_____

_____

_____

_____

Psalm 111[a]

[1] Praise the Lord.[b]

I will extol the Lord with all my heart
 in the council of the upright and in the
  assembly.

[2] Great are the works of the Lord;
 they are pondered by all who delight in
  them.
[3] Glorious and majestic are his deeds,
 and his righteousness endures forever.
[4] He has caused his wonders to be
  remembered;
 the Lord is gracious and compassionate.
[5] He provides food for those who fear him;
 he remembers his covenant forever.

[6] He has shown his people the power of his
  works,
 giving them the lands of other nations.
[7] The works of his hands are faithful and just;
 all his precepts are trustworthy.
[8] They are established for ever and ever,
 enacted in faithfulness and uprightness.
[9] He provided redemption for his people;
 he ordained his covenant forever—
 holy and awesome is his name.

[10] The fear of the Lord is the beginning of
  wisdom;
 all who follow his precepts have good
  understanding.
 To him belongs eternal praise.

Psalm 112[a]

[1] Praise the Lord.[b]

Blessed are those who fear the Lord,
 who find great delight in his commands.

[2] Their children will be mighty in the land;
 the generation of the upright will be
  blessed.
[3] Wealth and riches are in their houses,
 and their righteousness endures forever.

---

[a] This psalm is an acrostic poem, the lines of which begin with the successive letters of the Hebrew alphabet.
[b] 1 Hebrew *Hallelu Yah*

Ps 111–119 A cluster of nine psalms framed by unusual alphabetic acrostics (see Introduction: Literary Features) that enclose the "Egyptian Hallel" (see introduction to Ps 113–118). The framing psalms that enclose the celebration of redemption contained in the Hallel (which means "praise" in Hebrew) offer instruction in the piety that must characterize those who join in the celebration of God's saving acts in behalf of his people.

Ps 111 A hymn of praise to God for his unfailing righteousness. The psalm combines hymnic praise with wisdom instruction, as its first and last verses indicate. Close comparison with Ps 112 shows that these two psalms are twins, probably written by the same author and intended to be kept together. The two psalms are most likely postexilic

111:1 *I will extol.* Introductory to the praise that follows in vv. 2–9. *with all my heart.* A verbal link with a recurring phrase in Ps 119 (vv. 2,10,34,58,69,145). *council of the upright.* Probably a more intimate circle than the assembly (see 107:32 for a similar distinction) and referring to those who are truly godly—such as the "upright" of 112:2,4 (11:7; 33:1; 49:14; 97:11; 107:42; 140:13). *in the assembly.* See note on 9:1.

111:2–5 The stanza is framed by references to the Lord's "works" and "his covenant."

111:3 *righteousness.* As embodied in his deeds (see note on 4:1).

111:5 *provides food.* Illustrative of his bountiful provisions for the daily needs of his people (as in the Lord's prayer: "Give us today our daily bread," Mt 6:11). *fear.* See v. 10 and note. *his covenant.* The Lord remembers "forever" the covenant he "ordained . . . forever" (v. 9; see also 105:8–11).

111:7 *faithful and just.* Cf. "Glorious and majestic" (v. 3). *precepts are trustworthy.* See note on 93:5.

111:10 Concluding word of godly wisdom. *The fear of the Lord is the beginning of wisdom.* The classic OT statement concerning the religious basis of what it means to be wise (see Job 28:28; Pr 1:7; 9:10). *precepts.* Refers back to the "precepts" in v. 7 (see 19:7–9, where "The fear of the Lord" stands parallel to "statutes," "precepts," "commands," "decrees"; see also 112:1).

Ps 112 A eulogy to the godly—in the spirit of Ps 1 but formed after the pattern of Ps 111 and likely intended as its complement (see introduction to Ps 111).

112:1 The basic theme, developed more fully in vv. 2–9. Verse 10 states its converse. See 1:1–2; 128:1. *Blessed.* See note on 1:1. *delight . . . commands.* A verbal and conceptual link with Ps 119 (see 119:35).

112:2 *children.* The godly bring blessing to their children and to themselves—not least in the fact that through their children they are "remembered" in the community (see v. 6; see also Dt 25:6; Ru 4:10; see further

4Even in darkness light dawns for the upright,
   for those who are gracious and
      compassionate and righteous.
5Good will come to those who are generous and
      lend freely,
   who conduct their affairs with justice.

6Surely the righteous will never be shaken;
   they will be remembered forever.
7They will have no fear of bad news;
   their hearts are steadfast, trusting in the
      LORD.
8Their hearts are secure, they will have no fear;
   in the end they will look in triumph on
      their foes.
9They have freely scattered their gifts to the poor,
   their righteousness endures forever;
   their horn*a* will be lifted high in honor.

10The wicked will see and be vexed,
   they will gnash their teeth and waste away;
   the longings of the wicked will come to
      nothing.

Psalm 113

1Praise the LORD.*b*

Praise the LORD, you his servants;
   praise the name of the LORD.
2Let the name of the LORD be praised,
   both now and forevermore.
3From the rising of the sun to the place where
      it sets,
   the name of the LORD is to be praised.

4The LORD is exalted over all the nations,
   his glory above the heavens.
5Who is like the LORD our God,
   the One who sits enthroned on high,
6who stoops down to look
   on the heavens and the earth?

7He raises the poor from the dust
   and lifts the needy from the ash heap;
8he seats them with princes,
   with the princes of his people.
9He settles the childless woman in her home
   as a happy mother of children.

Praise the LORD.

Psalm 114

1When Israel came out of Egypt,
   Jacob from a people of foreign tongue,

---

a 9 Horn here symbolizes dignity.   *b 1* Hebrew *Hallelu Yah;* also in verse 9

Ps 37:26; 127:3–5; 128:3 and note on 109:12). *will be mighty.* Will be persons of influence and reputation.
112:3 Cf. 111:3. *Wealth and riches.* See 1:3; 128:2. *righteousness.* See v. 9; see also note on 1:5. *endures.* It is not just an occasional characteristic of their actions (see "steadfast," v. 7).
112:5 *Good.* Well-being and prosperity (see 34:8–14 and note). *are generous and lend freely.* See v. 9; see also 111:5.
112:6–9 The stanza is framed by reference to the righteous being "remembered" (see note on v. 2) and to their generosity.
112:7 Shares with 111:7 the basic theme of reliability. *hearts.* See v. 8; see also note on 4:7. *trusting.* Their trust in God will be as steadfast as their righteousness is enduring (v. 3). For trust and obedience to God's righteous will as the sum of true godliness, see 34:8–14 and note.
112:9 *their righteousness.* Just as the Lord remembers his covenant (111:5,9), so the righteous act according to "justice" (v. 5) and "righteousness" (v. 9), two of the prime moral virtues the Lord requires of his covenant servant (see Ge 18:19; Ps 106:3; Isa 5:7; 56:1; Eze 18:5,21; 33:14,16,19; 45:9; Am 5:24; 6:12; see also 2Sa 8:15; Pr 1:3; 21:3; Jer 22:15; 32:15—sometimes rendered "just" and "right").
Ps 113–118 The "Egyptian Hallel," a collection of psalms celebrating Israel's deliverance from Egypt, which came to be used in Jewish liturgy at the great religious festivals (Passover, Weeks, Tabernacles, Dedication, New Moon; see Lev 23; Nu 10:10; Jn 10:22). At Passover, Ps 113 and 114 were sung before the meal (before the second cup was passed) and Ps 115–118 after the meal (when the fourth cup had been filled). For the frame within which the "Hallel" has been set, see introduction to Ps 111–119.
Ps 113 A hymn to the Lord celebrating his high majesty and his mercies to the lowly (138:6). It was probably composed originally for the temple liturgy. Thematically, the psalm has strong links with the song of Hannah (1Sa 2:1–15) and the song of Mary (Lk 1:46–55).
113:1 *name of the LORD.* See vv. 2–3. Triple repetition was a common liturgical convention (see note on 96:1–3).
113:2 *now and forevermore.* The praise of those who truly praise the Lord cannot rest content until it fills all time—and space (v. 3).
113:3 The psalmist employs an ancient formula for indicating universal space. Canaanite Amarna letter No. 288 reads as follows: "Behold, the king, my lord, has set his name at the rising of the sun and at the setting of the sun" (cf. Ps 139:9 and note).
113:4–6 The Lord is enthroned on high, exalted over all creation.
113:5 The rhetorical center (see note on 6:6). *our God.* What grace, that he has covenanted to be "our" God (Ge 17:7; Ex 19:5–6; 20:2)!
113:7–9 The Lord exalts the lowly—the God of highest majesty does not ally himself with the high and mighty of the earth but stands with and raises up the poor and needy (1Sa 2:3–8; Lk 1:46–55). Cf. the deliverance celebrated in Ps 118.
113:7–8 Repeated almost verbatim from Hannah in 1Sa 2:8.
113:9 *childless woman.* In that ancient society barrenness was the greatest disgrace and the deepest tragedy for a

²Judah became God's sanctuary,
    Israel his dominion.

³The sea looked and fled,
    the Jordan turned back;
⁴the mountains leaped like rams,
    the hills like lambs.

⁵Why was it, sea, that you fled?
    Why, Jordan, did you turn back?
⁶Why, mountains, did you leap like rams,
    you hills, like lambs?

⁷Tremble, earth, at the presence of the Lord,
    at the presence of the God of Jacob,
⁸who turned the rock into a pool,
    the hard rock into springs of water.

Psalm 115

¹Not to us, LORD, not to us
    but to your name be the glory,
    because of your love and faithfulness.

²Why do the nations say,
    "Where is their God?"
³Our God is in heaven;
    he does whatever pleases him.
⁴But their idols are silver and gold,
    made by human hands.
⁵They have mouths, but cannot speak,
    eyes, but cannot see.
⁶They have ears, but cannot hear,
    noses, but cannot smell.
⁷They have hands, but cannot feel,
    feet, but cannot walk,
    nor can they utter a sound with their throats.
⁸Those who make them will be like them,
    and so will all who trust in them.

⁹All you Israelites, trust in the LORD—
    he is their help and shield.
¹⁰House of Aaron, trust in the LORD—
    he is their help and shield.
¹¹You who fear him, trust in the LORD—
    he is their help and shield.

¹²The LORD remembers us and will bless us:
    He will bless his people Israel,
    he will bless the house of Aaron,
¹³he will bless those who fear the LORD—
    small and great alike.

¹⁴May the LORD cause you to flourish,
    both you and your children.
¹⁵May you be blessed by the LORD,
    the Maker of heaven and earth.

¹⁶The highest heavens belong to the LORD,
    but the earth he has given to mankind.

woman (Ge 30:1; 1Sa 1:6–7,10); in her old age she would be as desolate as Naomi because she would have no one to sustain her (see Ru 1:11–13; see also 2Ki 4:14).

Ps 114 A hymnic celebration of the exodus, the second psalm in the "Egyptian Hallel" (see introduction to Ps 113–118). It is one of the most exquisitely fashioned songs of the Psalter. It probably dates from the period of the monarchy sometime after the division of the kingdom (v. 2). No doubt it was composed for liturgical use at the temple during one of the annual religious festivals (see introduction to Ps 113).

114:1–2 The great OT redemptive event.

114:1 *Israel . . . Jacob.* Synonyms (Ex 19:3). *came out of Egypt.* Recalls the exodus and all the great events of the wilderness journey. According to 105:37, it was *God* who brought them out.

114:2 *Judah . . . Israel.* The southern and northern kingdoms, viewed here as the one people of God. *became.* The crucial event was the establishment of the covenant at Sinai, where Israel became bound to the Lord as a "kingdom of priests and a holy nation" (Ex 19:3–6).

114:3 *sea . . . Jordan.* The Red Sea and the Jordan River, through which the Lord brought his people, are here personified. *looked and fled.* Saw the mighty God approach in his awesome pillar of cloud and fled.

114:4 *leaped.* The mountains and hills quaked at God's approach (29:6).

114:7–8 The Lord of yesterday (vv. 5–6)—"The God of Jacob"—is still with us.

114:7 *Tremble.* In awesome recognition. *earth.* All creation. *Jacob.* A synonym for Israel (Ge 32:28).

Ps 115 This third psalm in the "Egyptian Hallel" (see introduction to Ps 113–118) offers praise to the Lord, the one true God, for his love and faithfulness toward his people. It may have been a liturgy of praise for the temple worship, written for use at the dedication of the second temple (Ezr 6:16) when Israel was beginning to revive after the disruption of the exile.

115:1–8 Praise of God's love and faithfulness toward his people, which silences the taunts of the nations.

115:2 *Where is their God?* The taunt of the nations when Israel is decimated by natural disasters (Joel 2:17) or crushed by enemies, especially when Judah is destroyed and the temple of God razed (see 3:2; 10:11 and notes; 42:3; 79:10; Mic 7:10).

115:3 *is in heaven.* Sits enthroned (113:5) in the "highest heavens" (v. 16). *whatever pleases him.* If Israel is decimated or destroyed, it is God's doing; it is not his failure or inability to act, nor is it the achievement of the idols the nations worship. When Israel is revived, that is also God's doing, and no other god can oppose him.

115:4–7 Whatever glory and power the false gods are thought to have (as symbolized in the images made to represent them), they are mere figments of human imagination and utterly worthless (135:15–18; Isa 46:1–7).

115:8 *Those who make them.* The taunting nations (cf. v. 2). *like them.* Powerless and ineffectual. For a graphic elaboration of this truth, see Isa 44:9–20.

115:9–11 The call to trust in the Lord, not in idols (v. 8). For triple repetition as a liturgical convention, see note on 96:1–3. For the same groupings, see 118:2–4; see also 135:19–20.

¹⁷ It is not the dead who praise the LORD,
     those who go down to the place of silence;
¹⁸ it is we who extol the LORD,
     both now and forevermore.

  Praise the LORD.^a

Psalm 116

¹ I love the LORD, for he heard my voice;
     he heard my cry for mercy.
² Because he turned his ear to me,
     I will call on him as long as I live.

³ The cords of death entangled me,
     the anguish of the grave came over me;
     I was overcome by distress and sorrow.
⁴ Then I called on the name of the LORD:
     "LORD, save me!"

⁵ The LORD is gracious and righteous;
     our God is full of compassion.
⁶ The LORD protects the unwary;
     when I was brought low, he saved me.

⁷ Return to your rest, my soul,
     for the LORD has been good to you.

⁸ For you, LORD, have delivered me from death,
     my eyes from tears,
     my feet from stumbling,
⁹ that I may walk before the LORD
     in the land of the living.

¹⁰ I trusted in the LORD when I said,
     "I am greatly afflicted";
¹¹ in my alarm I said,
     "Everyone is a liar."

¹² What shall I return to the LORD
     for all his goodness to me?

¹³ I will lift up the cup of salvation
     and call on the name of the LORD.
¹⁴ I will fulfill my vows to the LORD
     in the presence of all his people.

¹⁵ Precious in the sight of the LORD
     is the death of his faithful servants.
¹⁶ Truly I am your servant, LORD;
     I serve you just as my mother did;
     you have freed me from my chains.

¹⁷ I will sacrifice a thank offering to you
     and call on the name of the LORD.
¹⁸ I will fulfill my vows to the LORD
     in the presence of all his people,
¹⁹ in the courts of the house of the LORD —
     in your midst, Jerusalem.

  Praise the LORD.^a

^a 18,19 Hebrew *Hallelu Yah*

115:12–13 The people's confession of trust.
115:14–15 The priestly blessing.
115:14 *cause you to flourish.* In numbers, wealth and strength.
115:16–18 The people's concluding doxology.
  115:16 *highest heavens . . . earth.* The heavens are the exclusive realm of the exalted, all-sovereign God; the earth is the divinely appointed place for human beings, where they live under God's rule and care, enjoy his abundant blessings (vv. 12–13) and celebrate his praise (v. 18).
115:17 *not the dead.* The dead no longer live in "the earth" (v. 16) but have descended to the silent realm below, where blessings are no longer enjoyed and hence praise is absent (see notes on 6:5; 30:1).
Ps 116 The fourth of the "Egyptian Hallel" psalms (see note on Ps 113–118) praises the Lord for deliverance from death. It may have been written by a king (see v. 16 and note; cf. also Hezekiah's thanksgiving, Isa 38:10–20); its language echoes many of the psalms of David. In Jewish liturgy (see introduction to Ps 113–118), the singular personal pronoun must have been used corporately (see note on Ps 30 title), and the references to "death" may have been understood as alluding to the Egyptian bondage and/or the exile.
  116:1–2 I love the Lord because he has heard and saved me (cf. 18:1).
  116:2 *I will call on him.* In him I will trust, and my prayers will ever be to him. "I will call/I called" is a key thematic phrase (in Hebrew one word, and always in the same form as here), occurring twice in each half of the psalm (vv. 2,4,13,17).
116:5–6 Testimony to God's goodness—echoing Ex 34:6.
116:5 *gracious . . . righteous . . . compassion.* See 145:8,17; cf. 112:4. *our God.* The author is conscious of those about him; he is praising the Lord "in the presence of all his people" (vv. 14,18).
  116:6 *unwary.* Those who are childlike in their sense of dependence on and trust in the Lord (see note on 19:7).
116:10–11 Introduction to the second half of the psalm, an elaboration on the introduction to the first half (vv. 1–2).
116:10 *I am greatly afflicted.* This and the quotation in v. 11 should perhaps be taken, together with the one in v. 4, as a brief recollection of the prayer offered when the psalmist was in distress. The threat of death from which he had been delivered was brought on by the false accusations of enemies, as in Ps 109 (see notes on 5:9; 10:7). (For another interpretation, see following note.)
116:11 *Everyone is a liar.* The heart of the accusation he had lodged against his false accusers (for examples of similar accusations, see 5:9–10; 35:11,15; 109:2–4). Others interpret these words as a declaration that all people offer but a false hope for deliverance (60:11; 118:8–9)—therefore the psalmist called on the Lord.
116:12 *goodness.* The Hebrew for this word occurs only here in the OT but represents the same basic root as "has been good" in v. 7. Verses 7,12, taken together, concisely focus the central movement of the psalm's theme (cf. 13:6).
116:13 *cup of salvation.* Often thought to be related to the cup of the Passover meal referred to in Mt 26:27 and parallels, but far more likely the cup of wine drunk at the

¹Praise the LORD, all you nations;
  extol him, all you peoples.
²For great is his love toward us,
  and the faithfulness of the LORD endures
    forever.

Praise the LORD.[a]

¹Give thanks to the LORD, for he is good;
  his love endures forever.

²Let Israel say:
  "His love endures forever."
³Let the house of Aaron say:
  "His love endures forever."
⁴Let those who fear the LORD say:
  "His love endures forever."

⁵When hard pressed, I cried to the LORD;
  he brought me into a spacious place.
⁶The LORD is with me; I will not be afraid.
  What can mere mortals do to me?
⁷The LORD is with me; he is my helper.
  I look in triumph on my enemies.

⁸It is better to take refuge in the LORD
  than to trust in humans.
⁹It is better to take refuge in the LORD
  than to trust in princes.
¹⁰All the nations surrounded me,
  but in the name of the LORD I cut them down.
¹¹They surrounded me on every side,
  but in the name of the LORD I cut them down.
¹²They swarmed around me like bees,
  but they were consumed as quickly as
    burning thorns;
  in the name of the LORD I cut them down.
¹³I was pushed back and about to fall,
  but the LORD helped me.
¹⁴The LORD is my strength and my defense[b];
  he has become my salvation.

¹⁵Shouts of joy and victory
  resound in the tents of the righteous:
  "The LORD's right hand has done mighty
    things!
¹⁶ The LORD's right hand is lifted high;
  the LORD's right hand has done mighty
    things!"
¹⁷I will not die but live,
  and will proclaim what the LORD has done.
¹⁸The LORD has chastened me severely,
  but he has not given me over to death.

a 2 Hebrew *Hallelu Yah*   b 14 Or *song*

festal meal that climaxed a thank offering (cf. 22:26,29; Lev 7:11–21)—called the "cup of salvation" because the thank offering and its meal celebrated deliverance by the Lord. See the parallel with "sacrifice a thank offering" in the corresponding series in vv. 17–18.

116:14 *vows.* To praise the Lord (see note on 7:17).

116:15–16 Elaboration on vv. 3–4. Note the references to "death" in vv. 3,15; cf. vv. 8–9.

116:15 *Precious . . . is the death.* The death of his servants is of great concern to the Lord; cf. the analogous expression, "precious is their blood in his sight" (72:14). *his faithful servants.* See note on 4:3.

116:16 *your servant.* This may identify the psalmist as the Lord's anointed (78:70), but in any event as one devoted to the Lord (19:11,13).

116:17–19 Reiteration of the vows of vv. 13–14.

🍃 **Ps 117** The fifth of the "Egyptian Hallel" psalms (see note on Ps 113–118), the shortest psalm in the Psalter and the shortest chapter in the Bible. Psalm 117 is an expanded Hallelujah (cf. introduction to Ps 119). It may originally have served as the conclusion to the preceding collection of Hallelujah psalms (Ps 111–116)—of which it is the seventh. All nations and peoples are called on to praise the Lord (as in 47:1; 67:3–5; 96:7; 98:4; 100:1; see note on 9:1) for his great love and enduring faithfulness toward Israel (Isa 12:4–6). Thus the Hallelujahs of the OT Psalter, when fully expounded, express that great truth, so often emphasized in the OT, that the destiny of all peoples is involved in what God was doing in and for his people Israel (see, e.g., 2:8–12; 47:9; 67:2; 72:17; 102:15; 110). See introduction to Ps 113–118.

🍃 **117:1** Quoted in Ro 15:11 as proof that the salvation of Gentiles and the glorifying of God by Gentiles was not a divine afterthought.

🍃 **Ps 118** A hymn of thanksgiving for deliverance from enemies. The setting may be that of a Davidic king leading the nation in a liturgy of thanksgiving for deliverance and victory after a hard-fought battle with a powerful confederacy of nations (cf. 2Ch 20:27–28). The speaker in vv. 5–21 is the king. As the last song of the "Egyptian Hallel" (see note on Ps 113–118), this psalm may have been the hymn sung by Jesus and his disciples at the conclusion of the Last Supper (see Mt 26:30).

118:1 A conventional call to praise (shared in whole or in part with Ps 105–107; 136; 1Ch 16:8,34; 2Ch 20:21). *Give thanks.* See note on Ps 100 title. This, together with vv. 2–4 (except for the refrain) and 29, may have been by the same voice that speaks in vv. 5–21. *love.* See vv. 2–4,29; see also article, p. 16.

118:2–4 *Israel . . . house of Aaron . . . those who fear the LORD.* See 115:9–11 and note. Triple repetition is a common feature in this psalm (see note on 96:1–3).

118:5–21 The king's song of thanksgiving for deliverance and victory.

118:5–7 The introduction: I cried to the Lord; he answered; I need fear no one.

118:8–14 Reflection on the experience of the Lord's saving help—framed by vv. 8–9 and v. 14.

118:12 *as burning thorns.* See 58:9 and note.

118:13 *fall.* Be killed (see vv. 17–18).

118:14 Perhaps recalls the triumph song of Ex 15, but more

¹⁹Open for me the gates of the righteous;
  I will enter and give thanks to the Lord.
²⁰This is the gate of the Lord
  through which the righteous may enter.
²¹I will give you thanks, for you answered me;
  you have become my salvation.

²²The stone the builders rejected
  has become the cornerstone;
²³the Lord has done this,
  and it is marvelous in our eyes.
²⁴The Lord has done it this very day;
  let us rejoice today and be glad.

²⁵Lord, save us!
  Lord, grant us success!

²⁶Blessed is he who comes in the name of the Lord.
  From the house of the Lord we bless you.^a
²⁷The Lord is God,
  and he has made his light shine on us.
  With boughs in hand, join in the festal procession
  up^b to the horns of the altar.

²⁸You are my God, and I will praise you;
  you are my God, and I will exalt you.

²⁹Give thanks to the Lord, for he is good;
  his love endures forever.

^a 26 The Hebrew is plural.   ^b 27 Or *Bind the festal sacrifice
with ropes / and take it*

Four-horned altar from Ekron. Ps 118:27
mentions "the horns of the altar."

© Phoenix Data Systems

likely the verse had become a widely used testimony of
praise to the Lord (Isa 12:2).

118:15–21 Celebration of the Lord's deliverance—framed
by vv. 15–16 and v. 21.

118:15 *tents.* Dwellings. *righteous.* Israel as the people (ideally) committed in heart and life to the Lord (see v. 20; see
also 68:3 and note). Cf. "the tents of the wicked" (84:10).

118:18 *chastened me.* The king acknowledges that
the grave threat through which he has passed has
also served God's purpose—to discipline him and teach
him humble godliness (6:1; 38:1; 94:12; Dt 4:36; 8:5).

118:19 *Open for me.* This line suggests a liturgical procession (v. 27) in which the king approaches the inner court
of the temple at the head of the jubilant worshipers (Ps
24; 68). *gates.* Those leading to the inner temple court. *of
the righteous.* Often thought to be the name of a particular gateway, but more likely only descriptive here of the
gate "through which the righteous may enter" (v. 20). It
is possible that the procession began outside the city
and that "the gates of the righteous" are the gates of
Jerusalem, the city of God (see also Isa 26:2).

118:21 This closing verse of the thanksgiving song echoes
the "Give thanks" of v. 1, the "brought me" of v. 5 and the
testimony of v. 14.

118:22–27 The people's exultation.

118:22 *The stone the builders rejected.* Most likely a
reference to the king (whose deliverance and victory
are being celebrated), who had been looked on with disdain by the kings invading his realm—the builders of
worldly empires. Others suppose that the stone refers to
Israel, a nation held in contempt by the world powers. *cornerstone.* Either (1) a capstone over a door (a large stone
used as a lintel), (2) a large stone used to anchor and align
the corner of a wall or (3) the keystone of an arch (Zec 4:7;
10:4). By a wordplay (pun) the author hints at "chief ruler"
(the Hebrew word for "corner" is sometimes used as a
metaphor for leader/ruler; see Isa 19:13; see also Jdg 20:2;
1Sa 14:38). This stone, disdained by the worldly powers,
has become the most important stone in the structure of
the new world order that God is bringing about through
Israel. Jesus applied this verse (and v. 23) to himself (see
Mt 21:42; Mk 12:10–11; Lk 20:17; see also Ac 4:11; Eph 2:20;
1Pe 2:7).

118:24 *The Lord has done it this very day . . . rejoice.* This
day of rejoicing was made possible by God's deliverance in
the victory being celebrated. Others suppose a reference
to Passover or the Festival of Tabernacles. *has done it.* Has
made the "stone" the "cornerstone" (v. 22; see also vv. 15–17,
23).

118:25 Prayer for the Lord to continue to save and sustain
his people.

118:26 *who comes in the name of the Lord.* The one
who with God's help had defeated the enemies "in
the name of the Lord" (vv. 10–12). *From the house of the
Lord.* From God's very presence (134:3). *you.* The plural
(see NIV text note) may have been used to exalt the king
(the plural was often used with reference to God), whom
God had so singularly blessed (see NIV text note on 1Ki
9:6). Alternatively, it may refer to those who have come
with the king victoriously from the battle. The crowds
who greeted Jesus at his entrance into Jerusalem as King
used the words of vv. 25–26 (Jn 12:13).

Psalm 119[a]

א Aleph

[1] Blessed are those whose ways are blameless,
   who walk according to the law of the LORD.
[2] Blessed are those who keep his statutes
   and seek him with all their heart —
[3] they do no wrong
   but follow his ways.
[4] You have laid down precepts
   that are to be fully obeyed.
[5] Oh, that my ways were steadfast
   in obeying your decrees!
[6] Then I would not be put to shame
   when I consider all your commands.

[a] This psalm is an acrostic poem, the stanzas of which begin with successive letters of the Hebrew alphabet; moreover, the verses of each stanza begin with the same letter of the Hebrew alphabet.

> ### In what ways do you obey God's Word?

_____

_____

_____

_____

_____

_____

_____

_____

_____

_____

_____

_____

_____

_____

_____

_____

118:27 *made his light shine on us.* An echo of the priestly benediction (see Nu 6:25). *With boughs . . . up.* Apparently a call to complete the climax of the liturgy of a thank offering (Lev 7:11–21), though others suggest the liturgy of the Festival of Tabernacles. *horns of the altar.* See photo, p. 152.

118:28 The king's closing reiteration of his vow in v. 21.

118:29 Renewal of the opening call to grateful praise (see v. 1 and note).

Ps 119 The longest psalm in the Psalter—and the longest chapter in the Bible—is a hymn celebrating the word of God (cf. introduction to Ps 117). The author was an Israelite of exemplary piety who (1) was passionately devoted to the word of God as the word of life; (2) humbly acknowledged, nevertheless, the errant ways of his heart and life; (3) knew the pain—but also the fruits—of God's corrective discipline; and (4) had suffered much at the hands of those who arrogantly disregarded God's word and made him the target of their hostility, ridicule and slander. It is possible that he was a priest (see notes on vv. 23,57)—and the psalm might well be a vehicle for priestly instruction in godliness. He elaborated on the themes of 19:7–13 and interwove with them many prayers for deliverance, composing a massive alphabetic acrostic (see NIV text note; see also Introduction: Literary Features) that demands patient, meditative reading. Most of its lines are addressed to God, mingling prayers with professions of devotion to God's law. Yet, as the opening verses (and perhaps also its elaborate acrostic form) make clear, it was intended for godly instruction (in the manner of Ps 1; see v. 9 and note). For its placement in the Psalter, see introduction to Ps 111–119. See also notes on 111:1; 112:1.

Whereas elsewhere in the Psalter the focus falls primarily on God's mighty acts of creation and redemption and his rule over all the world, here devotion to the word of God (and the God of the word) is the dominant theme. The author highlights two aspects of that word: (1) God's directives for life and (2) God's promises—the one calling for obedience, the other for faith. In referring to these, he makes pervasive use of eight Hebrew terms: *torah*, "law"; *'edot*, "statutes"; *piqqudim*, "precepts"; *miṣwot*, "commands, commandments"; *mishpaṭim*, "laws"; *huqqim*, "decrees"; *dabar*, "word" (in the sense of either "law" or "promise"); *'imrah*, "word," but more often "promise."

119:1–3 General introduction.

119:1–2 *Blessed.* See note on 1:1.

119:1 *whose ways are blameless.* This opening general description is further elaborated in the rest of the introduction, which concludes with an equally general statement: "follow his ways" (v. 3). See Ge 17:1; cf. Ge 26:5. *law.* Hebrew *torah*, a collective term for God's covenant directives for his people (see Dt 4:44). "Law" often came, especially later, to have a whole broader reference—the whole Pentateuch (see Lk 24:44) or even the whole OT (see Jn 10:34; 12:34; 15:25; 1Co 14:21)—but here it is limited by the synonyms with which it is used interchangeably.

119:2 *statutes.* Hebrew *'edot*, a specifically covenantal term referring to stipulations laid down by the covenant Lord (see 25:10, "demands"; Dt 4:45, "stipulations"). *seek him with all their heart.* See Dt 4:29. *heart.* See v. 7; see also note on 4:7.

7 I will praise you with an upright heart
    as I learn your righteous laws.
8 I will obey your decrees;
    do not utterly forsake me.

ב Beth 2

9 How can a young person stay on the path of
        purity?
    By living according to your word.
10 I seek you with all my heart;
    do not let me stray from your commands.
11 I have hidden your word in my heart
    that I might not sin against you.
12 Praise be to you, LORD;
    teach me your decrees.
13 With my lips I recount
    all the laws that come from your mouth.
14 I rejoice in following your statutes
    as one rejoices in great riches.
15 I meditate on your precepts
    and consider your ways.
16 I delight in your decrees;
    I will not neglect your word.

ג Gimel 3

17 Be good to your servant while I live,
    that I may obey your word.
18 Open my eyes that I may see
    wonderful things in your law.
19 I am a stranger on earth;
    do not hide your commands from me.
20 My soul is consumed with longing
    for your laws at all times.
21 You rebuke the arrogant, who are accursed,
    those who stray from your commands.
22 Remove from me their scorn and contempt,
    for I keep your statutes.
23 Though rulers sit together and slander me,
    your servant will meditate on your decrees.
24 Your statutes are my delight;
    they are my counselors.

Additional Insights

God's election of Israel, together with the giving of his word, represents the renewed inbreaking of God's righteous kingdom into this world of rebellion and evil.

119:3 *ways.* The Hebrew for this word occurs only rarely in this psalm but is common in Deuteronomy and elsewhere as a general reference to God's covenant requirements—used here to balance "ways" in v. 1.

119:4–8 Those who obey God's law (vv. 4–5,8) can hope for God's help (vv. 6–8).

119:4 *precepts.* Hebrew *piqqudim,* covenant regulations laid down by the Lord (19:8; 111:7).

119:5 *decrees.* Hebrew *ḥuqqim,* covenant directives (Dt 6:2; 28:15,45; 30:10,16; 1Ki 11:11), emphasizing their fixed character.

119:6 *not be put to shame.* The psalmist would not suffer poverty, sickness or humiliation at the hands of his enemies and so become the object of sneers (see vv. 31,46,80; 25:2–3,20; see also introduction to this psalm), but he would have reason to praise the Lord (v. 7) for blessings received and deliverances granted because the Lord does not forsake him (v. 8). *consider.* Respect, have regard for (v. 15; 74:20). *commands.* Hebrew *miṣwot,* covenant directives (Ex 20:6; 24:12; Dt 4:2) designated specifically as that which God has commanded.

119:7 *righteous.* One of the author's favorite characterizations of God's law (see vv. 62,75,106,123,138,144,160,164,172; see also 19:9). *laws.* Hebrew *mishpaṭim,* covenant directives (Ex 21:1; 24:3; Dt 4:1), as the laws laid down by a ruler (king).

119:8 *not . . . forsake me.* To poverty, sickness or my enemies (cf. 9:10; 22:1; 27:9–10; 38:21; 71:9,11,18).

119:9 *a young person.* Indicates instruction addressed to the young after the manner of the wisdom teachers (see 34:11; Pr 1:4; Ecc 11:9; 12:1). *purity.* Free from all moral taint (73:13). *word.* Hebrew *dabar,* a general designation for God's (word) revelation but here used with special reference to his law (sometimes promises).

119:10 *I seek you.* The author's devotion is first of all to the God of the law and the promises; they have meaning for him only because they are *God's* word of life for him. *heart.* See v. 11; see also note on 4:7.

119:11 *word.* Hebrew *'imrah,* a synonym of *dabar* ("word"; see note on v. 9; see also Dt 33:9; Pr 30:5). Except where noted, as here, "word" in this psalm is *dabar; 'imrah* is usually translated "promise."

119:13 *recount.* Either in meditation or in liturgies of covenant commitment to the Lord (see 50:16, "recite").

119:14 *as one rejoices in great riches.* See vv. 72,111,162.

119:15 *ways.* The Hebrew for this word is a synonym of the Hebrew for "ways" in v. 3.

119:17–24 Devotion to God's law marks the Lord's servant but alienates him from the arrogant (v. 21) of the world.

119:17 *that I may obey.* Out of gratitude for God's care and blessing.

119:18 *wonderful things.* Usually ascribed to God's redeeming acts (see 9:1 and note)—but God's law also contains wonders (v. 27) to contemplate, if only God opens a person's eyes.

119:19 *stranger on earth.* As a servant of the Lord, i.e., a citizen of his kingdom, the psalmist is not at home in any of the kingdoms of the world (see 39:12 and note; see also note on v. 54).

119:20 *My soul is.* I am (see vv. 28,81; see also note on 6:3).

119:21 *the arrogant.* Those who are a law to themselves, most fully described in 10:2–11 (see vv. 51,69,78,85,122; see also note on 31:23). The author

4 ד Daleth

25 I am laid low in the dust;
      preserve my life according to your word.
26 I gave an account of my ways and you
            answered me;
      teach me your decrees.
27 Cause me to understand the way of your
            precepts,
      that I may meditate on your wonderful deeds.
28 My soul is weary with sorrow;
      strengthen me according to your word.
29 Keep me from deceitful ways;
      be gracious to me and teach me your law.
30 I have chosen the way of faithfulness;
      I have set my heart on your laws.
31 I hold fast to your statutes, LORD;
      do not let me be put to shame.
32 I run in the path of your commands,
      for you have broadened my understanding.

5 ה He

33 Teach me, LORD, the way of your decrees,
      that I may follow it to the end.[a]
34 Give me understanding, so that I may keep
            your law
      and obey it with all my heart.
35 Direct me in the path of your commands,
      for there I find delight.
36 Turn my heart toward your statutes
      and not toward selfish gain.
37 Turn my eyes away from worthless things;
      preserve my life according to your word.[b]
38 Fulfill your promise to your servant,
      so that you may be feared.
39 Take away the disgrace I dread,
      for your laws are good.
40 How I long for your precepts!
      In your righteousness preserve my life.

6 ו Waw

41 May your unfailing love come to me, LORD,
      your salvation, according to your promise;
42 then I can answer anyone who taunts me,
      for I trust in your word.
43 Never take your word of truth from my mouth,
      for I have put my hope in your laws.
44 I will always obey your law,
      for ever and ever.
45 I will walk about in freedom,
      for I have sought out your precepts.
46 I will speak of your statutes before kings
      and will not be put to shame,

---

a 33 Or *follow it for its reward*   b 37 Two manuscripts of the
Masoretic Text and Dead Sea Scrolls; most manuscripts of
the Masoretic Text *life in your way*

---

has suffered much from their hostility because of his zeal for God and his law, as the next two verses and many others indicate. *accursed.* Ripe for God's judgment.

119:22 *scorn and contempt.* Of the arrogant.

119:23 *rulers.* Because the author mentions also speaking "before kings" (v. 46) and being persecuted by "rulers" (v. 161), it may be that he held some official position, such as priest (one of whose functions it would have been to teach God's law; see Lev 10:11; Ezr 7:6; Ne 8:2–8; Jer 2:8; 18:18; Mal 2:7; see also note on v. 57). The kings and rulers referred to may have been Israelite in the time of the monarchy but more likely were local rulers in the postexilic Persian imperial system. *sit.* As those securely settled in the world—not as strangers (cf. v. 19). *together and slander.* As they share their worldly counsels, they speak derisively of the one who stands apart because he delights in God's statutes and makes them his "counselors" (v. 24).

119:25–32 Whether "laid low" (v. 25) or having his understanding broadened (v. 32), he is determined to "hold fast" (v. 31) to God's word.

119:25 *laid low.* The author speaks much of his sorrow, suffering and affliction (vv. 28,50,67,71, 75,83,92,107,143,153). Ridicule, slander and persecution from his adversaries often accompany this suffering of God's devoted servant, who makes God's word (his law and promises) the hope of his life (see vv. 42,51,65,69,78, 85,95,110,134,141,150,154,157,161; see also notes on v. 6; 5:9; 31:11–12). *in the dust.* See 44:25 and note. *word.* Especially its promises, as also in vv. 28,37,42,49,65,74,81,107,114,147.

119:27 *wonderful deeds.* See note on v. 18.

119:29 *deceitful ways.* Ways that seem right but lead to death (see Pr 14:12)—in contrast to the ways prescribed by God's law, which are trustworthy (vv. 86,138) and true (vv. 142,151,160). *teach me your law.* By keeping me true to your law, let me enjoy your blessings.

119:30 *way of faithfulness.* See note on v. 29.

119:31 *put to shame.* See note on v. 6.

119:32 *broadened my understanding.* See 1Ki 4:29, "breadth of understanding."

119:33–40 Prayer for instruction in God's will as he longs for his precepts.

119:34 *heart.* See v. 36; see also note on 4:7.

119:36–37 *heart . . . eyes.* See 101:2b–3a and note.

119:38 *that you may be feared.* The Lord's saving acts in fulfillment of his promises contribute to the recognition that he is the true God (130:4; 2Sa 7:25–26; 1Ki 8:39–40; Jer 33:8–9).

119:39 *disgrace I dread.* See notes on vv. 6,25.

119:40 *righteousness.* See note on 4:1.

119:41–48 May the Lord deliver me and not take his truth from my mouth; then I will honor his law in my

Additional Insights

God opposes the proud and exalts the humble.

47 for I delight in your commands
　　because I love them.
48 I reach out for your commands, which I love,
　　that I may meditate on your decrees.

7　　ז Zayin

49 Remember your word to your servant,
　　for you have given me hope.
50 My comfort in my suffering is this:
　　Your promise preserves my life.
51 The arrogant mock me unmercifully,
　　but I do not turn from your law.
52 I remember, LORD, your ancient laws,
　　and I find comfort in them.
53 Indignation grips me because of the wicked,
　　who have forsaken your law.
54 Your decrees are the theme of my song
　　wherever I lodge.
55 In the night, LORD, I remember your name,
　　that I may keep your law.
56 This has been my practice:
　　I obey your precepts.

8　　ח Heth

57 You are my portion, LORD;
　　I have promised to obey your words.
58 I have sought your face with all my heart;
　　be gracious to me according to your promise.
59 I have considered my ways
　　and have turned my steps to your statutes.
60 I will hasten and not delay
　　to obey your commands.
61 Though the wicked bind me with ropes,
　　I will not forget your law.
62 At midnight I rise to give you thanks
　　for your righteous laws.
63 I am a friend to all who fear you,
　　to all who follow your precepts.
64 The earth is filled with your love, LORD;
　　teach me your decrees.

9　　ט Teth

65 Do good to your servant
　　according to your word, LORD.
66 Teach me knowledge and good judgment,
　　for I trust your commands.
67 Before I was afflicted I went astray,
　　but now I obey your word.
68 You are good, and what you do is good;
　　teach me your decrees.
69 Though the arrogant have smeared me
　　　with lies,
　　I keep your precepts with all my heart.
70 Their hearts are callous and unfeeling,
　　but I delight in your law.

life and speak of it before kings, for I love his commands.

119:41 *love.* See vv. 64,76,88,124,149,159; see also article, p. 16.

119:42 *anyone who taunts me.* See note on v. 25 ("laid low"). *word.* See note on v. 25.

119:43 *word of truth from my mouth.* See v. 13 and note; see also v. 46.

119:45 *freedom.* Unconfined by affliction or oppression (see 18:19 and note).

119:46 *before kings.* Such will be his boldness (see note on v. 23).

119:48 *I reach out for.* An act accompanying praise (as in 63:4; 134:2); so the sense may be: I praise.

119:49–56 God's word is my comfort and my guide, whatever my circumstances.

119:49 *word.* See note on v. 25.

119:50–51 *in my suffering . . . The arrogant mock.* See note on v. 25 ("laid low").

119:51 *arrogant.* See note on v. 21.

119:52 *ancient.* God's law is not fickle but is grounded firmly in his unchanging moral character. This is a major source of the author's comfort and one of the main reasons he cherishes the law so highly (vv. 89,144,152,160).

119:53 *Indignation grips me.* Zeal for God's law (vv. 136,139) awakens righteous anger against those who reject it (vv. 113,115,158) and brings abhorrence of all that is contrary to it (vv. 104,128,163), but it draws together those who honor it (v. 63).

119:54 *wherever I lodge.* The sense may be that of v. 19 (see note there).

119:57–64 The Lord is the psalmist's true homestead because it is God's law that fills the earth with all that makes life secure and joyous. So God's promises are his hope and God's righteous laws his delight.

119:57 *portion.* May identify the author as a priest or Levite (see 73:26 and note).

119:58 *heart.* See note on 4:7.

119:61 *bind me with ropes.* Oppress me.

119:62 *give you thanks.* See note on Ps 100 title. *righteous.* See note on v. 7.

119:65–72 Do good to me in accordance with your goodness, even if that means affliction, because your affliction is good for me; it teaches me knowledge and good judgment from your law.

Additional Insights

When in the Psalms righteous sufferers cry out to God in their distress, they give voice to the sufferings of God's servants in a hostile and evil world. These cries became the prayers of God's oppressed people, and as such they were taken up into Israel's book of prayers.

71 It was good for me to be afflicted
    so that I might learn your decrees.
72 The law from your mouth is more precious
       to me
    than thousands of pieces of silver and gold.

10   י Yodh

73 Your hands made me and formed me;
    give me understanding to learn your
       commands.
74 May those who fear you rejoice when they
       see me,
    for I have put my hope in your word.
75 I know, LORD, that your laws are righteous,
    and that in faithfulness you have afflicted me.
76 May your unfailing love be my comfort,
    according to your promise to your servant.
77 Let your compassion come to me that I may
       live,
    for your law is my delight.
78 May the arrogant be put to shame for
       wronging me without cause;
    but I will meditate on your precepts.
79 May those who fear you turn to me,
    those who understand your statutes.
80 May I wholeheartedly follow your decrees,
    that I may not be put to shame.

11   כ Kaph

81 My soul faints with longing for your salvation,
    but I have put my hope in your word.
82 My eyes fail, looking for your promise;
    I say, "When will you comfort me?"
83 Though I am like a wineskin in the smoke,
    I do not forget your decrees.
84 How long must your servant wait?
    When will you punish my persecutors?
85 The arrogant dig pits to trap me,
    contrary to your law.
86 All your commands are trustworthy;
    help me, for I am being persecuted without
       cause.
87 They almost wiped me from the earth,
    but I have not forsaken your precepts.
88 In your unfailing love preserve my life,
    that I may obey the statutes of your mouth.

12   ל Lamedh

89 Your word, LORD, is eternal;
    it stands firm in the heavens.
90 Your faithfulness continues through all
       generations;
    you established the earth, and it endures.
91 Your laws endure to this day,
    for all things serve you.

119:65 *Do good.* Cf. v. 68; see 31:19; 86:17 and notes. *to your servant.* To me. *word.* See note on v. 25.
119:66 *trust.* Have confidence in; God's commands are not deceitful (see note on v. 29) or fickle (see note on v. 52).
119:67 *afflicted.* At the hands of God (see v. 71; see also note on v. 25, "laid low"). *word.* See note on v. 11.
119:69 *arrogant.* See note on v. 21.
119:71 While one cannot assume that all or even most affliction is designed to teach God's people lessons they should learn, at times it is (Heb 12:5–11).
119:72 *than thousands . . . of silver and gold.* See vv. 14, 57,111,162.
119:73–80 Complete your forming of me by helping me to conform to your righteous laws so that the arrogant may be put to shame and those who fear you may rejoice with me. (The stanza has a concentric structure; compare vv. 73 and 80, 74 and 79, 75 and 78, 76 and 77.)
119:73 *understanding.* What I need to perfect the work you began when you formed me.
119:74 *fear you.* See v. 79; see also note on 34:8–14. *when they see me.* When I am perfectly formed and enjoying the blessings of the godly. *word.* See note on v. 25.
119:75 *laws.* Here the Hebrew for this word (*mishpaṭim*) may refer to God's just decisions in dealing with his servant, as the rest of the verse implies. *you have afflicted me.* See vv. 67,71.
119:76 *unfailing love.* See article, p. 16. *my comfort.* In my affliction.
119:77 *that I may live.* And not perish in my affliction.
119:78 *the arrogant.* See note on v. 21. *be put to shame.* As they have subjected me to shame (see note on 5:10). *for wronging me.* See note on v. 25 ("laid low").
119:79 *turn to me.* See v. 63 and note on v. 53.
119:80 *not be put to shame.* See note on v. 6.
119:81–88 Save me from my affliction and my persecutors, according to your promises, and I will obey your statutes. This last stanza of the first half of the psalm, like the closing stanza, is dominated by prayer for God's help (see note on v. 25).
119:81 *soul.* See note on 6:3.
119:83 *like a wineskin in the smoke.* As a wineskin hanging in the smoke and heat above a fire becomes smudged and shriveled, so the psalmist bears the marks of his affliction.
119:85 *The arrogant.* See note on v. 21. *dig pits.* Probably referring to slander—public accusations that the psalmist must be guilty of vile sins or he would not be suffering such affliction (see notes on 5:9; 9:15). *contrary to your law.* See Ex 20:16.
119:86 *trustworthy.* See note on v. 29 ("deceitful ways").
119:88 *love.* See article, p. 16.
119:89–91 God's sovereign and unchanging word governs and maintains all creation. (These first three verses of the second half of the psalm teach a general truth; cf. vv. 1–3.)
119:89 *Your word.* Here God's word by which he created, maintains and governs all things (33:4,6; 107:20; 147:15,18). *stands firm in the heavens.* The secure order of the heavens and the earth (v. 90) declares (19:1–4) the reassuring truth that God's word (his "laws," v. 91), by which he upholds and governs all things, is enduring (eternal) and trustworthy ("your faithfulness," v. 90). And that is the larger truth that confirms the confidence of

⁹²If your law had not been my delight,
    I would have perished in my affliction.
⁹³I will never forget your precepts,
    for by them you have preserved my life.
⁹⁴Save me, for I am yours;
    I have sought out your precepts.
⁹⁵The wicked are waiting to destroy me,
    but I will ponder your statutes.
⁹⁶To all perfection I see a limit,
    but your commands are boundless.

13   מ Mem

⁹⁷Oh, how I love your law!
    I meditate on it all day long.
⁹⁸Your commands are always with me
    and make me wiser than my enemies.
⁹⁹I have more insight than all my teachers,
    for I meditate on your statutes.
¹⁰⁰I have more understanding than the elders,
    for I obey your precepts.
¹⁰¹I have kept my feet from every evil path
    so that I might obey your word.
¹⁰²I have not departed from your laws,
    for you yourself have taught me.
¹⁰³How sweet are your words to my taste,
    sweeter than honey to my mouth!
¹⁰⁴I gain understanding from your precepts;
    therefore I hate every wrong path.

14   נ Nun

¹⁰⁵Your word is a lamp for my feet,
    a light on my path.
¹⁰⁶I have taken an oath and confirmed it,
    that I will follow your righteous laws.
¹⁰⁷I have suffered much;
    preserve my life, Lord, according to
       your word.
¹⁰⁸Accept, Lord, the willing praise of my
       mouth,
    and teach me your laws.
¹⁰⁹Though I constantly take my life in my
       hands,
    I will not forget your law.
¹¹⁰The wicked have set a snare for me,
    but I have not strayed from your
       precepts.
¹¹¹Your statutes are my heritage forever;
    they are the joy of my heart.
¹¹²My heart is set on keeping your decrees
    to the very end.ᵃ

15   ס Samekh

¹¹³I hate double-minded people,
    but I love your law.

ᵃ 112 Or *decrees / for their enduring reward*

the godly in the trustworthiness of God's word (his laws and promises) of special revelation (see notes on 93:5; 96:10; see also note on v. 29, "deceitful ways").
119:90 *Your faithfulness.* An indirect reference to God's word (see v. 89 and note).
119:92 *would have perished in my affliction.* Would not have learned the way of life (v. 93) from your law (see vv. 67,71 and note on vv. 65–72).
119:95 *The wicked.* See note on v. 21 ("the arrogant"). *waiting to destroy me.* See note on v. 25 ("laid low").
119:96 *perfection.* Probably that which has been perfected in the sense of completed, given fixed bounds so that it is no longer open-ended. *boundless.* An inexhaustible source of wise counsel for life.
🌿 **119:97–104** Meditation on God's law yields the highest wisdom.
119:98 *my enemies.* Those arrogant ones (see note on v. 21) who place confidence in worldly wisdom.
119:99 *teachers.* Merely human teachers (cf. v. 102).
119:100 *elders.* Older men, taught by experience.
119:102 *you . . . have taught me.* Through your laws.
119:103 *words.* Perhaps better understood here as "laws" (see vv. 67,133,158,172 and note on v. 11).
119:104 *hate every wrong path.* See note on v. 53.
🌿 **119:105** *lamp . . . light.* Apart from which I could only grope about in the darkness (see photo, below).
119:106 *have taken an oath and confirmed it.* Have covenanted (Ne 10:29).
119:107 See v. 25 and note.
119:109 *take my life in my hands.* By publicly honoring God's law even in the face of threats and hostility (see especially vv. 23,46,161).
119:110 *set a snare.* See v. 85 and note.
119:111–112 *heart.* See note on 4:7.

In Old Testament times oil lamps were made of clay and shaped like saucers. "Your word is a lamp for my feet, a light on my path" (Ps 119:105).
© 2018 by Zondervan

114 You are my refuge and my shield;
    I have put my hope in your word.
115 Away from me, you evildoers,
    that I may keep the commands of my God!
116 Sustain me, my God, according to your
        promise, and I will live;
    do not let my hopes be dashed.
117 Uphold me, and I will be delivered;
    I will always have regard for your decrees.
118 You reject all who stray from your decrees,
    for their delusions come to nothing.
119 All the wicked of the earth you discard like dross;
    therefore I love your statutes.
120 My flesh trembles in fear of you;
    I stand in awe of your laws.

16   ע Ayin

121 I have done what is righteous and just;
    do not leave me to my oppressors.
122 Ensure your servant's well-being;
    do not let the arrogant oppress me.
123 My eyes fail, looking for your salvation,
    looking for your righteous promise.
124 Deal with your servant according to your love
    and teach me your decrees.
125 I am your servant; give me discernment
    that I may understand your statutes.
126 It is time for you to act, LORD;
    your law is being broken.
127 Because I love your commands
    more than gold, more than pure gold,
128 and because I consider all your precepts right,
    I hate every wrong path.

17   פ Pe

129 Your statutes are wonderful;
    therefore I obey them.
130 The unfolding of your words gives light;
    it gives understanding to the simple.
131 I open my mouth and pant,
    longing for your commands.
132 Turn to me and have mercy on me,
    as you always do to those who love your
        name.
133 Direct my footsteps according to your word;
    let no sin rule over me.
134 Redeem me from human oppression,
    that I may obey your precepts.
135 Make your face shine on your servant
    and teach me your decrees.
136 Streams of tears flow from my eyes,
    for your law is not obeyed.

18   צ Tsadhe

137 You are righteous, LORD,
    and your laws are right.

119:111 *my heritage.* The possession I have received from God as my homestead and that from which I draw the provisions for my life (see note on vv. 57–64).

119:113 *hate double-minded people.* See v. 115; see also note on v. 53. "Double-minded" people are "unstable in all they do" (Jas 1:8).

119:114 *word.* See note on v. 25.

119:118 *reject.* Or "shake off" or "make light of." *their delusions.* Probably their deceitful ways (see note on v. 29).

119:119 *dross.* Scum removed from molten ore or metal. The Hebrew for this word is a pun on the word for "stray" in v. 118: Those who stray are treated like dross.

119:120 *My flesh trembles.* He quivers out of his deep reverence for God.

119:121–128 As your faithful servant, I pray for deliverance from my oppressors—another stanza in which prayer for deliverance is dominant (see vv. 81–88 and note; see also note on v. 25, "laid low").

119:121 *what is righteous and just.* A phrase commonly used to sum up the whole will of God for moral action (106:3; Ge 18:19; 2Sa 8:15; Pr 1:3; 21:3; Isa 56:1; Jer 22:15; 33:15; Eze 18:5,19,21,17; 33:14,16,19; 45:9).

119:122 The only verse in this psalm that does not have either a direct or an indirect (as in vv. 90,121,132; see note on v. 75) reference to God's word. *the arrogant.* See note on v. 21.

119:124 *love.* See article, p. 16.

119:126 *act.* Either in defense of his servant or in judgment on the lawbreakers or both. Cf. Hab 1:2–4.

119:127 *more than gold.* See vv. 14,57,72,111.

119:128 *I hate every wrong path.* See note on v. 53.

119:129 *wonderful.* See v. 18 and note.

119:130 *unfolding.* Meaning (1) the revelation of your words, (2) the interpretation (see "expound," 49:4) of your words or (3) the entering of your words into the heart. *the simple.* See 19:7 and note.

119:132 *as you always do.* Or "as is (your) custom" (the Hebrew for "custom" is *mishpaṭ*); hence an indirect reference (see note on v. 122) to God's law (see note on v. 7).

119:134,154 *Redeem.* Here, as often, a synonym for "deliver."

119:134 *oppression.* See note on v. 25 ("laid low").

How does God's word help you make decisions?

_____

_____

_____

_____

_____

_____

¹³⁸ The statutes you have laid down are righteous;
    they are fully trustworthy.
¹³⁹ My zeal wears me out,
    for my enemies ignore your words.
¹⁴⁰ Your promises have been thoroughly tested,
    and your servant loves them.
¹⁴¹ Though I am lowly and despised,
    I do not forget your precepts.
¹⁴² Your righteousness is everlasting
    and your law is true.
¹⁴³ Trouble and distress have come upon me,
    but your commands give me delight.
¹⁴⁴ Your statutes are always righteous;
    give me understanding that I may live.

19   ק Qoph

¹⁴⁵ I call with all my heart; answer me, LORD,
    and I will obey your decrees.
¹⁴⁶ I call out to you; save me
    and I will keep your statutes.
¹⁴⁷ I rise before dawn and cry for help;
    I have put my hope in your word.
¹⁴⁸ My eyes stay open through the watches of the
        night,
    that I may meditate on your promises.
¹⁴⁹ Hear my voice in accordance with your love;
    preserve my life, LORD, according to your laws.
¹⁵⁰ Those who devise wicked schemes are near,
    but they are far from your law.
¹⁵¹ Yet you are near, LORD,
    and all your commands are true.
¹⁵² Long ago I learned from your statutes
    that you established them to last forever.

20   ר Resh

¹⁵³ Look on my suffering and deliver me,
    for I have not forgotten your law.
¹⁵⁴ Defend my cause and redeem me;
    preserve my life according to your promise.
¹⁵⁵ Salvation is far from the wicked,
    for they do not seek out your decrees.
¹⁵⁶ Your compassion, LORD, is great;
    preserve my life according to your laws.
¹⁵⁷ Many are the foes who persecute me,
    but I have not turned from your statutes.
¹⁵⁸ I look on the faithless with loathing,
    for they do not obey your word.
¹⁵⁹ See how I love your precepts;
    preserve my life, LORD, in accordance with
        your love.
¹⁶⁰ All your words are true;
    all your righteous laws are eternal.

21   ש Sin and Shin

¹⁶¹ Rulers persecute me without cause,
    but my heart trembles at your word.

119:135 *your face shine.* See note on 13:1 ("hide your face").
119:136 See v. 53 and note.
119:137–144 The Lord and his laws are righteous.
119:137 *righteous.* See note on 4:1.
119:138 *trustworthy.* See v. 142; see also note on v. 29 ("deceitful ways").
119:139 *My zeal.* See note on v. 53.
119:141 *lowly and despised.* Cf. v. 143; see also note on v. 25.
119:145–152 Save me, Lord, and I will keep your law. As the psalm draws to a close, prayer for deliverance becomes more dominant (see note on v. 25, "laid low").
119:148 *watches of the night.* See La 2:19.
119:149 *love.* See article, p. 16. *your laws.* Or "your justice" (complementing "your love"); Hebrew *mishpaṭ* (see note on v. 75).
119:150 *far from your law.* See vv. 21,53,85,118,126,139,155, 158.
119:151 *are true.* See note on v. 29 ("deceitful ways").
119:152 *last forever.* See note on v. 52.
119:153–160 See note on vv. 145–152.
119:155 *the wicked.* See note on v. 21 ("the arrogant").
119:156 *your laws.* See v. 149 and note.
119:158 *word.* Hebrew *'imrah* (see note on v. 11).
119:160 *true.* See note on v. 29 ("deceitful ways"). *eternal.* See note on v. 52.
119:161–168 See note on vv. 145–152.
119:161 *Rulers.* See note on v. 23. *heart.* See note on 4:7.

> ### What do you learn about God's character from the Psalms?

_____

_____

_____

_____

_____

_____

_____

_____

_____

_____

_____

¹⁶² I rejoice in your promise
   like one who finds great spoil.
¹⁶³ I hate and detest falsehood
   but I love your law.
¹⁶⁴ Seven times a day I praise you
   for your righteous laws.
¹⁶⁵ Great peace have those who love your law,
   and nothing can make them stumble.
¹⁶⁶ I wait for your salvation, LORD,
   and I follow your commands.
¹⁶⁷ I obey your statutes,
   for I love them greatly.
¹⁶⁸ I obey your precepts and your statutes,
   for all my ways are known to you.

22   ת Taw

¹⁶⁹ May my cry come before you, LORD;
   give me understanding according to your
      word.
¹⁷⁰ May my supplication come before you;
   deliver me according to your promise.
¹⁷¹ May my lips overflow with praise,
   for you teach me your decrees.
¹⁷² May my tongue sing of your word,
   for all your commands are righteous.
¹⁷³ May your hand be ready to help me,
   for I have chosen your precepts.
¹⁷⁴ I long for your salvation, LORD,
   and your law gives me delight.
¹⁷⁵ Let me live that I may praise you,
   and may your laws sustain me.
¹⁷⁶ I have strayed like a lost sheep.
   Seek your servant,
   for I have not forgotten your commands.

Psalm 120

A song of ascents.

¹ I call on the LORD in my distress,
   and he answers me.
² Save me, LORD,
   from lying lips
   and from deceitful tongues.

³ What will he do to you,
   and what more besides,
      you deceitful tongue?
⁴ He will punish you with a warrior's sharp arrows,
   with burning coals of the broom bush.

⁵ Woe to me that I dwell in Meshek,
   that I live among the tents of Kedar!
⁶ Too long have I lived
   among those who hate peace.
⁷ I am for peace;
   but when I speak, they are for war.

119:162 *great spoil.* See vv. 14,72,111.
119:163 *I hate.* See note on v. 53. *falsehood.* Or "that which is (ways that are) deceitful" (see v. 29 and note).
119:164 *Seven.* A number signifying completeness—he praises God throughout the day.
119:165 *Great peace.* Complete security and well-being.
119:169–176 See note on vv. 145–152.
119:171 *overflow with praise.* Because you have delivered me.
119:172 *righteous.* See note on v. 7.
119:174–176 The conclusion to the psalm.
119:176 *I have strayed.* See Isa 53:6; the clearest expression of the author's acknowledgment that, for all his devotion to God's law, he has again and again wandered into other (deceitful) ways and, like a lost sheep, must be brought back by his heavenly Shepherd. For one who has made God's law the guide and dearest treasure of his life, the last word can only be such a confession—and such a prayer.
Ps 120–137 A collection of 15 psalms (120–134), each bearing the title "song of ascents," to which has been attached Ps 135–137. Ps 120–136 have been referred to in some Jewish traditions as the "Great Hallel" (in distinction from the "Egyptian Hallel"; see introduction to Ps 113–118). Ps 137, expressive of deep devotion to Zion/Jerusalem, the city containing the great symbols of the Lord's presence with his people, brings the collection to its close. These "songs of ascents" most likely refer to the annual religious pilgrimages to Jerusalem (see 84:5–7; Ex 23:14–17; Dt 16:16; Mic 4:2; Zec 14:16), which brought the singing worshipers to Mount Zion (Isa 30:29). The spirit of these songs is similar to that of Ps 84 (cf. Ps 42–43).
Ps 120 The lament of an individual asking for deliverance from false accusers (see 5:9 and note). The reference to "war" (v. 7) is probably metaphorical. The theme is developed in three short stanzas: The prayer uttered (vv. 1–2), the adversaries addressed (vv. 3–4), the circumstances lamented (vv. 5–7).
120 title See introduction to Ps 120–137.
120:1–2 The prayer.
120:1 *I call . . . he answers.* See note on 118:5.
120:2 *lying lips . . . deceitful tongues.* See note on 5:9.
120:3–4 Assurance that God will act (see 6:8–10 and note on 3:8).
120:3 *he.* The Lord. *what more besides.* An echo of a common oath formula, thus suggesting the certainty and severity of God's judgment on the enemies.
120:4 *sharp arrows . . . burning coals.* As a weapon, the tongue is a sharp arrow (see Pr 25:18; Jer 9:8; see also 57:4; 64:3) and a searing fire (Pr 16:27; Jas 3:6), and God's judgment will answer in kind (7:11–13; 11:6; 64:7). For judgment in kind, see 63:9–10; 64:7–8 and notes. *broom bush.* A desert shrub, sometimes large enough to provide shade. Charcoal made from its wood produced an especially hot and durable fire.
120:5–7 Complaint over prolonged harassment.
120:5 *Meshek . . . Kedar.* The former was in central Asia Minor, the latter in Arabia. Besieged by slanderers, the psalmist feels as though he is far from home, surrounded by barbarians.

▶ How does Psalm 112 use hyperbole to make a point?

_____

_____

_____

_____

_____

▶ Why is it sometimes easier to put our trust in people rather than God (118:8–9)?

_____

_____

_____

_____

_____

▶ What are some benefits of God's Word, according to Psalm 119?

_____

_____

_____

_____

▶ How can you love the word of God like the psalmist (119:20)?

_____

_____

_____

_____

_____

Psalm 121

A song of ascents.

¹I lift up my eyes to the mountains —
　where does my help come from?
²My help comes from the LORD,
　the Maker of heaven and earth.

³He will not let your foot slip —
　he who watches over you will not slumber;
⁴indeed, he who watches over Israel
　will neither slumber nor sleep.

⁵The LORD watches over you —
　the LORD is your shade at your right hand;
⁶the sun will not harm you by day,
　nor the moon by night.

⁷The LORD will keep you from all harm —
　he will watch over your life;
⁸the LORD will watch over your coming and going
　both now and forevermore.

Psalm 122

A song of ascents. Of David.

¹I rejoiced with those who said to me,
　"Let us go to the house of the LORD."
²Our feet are standing
　in your gates, Jerusalem.

³Jerusalem is built like a city
　that is closely compacted together.
⁴That is where the tribes go up —
　the tribes of the LORD —
to praise the name of the LORD
　according to the statute given to Israel.
⁵There stand the thrones for judgment,
　the thrones of the house of David.

Additional Insights

As the Great King, God (who had chosen David and his dynasty to be his royal representatives) also chose Jerusalem as his own royal city.

Ps 121 A dialogue (perhaps liturgical) of confession and assurance. Its use as a pilgrimage song provides the key to its understanding. Whether the dialogue takes place in a single heart (cf. the refrain in Ps 42–43) or between individuals in the caravan is of no great consequence since all would share the same convictions. The comforting assurance expressed (Ps 33) is equally appropriate for the pilgrimage to Jerusalem and for the pilgrimage of life to the "glory" into which the faithful will be received (see notes on 49:15; 73:24).

121:1–2 Confession of trust in the Lord.

121:1 *mountains.* Those in the vicinity of Jerusalem, of which Mount Zion is one (125:2), or, if the plural indicates majesty (as in the Hebrew in 87:1; 133:3), Mount Zion itself.

121:2 *Maker of heaven and earth.* The one true God, the King of all creation (see 124:8; 134:3; see also 33:6; 89:11–13; 96:4–5; 104:2–9; 136:4–9).

121:3–4 Assurance concerning the unsleeping guardian over Israel.

121:3 *not let your foot slip.* Not even where the way is treacherous. *not slumber.* Like the pagan god Baal (1Ki 18:27)—though sometimes he seemed to (44:23; 78:65).

121:4 *he who watches over Israel.* The Lord of all creation and the guardian over Israel—the One in whom the faithful may put unfaltering trust.

121:5–6 Assurance concerning unfailing protection.

121:5 *shade.* See 91:1 ("shadow") and note on 17:8.

121:7–8 Assurance concerning all of life.

Ps 122 A hymn of joy over Jerusalem (see Ps 42–43; 46; 48; 84; 87; 137). Sung by a pilgrim in Jerusalem (very likely at one of the three annual festivals, Dt 16:16), it expresses deep joy over the city and offers a prayer for its welfare. As the third of the pilgrimage psalms (see introduction to Ps 120–137), it shares many dominant themes with Ps 132, the third from the end of this collection—possibly a deliberate arrangement

122 title *ascents.* See introduction to Ps 120–137. *Of David.* This element is not present in all ancient witnesses to the text, and the content suggests a later date.

122:1 *the house of the LORD.* The temple (2Sa 7:5,13; 1Ki 5:3,5; 8:10, "temple"). That Jerusalem became the city of pilgrimage before the dedication of the temple is doubtful in light of 1Ki 3:4; 8:1–11.

122:2 *gates.* Gateways.

122:3–5 Jerusalem's significance for the faithful.

122:4 *to praise . . . the LORD.* For his saving acts in behalf of Israel and his blessings on the nation. *statute given to Israel.* See 81:3–5; Dt 16:1–17.

122:5 *There . . . the thrones of the house of David.* Jerusalem is both the city of the Lord and the royal city of his chosen dynasty, through which he (ideally) protects and governs the nation (see 2:2,6–7; 89:3–4,19–37; 110; 2Sa 7:8–16). In postexilic times it remained, though now in Messianic hope, the city of David.

⁶Pray for the peace of Jerusalem:
  "May those who love you be secure.
⁷May there be peace within your walls
  and security within your citadels."
⁸For the sake of my family and friends,
  I will say, "Peace be within you."
⁹For the sake of the house of the LORD our God,
  I will seek your prosperity.

Psalm 123

A song of ascents.

¹I lift up my eyes to you,
  to you who sit enthroned in heaven.
²As the eyes of slaves look to the hand of their master,
  as the eyes of a female slave look to the hand
    of her mistress,
 so our eyes look to the LORD our God,
  till he shows us his mercy.

³Have mercy on us, LORD, have mercy on us,
  for we have endured no end of contempt.
⁴We have endured no end
  of ridicule from the arrogant,
  of contempt from the proud.

Psalm 124

A song of ascents. Of David.

¹If the LORD had not been on our side—
  let Israel say—
²if the LORD had not been on our side
  when people attacked us,
³they would have swallowed us alive
  when their anger flared against us;
⁴the flood would have engulfed us,
  the torrent would have swept over us,
⁵the raging waters
  would have swept us away.

⁶Praise be to the LORD,
  who has not let us be torn by their teeth.
⁷We have escaped like a bird
  from the fowler's snare;
 the snare has been broken,
  and we have escaped.
⁸Our help is in the name of the LORD,
  the Maker of heaven and earth.

Psalm 125

A song of ascents.

¹Those who trust in the LORD are like Mount Zion,
  which cannot be shaken but endures forever.

122:6–9 Prayers for Jerusalem's peace.

122:6 In Hebrew a beautiful wordplay tightly binds together "Pray," "peace," "Jerusalem" and "be secure." *peace.* See vv. 7–8; includes both security and prosperity. *those who love you.* The psalmist, those referred to in vv. 1,8 and all who love Jerusalem because they are devoted to the Lord and his chosen king. These constitute a loving fellowship of those who worship together, pray together and seek each other's welfare as the people of God (Ps 133).
122:7 *walls . . . citadels.* See 48:13 ("ramparts . . . citadels").
Ps 123 A lament of God's humble people asking him to show mercy and so foil the contempt of the proud. See introduction to Ps 124. As to its structure, a one-verse introduction is followed by two brief stanzas, each developing its own theme.
123:1 *I lift up my eyes.* The psalmist speaks as a representative member of or as spokesperson for the community—see the first-person plurals that follow. *who sit enthroned in heaven.* The same God whose earthly throne is in the temple on Mount Zion (see 122:5 and note; see also 2:4; 9:11; 11:4; 80:1; 99:1; 113:5; 132:14).
123:2 With the use of two similes drawn from domestic life, the faithful (men and women alike) present themselves as dependent and confidently reliant on God.
123:4 *the arrogant . . . the proud.* Those who live by their own wits and strength (see notes on 10:2–11; 31:23) and pour contempt on those who humbly rely on the Lord. For examples, see those with whom King Hezekiah (2Ki 18:17—19:19) or Governor Nehemiah (Ne 4; 6:1–4) had to contend.
Ps 124 Israel's praise of the Lord for deliverance from powerful enemies—an appropriate sequel to Ps 123. Very likely a Levite speaks in vv. 1–5, while the worshipers answer in vv. 6–8. That it shares with Ps 129 a similar introduction and a theme focused on Zion's deliverance from powerful enemies suggests that these two psalms were arranged to frame the intervening four (see note on 125:5).
124 title *ascents.* See introduction to Ps 120–137. *Of David.* Not all ancient witnesses to the text contain this element, and both language and theme may suggest a postexilic date (see note on Ps 122 title). It may have been assigned to David because of supposed echoes of Ps 18; 69.
124:1–5 Let Israel acknowledge that the Lord alone has saved them from extinction (20:7; 94:17).
124:2 *people attacked.* Proud and arrogant people (123:4) may attack, but the Lord is Israel's help (v. 8).
124:3 *swallowed us.* Like death (see note on 49:14). But see 69:15.
124:6–8 Response of praise for deliverance—with a vivid enrichment of the imagery.
124:7 *escaped like a bird from the fowler's snare.* A most apt figure for Israel's release from Babylonian captivity (cf. notes on 9:15; 91:3).
124:8 In climax, the great confession.
Ps 125 Israel's security celebrated in testimony, prayer and benediction. Ps 125 and 126 are thematically linked and precisely balanced, each being composed (in Hebrew) of 116 syllables. Their juxtaposition was no doubt deliberate.
125:1–2 The solid security of God's people.
125:1 *Those who trust in the LORD.* God's "people" (v. 2) are also characterized as "the righteous" (v. 3;

²As the mountains surround Jerusalem,
 so the LORD surrounds his people
 both now and forevermore.

³The scepter of the wicked will not remain
 over the land allotted to the righteous,
for then the righteous might use
 their hands to do evil.

⁴LORD, do good to those who are good,
 to those who are upright in heart.
⁵But those who turn to crooked ways
 the LORD will banish with the
  evildoers.

Peace be on Israel.

Psalm 126

A song of ascents.

¹When the LORD restored the fortunes
 of*ᵃ* Zion,
 we were like those who dreamed.*ᵇ*
²Our mouths were filled with laughter,
 our tongues with songs of joy.
Then it was said among the nations,
 "The LORD has done great things for
  them."
³The LORD has done great things for us,
 and we are filled with joy.

⁴Restore our fortunes,*ᶜ* LORD,
 like streams in the Negev.
⁵Those who sow with tears
 will reap with songs of joy.
⁶Those who go out weeping,
 carrying seed to sow,
will return with songs of joy,
 carrying sheaves with them.

Psalm 127

A song of ascents. Of Solomon.

¹Unless the LORD builds the house,
 the builders labor in vain.
Unless the LORD watches over the city,
 the guards stand watch in vain.
²In vain you rise early
 and stay up late,
toiling for food to eat—
 for he grants sleep to*ᵈ* those he loves.

³Children are a heritage from the LORD,
 offspring a reward from him.

---

*ᵃ 1 Or LORD brought back the captives to ᵇ 1 Or those
restored to health   ᶜ 4 Or Bring back our captives
ᵈ 2 Or eat — / for while they sleep he provides for*

---

see note on 1:5) and "those who are good," "who are upright in heart" (v. 4). For a similar description of the "righteous," see 34:8–14 and note. *like Mount Zion.* In their security (Ps 46; 48).

125:2 *mountains surround Jerusalem.* The city is located in
what OT writers called a mountainous region. *so the LORD
surrounds his people.* As surely, as substantially and as im-
movably (2Ki 6:17; Zec 2:5).

125:3 Wicked rulers, whether by example or by oppression,
tend to corrupt even the righteous, but the Lord will preserve his people also from this corrosive threat. *scepter of
the wicked.* Probably referring to Persian rule (Ne 9:36–37)
and its appointed authorities, such as those Nehemiah had
to contend with (Ne 2:19; 4:1–3,7–8; 6:1–14,17–19; 13:7–8,28).
land allotted to the righteous. The promised land (78:55).

125:4 *heart.* See note on 4:7.

125:5 *Peace be on Israel.* Perhaps a concise form of the
priestly benediction (Nu 6:24–26). This benediction has
its counterpart in the prayer of 126:4–6. Its repetition at
the end of Ps 128 suggests a frame around the four closely
balanced psalms (made up of two pairs: 125–126; 127–128).

Ps 126 A hymn of joy for the restoration of the exiled community to Zion (cf. Ps 42–43; 84; 137). The psalm divides
into two stanzas of four (Hebrew) lines each, with their
initial lines sharing a common theme. Thematic unity is
further served by repetition (cf. vv. 2–3) and other key
words ("the LORD," "songs of joy," "carrying"). References
to God's action (vv. 1,3) frame the first stanza, while v. 2 offers exposition. For this psalm's relationship to Ps 125, see
introduction to that psalm.

126 title See introduction to Ps 120–137.

126:1–3 Joy over restoration experienced.

126:1 *restored the fortunes of.* This translation and its alternative (see NIV text note here and on v. 4) have essentially
the same result. *dreamed.* The wonder and joy of the reality were so marvelous that they hardly dared believe it.
It seemed more like the dreams with which they had so
long been tantalized.

126:4–6 Prayer for restoration to be completed.

126:4 *Restore our fortunes.* Either complete the repatria-
tion of exiles (see NIV text note) or fully restore the security and prosperity of former times. *like streams in the
Negev.* Which are bone-dry in summer, until the winter
rains renew their flow.

126:5–6 An apt metaphorical portrayal of the joy already
experienced and the joy anticipated. *with tears . . . weeping.* Even when sowing is accompanied by trouble or sorrow, harvest brings joy. For a related figure, see 20:5.

Ps 127 Godly wisdom concerning home and hearth.
Its theme is timeless; it reminded the pilgrims on
their way to Jerusalem that all of life's securities and
blessings are gifts from God rather than their own
achievements (Dt 28:1–14).

127 title *ascents.* See introduction to Ps 120–137. *Of Solomon.* If Solomon was not the author (not all witnesses
to the text ascribe it to him), it is easy to see why some
thought him so.

127:1–2 It is the Lord who provides shelter, security
and sustenance.

127:2 *he grants sleep.* A good harvest is not the achievement of endless toil but the result of God's blessing

⁴Like arrows in the hands of a warrior
   are children born in one's youth.
⁵Blessed is the man
   whose quiver is full of them.
 They will not be put to shame
   when they contend with their opponents
     in court.

Psalm 128

A song of ascents.

¹Blessed are all who fear the LORD,
   who walk in obedience to him.
²You will eat the fruit of your labor;
   blessings and prosperity will be yours.
³Your wife will be like a fruitful vine
   within your house;
 your children will be like olive shoots
   around your table.
⁴Yes, this will be the blessing
   for the man who fears the LORD.

⁵May the LORD bless you from Zion;
   may you see the prosperity of
     Jerusalem
 all the days of your life.
⁶May you live to see your children's
     children —
   peace be on Israel.

Psalm 129

A song of ascents.

¹"They have greatly oppressed me from my
     youth,"
   let Israel say;
²"they have greatly oppressed me from my
     youth,
   but they have not gained the victory
     over me.
³Plowmen have plowed my back
   and made their furrows long.
⁴But the LORD is righteous;
   he has cut me free from the cords of the
     wicked."

⁵May all who hate Zion
   be turned back in shame.
⁶May they be like grass on the roof,
   which withers before it can grow;
⁷a reaper cannot fill his hands with it,
   nor one who gathers fill his arms.
⁸May those who pass by not say to them,
   "The blessing of the LORD be on you;
   we bless you in the name of the LORD."

(Pr 10:22; Mt 6:25–34; 1Pe 5:7). *those he loves.* See especially Dt 33:12; Jer 11:15.

127:3–5 Children are God's gift and a sign of his favor.

127:3 *Children.* Children too are a gift—not the mere product of virility and fertility (see 113:9 and note; Ge 30:2). *heritage.* Emphasis here is on gift rather than possession. But perhaps more is implied. In the OT economy an Israelite's "inheritance" from the Lord was first of all property in the promised land (Nu 26:53; Jos 11:23; Jdg 2:6), which provided a sure place in the life and "rest" (Jos 1:13) of the Lord's kingdom. But without children the inheritance in the land would be lost (Nu 27:8–11), so that offspring were a heritage in a double sense. *reward from him.* Bestowed by God on one who stands in his favor because he has been faithful.

127:5 *when they contend with their opponents.* Fathers with many children have many defenders when falsely accused in court. Moreover, the very fact that they have many children as God's "reward" (v. 3) testifies to God's favor toward them (in effect, they are God-provided character witnesses; see 128:3–4). *in court.* Or "in the gate." For "[city/town] gate" as court, see Dt 17:5; 21:19; 22:15,24; 25:7; Ru 4:1; Isa 29:21 ("court"); Am 5:12 ("courts").

Ps 128 The blessedness of the godly man; another word of wisdom concerning hearth and home (see introduction to Ps 127). Structurally, the frame ("who fear[s] the LORD") around vv. 1–4 sets off those verses as the main body of the psalm.

128 title See introduction to Ps 120–137.

128:2 Blessings upon labor.

128:3 *fruitful vine.* Bearing many children, productive and beneficial to her husband and family. *within your house.* She is not like the faithless wife whose "feet never stay at home" (Pr 7:11). *olive shoots.* Ever green and with the promises of both long life and productivity (of staples: wood, fruit, oil). The vine and the olive tree are frequently paired in the OT (as, e.g., in Ex 23:11). Both were especially long-lived, and they produced the wine and the oil that played such a central role in the lives of the people.

128:5–6 The benediction pronounced—completing the scope of true blessedness: unbroken prosperity, secure relationship with God and secure national existence (the prosperity of Jerusalem entailed both), and long life.

128:5 *from Zion.* See 9:11 and note; 20:2; 135:21.

128:6 *peace be on Israel.* See 125:5 and note.

Ps 129 Israel's prayer for the continued withering of all their powerful enemies. The rescue celebrated (v. 4) is probably from Babylonian exile. Against the background of Ps 124–128, this prayer for the withholding of God's blessing (v. 8) is set in sharp relief. Like Ps 127, its two main stanzas (vv. 1–4,5–8a) are perfectly balanced, having a total of 59 Hebrew syllables each. Its total syllable count (127) closely matches that of Ps 130 (128 syllables). For its apparent link with Ps 124, see introduction to that psalm.

129 title See introduction to Ps 120–137.

129:1–4 The wicked oppressors have not prevailed.

129:1 *from my youth.* From the time Israel was enslaved in Egypt, they have suffered much at the hands of hostile powers.

129:2 *have not gained the victory.* Have not succeeded

Psalm 130

A song of ascents.

¹Out of the depths I cry to you, LORD;
²   Lord, hear my voice.
  Let your ears be attentive
    to my cry for mercy.

³If you, LORD, kept a record of sins,
    Lord, who could stand?
⁴But with you there is forgiveness,
    so that we can, with reverence, serve you.

⁵I wait for the LORD, my whole being waits,
    and in his word I put my hope.
⁶I wait for the Lord
    more than watchmen wait for the morning,
    more than watchmen wait for the morning.

⁷Israel, put your hope in the LORD,
    for with the LORD is unfailing love
    and with him is full redemption.
⁸He himself will redeem Israel
    from all their sins.

in their efforts to destroy Israel totally or to hold God's people permanently in bondage.

129:4 *righteous.* See note on 4:1.

129:5–8 May all those oppressors who have shown hatred toward Zion wither away (Ps 137).

129:5 See note on 5:10.

129:6 *like grass on the roof.* May those who attack or oppress Israel (vv. 2–3) wither like grass that sprouts on the flat, sunbaked housetops, where no plow can prepare a nurturing soil to sustain the young shoots—and so there is no harvest (v. 7).

129:8 *those who pass by.* Whoever may pass by the harvesters in the fields will exchange no joyful greetings (Ru 2:4) because the hands of the harvesters will be empty.

Ps 130 A lament by one who knows that even though he is a sinner, the Lord hears his cry out of the depths. This is the sixth of seven penitential psalms.

130 title See introduction to Ps 120–137.

130:1–4 A prayer for mercy and grounds for assurance.

130:4 *there is forgiveness.* No doubt recalling such reassuring words as Ex 34:6–7. *with reverence, serve you.* Honor, worship, trust and serve you as the one true God (see Ps 34:8–14 and note). If God were not forgiving, people could only flee from him in terror.

130:5–8 Trust in the Lord: a personal testimony, expanding into a reassuring invitation (131:3).

130:7 See 131:3. *unfailing love.* See article, p. 16.

130:8 *from all their sins.* From the root of trouble—but also from all its consequences. This greatest of all hopes has been fulfilled in Christ.

How can you respond to God's mercy?

_____

_____

_____

_____

_____

_____

_____

_____

_____

_____

▶ How can you read the psalms in context to make sense of verses like 121:7, which is not a general promise for all believers that they will live a life of ease.

_____

_____

_____

_____

_____

▶ What are some characteristics of people who trust in God (Ps 125)?

_____

_____

_____

_____

_____

▶ Is it okay for believers today to pray for judgment on other people (Ps 129)?

_____

_____

_____

_____

_____

▶ For what in your life do you need to wait for the Lord (130:5)?

_____

_____

_____

_____

_____

Psalm 131

A song of ascents. Of David.

¹My heart is not proud, LORD,
   my eyes are not haughty;
I do not concern myself with great matters
   or things too wonderful for me.
²But I have calmed and quieted myself,
   I am like a weaned child with its mother;
   like a weaned child I am content.

³Israel, put your hope in the LORD
   both now and forevermore.

Psalm 132

A song of ascents.

¹LORD, remember David
   and all his self-denial.

²He swore an oath to the LORD,
   he made a vow to the Mighty One of Jacob:
³"I will not enter my house
   or go to my bed,
⁴I will allow no sleep to my eyes
   or slumber to my eyelids,
⁵till I find a place for the LORD,
   a dwelling for the Mighty One of Jacob."

⁶We heard it in Ephrathah,
   we came upon it in the fields of Jaar:ᵃ
⁷"Let us go to his dwelling place,
   let us worship at his footstool, saying,
⁸'Arise, LORD, and come to your resting place,
   you and the ark of your might.
⁹May your priests be clothed with your
         righteousness;
   may your faithful people sing for joy.'"

¹⁰For the sake of your servant David,
   do not reject your anointed one.

¹¹The LORD swore an oath to David,
   a sure oath he will not revoke:
"One of your own descendants
   I will place on your throne.
¹²If your sons keep my covenant
   and the statutes I teach them,

ᵃ 6 Or *heard of it in Ephrathah, / we found it in the fields of Jearim.* (See 1 Chron. 13:5,6) (And no quotation marks around verses 7-9)

Ps 131 A hymn of humble trust in the Lord—appropriately placed next to Ps 130.
131 title *ascents.* See introduction to Ps 120–137. *Of David.* See Introduction: Authorship and Titles (or Superscriptions).

131:1 *heart.* See note on 4:7. *proud . . . haughty.* Pride in humanity's presumed ability to master the whole creation, design its own moral world and control its own destiny (of which Babel is the prime biblical example; see Ge 11:1–9) is that which, more than all else, alienates humans from God. *concern myself with.* (Presume to) walk among, live among, be party to. *great matters . . . too wonderful for me.* Heroic exploits or achievements to rival, if not substitute for, the mighty works of God.
131:2 *weaned child.* A child who no longer nurses but remains quiet and content in the presence of their mother.
Ps 132 A prayer for God's favor on the reigning son of David and on the regime that David founded—as the structure makes clear. Its language suggests a date early in the monarchy. The venerable belief that it was composed for the dedication of the temple may be correct (compare vv. 8–10 with 2Ch 6:41–42), but the possibility cannot be ruled out that it was used in the coronation ritual (cf. Ps 2; 72; 110). The author of Chronicles places the prayer (or a portion of it) on the lips of the king himself. As used in postexilic liturgies, it had Messianic implications.
132:1 The initial petition (v. 10). *remember.* See 20:3; see also 1Ki 11:12–13; 15:4–5. *self-denial.* What David took on himself in his vow (vv. 2–5; see Nu 30:13, where the same technical term for a self-denying oath is used).
132:2 *He swore an oath.* This prayer for David's son is grounded in the special relationship between David and the Lord, as epitomized in their mutual oaths (vv. 11–12). In 2Sa 6–7, which narrates the events here recalled, David's oath is not mentioned.
132:6–9 Moments in the people's procession to the temple for worship are recalled.
132:6 *it . . . it.* Often thought to refer to the ark (see NIV text note), but more likely it refers to the call to worship that follows (in Hebrew the pronoun is feminine, but the Hebrew for "ark" is masculine).
132:8 *Arise.* Although (in accordance with a common feature in Hebrew poetry) the Hebrew omits an introductory word, such as "saying" (which the NIV supplies at the end of v. 7 for clarity), vv. 8–9 are probably words on the lips of the worshipers. See introduction to Ps 24. *resting place.* As the promised land was Israel's place of rest at the end of their wanderings (Nu 10:33; Jos 1:13; Mic 2:10), so the temple was the Lord's resting place after he had been moving about in a tent (see 2Sa 7:6; see also 1Ch 28:2). The expression may suggest that the temple was the place of God's throne (v. 14).
132:9 *clothed with.* Beyond their normal priestly garb—

then their sons will sit
  on your throne for ever and ever."

13 For the LORD has chosen Zion,
  he has desired it for his dwelling, saying,
14 "This is my resting place for ever and ever;
  here I will sit enthroned, for I have desired it.
15 I will bless her with abundant provisions;
  her poor I will satisfy with food.
16 I will clothe her priests with salvation,
  and her faithful people will ever sing for joy.

17 "Here I will make a horn[a] grow for David
  and set up a lamp for my anointed one.
18 I will clothe his enemies with shame,
  but his head will be adorned with a radiant
    crown."

Psalm 133

A song of ascents. Of David.

1 How good and pleasant it is
  when God's people live together in unity!

2 It is like precious oil poured on the head,
  running down on the beard,
running down on Aaron's beard,
  down on the collar of his robe.
3 It is as if the dew of Hermon
  were falling on Mount Zion.
For there the LORD bestows his blessing,
  even life forevermore.

Psalm 134

A song of ascents.

1 Praise the LORD, all you servants of the LORD
  who minister by night in the house of the
    LORD.
2 Lift up your hands in the sanctuary
  and praise the LORD.

3 May the LORD bless you from Zion,
  he who is the Maker of heaven and earth.

[a] 17 *Horn* here symbolizes strong one, that is, king.

Additional Insights

Jerusalem became the earthly capital and symbol of the kingdom of God. There in his temple he ruled his people. There his people could meet with him to bring their prayers and praise and to see his power and glory.

may their ministry be characterized by, i.e., result in, righteousness. *righteousness.* Since the corresponding word in v. 16 is "salvation," the same word used by the author of Chronicles when quoting this verse (2Ch 6:41), and since "righteousness" and "salvation" are often paralleled (40:10; 51:14; 71:15; 98:2; Isa 45:8; 46:13; 51:5–6; 56:1; 59:17; 60:17–18; 61:10; 62:1), the reference is clearly to God's righteousness that effects the salvation of his people (see note on 4:1).
132:11–12 The Lord's covenant with David is recalled, as grounds for the prayer. These and vv. 13–18 are a poetic recollection of 1Ki 9:1–5 (2Ch 7:11–18).
132:11 *swore an oath.* See v. 2 and note. 2Sa 7 does not mention an oath, but elsewhere God's promise to David is called a covenant (89:3,28,34,39; 2Sa 23:5; Isa 55:3), and covenants were made on oath. *will not revoke.* See 110:4. *One of your own descendants . . . on your throne.* Peter alludes to this verse with reference to Jesus in Ac 2:30.
132:13–16 The Lord's election of Zion recalled, as grounds for the prayer (see Introduction: Theology: Major Themes, 7).
132:13 *desired it for his dwelling.* David's and the Lord's desires harmonize (Dt 12:5–14).
132:15 The Lord, enthroned in his resting place (vv. 8,14), will bless the land, making it a place of rest for his people (see Dt 12:9; Jos 1:13).
132:17–18 Concluding word of assurance, which addresses the petition (vv. 1,10) directly and climactically.
Ps 133 A hymn in praise of unity among the people of God. If David was the author, he may have been moved to write it by some such occasion as when, after many years of conflict, all Israel came to Hebron to make him king (2Sa 5:1–3). Other historical possibilities are after the influx of many refugees from the northern tribes into the kingdom of Judah during the great Assyrian invasions (see introduction to Ps 80) or the postexilic regathering of representatives of "all Israel," as reflected in Ezra and Nehemiah (Ezr 8:25; Ne 12:47).
133:2 *like precious oil . . . on Aaron's beard . . . on the collar of his robe.* The oil of Aaron's anointing (Ex 29:7; Lev 21:10) saturated all the hair of his beard and ran down on his priestly robe, signifying his total consecration to holy service. Similarly, communal harmony sanctifies God's people.
133:3 *dew of Hermon . . . on Mount Zion.* A dew as profuse as that of Mount Hermon would make Mount Zion (or the mountains of Zion) richly fruitful (Ge 27:28; Hag 1:10; Zec 8:12). So would communal unity make Israel richly fruitful. The two similes (vv. 2–3) are well chosen: God's blessings flowed to Israel through the priestly ministrations at the sanctuary (Ex 29:44–46; Lev 9:22–24; Nu 6:24–26)— epitomizing God's redemptive mercies— and through heaven's dew that sustained life in the fields—epitomizing God's providential mercies in the creation order.
Ps 134 A hymn of praise possibly comprised of a brief exchange between the worshipers, as they are about to leave the temple after the evening service, and the Levites, who kept the temple watch through the night. In the Psalter it concludes the "songs of ascents," as Ps 117 concludes a collection of Hallelujah psalms (Ps 111–117). Its date is probably postexilic.

¹Praise the LORD.ᵃ

Praise the name of the LORD;
    praise him, you servants of the LORD,
²you who minister in the house of the LORD,
    in the courts of the house of our God.

³Praise the LORD, for the LORD is good;
    sing praise to his name, for that is pleasant.
⁴For the LORD has chosen Jacob to be his own,
    Israel to be his treasured possession.

⁵I know that the LORD is great,
    that our Lord is greater than all gods.
⁶The LORD does whatever pleases him,
    in the heavens and on the earth,
    in the seas and all their depths.
⁷He makes clouds rise from the ends of the earth;
    he sends lightning with the rain
    and brings out the wind from his storehouses.

⁸He struck down the firstborn of Egypt,
    the firstborn of people and animals.
⁹He sent his signs and wonders into your midst,
    Egypt,
    against Pharaoh and all his servants.
¹⁰He struck down many nations
    and killed mighty kings —
¹¹Sihon king of the Amorites,
    Og king of Bashan,
    and all the kings of Canaan —
¹²and he gave their land as an inheritance,
    an inheritance to his people Israel.

¹³Your name, LORD, endures forever,
    your renown, LORD, through all generations.
¹⁴For the LORD will vindicate his people
    and have compassion on his servants.

¹⁵The idols of the nations are silver and gold,
    made by human hands.
¹⁶They have mouths, but cannot speak,
    eyes, but cannot see.
¹⁷They have ears, but cannot hear,
    nor is there breath in their mouths.
¹⁸Those who make them will be like them,
    and so will all who trust in them.

¹⁹All you Israelites, praise the LORD;
    house of Aaron, praise the LORD;
²⁰house of Levi, praise the LORD;
    you who fear him, praise the LORD.
²¹Praise be to the LORD from Zion,
    to him who dwells in Jerusalem.

Praise the LORD.

ᵃ 1 Hebrew *Hallelu Yah*; also in verses 3 and 21

134:1–2 The departing worshipers call on the Levites to continue the praise of the Lord through the night (1Ch 9:33).

134:2 *Lift up your hands.* See 63:4 and note.

134:3 Possibly one of the Levites responds with a benediction on the worshipers (see 124:8; 128:5).

Ps 135 A salvation-history hymn, calling Israel to praise the Lord—the one true God: Lord of all creation, Lord over all the nations, Israel's Redeemer. No doubt postexilic, it echoes many lines found elsewhere in the OT. It was clearly composed for the temple liturgy. Framed with "Praise the LORD" (as are also Ps 146–150), its first and last stanzas are also calls to praise God. Recital of God's saving acts for Israel in Egypt and Canaan (vv. 8–12) makes up the middle of seven stanzas, while the remaining four constitute two pairs related to each other by theme and language (vv. 3–4,13–14; vv. 5–7,15–18).

135:1–2 Initial call to praise, addressed to priests and Levites (134:1–2).

135:3–4 A central reason for Israel to praise the Lord (vv. 13–14).

135:3 *that is pleasant.* See 133:1.

135:4 *Jacob.* A synonym for Israel (Ge 32:28).

135:5–7 The Lord is great, as well as good (v. 3); he is the absolute Lord in all creation (cf. the word about idols in vv. 15–18; see Jer 10:11–16; see also 96:5; 97:7 ; 115:3 and notes).

135:6 *does whatever pleases him.* The idols can do nothing (vv. 16–17); they are themselves done (made) by their worshipers (v. 18). *heavens . . . earth . . . seas.* The three great domains of the visible creation, as the ancients viewed it (see Ge 1:8–10 and introduction to Ps 104).

135:7 *He makes clouds.* The Lord, not Baal or any other god, brings the life-giving rains (see Ps 29 and its introduction; see also Jer 14:22; Zec 10:1). *wind.* See 104:4; 148:8. The idols do not even have any "wind" (breath) in their mouths (v. 17).

135:8–12 The Lord's triumph over Egypt and over the kings whose lands became Israel's inheritance, a concise recollection of Ex 7–14; Nu 21:21–35; Joshua.

135:14 *vindicate.* Uphold against all attacks by the world powers both Israel's cause and their claim that the Lord is the only true God. *have compassion on.* See Ex 34:6–7. *his servants.* His covenant people.

135:15–18 The powerlessness of the false gods and of those who trust in them (see vv. 5–7 and note; see also 115:4–8).

Additional Insights

Hymns are characterized by exuberant praise to God motivated by specific reasons outlined by the psalmist. Thus, hymns usually contain (1) a call to praise God; (2) reasons for that praise; and (3) often an additional call to praise God.

¹Give thanks to the LORD, for he is good.
His love endures forever.
²Give thanks to the God of gods.
His love endures forever.
³Give thanks to the Lord of lords:
His love endures forever.

⁴to him who alone does great wonders,
His love endures forever.
⁵who by his understanding made the heavens,
His love endures forever.
⁶who spread out the earth upon the waters,
His love endures forever.
⁷who made the great lights —
His love endures forever.
⁸the sun to govern the day,
His love endures forever.
⁹the moon and stars to govern the night;
His love endures forever.

¹⁰to him who struck down the firstborn of Egypt
His love endures forever.
¹¹and brought Israel out from among them
His love endures forever.
¹²with a mighty hand and outstretched arm;
His love endures forever.

¹³to him who divided the Red Sea*ᵃ* asunder
His love endures forever.
¹⁴and brought Israel through the midst of it,
His love endures forever.
¹⁵but swept Pharaoh and his army into the Red Sea;
His love endures forever.

¹⁶to him who led his people through the wilderness;
His love endures forever.

¹⁷to him who struck down great kings,
His love endures forever.
¹⁸and killed mighty kings —
His love endures forever.
¹⁹Sihon king of the Amorites
His love endures forever.
²⁰and Og king of Bashan —
His love endures forever.
²¹and gave their land as an inheritance,
His love endures forever.
²²an inheritance to his servant Israel.
His love endures forever.

²³He remembered us in our low estate
His love endures forever.
²⁴and freed us from our enemies.
His love endures forever.

ᵃ 13 Or *the Sea of Reeds*; also in verse 15

135:19–21 Concluding call to praise, addressed to all who are assembled at the temple (115:9–11; 118:2–4).
135:20 *house of Levi.* Mentioned expressly only here in the Psalter (cf. 1Ch 23:4,30–31; 25:1; 2Ch 20:19,21).
135:21 *from Zion.* Not only in Zion but also from Zion—to the ends of the earth (see notes on 9:1; 22:22–31).
Ps 136 A salvation-history liturgy of praise to the Lord as Creator and as Israel's Redeemer. Its theme and many of its verses parallel much of Ps 135. Most likely a Levitical song leader led the recital, while the Levitical choir (1Ch 16:41; 2Ch 5:13; Ezr 3:11) or the worshipers (2Ch 7:3,6; 20:21) responded with the refrain (106:1; 107:1; 118:1–4,29). Following the initial call to praise God (vv. 1–3), the recital devotes six verses to God's creation acts (vv. 4–9), six to his deliverance of Israel out of Egypt (vv. 10–15), one to the wilderness journey (v. 16) and six to the conquest (vv. 17–22). The four concluding verses return to the same basic themes in reverse order: God's action in history in behalf of his people (vv. 23–24), God's action in the creation order (v. 25) and a closing call to praise God (v. 26). The echoing response ("*His love endures forever*") occurs 26 times, the numerical value of the divine name Yahweh (when the Hebrew letters were used as numbers). This psalm is the only one that repeats the same refrain after each verse.
136:1–3,26 *Give thanks to.* Or "Praise" (see 7:17 and note).
136:6 *upon the waters.* See 24:2 and note.
136:7–9 Direct echoes of Ge 1:16.
136:15 *Pharaoh and his army.* Probably a hendiadys (two words expressing a single idea) for "Pharaoh's army," since pharaohs did not usually march with their armies.
136:23–24 Probably a concluding summary of the deliverance recalled above, but may allude also to the deliverances experienced during the period of the judges and the reign of David.

▶ **List some things you can thank God for.**

_____

_____

_____

_____

_____

_____

_____

_____

25 He gives food to every creature.
> *His love endures forever.*

26 Give thanks to the God of heaven.
> *His love endures forever.*

Psalm 137

1 By the rivers of Babylon we sat and wept
  when we remembered Zion.
2 There on the poplars
  we hung our harps,
3 for there our captors asked us for songs,
  our tormentors demanded songs of joy;
  they said, "Sing us one of the songs of
    Zion!"

4 How can we sing the songs of the LORD
  while in a foreign land?
5 If I forget you, Jerusalem,
  may my right hand forget its skill.
6 May my tongue cling to the roof of my
    mouth
  if I do not remember you,
 if I do not consider Jerusalem
  my highest joy.

136:26 *the God of heaven.* A Persian title for God found frequently in Ezra, Nehemiah and Daniel. Its intent is similar to that of the language of vv. 2–3.

Ps 137 A plaintive lament of one who has recently returned from Babylon but in whose soul there lingers the bitter memory of the years in a foreign land and of the cruel events that led to that enforced stay. Here speaks the same deep love of Zion as that found in Ps 42–43; 46; 48; 84; 122; 126. The editors of the Psalter attached this song to the Great Hallel as a closing expression of supreme devotion to the city at the center of Israel's worship of the Lord (see introduction to Ps 120–137). The 12 poetic lines of the Hebrew song divide symmetrically into three stanzas of four lines each: the remembered sorrow and torment (vv. 1–3), an oath of total commitment to Jerusalem (vv. 4–6) and a call for retribution on Edom and Babylon (vv. 7–9).

137:1 *rivers.* The Tigris and Euphrates and the many canals associated with them (see photo, below). *we sat.* Again and again the thought of their forced separation from Zion brought them down to the posture of mourning (Job 2:8,13; La 2:10).

137:4–6 Only someone whose heart had disowned the Lord and his holy city, Jerusalem, could play the puppet on a Babylonian stage. But may I never play the harp again or sing another syllable if I am untrue to that beloved city!

Town along the Euphrates River. Babylon was located between the Euphrates and Tigris Rivers. "By the rivers of Babylon we sat and wept when we remembered Zion" (Ps 137:1), but the "rivers" (or "streams") may have also included irrigation canals.

MehmetO/Shutterstock

⁷Remember, LORD, what the Edomites did
  on the day Jerusalem fell.
 "Tear it down," they cried,
  "tear it down to its foundations!"
⁸Daughter Babylon, doomed to destruction,
  happy is the one who repays you
  according to what you have done to us.
⁹Happy is the one who seizes your infants
  and dashes them against the rocks.

Psalm 138

Of David.

¹I will praise you, LORD, with all my heart;
  before the "gods" I will sing your praise.
²I will bow down toward your holy temple
  and will praise your name
 for your unfailing love and your faithfulness,
 for you have so exalted your solemn decree
  that it surpasses your fame.
³When I called, you answered me;
  you greatly emboldened me.

> **How do you respond to the psalmist's prayers for revenge in the context of New Testament teachings on love?**

_____

_____

_____

_____

_____

_____

_____

_____

_____

_____

_____

137:7–9 Lord, remember Edom; and as for you, Babylon, I bless whoever does to you what you did to Jerusalem: a passionate call for redress from a loyal son of the ravaged city (see note on 5:10).

137:7 *Edomites.* The agelong animosity of Edom—descendants of Esau, Jacob's brother—showed its most dastardly face in Jerusalem's darkest hour. No doubt the author knew the Lord's judgments against that nation announced by the prophets (Isa 63:1–4; Jer 49:7–22; Eze 25:8,12–14; 35; Obadiah). *Tear it down.* Or "Strip her"—cities were conventionally portrayed as women. La 4:21 anticipates that Edom will be punished by suffering the same humiliation.

137:8 *Daughter Babylon.* A personification of Babylon. *doomed to destruction.* The author and those who took up this psalm surely knew of the Lord's announced judgments on this cruel destroyer (Isa 13; 47; Jer 50–51). In the day of the Lord's judgment Babylon was to receive what she had done to others (see Jer 50:15,29; 51:24,35,49; cf. Rev 18:5–6). *happy is the one who repays you.* Because a cruel international predator has been removed from the earth (see Isa 14:3–8; cf. Jer 51:47–48; Rev 19:1–3).

137:9 *your infants.* War was as cruel then as now; women and children were not spared (2Ki 8:12; 15:16; Isa 13:16,18; Hos 10:14; 13:16; Am 1:13; Na 3:10). For the final announcement of the destruction of the "Babylon" that persists in its warfare against the City of God, and the joy with which that announcement is greeted, see Rev 14:18; 18:1—19:4.

Ps 138–145 A final collection of eight Davidic psalms brings the Psalter toward its close. While much in some of these psalms points to a later, even postexilic, date, they clearly stand in the tradition of psalmody of which David was the reputed father and echo the language and concerns of the earlier Davidic psalms. The collection is framed by songs of praise (Ps 138; 145). The first of these extols the greatness of the Lord's glory as displayed in his answering the prayer ("call") of the "lowly" when suffering at the hands of the proud. The last, employing a grand and intricately woven alphabetic acrostic design (see Introduction: Literary Features), extols the glorious majesty of the Lord as displayed in his benevolent care over all his creatures—especially those who "call" on him (look to him in every need). Within this frame have been placed six psalms—with certain interlocking themes that will be pointed out in the notes on the individual psalms.

This final Davidic collection contains the Psalter's two most magnificent expositions of the greatness and goodness of God, one of them (Ps 139) focusing on his relationship with an individual, the other (Ps 145) on his relationship with his whole creation.

Ps 138 A psalm of thanksgiving for God's saving help against threatening foes—understood by many to have been originally on the lips of a king. In some respects it is like Ps 18, though in style and scope much less grand.

138:1–3 Praise for God's faithful covenant love shown in answer to prayers for help.

138:1 *heart.* See note on 4:7. *"gods."* Either pagan kings (vv. 4–5) or the "gods" they claimed to represent (see introduction to Ps 82; see also note on 82:1).

138:2 *your holy temple.* If David is in fact the author, reference is to the tent he set up for the ark (2Sa 6:17)—many psalms ascribed to David refer to the "tem-

⁴May all the kings of the earth praise you, LORD,
    when they hear what you have decreed.
⁵May they sing of the ways of the LORD,
    for the glory of the LORD is great.

⁶Though the LORD is exalted, he looks kindly on
    the lowly;
    though lofty, he sees them from afar.
⁷Though I walk in the midst of trouble,
    you preserve my life.
You stretch out your hand against the anger of
    my foes;
    with your right hand you save me.
⁸The LORD will vindicate me;
    your love, LORD, endures forever —
    do not abandon the works of your hands.

Psalm 139

For the director of music. Of David. A psalm.

¹You have searched me, LORD,
    and you know me.
²You know when I sit and when I rise;
    you perceive my thoughts from afar.
³You discern my going out and my lying down;
    you are familiar with all my ways.
⁴Before a word is on my tongue
    you, LORD, know it completely.
⁵You hem me in behind and before,
    and you lay your hand upon me.
⁶Such knowledge is too wonderful for me,
    too lofty for me to attain.

⁷Where can I go from your Spirit?
    Where can I flee from your presence?
⁸If I go up to the heavens, you are there;
    if I make my bed in the depths, you are there.
⁹If I rise on the wings of the dawn,
    if I settle on the far side of the sea,
¹⁰even there your hand will guide me,
    your right hand will hold me fast.
¹¹If I say, "Surely the darkness will hide me
    and the light become night around me,"
¹²even the darkness will not be dark to you;
    the night will shine like the day,
    for darkness is as light to you.

¹³For you created my inmost being;
    you knit me together in my mother's womb.
¹⁴I praise you because I am fearfully and
    wonderfully made;
    your works are wonderful,
    I know that full well.
¹⁵My frame was not hidden from you
    when I was made in the secret place,
    when I was woven together in the depths of
    the earth.

ple" (see, e.g., 5:7; 11:4; 18:6; 27:4; see also Ps 30 title). *love.* See v. 8; see also article, p. 16.

138:4–5 The center of the poem (see note on 6:6): a wish that all the kings of earth may come to join in praising the Lord (see note on 9:1). The verbs, however, could be read as simple futures. In that case, these verses voice a confident expectation.

138:4 *what you have decreed.* God's grand commitments either to his people or to the royal house of David (see 18:30 and note; there, too, God's word and "ways" [v. 5] are linked).

138:5 *ways of the LORD.* See 25:10 and note. God's words and his ways are in harmony, and together they display his great glory (cf. Ps 145).

138:6–8 A testimony to God's condescending and faithful love, concluded with a prayer.

138:6 See 113:4–9 and notes. *sees them from afar.* Cf. the acknowledgment of the psalmist in 139:2.

138:8 *will vindicate me.* See 57:2 and note. *do not abandon the works of your hands.* A concluding prayer that the faithfulness of God celebrated here truly "endures forever."

Ps 139 A prayer for God to examine the heart and see its true devotion. Like Job, the author firmly claims his loyalty to the Lord. Nowhere (outside Job) does one find expressed such profound awareness of how awesome it is to ask God to examine not only one's life but also one's soul. The thought progresses steadily in four poetic paragraphs of six verses each (vv. 1–6,7–12,13–18,19–24), and each paragraph is concluded with a couplet that elaborates on the unit's central theme. References to God's searching and knowing begin and end the prayer.

139 title *For the director of music.* See note on Ps 4 title. *Of David.* See introduction to Ps 138–145.

139:1–6 God knows David perfectly—far beyond David's knowledge of himself: his every action (v. 2a), his every undertaking (v. 3a) and the manner in which he pursues it (v. 3b), even his thoughts before they are fully crystallized (v. 2b) and his words before they are uttered (v. 4). See also v. 23.

139:5–6 The psalmist's response to the fact that God knows him so well.

139:6 *too wonderful for me.* Beyond human capacity. The Hebrew term regularly applies to God's wondrous acts (see 77:11,14, "miracles"; Ex 15:11).

139:9 *wings of the dawn . . . far side of the sea.* The two horizontal extremes: east and west (the sea is the Mediterranean). Using a literary figure in which the totality is denoted by referring to its two extremes (merism), vv. 8–9 specify all spatial reality, the whole creation.

139:10 *guide me . . . hold me fast.* Though this language occurs in 73:23–24 to indicate God's solicitous care, it here denotes God's inescapable supervision, not unlike the thought of v. 5.

139:13–18 God himself put David together in the womb and ordained the span of David's life before he was born. God knew him so thoroughly because he made him.

139:13 *created.* The Hebrew for this verb is the same as in Ge 14:19,22; Pr 8:22 ("brought . . . forth"), not as in Ge 1:1,21,27.

139:14 *fearfully . . . wonderfully . . . wonderful.* You know me as the One who formed me (vv. 15–16), but

¹⁶Your eyes saw my unformed body;
>   all the days ordained for me were written in
>   your book
>   before one of them came to be.
¹⁷How precious to me are your thoughts,^a God!
>   How vast is the sum of them!
¹⁸Were I to count them,
>   they would outnumber the grains of sand —
>   when I awake, I am still with you.

¹⁹If only you, God, would slay the wicked!
>   Away from me, you who are bloodthirsty!
²⁰They speak of you with evil intent;
>   your adversaries misuse your name.
²¹Do I not hate those who hate you, LORD,
>   and abhor those who are in rebellion
>   against you?
²²I have nothing but hatred for them;
>   I count them my enemies.
²³Search me, God, and know my heart;
>   test me and know my anxious thoughts.
²⁴See if there is any offensive way in me,
>   and lead me in the way everlasting.

Psalm 140^b

For the director of music. A psalm of David.

¹Rescue me, LORD, from evildoers;
>   protect me from the violent,
²who devise evil plans in their hearts
>   and stir up war every day.
³They make their tongues as sharp as a
>   serpent's;
>   the poison of vipers is on their lips.^c

⁴Keep me safe, LORD, from the hands of the
>   wicked;
>   protect me from the violent,
>   who devise ways to trip my feet.
⁵The arrogant have hidden a snare for me;
>   they have spread out the cords of their net
>   and have set traps for me along my path.

⁶I say to the LORD, "You are my God."
>   Hear, LORD, my cry for mercy.
⁷Sovereign LORD, my strong deliverer,
>   you shield my head in the day of battle.
⁸Do not grant the wicked their desires, LORD;
>   do not let their plans succeed.

⁹Those who surround me proudly rear their
>   heads;
>   may the mischief of their lips engulf them.

I cannot begin to comprehend this creature you have fashioned. I can only look upon him with awe and wonder (see note on v. 6)—and praise you (Ecc 11:5).

139:15 *secret place . . . depths of the earth.* Reference is to the womb: called "the secret place" because it normally conceals (2Sa 12:12), and it shares with "the depths of the earth" (see note on 30:1) associations with darkness, dampness and separation from the visible realm of life. Moreover, both phrases refer to the place of the dead (63:9; Job 14:13; Isa 44:23; 45:19), with which on one level the womb appears to have been associated: Humans come from the dust and return to the dust (90:3; Ge 3:19; Ecc 3:20; 12:7), and the womb is the "depth"-like place where they are formed (Isa 44:2,24; 49:5; Jer 1:5).

139:16 *all the days ordained.* The span of life and its events sovereignly determined.

139:17 *your thoughts.* As expressed in his works—and in contrast with "my thoughts" (v. 2).

139:18 *when I awake.* The sleep of exhaustion overcomes every attempt to count God's thoughts/works (63:6; 119:148), and waking only floods my soul once more with the sense of the presence of this God. On the other hand, reference may be to "awaking" from the sleep of death, as in Ps 17:15 (see also 2Ki 4:31; Job 14:12; Isa 26:9; Jer 51:39,57; Da 12:2). If so, the psalmist extends the sphere of God's presence to beyond death.

139:19–24 David's zeal for God and his loyalty to God set him against all God's adversaries (see 5:10 and note).

139:21–22 A declaration of loyalty that echoes the pledge required by ancient Near Eastern kings of their vassals (e.g., "With my friend you shall be friend, and with my enemy you shall be enemy," from a treaty between Mursilis II, a Hittite king, and Tette of Nuhassi, fourteenth century BC).

139:23–24 A concluding prayer, submitting to God's penetrating examination: Examine me, see the integrity of my devotion and keep me true (see v. 1; 17:3–5).

139:23 *Search me . . . know my heart.* After David calls for redress against God's and his enemies (vv. 19–22), he then asks God to see if he has said or done anything offensive (vv. 23b–24). *heart.* See note on 4:7. *anxious thoughts.* See 94:19. It is no light matter to be examined by God.

Ps 140 A lament to God asking for deliverance from the plots and slander of unscrupulous enemies. It recalls Ps 58 and 64 but employs a number of words found nowhere else in the OT.

140:1–3 Rescue me from those "vipers."

140:1 *LORD.* Hebrew *Yahweh*; God's personal name occurs seven times (the number of completeness) in this psalm.

140:4–5 Protect me from those proud and wicked hunters (see 10:2–11 and notes).

140:6–8 Do not let these wicked men attain their evil designs against me.

140:6 *Hear, LORD, my cry for mercy.* A thematic and verbal link with 141:1; 142:1; 143:1.

140:9–11 Let the harm they plot against me recoil on their heads (see note on 5:10).

---

^a 17 Or *How amazing are your thoughts concerning me*   ^b In Hebrew texts 140:1-13 is numbered 140:2-14.   ^c 3 The Hebrew has *Selah* (a word of uncertain meaning) here and at the end of verses 5 and 8.

¹⁰ May burning coals fall on them;
    may they be thrown into the fire,
    into miry pits, never to rise.
¹¹ May slanderers not be established in
      the land;
    may disaster hunt down the violent.

¹² I know that the Lord secures justice for the
      poor
    and upholds the cause of the needy.
¹³ Surely the righteous will praise your name,
    and the upright will live in your
      presence.

140:10 *burning coals.* For the reference, see Lev. 16:12; Job 41:21; Pr 6:28; Isa 47:14; Eze 24:11. Other examples of this imagery for divine judgment may be found in Ps 18:8; 120:4; Eze 10:2. *fire . . . miry pits.* This combination, together with the conjunction of fire and darkness in Job 15:30; 20:26, suggests the idea that the fire of God's judgment (see, e.g., 21:9; 97:3; Isa 1:31; 26:11; 33:14) reaches even into the realm of the dead (see Job 31:12 and note on Ps 30:1). *never to rise.* See 36:12; Isa 26:14.
140:12 *poor . . . needy.* See notes on 9:18; 34:6.
140:13 *the righteous.* See note on 1:5. *will praise.* Having experienced God's help (see notes on 7:17; 9:1). *will live in your presence.* In contrast to the wicked (v. 10; see notes on 11:7; 16:9–11).

> What weighs on your heart that you need to share with the Lord?

▶ How is today's church as important as the temple was in David's day (Ps 132)?

_____

_____

_____

_____

_____

▶ How can God's people live in unity (133:1)?

_____

_____

_____

_____

_____

▶ This well-known psalm expresses the lament of the exiled Israelites (Ps 137). What do you learn about the tragedy of war and its victims from it?

_____

_____

_____

_____

_____

▶ What do you learn about God's sovereignty from Psalm 139?

_____

_____

_____

_____

_____

Psalm 141

A psalm of David.

¹ I call to you, LORD, come quickly to me;
    hear me when I call to you.
² May my prayer be set before you like incense;
    may the lifting up of my hands be like the
      evening sacrifice.

³ Set a guard over my mouth, LORD;
    keep watch over the door of my lips.
⁴ Do not let my heart be drawn to what is evil
    so that I take part in wicked deeds
along with those who are evildoers;
    do not let me eat their delicacies.

⁵ Let a righteous man strike me — that is a
      kindness;
    let him rebuke me — that is oil on my head.
My head will not refuse it,
    for my prayer will still be against the deeds
      of evildoers.

⁶ Their rulers will be thrown down from the
      cliffs,
    and the wicked will learn that my words
      were well spoken.
⁷ They will say, "As one plows and breaks up the
      earth,
    so our bones have been scattered at the
      mouth of the grave."

⁸ But my eyes are fixed on you, Sovereign LORD;
    in you I take refuge — do not give me over to
      death.
⁹ Keep me safe from the traps set by evildoers,
    from the snares they have laid for me.
¹⁰ Let the wicked fall into their own nets,
    while I pass by in safety.

Psalm 142 [a]

A maskil [b] of David. When he was in the cave. A prayer.

¹ I cry aloud to the LORD;
    I lift up my voice to the LORD for mercy.
² I pour out before him my complaint;
    before him I tell my trouble.

---

[a] In Hebrew texts 142:1-7 is numbered 142:2-8.   [b] Title:
Probably a literary or musical term

Ps 141 A lament to God asking for deliverance from the wicked and their evil ways. Like Ps 140, the psalm is profuse in its physiological allusions: hands, mouth, lips, heart, head, bones, eyes.
141 title See introduction to Ps 138–145.
141:1–2 Initial appeal for God to hear.
141:2 *like the evening sacrifice.* See Ex 29:38–41; Nu 28:3–8. These sacrifices are frequently mentioned (1Ki 18:29; 2Ki 16:15; 1Ch 16:40; 2Ch 13:11; 31:3; Ezr 3:3; 9:4–5; Da 9:21).
141:1 *hear me when I call.* See 140:6 and note.
141:3–4 A plea that God will keep him from speaking, desiring or doing what is evil.
141:4 *Do not let my heart be drawn to . . . evil.* Keep me from yielding to the example and urgings of the wicked (Pr 1:10–16). *heart.* See note on 4:7. *their delicacies.* Usually taken to refer to the luxuriant tables the wicked set from their unjust gains—thus a prayer that the psalmist be kept from acquiring an appetite for such unholy dainties. But the noun occurs only here, and it may refer to the pleasant sounding, but deceptive and evil, words of the wicked—thus a prayer that the psalmist be kept from taking into his mouth the talk of the wicked that corresponds with their evil way of life (cf. v. 6 and note). Words related to this noun are elsewhere used to characterize words/thoughts (Pr 15:26; 16:21; 23:8).
141:5 The center of the poem (see note on 6:6). *Let a righteous man strike me.* The disciplining blows and rebukes of the righteous are the true "kindness" (Hebrew *ḥesed*, meaning "love" or "acts of authentic friendship"; see Pr 27:6; see also article, p. 16). *oil on my head.* See note on 23:5.
141:6–7 The destiny of the wicked.
141:6 *my words.* Of commitment to righteousness, as in vv. 3–5. *well spoken.* Good and right.
141:8–10 A plea that God will deliver from the designs of the wicked.
141:8 *do not give me over to death.* As you do the wicked (see v. 7; see also 73:18–20,23–26 and notes).
141:9 *traps . . . snares.* Perhaps, as usual, the plots of enemies to bring him down (as in 38:12; 64:5; 91:3; 140:5; 142:3; see note on 9:15)—note this link with Ps 140; 142.
141:10 *Let the wicked fall.* See note on 5:10. *fall into their own nets.* In Hebrew a verbal echo of 140:10 ("thrown into . . . miry pits").
Ps 142 A plaintive lament to God requesting deliverance from powerful enemies—when powerless, alone and without refuge. Much of its language echoes that of other psalms (see notes below).
142:1–2 Initial appeal—using the formal third person "I cry aloud to the LORD" (as was often done when addressing kings), equivalent to: "I cry aloud to you, LORD."
142:1 Very similar to 77:1. *lift up my voice to the LORD for mercy.* See 140:6 and note.
142:2 *I pour out before him my complaint.* Very similar to language found in the title of Ps 102.

³When my spirit grows faint within me,
 it is you who watch over my way.
In the path where I walk
 people have hidden a snare for me.
⁴Look and see, there is no one at my right hand;
 no one is concerned for me.
I have no refuge;
 no one cares for my life.

⁵I cry to you, LORD;
 I say, "You are my refuge,
 my portion in the land of the living."

⁶Listen to my cry,
 for I am in desperate need;
rescue me from those who pursue me,
 for they are too strong for me.
⁷Set me free from my prison,
 that I may praise your name.
Then the righteous will gather about me
 because of your goodness to me.

Psalm 143

A psalm of David.

¹LORD, hear my prayer,
 listen to my cry for mercy;
in your faithfulness and righteousness
 come to my relief.
²Do not bring your servant into judgment,
 for no one living is righteous before you.
³The enemy pursues me,
 he crushes me to the ground;
he makes me dwell in the darkness
 like those long dead.
⁴So my spirit grows faint within me;
 my heart within me is dismayed.
⁵I remember the days of long ago;
 I meditate on all your works
 and consider what your hands have done.
⁶I spread out my hands to you;
 I thirst for you like a parched land.ᵃ

⁷Answer me quickly, LORD;
 my spirit fails.
Do not hide your face from me
 or I will be like those who go down to the pit.
⁸Let the morning bring me word of your
  unfailing love,
 for I have put my trust in you.
Show me the way I should go,
 for to you I entrust my life.
⁹Rescue me from my enemies, LORD,
 for I hide myself in you.

ᵃ 6 The Hebrew has *Selah* (a word of uncertain meaning) here.

142:3–4 Description of his "desperate need" (v. 6).
142:3 *When my spirit grows faint.* Because he is overwhelmed by his situation (22:14–15)—a thematic and verbal link with 143:6 (see also 77:3; Ps 102 title; Jnh 2:7). *you who watch over.* And are concerned about (cf. v. 4). *hidden a snare for me.* A thematic and verbal link with 140:5; 141:9–10 (see note on 9:15).
142:4 *right hand.* Where one's helper or defender stands. *is concerned.* In Hebrew a less common synonym of "know" (v. 3, "watch over"); see Ru 2:10,19 ("notice"). *cares for.* See Dt 11:12.
142:5–7 Prayer for rescue.
142:5 *You are my refuge.* See 71:7; Jer 17:17. *portion.* The sustainer and preserver of his life (see 73:26 and note). *in the land of the living.* See 27:13; 52:5; 116:9.
142:6 *Listen to my cry.* See 17:1. *rescue me.* See 143:9; 144:7.
142:7 *prison.* Metaphor for the sense of being fettered by affliction (see note on 18:19; see also Job 36:8). *that I may praise your name.* In celebration of your saving help (see note on 7:17). *righteous.* See note on 1:5. *will gather about me.* He will no longer be alone. The conclusion expresses an expectant word of confidence (see note on 3:8). *your goodness to me.* See 13:6; 116:7.
Ps 143 A lament to God asking for deliverance from enemies and for divine leading. This is the seventh and final penitential psalm.
143 title See introduction to Ps 138–145.
143:1–2 Initial appeal.
143:1 *my cry for mercy.* See 140:6 and note. *righteousness.* See note on 4:1.
143:2 As he begins his prayer, he pleads that God not sit in judgment over his servant (he knows his own failings; see also v. 10) but that he focus his judicial attention on the enemy's harsh and unwarranted attacks. *your servant.* A verbal link with 144:10—which suggests why this psalm was traditionally ascribed to David (see also 78:70; 132:10).
143:3–4 The distress he suffers.
143:3 The last half of this verse appears almost verbatim in La 3:6. *in the darkness.* As one cut off from the enjoyments of life (see v. 7; see also notes on 27:1; 30:1).
143:4 *my spirit grows faint.* See note on 142:3. *heart.* See note on 4:7.
143:5–6 Remembrance of God's past acts of deliverance encourages him in his appeal.
143:6 *spread out my hands.* In prayer (44:20; 88:9; Ex 9:29). *thirst for you.* See note on 63:1. For *Selah*, see NIV text note and note on 3:2.
143:7–10 The prayer.
143:7 *my spirit fails.* Or perhaps: "my spirit faints with longing," which parallels the construction in 119:81. Ultimately, the failing of "my spirit" will be healed by the leading of "your good Spirit" (v. 10)—the two references enclose the prayer. *hide your face.* See note on 13:1. *the pit.* See v. 3 and note on 30:1.
143:8 *the morning.* Of salvation from the present "darkness" (v. 3; see introduction to Ps 57; see also note on 101:8). *unfailing love.* See v. 12; see also article, p. 16. *I have put my trust in you . . . to you I entrust my life.* See 25:1–2. *Show me the way.* See v. 10. Deliverance from the enemy is not enough—either for God's "servant" (vv. 2,12) or for entrance into life.

• ¹⁰ Teach me to do your will,
    for you are my God;
  may your good Spirit
    lead me on level ground.

¹¹ For your name's sake, LORD, preserve my life;
    in your righteousness, bring me out of
      trouble.
¹² In your unfailing love, silence my enemies;
    destroy all my foes,
    for I am your servant.

Psalm 144

Of David.

¹ Praise be to the LORD my Rock,
    who trains my hands for war,
    my fingers for battle.
² He is my loving God and my fortress,
    my stronghold and my deliverer,
  my shield, in whom I take refuge,
    who subdues peoples*ᵃ* under me.

ᵃ 2 Many manuscripts of the Masoretic Text, Dead Sea Scrolls, Aquila, Jerome and Syriac; most manuscripts of the Masoretic Text *subdues my people*

143:11–12 Concluding reiteration of the prayer. Note how "your righteousness," "your unfailing love" and "your servant" all establish links with vv. 1–2.
143:11 *For your name's sake.* See note on 23:3.
143:12 *destroy all my foes.* See note on 5:10.
Ps 144 A lament to God requesting deliverance from treacherous enemies, composed in the mode of a royal prayer. Verses 1–10 show much affinity to Ps 18, with vv. 5–7 all appearing to be variations on lines found there (see notes below). The remaining lines of this section contain similar echoes of other psalms, and the author may have drawn directly on them. This first part of the psalm is fairly typical of the laments of the Psalter. Verse 11 recapitulates the prayer of vv. 5–8; vv. 12–14 describe a people enjoying ideal conditions; v. 15 closes the psalm with an echo of 33:12. For thematic continuities, see notes below.
144 title See introduction to Ps 138–145.
144:1–2 Praise of the Lord. As the opening words of a prayer, it seems to function both as an initial appeal (143:1–2) and as a confession of confidence that the prayer will be heard. The unusual piling up of epithets for God echoes Ps 18 (see note on 18:2).
144:2 *my loving God.* More formally, "My unfailing love," so called because God is the source of benevolent acts of love that David can count on—just as God can be called "my salvation" because he is the source of salvation (27:1; 35:3; 62:2; see article, p. 16).

Detail of the Porch of the Caryatids on the Acropolis of Athens, Greece. Psalm 144:12 mentions daughters being "like pillars carved to adorn a palace."
Rob & Lisa Meehan/Wikimedia Commons, CC BY 2.0

³LORD, what are human beings that you care for
them,
mere mortals that you think of them?
⁴They are like a breath;
their days are like a fleeting shadow.

⁵Part your heavens, LORD, and come down;
touch the mountains, so that they smoke.
⁶Send forth lightning and scatter the enemy;
shoot your arrows and rout them.
⁷Reach down your hand from on high;
deliver me and rescue me
from the mighty waters,
from the hands of foreigners
⁸whose mouths are full of lies,
whose right hands are deceitful.

⁹I will sing a new song to you, my God;
on the ten-stringed lyre I will make music
to you,
¹⁰to the One who gives victory to kings,
who delivers his servant David.

From the deadly sword ¹¹deliver me;
rescue me from the hands of foreigners
whose mouths are full of lies,
whose right hands are deceitful.

¹²Then our sons in their youth
will be like well-nurtured plants,
and our daughters will be like pillars
carved to adorn a palace.
¹³Our barns will be filled
with every kind of provision.
Our sheep will increase by thousands,
by tens of thousands in our fields;
¹⁴ our oxen will draw heavy loads.^a
There will be no breaching of walls,
no going into captivity,
no cry of distress in our streets.
¹⁵Blessed is the people of whom this is true;
blessed is the people whose God is the LORD.

Psalm 145^b

A psalm of praise. Of David.

¹I will exalt you, my God the King;
I will praise your name for ever and ever.
²Every day I will praise you
and extol your name for ever and ever.

³Great is the LORD and most worthy of praise;
his greatness no one can fathom.
⁴One generation commends your works to another;
they tell of your mighty acts.

---

^a 14 Or *our chieftains will be firmly established*   ^b This psalm is an acrostic poem, the verses of which (including verse 13b) begin with the successive letters of the Hebrew alphabet.

144:3–4 Acknowledgment of the relative insignificance of human beings and an expression of wonder that God cares for them.
144:3 A variation of 8:4.
144:4 *breath.* See 39:4–6 and notes. *shadow.* See 102:11 and note.
144:5–8 Prayer for deliverance.
144:5 See 18:9 and note on 18:7–15; see also Isa 64:1.
144:6 See 18:14 and note.
144:7 See 18:16–17 and note on 32:6.
144:8 *mouths.* See note on 5:9. *right hands.* Hands raised to swear covenant oaths of allegiance or submission (106:26; Ex 6:8; Dt 32:40).
144:9–10 Vow to praise God (see note on 7:17).
144:9 *new song.* See note on 33:3.
144:10 *his servant David.* See 143:2 and note.
144:11 Repetition of the prayer in vv. 7–8, apparently to serve as transition to what follows: If God will deliver his servant David, the realm will prosper and be secure.
144:12–15 Many believe this to be a separate prayer ("May our sons . . ."), unrelated to vv. 1–11, but the apparently transitional function of v. 11 supports the NIV rendering.
144:12–14 Possibly a postexilic echo of Dt 28:3–8.
144:12 *sons . . . like . . . plants.* Strong and healthy. *daughters . . . like pillars carved.* An honor by which their beauty will be remembered. Temple columns in the shape of women were not uncommon (e.g., the caryatids on the Acropolis in Athens; see photo, p. 181).
144:14 *our oxen will draw heavy loads.* Or "our oxen will be heavy with flesh" or "our oxen will be heavy with young" (see also NIV text note).
144:15 *Blessed.* See note on 1:1. *the people of whom this is true.* Cf. 33:12; see Dt 28:3–8; 1Ki 5:4.
Ps 145 A magnificent hymn to the Lord, the Great King, for his mighty acts and benevolent virtues, which are the glory of his kingly rule. It exploits to the full the traditional language of praise and, as an alphabetic acrostic (see Introduction: Literary Features), reflects the care of studied composition. This care can be seen also in the manner in which the whole is structured. Between the two-line introduction (vv. 1–2) and one-line conclusion (v. 21), four main stanzas (vv. 3–7,9–13a,13b–16,17–20) describe these divine attributes: greatness, goodness, trustworthiness, righteousness.
145 title *praise.* Hebrew *tehillah,* occurring only here in the psalm titles, but from a plural form (*tehillim*) has come the traditional Hebrew name of the Psalter. *Of David.* See introduction to Ps 138–145.
145:1–2 Initial commitment to praise God. *name.* See v. 21, thus framing the psalm.
145:3–7 Praise of God's mighty acts, which display his greatness (v. 3) and his goodness (v. 7)—as the author underscores by framing the paragraph with these two references. For the same combination, see 86:10,17; 135:3,5.
145:4 *commends . . . tell.* See vv. 5–7,10–12,21; see also note on 9:1. *your works.* In creation, providence and redemption.

⁵ They speak of the glorious splendor of your
    majesty —
    and I will meditate on your wonderful works.^a
⁶ They tell of the power of your awesome works —
    and I will proclaim your great deeds.
⁷ They celebrate your abundant goodness
    and joyfully sing of your righteousness.

⁸ The LORD is gracious and compassionate,
    slow to anger and rich in love.

⁹ The LORD is good to all;
    he has compassion on all he has made.
¹⁰ All your works praise you, LORD;
    your faithful people extol you.
¹¹ They tell of the glory of your kingdom
    and speak of your might,
¹² so that all people may know of your mighty acts
    and the glorious splendor of your kingdom.
¹³ Your kingdom is an everlasting kingdom,
    and your dominion endures through all
      generations.

The LORD is trustworthy in all he promises
    and faithful in all he does.^b
¹⁴ The LORD upholds all who fall
    and lifts up all who are bowed down.
¹⁵ The eyes of all look to you,
    and you give them their food at the proper time.
¹⁶ You open your hand
    and satisfy the desires of every living thing.

¹⁷ The LORD is righteous in all his ways
    and faithful in all he does.
¹⁸ The LORD is near to all who call on him,
    to all who call on him in truth.
¹⁹ He fulfills the desires of those who fear him;
    he hears their cry and saves them.
²⁰ The LORD watches over all who love him,
    but all the wicked he will destroy.

²¹ My mouth will speak in praise of the LORD.
    Let every creature praise his holy name
    for ever and ever.

Psalm 146

¹ Praise the LORD.^c

Praise the LORD, my soul.

² I will praise the LORD all my life;
    I will sing praise to my God as long as I live.
³ Do not put your trust in princes,
    in human beings, who cannot save.

---

^a 5 Dead Sea Scrolls and Syriac (see also Septuagint); Masoretic
Text *On the glorious splendor of your majesty / and on your
wonderful works I will meditate*   ^b 13 One manuscript of the
Masoretic Text, Dead Sea Scrolls and Syriac (see also Septuagint);
most manuscripts of the Masoretic Text do not have the last two
lines of verse 13.   ^c 1 Hebrew *Hallelu Yah*; also in verse 10

145:7 *righteousness.* See v. 17; see also note on 4:1.
145:8 This centered line (see introduction) is equal in thematic importance to vv. 3,9,13b,17. It echoes the classic exposition of the divine attributes in Ex 34:6–7.
145:9–13a Praise of God's benevolent virtues, which move all creatures to celebrate the glory of his kingdom.
145:10 *All your works praise you.* See v. 21; see also note on 65:13. *faithful people.* See note on 4:3.
145:13b–16 Praise of God's faithfulness.
145:13b,17 *faithful.* See article, p. 16.
145:17–20 Praise of God's righteousness.
145:18 *in truth.* With godly integrity.
145:21 The praise of God must continue, and every creature take it up—forever. *every creature.* Or perhaps "every human" (see 65:2, "all people"; but see also 150:6).
Ps 146–150 A final cluster of five hymns all bracketed by shouts of Hallelujah! ("Praise Yahweh!")—which may have been added by the final editors (see introductions to Ps 105–106; see also Ps 111–117). The Psalter collection begins with two psalms that address the reader and whose function is to identify those to whom the collections specifically belong (see introduction to Ps 1–2). Here, at the collection's end, that congregation gives voice to its final themes. They are the themes of praise—and calls to praise—of Zion's heavenly King (146:10; 147:12; 149:2), the Maker, Sustainer and Lord over all creation (146:6; 147:4,8–9,15–18; 148:5–6); the one sure hope of those who in their need and vulnerability look to him for help (146:5–9; 147:2–3,6,11,13–14; 149:4); the Lord of history whose commitment to his people is their security and the guarantee that, as his kingdom people (see especially 147:19–20), they will ultimately triumph over all the forces of this world arrayed against them (146:3,10; 147:2,6,10,13–14; 148:14; 149:4–9).
Ps 146 A hymn in praise of Zion's heavenly King, with special focus on his powerful and trustworthy care for Zion's citizens who look to him when oppressed, broken or vulnerable. It has many thematic links with Ps 33; 62; 145. For its placement, see introduction to Ps 146–150.
146:1–2 Initial vow to praise God—as long as life continues (see 145:21 and note on 7:17).
146:1 *Praise the LORD, my soul.* See the frames around Ps 103–104. *soul.* See note on 6:3.
146:3–4 A call to trust ultimately in the Lord rather than in any human help (see 118:10–11; 147:10–11).

Additional Insights

All creation is Yahweh's one kingdom. To be a creature in the world is to be a part of his kingdom and under his rule.

⁴When their spirit departs, they return to the
ground;
on that very day their plans come to nothing.
⁵Blessed are those whose help is the God of Jacob,
whose hope is in the LORD their God.

⁶He is the Maker of heaven and earth,
the sea, and everything in them —
he remains faithful forever.
⁷He upholds the cause of the oppressed
and gives food to the hungry.
The LORD sets prisoners free,
⁸ the LORD gives sight to the blind,
the LORD lifts up those who are bowed down,
the LORD loves the righteous.
⁹The LORD watches over the foreigner
and sustains the fatherless and the widow,
but he frustrates the ways of the wicked.

¹⁰The LORD reigns forever,
your God, O Zion, for all generations.

Praise the LORD.

Psalm 147

¹Praise the LORD.ᵃ

How good it is to sing praises to our God,
how pleasant and fitting to praise him!

²The LORD builds up Jerusalem;
he gathers the exiles of Israel.
³He heals the brokenhearted
and binds up their wounds.
⁴He determines the number of the stars
and calls them each by name.
⁵Great is our Lord and mighty in power;
his understanding has no limit.
⁶The LORD sustains the humble
but casts the wicked to the ground.

⁷Sing to the LORD with grateful praise;
make music to our God on the harp.

⁸He covers the sky with clouds;
he supplies the earth with rain
and makes grass grow on the hills.
⁹He provides food for the cattle
and for the young ravens when they call.

¹⁰His pleasure is not in the strength of the horse,
nor his delight in the legs of the warrior;
¹¹the LORD delights in those who fear him,
who put their hope in his unfailing love.

¹²Extol the LORD, Jerusalem;
praise your God, Zion.

¹³He strengthens the bars of your gates
and blesses your people within you.

ᵃ 1 Hebrew *Hallelu Yah*; also in verse 20

146:5–9 Encouragement to trust in the covenant God of Jacob, who as Creator is Lord over all, as the Faithful One defends the defenseless and provides for the needy, and as the Righteous One shows favor to the righteous but checks the wicked in their pursuits.
146:7 *upholds the cause of the oppressed.* See 9:9; 10:18; 103:6. *gives food to the hungry.* See 17:14; 34:10; 107:9; cf. Isa 49:10. *sets prisoners free.* See 68:6; 79:11; 102:20; 107:10,14; cf. Isa 42:7; 61:1.
146:8 *gives sight to the blind.* See Isa 29:18; 35:5; cf. Isa 42:7; 43:8. *lifts up those who are bowed down.* See 145:14. *righteous.* See note on 1:5.
146:9 *watches over the foreigner . . . fatherless . . . widow.* See Dt 10:18; cf. Isa 1:17; 9:17; cf. also Jer 22:16; Jas 1:17. *frustrates the ways of the wicked.* Cf. 104:35; 145:20.
146:10 Concluding exultant testimony to the citizens of God's royal city. *The LORD reigns forever.* See 93:1 and note. *Zion.* See note on 9:11.
Ps 147 A hymn of praise to God, the Creator and Lord over all, for his special mercies to Israel—possibly composed for the Levitical choirs on the joyous occasion of the dedication of the rebuilt walls of Jerusalem (Ne 12:27–43). Following the introduction (v. 1), two couplets in which the Lord's unique favors to Israel are celebrated (vv. 2–3,19–20) frame its main body, while at the center another couplet (vv. 10–11) highlights the Lord's special pleasure in those who rely finally on him rather than on any of his creatures. In the balanced stanzas that intervene (vv. 4–9,12–18), this thematic core is placed in the larger context of God's works and ways. See introduction to Ps 146–150.
147:1 See note on 135:3.
147:2 *builds up.* Refers to the postexilic rebuilding of Jerusalem. *exiles.* Translates an unusual Hebrew word found also in Isa 11:10; 56:8—all of which speak of gathering (restoring) "the exiles of Israel."
147:3 *brokenhearted.* Such as the exiles (see Ps 137; cf. Ps 126) and those who struggled in the face of great opposition to rebuild Jerusalem's walls (Ne 2:17–20; 4:1–23).
147:4–6 He whose power and understanding are such that he fixes the number of (or counts) the stars and names them is able to sustain his humble ones and bring the wicked down (see 20:8; 146:9; see also Isa 40:26–29).
147:6 *humble.* Those who acknowledge that they are without resources to deliver or maintain themselves—those who, as God's people, put their trust in him (see 149:4; see also 22:26, "the poor"; 37:11, "the meek," and note; 69:32, "the poor"). *ground.* Probably the grave (see note on 61:2).
147:7–9 Israel's God is Lord of creation, the one who provides for all living things.
147:10–11 The central couplet (see note on 6:6), thematically linked with vv. 2–3 and vv. 19–20 (see introduction to Ps 147). Israel's God is not particularly impressed by the creaturely capacities that humans are prone to rely on (cf. 146:3–4 and note); it gives him delight when his people rely on him (cf. 146:5–9).
147:11 *fear.* See note on 34:8–14. *unfailing love.* See article, p. 16.
147:12–18 The Lord of all creation, Zion's God, secures his people's defenses and prosperity, their peace and abun-

¹⁴He grants peace to your borders
  and satisfies you with the finest of wheat.

¹⁵He sends his command to the earth;
  his word runs swiftly.
¹⁶He spreads the snow like wool
  and scatters the frost like ashes.
¹⁷He hurls down his hail like pebbles.
  Who can withstand his icy blast?
¹⁸He sends his word and melts them;
  he stirs up his breezes, and the waters flow.

¹⁹He has revealed his word to Jacob,
  his laws and decrees to Israel.
²⁰He has done this for no other nation;
  they do not know his laws.ᵃ

Praise the LORD.

Psalm 148

¹Praise the LORD.ᵇ

Praise the LORD from the heavens;
  praise him in the heights above.
²Praise him, all his angels;
  praise him, all his heavenly hosts.
³Praise him, sun and moon;
  praise him, all you shining stars.
⁴Praise him, you highest heavens
  and you waters above the skies.

⁵Let them praise the name of the LORD,
  for at his command they were created,
⁶and he established them for ever and ever—
  he issued a decree that will never pass away.

⁷Praise the LORD from the earth,
  you great sea creatures and all ocean depths,
⁸lightning and hail, snow and clouds,
  stormy winds that do his bidding,
⁹you mountains and all hills,
  fruit trees and all cedars,
¹⁰wild animals and all cattle,
  small creatures and flying birds,
¹¹kings of the earth and all nations,
  you princes and all rulers on earth,
¹²young men and women,
  old men and children.

¹³Let them praise the name of the LORD,
  for his name alone is exalted;
  his splendor is above the earth and the heavens.
¹⁴And he has raised up for his people a horn,ᶜ
  the praise of all his faithful servants,
  of Israel, the people close to his heart.

Praise the LORD.

ᵃ 20 Masoretic Text; Dead Sea Scrolls and Septuagint *nation; /
he has not made his laws known to them*   ᵇ 1 Hebrew *Hallelu
Yah*; also in verse 14   ᶜ 14 *Horn* here symbolizes strength.

dant provision. The verses mention clouds and rain (v. 8); snow, frost and hail (vv. 16–17); icy winds and warm breezes (vv. 17–18)—the whole range of weather.
147:15 *his command . . . his word.* Personified as messengers commissioned to carry out a divine order (see v. 18; see also notes on 23:6; 104:4).
147:19–20 God's most unique gift to Israel: his redemptive word, by which he makes known his program of salvation and his holy will. These verses constitute the end frame, thematically linked with vv. 2–3 and vv. 10–11 (see introduction to Ps 147 and note on vv. 10–11).
Ps 148 A hymn that calls all things in creation to praise the Lord. Whatever its original liturgical purpose, its placement here at the center of the five concluding hymns serves to complete the scope of the calls to praise with which the Psalter closes (see introduction to Ps 146–150). Two similarly constructed stanzas call on all creatures in the heavens (vv. 1–6) and all creatures beneath the heavens (vv. 7–14) to join in the chorus of praise (see 103:20–22 and note). Both stanzas end with a couplet setting forth the motivation for praise. The second of these (vv. 12–14), made up of extended lines, clearly constitutes the climax.
148:1–6 Let all creatures in the heavens praise the Lord.
148:3 *sun and moon . . . shining stars.* See note on 65:13.
148:4 *waters above the skies.* The "deep" above (see Ge 1:7; cf. "ocean depths" in v. 7; see also note on 42:7).
148:5–6 Motivation ("for," v. 5) for the heavenly creatures to praise the Lord (cf. vv. 13–14 and "for," v. 13).
148:5,13 *name of the LORD.* They are to praise the Lord because he has created them and made their existence secure.
148:7–14 Let all creatures of earth praise the Lord ("the earth and the heavens" [v. 13] are the sum of all creation; see 89:11; 113:6; 136:5–6; Ge 2:1,4).
148:7 *sea creatures and all ocean depths.* Likely with Ge 1 in mind (Ge 1:7,10,21), the call begins with these and moves toward the human components. This and the pairs that follow employ a figure of speech that refers to all reality pertaining to the sphere to which they belong—here, all creatures great and small that belong to the realm of lakes and seas.
148:8 *his bidding.* Or "his word" (see 147:15 and note).
148:13–14 Climactic conclusion, with focus again on motivation for praising God (cf. vv. 5–6 and note).
148:13 *his name . . . his splendor.* As shown in the glory of his creation. *is above.* The glory of the Creator is greater than the glory of the creation.
148:14 *horn.* The Lord's anointed (see NIV text note; 132:17; see also notes on 2:2; Ps 18 title). It may be, however, that "horn" here represents the strength and vigor of God's people (92:10; 1Sa 2:1; Jer 48:25; La 2:17). In any event, reference is to God's saving acts for Israel—God is to be praised for his works in creation and redemption (see note on 65:6–7). *praise.* See 22:3 and note. *faithful servants.* See note on 4:3.

Psalm 149

[1] Praise the Lord.[a]

Sing to the Lord a new song,
    his praise in the assembly of his faithful people.

[2] Let Israel rejoice in their Maker;
    let the people of Zion be glad in their King.
[3] Let them praise his name with dancing
    and make music to him with timbrel and harp.
[4] For the Lord takes delight in his people;
    he crowns the humble with victory.
[5] Let his faithful people rejoice in this honor
    and sing for joy on their beds. •

[6] May the praise of God be in their mouths
    and a double-edged sword in their hands,
[7] to inflict vengeance on the nations
    and punishment on the peoples,
[8] to bind their kings with fetters,
    their nobles with shackles of iron,
[9] to carry out the sentence written against them —
    this is the glory of all his faithful people.

Praise the Lord.

Psalm 150

[1] Praise the Lord.[b]

Praise God in his sanctuary;
    praise him in his mighty heavens.
[2] Praise him for his acts of power;
    praise him for his surpassing greatness.
[3] Praise him with the sounding of the trumpet,
    praise him with the harp and lyre,
[4] praise him with timbrel and dancing,
    praise him with the strings and pipe,
[5] praise him with the clash of cymbals,
    praise him with resounding cymbals.

[6] Let everything that has breath praise the Lord.

Praise the Lord.

[a] 1 Hebrew *Hallelu Yah*; also in verse 9   [b] 1 Hebrew *Hallelu Yah*; also in verse 6

Additional Insights

The Psalter is not only the prayer book of the second temple; it is also the enduring prayer book of the people of God across generations.

Ps 149 A hymn of praise to God for the high honor bestowed on his people Israel. Israel's unique honor has two sides: They were granted salvation (in fact and in promise), and, under the particular administration of the emerging kingdom of God put in place in the inauguration of the Sinaitic covenant, they were armed to execute God's sentence of judgment on the world powers that have launched attacks against the kingdom of God. Under that arrangement, Israel served as the earthly contingent of the armies of the King of heaven (see 68:17 and note; see also Jos 5:14; 2Sa 5:23–24; 2Ch 20:15–17,22; Hab 3:3–15). This next-to-last psalm should be read in the light of the second psalm (see introduction to Ps 2; see also introduction to Ps 146–150).

149:1 *new song.* See note on 33:3. *in the assembly.* See note on 9:1. *his faithful people.* See vv. 5,9; see also note on 4:3.

149:2–5 Let Israel rejoice in their King, who has crowned them with the honor of salvation.

149:4 *crowns.* Endows with splendor (Isa 55:5; 60:9; 61:3). *humble.* Those who acknowledge that they are without resources (see 147:6 and note).

149:5 *on their beds.* The salvation (v. 4) so tangible in the daytime evokes songs in the night (42:8; 63:6; 77:6).

149:6–9 Let Israel praise their God, who has given them the glory of bearing the sword as his army in service (cf. Ps 137; 139:19–22; Eze 38–39; Da 2:44; 7:22,26–27; Am 9:12).

149:7 *vengeance.* God's just retribution on those who have attacked his kingdom. Of this divine retribution the OT speaks often: 58:10; 79:10; 94:1; Nu 31:2; Dt 32:35,41,43; 2Ki 9:7; Isa 34:8; 35:4; 47:3; 59:17; 61:2; 63:4; Jer 46:10; 50:15,28; 51:6,11,36; Eze 25:14,17; Mic 5:15; Na 1:2. In the NT age, however, God's people are armed with the "sword of the Spirit" for overcoming the powers arrayed against God's kingdom (2Co 6:7; 10:4; Eph 6:12,17; Heb 4:12); their participation in God's retribution on the world awaits the final judgment (1Co 6:2–3).

149:9 *sentence written.* God's firmly determined judgment (see 139:16 and note).

Ps 150 The final great Hallelujah—perhaps composed specifically to close the Psalter. See the doxologies that conclude the first four Books: 41:13; 72:18–19; 89:52; 106:48. This final call to praise God moves powerfully by stages from place to themes to orchestra to choir, framed with Hallelujahs. See introduction to Ps 146–150.

150:1 *Where* God should be praised. *his sanctuary.* At Jerusalem. *his mighty heavens.* Or "the vault of his power" (see 19:1, "skies"; Ge 1:6), i.e., the vault that displays or symbolizes his power or in which his power resides. Usually thought to refer to God's heavenly temple (11:4), it may signify the vaulted ceiling of the visible universe viewed as a cosmic temple.

150:2 *Why* God should be praised. *his acts of power.* What he does (in creation and redemption). *his surpassing greatness.* Who he is.

150:3–5 *How* God should be praised—with the whole orchestra (eight instruments: wind, string, percussion), with dancing aptly placed at the middle (see photos, pp. 2, 3).

150:6 *Who* should praise God. The choir, with articulate expression, celebrates God's "acts of power" and "surpassing greatness" (v. 2). *Praise the Lord.* Hebrew *Hallelu Yah.* For another final great Hallelujah (see introduction to this psalm), see Rev 19:1–8.

▶ What does it mean to you to be able to call on the Lord when you need him (141:1)?

_____

_____

_____

_____

▶ How does the Sprit lead believers (143:10)?

_____

_____

_____

_____

▶ For what can you give praise to God?

_____

_____

_____

_____

▶ How is the praise in Psalm 150 a fitting end to the book of Psalms?

_____

_____

_____

_____

TABLE OF WEIGHTS AND MEASURES

	Biblical Unit	Approximate American Equivalent	Approximate Metric Equivalent
Weights	talent (60 minas)	75 pounds	34 kilograms
	mina (50 shekels)	1 1/4 pounds	560 grams
	shekel (2 bekas)	2/5 ounce	11.5 grams
	pim (2/3 shekel)	1/4 ounce	7.8 grams
	beka (10 gerahs)	1/5 ounce	5.7 grams
	gerah	1/50 ounce	0.6 gram
	daric	1/3 ounce	8.4 grams
Length	cubit	18 inches	45 centimeters
	span	9 inches	23 centimeters
	handbreadth	3 inches	7.5 centimeters
	stadion (pl. stadia)	600 feet	183 meters
Capacity *Dry Measure*	cor [homer] (10 ephahs)	6 bushels	220 liters
	lethek (5 ephahs)	3 bushels	110 liters
	ephah (10 omers)	3/5 bushel	22 liters
	seah (1/3 ephah)	7 quarts	7.5 liters
	omer (1/10 ephah)	2 quarts	2 liters
	cab (1/18 ephah)	1 quart	1 liter
Liquid Measure	bath (1 ephah)	6 gallons	22 liters
	hin (1/6 bath)	1 gallon	3.8 liters
	log (1/72 bath)	1/3 quart	0.3 liter

The figures of the table are calculated on the basis of a shekel equaling 11.5 grams, a cubit equaling 18 inches and an ephah equaling 22 liters. The quart referred to is either a dry quart (slightly larger than a liter) or a liquid quart (slightly smaller than a liter), whichever is applicable. The ton referred to in the footnotes is the American ton of 2,000 pounds. These weights are calculated relative to the particular commodity involved. Accordingly, the same measure of capacity in the text may be converted into different weights in the footnotes.

This table is based upon the best available information, but it is not intended to be mathematically precise; like the measurement equivalents in the footnotes, it merely gives approximate amounts and distances. Weights and measures differed somewhat at various times and places in the ancient world. There is uncertainty particularly about the ephah and the bath; further discoveries may shed more light on these units of capacity.

A NOTE REGARDING THE TYPE

This Bible was set in the Zondervan NIV Typeface, commissioned by Zondervan, a division of HarperCollins Christian Publishing, and designed in Aarhus, Denmark, by Klaus E. Krogh and Heidi Rand Sørensen of 2K/DENMARK. The design takes inspiration from the vision of the New International Version (NIV) to be a modern translation that gives the reader the most accurate Bible text possible, reflects the very best of Biblical scholarship, and uses contemporary global English. The designers of the Zondervan NIV Typeface sought to reflect this rich, half-century-old tradition of accuracy, readability, and clarity while also embodying the best advancements in modern Bible typography. The result is a distinctive, open Bible typeface that is uncompromisingly beautiful, clear, readable at any size, and perfectly suited to the New International Version.

CPSIA information can be obtained
at www.ICGtesting.com
Printed in the USA
LVHW061411160222
711194LV00002B/4